Measurement Theory in ACTION

Case Studies and Exercises

D0011073

Kenneth S. Shultz
California State University, San Bernardino

◆

David J. Whitney
California State University, Long Beach

SAGE Publications
Thousand Oaks ▪ London ▪ New Delhi

For information:

Sage Publications, Inc.
2455 Teller Road
Thousand Oaks, California 91320
E-mail: order@sagepub.com

Sage Publications Ltd.
1 Oliver's Yard
55 City Road
London EC1Y 1SP
United Kingdom

Sage Publications India Pvt. Ltd.
B-42 Panchsheel Enclave
Post Box 4109
New Delhi 110 017 India

Printed in the United States of America on acid-free paper.

Library of Congress Cataloging-in-Publication Data

Shultz, Kenneth S.
Measurement theory in action: case studies and exercises / Kenneth S. Shultz, David J. Whitney.
    p. cm.
Includes bibliographical references and index.
ISBN 978-0-7619-2730-3 (pbk.)
    1. Psychometrics—Case studies. 2. Psychometrics—Problems, exercises, etc.
I. Whitney, David J. II. Title.
BF39.S55 2005
150'.28'7—dc22   2004004418

06 07 08 09 10 9 8 7 6 5 4 3 2

Acquisitions Editor:	Jim Brace-Thompson
Editorial Assistant:	Karen Ehrmann
Production Editors:	Claudia A. Hoffman/Tracy Alpern
Copy Editor:	Fran Andersen, Mattson Publishing Services
Typesetter:	C&M Digitals (P) Ltd.
Cover Designer:	Janet Foulger

We dedicate this book to our respective (and highly revered) spouses and sons who have provided endless support, encouragement, and understanding

Deborah Olson and Benjamin Olson Shultz—KSS
Michelle and Cole Whitney—DJW

Contents

Practical Issues in Test Construction

About the Authors

Kenneth S. Shultz, PhD, earned his MA and PhD degrees in Industrial/Organizational (I/O) Psychology from Wayne State University in Detroit, Michigan. He is currently a professor in the Psychology Department at California State University, San Bernardino (CSUSB), and serves as director of the Master of Science Program in I/O Psychology. He regularly teaches classes in undergraduate psychological statistics, tests and measurements, and industrial psychology. He also teaches graduate classes in correlation and regression statistics, applied psychological measurement, and personnel selection and test validation. Prior to joining CSUSB, he worked for four years for the City of Los Angeles as a personnel research analyst, where he conducted applied psychological measurement projects in job analysis, test validation, and other applied personnel psychology areas. He has also completed applied internships with United Airlines and UNISYS Corporation. He continues to engage in consulting assignments related to applied measurement issues for a variety of public and private agencies. He has presented papers and published articles on a variety of applied measurement and test construction issues, in addition to his substantive work in the areas of personnel selection, aging workforce issues, and retirement. When not teaching or writing, he enjoys running, watching sports, and generally hanging out with his wife and son. His Web site can be found at http://psychology.csusb.edu//faculty/kshultz/index.html.

David J. Whitney, PhD, earned his MA and PhD degrees in Industrial/Organizational Psychology at Michigan State University in East Lansing, Michigan. He is currently an associate professor of psychology at California State University, Long Beach (CSULB), where he is one of the core faculty members in the master's program in industrial/organizational psychology. He currently serves on the Board of Directors of the Personnel Testing Council of Southern California. He has also served as a program evaluator for a number of multiyear grants funded by the National Science Foundation. He regularly teaches an introductory I/O course at the undergraduate level and occasionally teaches introductory statistics. At the graduate level, he teaches classes in test construction, personnel selection, and employee training. He also instructs a course intended to provide assistance to graduate students in preparation of a thesis proposal. His research investigates applicant perceptions of employment tests, test-taking strategies, and the impact of test coaching on performance. Coincidental to CSULB's location along the Newport-Inglewood earthquake fault, his publication record also reflects his interest in the application of psychological theory to the promotion of seismic hazard preparedness. While he loves his adopted home of Southern California, his childhood roots are reflected in his undying (and some might say undeserved) devotion to New York Jets football. His Web site can be found at http://www.csulb.edu/~dwhitney.

Preface

*P*sychometric theory. Test theory. Measurement theory. A quick perusal of the major titles of advanced psychometrics textbooks reveals that most include the word *theory,* and this is for good reason. Upon opening these textbooks, we see clear evidence that the major emphasis of most advanced measurement texts is on explaining test theory. We acknowledge that this should be the case. Students certainly need a solid foundation in measurement theory in order to even begin to hope to apply what they have learned to actual test construction. In teaching our own advanced measurement classes, however, we have often sought to complement our consideration of test theory with applied examples and exercises. Doing such has not always been easy. Until now, few texts have provided students with much practice actually implementing the measurement theory they are so diligently learning about. The title of this book, *Measurement Theory in Action: Case Studies and Exercises,* discloses our major purpose as providing opportunities for students to apply and reinforce their newly found knowledge of psychometric theory. As such, our hope is that this text will be a great complement to the theoretical material students are exposed to elsewhere in their psychometrics class. The following sections explain how this text is organized to help achieve this goal.

Modules

The 20 modules that comprise this text each focus on a specific issue associated with test construction. It was our goal to ensure that these modules corresponded to entire chapters in most typical measurement theory texts. However, each module "stands alone" in that information from previous modules is not assumed in subsequent modules. This is intended to allow instructors to assign only those modules that seem relevant or to assign modules in an order that better fits their own course goals.

The initial four modules introduce the concept of measurement theory (Module 1), review essential foundational statistics (Module 2), explain the concept of psychological scaling (Module 3), and provide an overview of the necessity of developing clear test specifications in the development of a psychological measure (Module 4). Modules 5 through 10 discuss issues related to test reliability and validation. Module 5 discusses classical test theory (CTT) and reliability. Modules 6, 7, and 8 present issues related to traditional conceptions of content validation, criterion-related validation, and construct validation, respectively. However, we emphasize the contemporary approach, which asserts that all evidence examined in relation to the inferences and conclusions of test scores contributes to the same process, namely, validation. Module 9 examines validity generalization/meta-analysis, while Module 10 examines the psychometric conception of test bias. Practical issues in the construction of tests are examined in Modules 11 through 16. These issues include the development of measures of maximal performance (Module 11), CTT item analysis (Module 12), the scoring of tests (Module 13), issues of diversity in testing (Module 14), development of measures of typical performance (Module 15), and concerns related to response styles and guessing (Module 16). Modules 17 through 20 present more advanced topics in measurement theory, including multiple regression (Module 17), exploratory and confirmatory factor analysis (Module 18), an introduction to item response theory (IRT) (Module 19), and the application of IRT to computer adaptive testing (CAT) and differential item functioning (DIF) (Module 20).

Each module is composed of an overview, case studies, exercises, Internet Web site references, and suggested further readings. Further explanation of each of these components is presented below.

Overviews

If you are hoping the overview of each module will provide an extensive and in-depth explanation of the substantive elements of each particular aspect of measurement theory, then you will certainly be disappointed. As noted earlier, our purpose is to focus on the *application* of measurement theory, not the theory itself. Thus, our intended purpose of the overviews is to provide a brief, simply stated summary of the major (not *all*) issues related to a particular topic in measurement theory. However, because we could not force applied case studies and exercises on students absent theory altogether, we felt it necessary to provide a bit of summary information on each major psychometric topic before launching into the applied case studies and exercises. In addition, many of the overviews include step-by-step examples of the application of measurement theory topics covered in that module. Each overview then concludes with a series of practical questions intended to assess understanding of the material presented.

We hope that those new to measurement theory will find the overviews easy to read and understand. Indeed, we would be especially proud if a student conscientiously pored over a number of primary readings on a psychometric topic, then read the corresponding chapter in a typical advanced measurement textbook, and then, after reading our brief overview on the same topic, exclaimed, "Aha. So that's what all that other stuff was about."

Case Studies

Each module contains two case studies that depict typical dilemmas and difficulties faced when applying measurement theory. In many cases, we have drawn these case studies from our own applied professional experiences, as well as the trials and tribulations of our students. In some instances, the case studies summarize an exemplar from the extant psychometric literature or discuss aspects of the development of a commercially available test. Others we completely made up after hours of staring at a blank computer screen. Nonetheless, in each case study we hoped to capture the questions and doubts many psychometric novices encounter when first attempting the application of measurement theory. The case studies rarely directly answer the questions they raise. Indeed, the "questions to ponder" that follow each case study serve only to further specify the issues raised by the case study. We believe that a thoughtful consideration of these issues will better prepare students for their own application of measurement theory.

Exercises

It is our firm belief that we learn best by actually doing. Therefore, each module contains two to four exercises intended to provide students with practical experience in the application of measurement theory. The purpose of each exercise is stated in a simple objective. Some exercises are amenable to in-class administration to groups, while others are best tackled individually outside the classroom environment. Many exercises require no computer access, while a number of exercises require access to the Internet or use of statistical analysis software such as SPSS. Appendix B presents a description of the data sets for the latter type of exercises. Exercises vary considerably in difficulty, although in no instance did we intend to include an exercise that was so difficult or so time consuming that students lost track of the relatively simple, straightforward objective.

While the vast majority of exercises require knowledge only of the material presented in that specific module, Appendix A presents a continuing exercise that incorporates many of the steps in the development of a measure of typical performance. This continuing exercise would appropriately serve as the basis of a term-long assignment.

Internet Web Site References

Academicians, academic publishers, test publishers, statistical software developers, and many other Web-savvy individuals and organizations have produced Web sites that help explain, illustrate, and depict psychometric-related material. All of this material is available free for the looking. Our goal in including Web references is to help direct you to some of the Web sites we have found to be particularly useful or interesting in teaching our own advanced psychometrics classes. Unfortunately, we understand that links may be broken or unreachable, and Web page content may change considerably over time. Please do not fault us too much if the really interesting sounding Web page we have directed you to no longer exists when you type out its uniform resource locator (URL). However, we would encourage you to further investigate what the Web has to offer in relation to psychometric-related material.

Further Readings

For each module, we have selected a number of additional readings we think you will find useful. These sometimes include classic readings on a topic; other times, they include the latest conceptualization of the topic or chapters that nicely summarize the topic. In many cases, we have recommended those authors who made very complex material somewhat understandable to us given our own admittedly limited cognitive abilities.

Glossary

At the back of the book, you will also find a glossary of important measurement terms. First usage of the glossary terms in the main text is in boldface type. We hope you'll find the glossary useful for defining terms presented throughout the text and in your other measurement theory–related readings. If you do not find what you are looking for, we welcome your suggestions for additional terms to add in future editions.

Additional Supplements

Instructors can request from Sage suggested answers to the questions posed after the overviews and case studies. In addition, answers to the exercises themselves as well as some example PowerPoint presentation slides for possible use in the classroom are available to instructors. An Instructor's Resources CD is available only to qualifying professors who adopt the book for use in the classroom.

Student Resources are available on Sage's Web site at www.sagepub.com/shultzdatasets.

Acknowledgments

We would like to thank a number of individuals who provided the necessary help to put this book together. We thank Kristin Olson and Sandy Wolfe for identifying relevant Web sites. We also thank Jennifer Mersman, Joel Wiesen, and several colleagues, who would prefer to remain anonymous, for providing the data used in several of the examples presented throughout the book. We are especially grateful to Stan Wakefield, the independent acquisitions editor who motivated and guided us as we took some very general ideas and put them on paper, turning them into a successful book prospectus. He also introduced us to Jim Brace-Thompson, our acquisitions editor at Sage Publications, to whom we are grateful for providing the gentle (and let's face it, not so gentle) push necessary to get this book done. We also thank our production editors, Claudia Hoffman and Tracy Alpern, as well as our copy editor, Fran Andersen. Finally, we are also very appreciative of the feedback from the reviewers who provided insightful comments on how we might improve earlier drafts of this book: Sebastiano Fiscaro, Wayne State University; Mike Aamodt, Radford University; Kevin Murphy, Pennsylvania State University; Keith F. Widaman, University of California at Davis; Jose Cortina, George Mason University; and additional reviewers.

From Ken Shultz

I would like to thank my colleagues Jan Kottke, Janelle Gilbert, Mark Agars, and Jodie Ullman in the psychology department at California State University, San Bernardino, for helping to shape, and often clarify, my thoughts on challenging statistics and measurement topics. I also appreciate the help of both current and former students in the master's program in industrial and organizational psychology at Cal State, San Bernardino, who let me "road test" many of the exercises and case studies in this book. I am particularly indebted to students in my graduate applied psychological measurement class in fall 2003 who helped to provide final revisions before this book went into production. On a personal note, I am also thankful for the support and love expressed by my wife Deborah Olson and son Benjamin as dad suddenly disappeared to his study to "work on his book." Last, but not least, I would like to thank my coauthor, Dave Whitney, for taking a chance on an untested collaborator and making the arduous process of writing a book both a little more fun and rewarding.

From Dave Whitney

I would like to thank several of my colleagues in the psychology department at California State University, Long Beach—Young-Hee Cho, Scott Hershberger, and Sherry Span—for their willingness to entertain the book-related questions I posed whenever I suddenly appeared at their office doors. I am especially grateful to Ken Shultz for asking me to serve as his coauthor. I am very fortunate to have undertaken this process with someone of Ken's keen mind and calm demeanor. But, Ken, next time we run a 10K together, let's make a pact to keep the discussion of psychometric issues to a minimum, okay? Finally, I'd like to thank my wife Michelle for supporting me in yet another example of my inability to just say "no."

—Kenneth S. Shultz
San Bernardino, California
kshultz@csusb.edu

—David J. Whitney
Long Beach, California
dwhitney@csulb.edu

Introduction

Module 1

Introduction and Overview

Thousands of important, and sometimes life-altering, decisions are made every day. Who should we hire? Which students should be placed in accelerated or remedial programs? Which defendants should be incarcerated and which paroled? Which treatment regimen will work best for a given client? Should custody of this child be granted to the mother or the father or the grandparents? In each of these situations, a "test" may be used to help provide guidance. There are many vocal opponents to the use of standardized tests to make such decisions. However, the bottom line is that these critical decisions will ultimately be made with or without the use of test information. The question we have to ask ourselves is, "Can a better decision be made with the use of relevant test information?" In many, although not all, instances, the answer will be yes, *if* a well-developed and appropriate test is used *in combination* with other relevant information available to the decision maker. The opposition that many individuals have to standardized tests is that they are the sole basis for making an important, sometimes life-altering, decision. Thus, it would behoove any decision maker to take full advantage of other relevant information, where available, to make the best and most well-informed decision possible.

What Makes Tests Useful

Tests can take many forms from traditional paper-and-pencil exams to portfolio assessments, job interviews, case histories, behavioral observations, and peer ratings—to name just a few. The common theme in all of these **assessment** procedures is that they represent a sample of behaviors from the test taker. Thus, psychological testing is similar to any science in that a sample

3

is taken to make inferences about a population. In this case, the sample consists of behaviors (e.g., test responses on a paper-and-pencil test or performance of physical tasks on a physical **ability test**) from a larger domain of all possible behaviors representing a construct. For example, the first test we take when we come into the world is called the APGAR test. That's right, just 1 minute into the world we get our first test. You probably do not remember your score on your APGAR test, but our guess is your mother does, given the importance this first test has in revealing your initial physical functioning. The purpose of the APGAR test is to assess a newborn's general functioning right after birth. Table 1.1 displays the five categories that newborn infants are tested on at 1 and 5 minutes after birth: Appearance, Pulse, Grimace, Activity, and Respiration (hence, the acronym APGAR). A score is obtained by summing the infant's assessed value on each of the dimensions. Scores can range from 0 to 10. A score of 7–10 is considered normal. A score of 4–6 indicates that the newborn infant may require some resuscitation, while a score of 3 or less means the newborn would require immediate and intensive resuscitation. The infant is then assessed again at 5 minutes, and if his or her score still is below a 7, he or she may be assessed again at 10 minutes. If the infant's APGAR score is 7 or above 5 minutes after birth, which is typical, then no further intervention is called for. Hence, by taking a relatively small sampling of behavior, we are (or at least a competent obstetrics nurse or doctor is) able to quickly, and quite accurately, assess the functioning of a newborn infant to determine if resuscitation interventions are required to get the newborn functioning properly.

Table 1.1   The APGAR Test Scoring Table

	Points		
Sign	*0*	*1*	*2*
Appearance (color)	Pale or blue	Body pink, extremities blue	Pink (normal for non-Caucasians)
Pulse (heartbeat)	Not detectible	Lower than 100 bpm	Higher than 100 bpm
Grimace (reflex)	No response	Grimace	Lusty cry
Activity (muscle tone)	Flaccid	Some movement	A lot of activity
Respiration (breathing)	None	Slow, irregular	Good (crying)

The **utility** of any assessment device, however, will depend on the qualities of the test and the intended use of the test (see Web References 1.1 and 1.2 for a discussion of these desired qualities). Test information can be used for a variety of purposes from making predictions about the likelihood that a patient will commit suicide to making personnel selection decisions by determining which entry-level workers to hire. Tests can also be used for classification purposes, as when students are designated as remedial, gifted, or somewhere in between. Tests can also be used for evaluation purposes, as in the use of a classroom test to evaluate performance of students in a given subject matter. Counseling psychologists routinely use tests to assess clients for emotional adjustment problems or possibly for help in providing vocational counseling. Finally, tests can also be used for research-only purposes such as when an experimenter uses a test to prescreen study participants to assign each one to an experimental condition. If the test is not used for its intended purpose, however, it will not be very useful and, in fact, may actually be harmful. As Anastasi and Urbina (1997) note, "Psychological tests are tools . . . Any tool can be an instrument of good or harm, depending on how it is used" (p. 2).

For example, most American children in grades 2–12 are required to take standardized tests on a yearly basis. These tests were initially intended for the sole purpose of assessing students' learning outcomes. Over time, however, a variety of other misuses for these tests have emerged. For instance, they are frequently used to determine school funding and, in some cases, teachers' or school administrators' "merit" pay. However, given that determining the pay levels of educational employees was not the intended use of such standardized educational tests when they were developed, they almost always serve poorly in this capacity. Thus, a test that was developed with good (i.e., appropriate) intentions can be used for inappropriate purposes, limiting the usefulness of the test. In this instance, however, not only is the test of little use in setting pay for teachers and administrators, it may actually be causing harm by coercing teachers to "teach to the test," thereby trading long-term gains in learning for short-term increases in standardized test performance.

In addition, no matter how the test is used, it will only be useful if it meets certain psychometric and practical requirements. From a psychometric or measurement standpoint, we want to know if the test is accurate, standardized, and reliable; if it demonstrates evidence of validity; and if it is free of both measurement and predictive bias. Procedures for determining these psychometric qualities form the core of the rest of this book (see also Web References 1.1–1.7). From a practical standpoint, the test must be cost effective as well as relatively easy to administer and score. Reflecting on our earlier example, we would surmise that the APGAR meets most of these qualities of being practical. Trained doctors and nurses in a hospital delivery room can administer the APGAR quickly and efficiently. Our key psychometric concern in this situation may be how often different doctors and nurses are able to provide similar APGAR scores in a given situation (i.e., the **inter-rater reliability** of the APGAR).

Individual Differences

Ultimately, when it comes right down to it, those interested in applied psychological measurement are usually interested in some form of **individual differences** (i.e., how individuals differ on test scores and the underlying **traits** being measured by those tests). If there are no differences in how target individuals score on the test, then the test will have little value to us. For example, if we give a group of elite athletes the standard physical ability test given to candidates for a police officer job, there will likely be very little variability in scores with all the athletes scoring extremely high on the test. Thus, the test data would provide little value in predicting which athletes would make good police officers. On the other hand, if we had a more typical group of job candidates who passed previous hurdles in the personnel selection process for police officer (e.g., cognitive tests, background checks, psychological evaluations) and gave them the same physical ability test, we would see much wider variability in scores. Thus, the test would at least have the potential to be a useful predictor of job success, as we would have at least some variability in the observed test scores.

Individual differences on psychological tests can take several different forms. Typically, we look at **inter-individual differences** where we examine differences on the same construct across individuals. In such cases, the desire is usually prediction. That is, how well does the test predict some criterion of interest? For example, in the preceding scenario, we would use the physical ability test data to predict who would be successful in police work. Typically, job candidates are rank ordered based on their test scores and selected in a top-down fashion, assuming the test is indeed linearly associated with job performance. As you will see as we move further into the book, however, it is rare that any single test will be sufficient to provide a complete picture of the test taker. Thus, more often than not, several tests (or at least several decision points) are incorporated into the decision-making process.

We may also be interested in examining **intra-individual differences**. These differences can take two forms. In the first situation, we may be interested in examining a single construct within the same individual across time. In this case, we are interested in how the individual changes or matures over time. For example, there have been longitudinal studies conducted by life-span developmental psychologists that have looked at how an individual's cognitive ability and personality change over the course of his or her lifetime. In particular, these researchers are interested in studying intra-individual differences in maturation. That is, why do some individuals' scores on cognitive ability tests go up dramatically over time, while the scores of other individuals only go up a little or not at all or maybe even go down? Thus, the focus is not on group mean differences (as in inter-individual differences); rather, we are looking for different rates of change within individuals over time.

In the second form of intra-individual differences, we are interested in looking at a given individual's strengths and weaknesses across a variety of constructs, typically at one point in time. Thus, the same individual is given a variety (or **battery**) of different tests. Here we are usually interested in classifying individuals based on their strengths and weaknesses. For example, hundreds of thousands of high school students take the **Armed Services Vocational Aptitude Battery (ASVAB)** every year. The ASVAB consists of a series of 10 subtests that assess individuals' strengths and weaknesses in a wide variety of aptitudes. Those not interested in pursuing a military career can use it for career counseling purposes, while individuals interested in military service can use it to be placed or classified within a particular branch of the armed services or career path within the military based on their relative strengths and weaknesses. The key is that the ASVAB consists of a **test battery** that allows test users to see how individuals differ in terms of the relative strength of different traits and characteristics. Hence, the ASVAB is useful for several different constituents in the testing process.

Constituents in the Testing Process

Because the decisions that result from the uses of test data are so often of great consequence, the testing process is very much a political process. Each of the **constituents** or stakeholders in the testing process will have a vested interest in the outcome, albeit for different reasons. Obviously, the **test takers** themselves have a strong vested interest in the outcome of the testing process. Because they are the ones who will be affected most by the use of the test, they tend to be most concerned with the procedural and distributive (i.e., outcome) fairness of the test and the testing process. The **test users** (those who administer, score, and use the test) may be less concerned with an individual's outcome per se, focusing more on making sure the test and testing process are as fair as possible to all test takers. They are using the test, no doubt, to help make a critical decision for both the individuals and the organization using the test. Thus, they will also be concerned with many of the psychometric issues that will be discussed throughout this book, such as reliability, validity, and test bias. The **test developer** tends to focus on providing the best possible test to the test user and test taker. This includes making sure the test is well designed and developed, in addition to being practical and effective. Test developers also need to collect and provide evidence that the test demonstrates consistency of scores (i.e., **reliability**) and that the concepts that are purported to be measured are, in fact, measured.

Thus, this book focuses on what you will need to know to be a qualified *test developer* and informed *test user*. You will learn how to develop test questions, determine the psychometric properties of a test, and evaluate test items and the entire test for potential biases. In addition, many practical issues such as test translation, dealing with response biases, and interpreting test scores will also be discussed. Each module includes case studies and hands-on exercises that will provide practice in thinking about and working through the many complicated psychometric processes you will learn about in the rest of the book. In addition, many modules also include step-by-step examples to walk you through the process that an applied practitioner would go through to evaluate the concepts discussed in that particular module. Thus, in short, conscientious use of this book will help you to better understand and apply the knowledge and skills you are developing as you study a wide variety of topics within advanced measurement theory.

Concluding Comments

Psychological testing, when done properly, can be a tremendous benefit to society. Competently developed and implemented assessment devices can provide valuable input to the critical decisions we are faced with everyday. However, poorly developed and implemented tests may, at best, be of little assistance and, in fact, may actually do more harm than good. Therefore, the rest of this book was written to help you become a more informed consumer of psychological tests as well as to prepare future test developers in terms of the critical competencies that are needed to develop tests that will be beneficial to society and acceptable (or at least tolerable) to all testing constituents.

Practical Questions

1. What specific goals do you want to achieve by taking a course in measurement?

2. What will likely be your major stake in the testing process once you finish your measurement course?

3. What alternative "test" to the APGAR could an obstetrics nurse or doctor use to assess newborn functioning? What would be the advantages and disadvantages compared to the APGAR test shown in Table 1.1?

4. Who are the major constituents or stakeholders in the psychological testing process?

5. What is the major purpose of examining inter-individual differences via test scores?

6. What are the different types of intra-individual differences?

7. What are the major purposes of the different forms of intra-individual differences in interpreting test data?

8. Can you provide examples of the uses of both inter-individual differences and intra-individual differences?

Case Studies

CASE STUDY 1.1: TESTING CONSTITUENTS AND THE STANFORD ACHIEVEMENT TEST

Professor Gilbert, an educational testing professor at a local state university, was contacted by a small school district that had decided to implement a Talented and Gifted (TAG) program for advanced students. The school district initially was going to use grade point average (GPA) as the sole basis for placement into the TAG program. However, several parents objected that the different tracks within the schools tended to grade using different standards. As a result, those students in Track A had much higher GPAs (on average) than those in the other two tracks. Thus, those in Track A were much more likely to be placed in the TAG program if only GPA was used than those in Tracks B and C.

Therefore, the school board decided to set up an ad hoc committee to provide recommendations to the board as to how entrance to the new TAG program would be determined. The committee was headed by Professor Gilbert (who also happened to have two sons in the school system) and included school psychologists, principals, parents, teachers, and students. The committee's initial report recommended that teacher written evaluations, test scores from the Stanford Achievement Test, version 9 (SAT-9), and letters of recommendations be used, in addition to GPA, to determine entrance into the TAG program. As you might have guessed, the next meeting of the school board, where these recommendations were presented and discussed, was a heated affair. Professor Gilbert was suddenly beginning to ponder whether she needed to raise her consulting fees.

Questions to Ponder

1. Who are the major constituents or stakeholders in the testing process in this scenario?

2. What is Professor Gilbert's "stake" in the testing process? Does she have more than one?

3. What form of individual differences is the committee most likely to be focusing on? Why?

4. Should all of the different assessment devices be equally weighted?

CASE STUDY 1.2: DEVELOPMENT OF A VOLUNTEER PLACEMENT TEST

A local volunteer referral agency was interested in using "tests" to place volunteer applicants in the volunteer organizations it served. In order to do so, however, the agency needed to assess each applicant to determine where his or her skills could best be used. As a first step, the director of the agency contacted a local university and found out that Professor Kottke's graduate practicum class in applied testing was in need of a community-based project. Soon thereafter, Professor Kottke and her students met with the director of the agency to determine what her needs were and how the class could help.

In the past, the agency first conducted a short 15-minute telephone interview as an initial screen for each volunteer applicant. Those applicants who appeared to be promising were asked to come in for a half-hour face-to-face interview with a member of the agency staff. If the applicant was successful at this stage, a brief background check was conducted, and the candidates who passed were placed in the first available opening. However, the agency was receiving feedback from the volunteer organizations that a large portion of the volunteers were participating for only a month or two and would then never return. In follow-up interviews with these volunteers, the most consistent reason given for not returning was that the volunteer placement was simply "not a good fit." Thus, Professor Kottke and her class were asked to improve the fit of candidates to the positions in which they were being placed. Unfortunately, Professor Kottke's 10-week course was already one third completed, so she and her students would have to work quickly.

Questions to Ponder

1. If you were in Professor Kottke's practicum class, where would you start in the process of trying to help this agency?

2. Does this seem to be more of an inter-individual differences or intra-individual differences issue? Explain.

3. Who are the constituents in this testing process?

4. What do you think Professor Kottke and her students can realistically accomplish in the six to seven weeks remaining in the term?

Exercises

EXERCISE 1.1: DIFFERENT USES FOR A GIVEN TEST

OBJECTIVE: To think critically about the wide variety of uses for a given test.

The Armed Services Vocational Aptitude Battery (ASVAB) was discussed in the module overview. Nearly one million people take this test each year, many of them high school students. The test consists of 10 different subtests measuring general science, arithmetic reasoning, word knowledge, paragraph comprehension, numerical operations, coding speed, auto and shop information, mathematics knowledge, mechanical comprehension, and electronics information. The ASVAB is used primarily to select recruits for the different branches of the armed services and then to place those individuals selected into various training programs based on their aptitude strengths and weaknesses. In fact, a subset of 100 items (called the Armed Forces Qualification Test—AFQT) from the ASVAB is used by all the branches of the military to select recruits. Each branch of the military employs a slightly different cutoff score to select recruits.

Given the 10 subtests listed previously, what other purposes could the ASVAB be used for besides selection and placement (i.e., career guidance)?

EXERCISE 1.2: WHO ARE THE MAJOR CONSTITUENTS IN THE TESTING PROCESS?

OBJECTIVE: To become familiar with the major constituents in the testing process.

As noted in the overview, there are typically numerous constituents in any given testing process. These constituents may include the test takers, test developers, test users, and, more broadly, society in general. Each of these constituents will have a varying degree of interest in a given assessment device.

Who are the major test constituents with regard to the Armed Services Vocational Aptitude Battery (ASVAB) discussed in the module overview and in Exercise 1.1? What would be the major concerns of each of these different constituents with regard to development, refinement, administration, and use of the ASVAB?

EXERCISE 1.3: TESTING AND INDIVIDUAL DIFFERENCES

OBJECTIVE: To identify the major forms of individual differences commonly assessed with psychological tests.

Most tests are administered to identify some form of individual differences. These can include inter-individual differences, intra-individual differences, or both. Again, looking at the Armed Services Vocational

Aptitude Battery (ASVAB), what forms of inter- and intra-individual differences might be assessed with this particular test?

Internet Web Site References

1.1. http://trochim.human.cornell.edu/kb/contents.htm

This Web page provides the table of contents for the online textbook, *The Research Methods Knowledge Base,* by Dr. William M. Trochim of Cornell University. A wealth of testing-related information is available from subsidiary links. Links from within this table of contents that are relevant to specific modules are cited throughout this book. An enhanced and revised version of Trochim's book is available in print. A hard copy of the book can be ordered online at http://trochim.omni.cornell.edu/kb/order.htm.

1.2. http://www.ed.gov/databases/ERIC_Digests/ed385607.html

This Web page, from the Educational Resources Information Center (ERIC), provides key standards to consider when evaluating a test. The standards are based on the AERA/APA/NCME (1999) *Standards for Educational and Psychological Testing.*

1.3. http://www.apa.org/science/fairtestcode.html

This Web page presents the Code of Fair Testing Practices in Education (1988) as developed by the Joint Committee on Testing Practices.

1.4. http://www.intestcom.org/test_use_full.htm

This Web page provides the International Test Commission's Guidelines on test use.

1.5. http://www.vanguard.edu/faculty/ddegelman/amoebaweb/index.cfm? doc_id=853

This Web page, maintained by Dr. Douglas Degelman of Vanguard University, presents links to a wide range of topics related to testing and research methods.

1.6. http://www.cpsimoes.net/artigos/art_psycho_eng.html

This Web page provides a brief introduction to the concept of psychological testing.

1.7. http://www.siop.org/_Principles/principlesdefault.htm

This Web page provides access to the fourth edition of the *Principles for the Validation and Use of Personnel Selection Procedures,* a guidebook of the accepted professional practices in the field of personnel selection psychology.

1.8. http://www.unl.edu/buros/

This Web page provides **Mental Measurement Yearbook (MMY)** reviews of nearly 4,000 commercially available tests. A fee is charged for each test review accessed. Your library, however, might subscribe to this service. Check with your instructor.

1.9. http://davidmlane.com/hyperstat/Statistical_analyses.html

This Web page provides links to several free statistical programs that can be used for analyzing test data.

Further Readings

Anastasi, A., & Urbina, S. (1997). *Psychological testing* (7th ed., pp. 2–31). Upper Saddle River, NJ: Prentice Hall.

Crocker, L. M., & Algina, J. (1986). *Introduction to classical and modern test theory* (pp. 3–15). Belmont, CA: Wadsworth.

Ghiselli, E. E., Campbell, J. P., & Zedeck, S. (1981). *Measurement theory for the behavioral sciences* (pp. 9–30). New York: W. H. Freeman.

Murphy, K. R., & Davidshofer, C. O. (2001). *Psychological testing: Principles and applications* (5th ed., pp. 49–66). Upper Saddle River, NJ: Prentice Hall.

Module 2

Statistics Review for Psychological Measurement

If you have already taken a statistics class, you probably spent a good portion of the term on statistical significance testing, learning about *t* tests, analysis of variance (ANOVA), and other such statistical tests. If you dreaded that part of your statistics class, you are in luck because in applied psychological measurement we typically do little in the way of statistical significance testing. Instead, we tend to focus on either descriptive statistics or estimation. For those of you who have not had an introductory statistics class or who have but are in need of a refresher, an abbreviated review follows. However, please see the Further Readings and the Internet Web Site References listed at the end of the module for a more detailed discussion and explanation of the statistics discussed below.

Organizing and Displaying Test Data

More often than not in applied psychological measurement, we are interested in simply describing a set of test data. For example, we may want to know how many people scored at a certain level, what the average score was for a group of test takers, or what the percentile rank equivalent is for a score of 84. Thus, we are most likely to be using univariate **descriptive statistics** to describe a set of test data. If we know the central tendency (e.g., mode, median, mean), variability or dispersion (e.g., range, interquartile range, standard deviation, variance), and shape (e.g., skew, kurtosis) of a distribution of scores, we can completely describe that distribution (at least as far as we are concerned in applied psychological measurement). In addition, we can standardize (e.g., Z scores, stanines, percentiles) a set of test scores to help us interpret a given score relative to other scores in the distribution or to some established group norm. Before we run any "numbers," however, we are best advised to draw some graphs (e.g., histograms, stem-and-leaf plots) to get a visual picture of what is going on with our test data. As has been said, a picture is worth a thousand words. That saying definitely applies to interpreting a set of test scores as well.

As an example, look at Table 2.1, which displays a distribution of examination scores obtained for an introductory tests and measurements class. What can we say about this distribution of scores? First, we see that we have a total of 25 scores. Next, we might notice that scores range from a low of 68 to a high of 93. In addition, we might notice that for many score values there is only one individual who obtained that score on the test. We may also notice that there is a clustering of scores in the high 80s. Looking at an individual score, say 80, we can see that two students obtained this score (see the Frequency column) and that two students represent 8% of all students (see the Percent column). We may also notice that 32% of students received a score lower than 80 (see the Cumulative Percent column). This latter figure is sometimes referred to as a score of 80 having a **percentile rank** of 32. Thus, by simply organizing the test scores into a simple frequency table as we did in Table 2.1, we can answer many questions about how the group did overall and how each individual performed on the test.

As noted previously, we could (and should) also graph the data before computing any statistics. It would be common to display test data as a frequency histogram or stem-and-leaf plot. Figure 2.1a shows a histogram of the **frequency distribution** of the data in Table 2.1. Again, we see that the low score is 68 and the high score is 93. We also notice the clustering of scores at 88 and 90. In addition, we may notice that no student received a score of 71, 75, 77, 78, 81–83, or 85. Thus, there is some "wasted space" in the graph where no students obtained a given score. While all this information is useful, we could have just as easily gleaned most of this information, and more, directly from Table 2.1. Thus, did we really need to go to the trouble of creating Figure 2.1a?

Now look at Figure 2.1b. How does this graph compare to Table 2.1 and Figure 2.1a? This is called a grouped frequency histogram. It is based on the data from Table 2.1; however, scores have been logically grouped into grade categories. In this case, because we are dealing with classroom test scores, most students (as well as the professor) will likely want to know how they did "gradewise" on the test. Thus, grouping the individual scores into grade

Table 2.1   Example Test Scores for a Classroom Examination With 25 Students

Test Scores	Frequency	Percent	Cumulative Percent	Z Score
68	1	4	4	−1.85
69	1	4	8	−1.73
70	1	4	12	−1.60
72	1	4	16	−1.36
73	1	4	20	−1.23
74	1	4	24	−1.11
76	1	4	28	−.86
79	1	4	32	−.48
80	2	8	40	−.36
84	1	4	44	.14
86	1	4	48	.39
87	2	8	56	.51
88	4	16	72	.64
89	1	4	76	.76
90	3	12	88	.89
91	1	4	92	1.01
92	1	4	96	1.14
93	1	4	100	1.26
Total	25			

categories provides a more informative picture of how students did on the test. In addition, notice the Y (vertical) axis now displays the percentage of scores as opposed to the simple frequency of scores. Although using percentages instead of frequencies is not necessary for a **grouped frequency distribution,** doing so is more informative as the number of test scores increases. Also, each bar on the graph lists the actual percentage of students who received that particular grade on the test. Imagine looking at the graph without the numbers in the bars (as in Figure 2.1a). Could you figure out exactly what percentage of students received an A⁻? It would be difficult. By

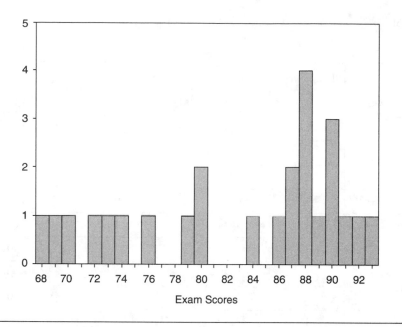

Figure 2.1a   Frequency Distribution for Exam Scores

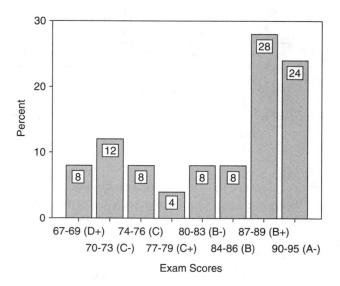

Figure 2.1b   Grouped Frequency Distribution for Exam Scores

the way, the change of the Y axis to percent and the addition of the numbers to the bars are not unique to the grouped frequency histogram. We simply added these features to this graph to highlight other ways of improving the presentation of the test data. Regardless, there are distinct advantages to using a grouped frequency histogram over an ungrouped frequency histogram, particularly when there is a wide range of test scores, several scores between the high and low score with no individuals obtaining that score, and many individuals who took the test. There is one major disadvantage, however. Can you guess what it is? That's right, you don't know exactly how many individuals received a specific score. You only know how many students fell within a given category. For example, in the C^+ grade category (without looking at Table 2.1), you do not know if the single score is a 77, 78, or 79 on the test. Looking at Table 2.1, we see that the lone individual received a 79; and there were no scores of 77 or 78. Thus, it would be wise to have both a frequency table like Table 2.1 to provide individual data *and* a grouped histogram like Figure 2.1b to allow us to obtain a general sense of what the distribution of test scores looks like.

An alternative to having both a table and a graph is to create a stem-and-leaf plot. Figure 2.2 displays the stem-and-leaf plot for the data in Table 2.1. Notice that we have retained both the ungrouped (i.e., individual) data and the grouped frequency count. In addition, if you turn your head to the right, you can get a sense of the shape of the distribution. How do you read a stem-and-leaf display? In this case, the "stem" is the 10s column (60, 70, 80, or 90), which is noted in the "Stem Width" line below the data, while the "leaf" is the 1s column (0–9). Thus, we can see that we have one score each of 68, 69, 70, 72, 73, 74, 76, and 79, but two scores of 80. We can also look in the Frequency column and see that we have two scores in the high 60s, four in the low 70s, two in the high 70s, and so on. Because we have a total of only 25 scores, each "leaf" is just one case. However, the more scores you have in your distribution, the less likely it is that each leaf will represent a single case. As a result, you may, in fact, not have individual-level data in your stem-and-leaf plot. In addition, the stem width is not always equal to 10; it depends on what you are measuring. For example, if your test scores are reaction times, then instead of the stems representing 10s, they may be 10ths or 100ths of a second. Therefore, be sure to read any stem-and-leaf plot carefully.

Univariate Descriptive Statistics

Now that we have obtained a general sense of the data by creating and looking at the frequency table and graphs such as the grouped frequency distribution

Frequency	Stem & Leaf
2 . 00	6 . 89
4 . 00	7 . 0234
2 . 00	7 . 69
3 . 00	8 . 004
8 . 00	8 . 67788889
6 . 00	9 . 000123
Stem width:	10 . 00
Each leaf:	1 case (s)

Figure 2.2   Exam 1 Test Scores Stem-and-Leaf Plot

and stem-and-leaf display, it would be nice to have just a couple of numbers (i.e., statistics) to summarize or describe how test scores tend to cluster (central tendency) and vary (variability or dispersion) within the sample. As noted at the beginning of the module, the three most common measures of **central tendency** are the mode, median, and mean. The **mode** represents the most frequently occurring score in the distribution. Can you tell what the mode is from looking at Table 2.1? Yes, it is a score of 88. It occurs most frequently, with four individuals obtaining this score. Often times, however, a set of scores may have more than one most frequently occurring score (i.e., mode). Such distributions are typically referred to as multimodal. If it has two modes, it is referred to as bimodal, three modes, trimodal, and so on. As a result, sometimes only the highest or lowest mode may be reported for a set of test scores.

The **median** is another measure of central tendency. It is the point in the distribution where half the scores are above and half below. Looking at Table 2.1, can you figure out the median? To do so, you would need to look at the Cumulative Percent column until you reached 50%. Looking at Table 2.1, you will notice that it skips from 48% at a score of 86 to 56% for a score of 87. So, what is the median? Remember, the cumulative percent represents the percentage of scores at or below that level, so in this instance the median would be a score of 87. More precise formulas for calculating the median are available in the Further Readings listed at the end of the module.

The **mean** is the most popular measure of central tendency for summarizing test data. It represents the arithmetic average of the test scores. The formula for the mean is $M = \sum X_i / n$, where M is the mean, $\sum X_i$ is the sum of the individual test scores, and n is the total number of persons for whom we have test scores. Using the data from Table 2.1, we see that the sum of test scores is 2072 and n is 25; thus, $M = 2072 / 25 = 82.88$. Be careful when computing the sum using a frequency table such as Table 2.1. A common mistake students (and sometimes professors) make is not counting all 25 scores. For example, students may forget to sum the two scores of 80, the two scores of 86, the four scores of 88, and the three scores of 90 in this example.

Knowing how scores tend to cluster (i.e., central tendency) is important. However, just as important is how scores tend to vary or spread out. If you do not know how scores vary, it would be difficult to determine how discrepant a given score is from the mean. For example, is a score of 84 all that discrepant from our mean of 82.88? We really cannot answer that question until we have some sense of how scores in this distribution tend to vary. Several common measures of **variability** include the range, interquartile range, standard deviation, and variance. The **range** is simply the high score minus the low score, which, in this case, would be $93 - 68 = 25$. However, whenever there are extreme scores, it is best to trim (i.e., drop) those extreme scores before computing the range. The **interquartile range** does just that. To compute the interquartile range, one subtracts the score at the 25th percentile from the score at the 75th percentile, instead of taking the highest and lowest scores as with the range. Thus, similar to how we found the median (i.e., the 50th percentile), we look at the Cumulative Percent column in Table 2.1 until we get to 25% (a score of 76 at the 28th percentile) and then 75% (a score of 89 at the 76th percentile). Thus, the interquartile range would be $89 - 76 = 13$. As with the median we computed previously, this is a somewhat crude estimate. More precise estimates are possible and methods to compute such estimates can be found in most introductory statistics books.

One of the most common forms of summarizing variability is to compute the variance. The **variance,** like the mean, is also an average, but in this case it is the average of the squared deviation of each score from the mean. The formula for a sample variance is $S^2 = \Sigma(X_i - M)^2 / n$, where S^2 is the sample variance estimate (note that you would have to divide by $n - 1$ if you were estimating a population variance), $(X_i - M)$ is the difference between each person's test score and the mean of the test scores, and n is the number of persons who took the test. You might be wondering why we square the deviation score. If we do not square the deviation score, our summed deviation scores will always sum to zero. Therefore, by squaring the deviation scores first, we get rid of all negative values and thus the problem of summing to zero is alleviated. However, we create a new problem by squaring each deviation score. Can you guess what it is? In interpreting our variance estimate, we are interpreting squared test scores, not our original test scores. As a result, we typically take the square root of our variance estimate. This is referred to as the **standard deviation** and labeled as S.

In our example, using the data from Table 2.1, the variance is $S^2 = 1544.64 / 25 = 61.79$. If we take the square root, the standard deviation will be $S = 7.86$. Thus, on average, scores tend to deviate about 7.86 points from the mean. How is this useful to us? Remember at the beginning of the module we said we could standardize our test scores in order to help us interpret the scores. One way of doing this is by converting each score to a **Z score**. The formula for a Z score is $Z = (X_i - M) / S$. Previously, we asked if a score of 84 is really all that different from our mean of 82.88. By converting our test score to a Z score, we can more readily answer that question. Thus, $Z = (84 - 82.88) / 7.86 = .14$. Thus, a score of 84 is only a little more than one tenth of a standard deviation above the mean, not a very large difference. Notice that all the standardized Z scores for all test values have been computed in the last column of Table 2.1. The farther the score is from the mean the larger its Z score will be. Z scores are also useful in identifying outlier cases in a set of data. A typical rule of thumb is any score more than 3 standard deviations away from the mean is considered an outlier. Can any individuals in Table 2.1 be considered outliers? Finally, Z scores also let us compare two scores that come from two different distributions, each with its own mean and standard deviation. This will be discussed in more detail later in this book.

At the beginning of this module, we said that if we knew the central tendency, variability, and shape of a distribution we could completely describe that distribution of scores. We have discussed the two former concepts, so it is time to discuss the latter. The first measure of shape is the skew statistic. It tells us how symmetrical the distribution is. Looking at Figure 2.1a, we see that our distribution of test scores is clearly not symmetrical. Scores tend to cluster at the upper end of the distribution and there is a bit of tail that goes off to the left. Thus, this is called a negatively skewed distribution. Distributions can vary in terms of both the direction of the skew (positive or negative) and the magnitude of the skew. Therefore, not surprisingly, statisticians created a skew statistic to quantify the degree of **skewness.** Similar to the variance, we look at the deviation scores, but this time we will cube the scores (i.e., take them to the third power) instead of squaring the scores. The formula is

$$Sk = \left[\sum (X_i - M)^3 / n \right] / S^3$$

where X_i is each individual test score, M is the mean test score, n is the total number of test scores, and S^3 is the standard deviation cubed. In our example, $Sk = -.626$. A skew of zero represents a symmetrical distribution of test scores; hence, our distribution has a slight negative skew.

Kurtosis is another measure of the shape of a distribution of scores. It describes how peaked (leptokurtic) or flat (platykurtic) a distribution of scores is. If the distribution follows a relatively normal (i.e., bell-shaped) curve, then it is said to be mesokurtic. Similar to the variance and skew statistic, we again use the deviation of each score from the mean, but now we take it to the fourth power. The formula for kurtosis is

$$\text{Ku} = \left\{\left[\sum(X_i - M)^4 / n\right] / S^4\right\} - 3$$

However, notice that, in order to have zero represent a mesokurtic distribution, we apply a correction factor of -3 at the end of the formula. Positive scores represent a leptokurtic distribution, while negative scores represent a platykurtic distribution. In our example, Ku = -1.085; hence, we have a slightly platykurtic distribution.

Bivariate Descriptive Statistics

We may also be interested in how strongly scores on a test are associated with some criterion variable. For example, are grades on this tests and measurements exam associated with overall grade point average (GPA)? In this instance, we would use a bivariate descriptive statistic (such as the Pearson product moment correlation coefficient) to describe the strength of the relationship between test scores and GPA (i.e., the **criterion**). If the association is sufficiently strong (this is a value judgment that depends on the context), we can then use one variable to predict the other variable using regression techniques. In our haste to compute the **correlation coefficient** and regression equations, however, we must not forget about graphical techniques such as bivariate **scatterplots.** Such plots will alert us to problems that will not be evident when we only examine the correlation coefficient. For example, outliers, possible subgroups, nonlinearity, and **heteroscedasticity** (i.e., the uniformity of the data points around a regression line) are best detected not with the correlation coefficient but rather with visual inspection of a scatterplot.

Data from Table 2.2 were used to create Figure 2.3. Figure 2.3 is a scatterplot that shows test scores on the X axis and GPA on the Y axis. Thus, each point on the graph represents a person's value on the test as well as his or her GPA (i.e., a **bivariate distribution**). Looking at Figure 2.3, we see that there is a very strong relationship between scores on the first examination and overall GPA. This is indicated by the positive linear relationship between the two variables. That is, as scores on the first exam get larger, so does one's overall GPA. Most data points on the scatterplot are represented by a single circle. However, notice that a few points (around a test score of 89 or 90 and an overall GPA of 3.50–4.00) have lines coming from them. Each line represents an individual who had the same combination of test score and GPA. Examining how the pairs of scores cluster around the line of the graph, we notice that most scores are fairly close to the line. There do not appear to be any bivariate outliers (extreme on both the test score and GPA). The points are also relatively uniform along the line (i.e., they exhibit **homoscedasticity**), and the relationship between test scores and GPA does appear to follow a linear trend. The graph would have to be constructed differently to discover possible subgroup differences (e.g., male versus female students). For example, red circles could represent men, while blue circles represent women. Then, separate regression lines could be constructed for each gender subgroup. We will discuss this issue in more detail in Module 10 when we discuss test bias and fairness.

The Pearson correlation coefficient is by far the most used "statistic" in all of applied psychological measurement. As you will see throughout this book or any book on **measurement theory** and testing, the Pearson correlation coefficient is used for a wide variety of purposes. For example, it is used in estimating reliability, the standard error of measurement, the standard error of prediction or estimate, validity, item analysis statistics, meta-analysis, factor analysis, utility analysis, and many other procedures conducted as part of applied psychological measurement. Therefore, if there is any one statistic you should know inside and out, it is the Pearson correlation. One simple formula (there are several more complex ones) for the Pearson correlation is

$$r_{xy} = \sum Z_x Z_y / n$$

where $\sum Z_x Z_y$ is the sum of the cross product of the two standardized variables and n is the number of pairs of scores. Using the data from Table 2.2, $r_{xy} = 23.22 / 25 = .93$. A score of zero represents no relationship, and a score of 1.0 or –1.0 indicates a perfect relationship. Thus, we clearly have a rather strong relationship between test scores and GPA (the interpretation of correlation coefficients is discussed in more detail in Module 7). One problem with actually using this formula in practice is the potential for rounding error. Substantial rounding error can occur when converting raw scores to Z scores. When we used a computer to calculate the Pearson correlation coefficient, we obtained a value of .967. This may represent a substantial difference in some circumstances. Thus, in practice, the preceding formula is really a conceptual formula; it is not meant for actual calculations. If you need to calculate a correlation coefficient by hand, we would suggest using one of the computational formulas presented in any introductory statistics textbook. Better yet, let a computer do it for you.

Table 2.2   Example Test Scores and GPAs for a Classroom Examination With 25 Students

Test Score	Z Test Score	GPA	Z GPA	$\Sigma Z_1 Z_2$
68	– 1.85	2.21	–2.05	3.80
69	–1.73	2.45	–1.59	2.76
70	–1.61	2.34	–1.80	2.89
72	–1.36	2.56	–1.38	1.88
73	–1.23	2.85	–.83	1.02
74	–1.11	2.75	–1.02	1.13
76	–.86	3.10	–.36	.31
79	–.48	2.95	–.64	.31
80	–.36	3.15	–.26	.09
80	–.36	3.23	–.11	.04
84	.14	3.35	.12	.02
86	.39	3.18	–.20	–.08
87	.51	3.39	.20	.10
87	.51	3.45	.31	.16
88	.64	3.56	.52	.33
88	.64	3.53	.46	.29
88	.64	3.48	.37	.23
88	.64	3.75	.88	.56
89	.76	3.68	.75	.57
90	.89	3.85	1.07	.95
90	.89	3.88	1.13	1.00
90	.89	3.91	1.19	1.05
91	1.01	3.67	.73	.74
92	1.14	3.95	1.26	1.43
93	1.26	3.96	1.28	1.62
Total	0		0	23.22

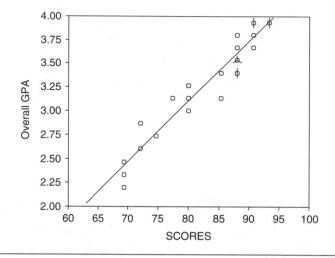

Figure 2.3   Bivariate Scatterplot of Exam 1 Test Scores and Overall GPA

Using univariate and bivariate descriptive statistics allows us both to interpret our test scores and to evaluate the test for its usefulness in predicting certain outcomes. Typically, we give a test not so much because we are interested in what the test tells us directly but rather in what it predicts. For example, you may have had to take the Graduate Record Examination (GRE) to get into a graduate program. Admissions officers are not so much interested in your GRE scores per se but rather in their ability to predict success in graduate school (or at least first-year grades). Thus, we typically are not interested in testing simply for the sake of testing; rather, we hope to use the test information to predict important outcomes. Thus, testing can be a powerful tool for decision makers if used judiciously and in combination with other relevant information. However, we often need strong statistical evidence to support our claims.

Estimation

In addition to describing a set of data, we may also be interested in estimating the underlying "true" ability level of individuals on different constructs. This will be what is referred to as an individual's true score in Module 5. Thus, with estimation, we use inferential statistics to build **confidence intervals** (e.g., 95% or 99%) around our observed test scores to estimate a population parameter. Again, using our data from Table 2.1, we know we have a sample mean of 82.88 and a standard deviation of 7.86 for a sample of

25 test scores. We would take a sample mean and, using the standard error of the mean (the standard deviation divided by the square root of the sample size), compute a 95% confidence interval around that mean to estimate the population parameter (population mean), such as

$$CI_{.95} = \bar{X} \pm t_{.05} * S_{\bar{X}} = 82.88 \pm 2.064 * (7.86/\sqrt{25}) = 79.64 \leq \mu_x \leq 86.13$$

where $t_{.05}$ is the tabled value for t at $\alpha = .05$, two tailed, for 24 ($n - 1$) degrees of freedom and $S_{\bar{X}}$ is the standard error of the mean, which is equal to the sample standard deviation divided by the square root of the sample size (n). This translates into English as, "We are 95% confident that the interval of 79.64 to 86.13 includes the true population mean for the test."

We may also take an individual score and use the standard error of measurement to estimate an individual's true score with regard to a specific construct of interest. In this case, we may have an individual score of 90. We also have to know the reliability of the test; in this case it is .88. Therefore,

$$CI_{.95} = X \pm Z_{.05} * (S_x * \sqrt{1 - r_{xx}}) = 90 \pm 1.96 * (7.86 * \sqrt{1 - .88})$$
$$= 84.63 \leq T \leq 95.37$$

where $Z_{.05}$ is the tabled value for Z at $\alpha = .05$, two tailed (note we use Z instead of t_{df} in this case because we are looking at individual scores), S_x is the sample standard deviation of the test, and r_{xx} is the reliability of the test. This translates into English as, "We are 95% confident that the interval of 84.63 to 95.37 includes the true score for an individual with an obtained score of 90 on the test."

You probably noticed that the interval for estimating an individual true score is much wider than the interval for estimating the population mean of a set of scores. In both cases (the 95% confidence interval for the population mean and the 95% confidence interval for the true score), we are interested in the observed score only to the extent it provides a meaningful estimate of the relevant value or population parameter of interest. Using the inferential statistic procedures of estimation allows us to do so.

Concluding Comments

Descriptive statistics play a large role in interpreting test scores. Both graphical (e.g., histograms, stem-and-leaf plots, scatterplots) and numerical (e.g., measures of central tendency, variability, and shape, as well as standardization of scores) techniques should be used to describe a set of test data fully. In particular, the Pearson product moment correlation coefficient is used in numerous procedures in psychological measurement, such as estimating reliability and validity, meta-analysis, and many other applications you will encounter throughout the rest of this book. In addition, inferential statistics, in the form of estimation procedures (e.g., confidence intervals), are also commonly used to interpret test data. This form of estimation can include estimating both population parameters, such as the population mean, as well as individual true scores.

Practical Questions

1. Are descriptive statistics or inferential statistics used more in applied psychological measurement?

2. Why are we more likely to use estimation rather than statistical significance testing in applied psychological measurement?

3. How do descriptive statistics and standardized scores allow us to interpret a set of test scores? Why?

4. What are the advantages of using a scatterplot in addition to the Pearson product moment correlation?

5. What does a 95% confidence interval of the mean tell us? How about a 99% confidence interval for an individual score?

Case Studies

CASE STUDY 2.1: DESCRIPTIVE STATISTICS FOR AN INTRODUCTORY PSYCHOLOGICAL STATISTICS TEST

Professor Ullman had just given the first examination in her introductory psychological statistics class. She passed the results on to Rudy, one of her graduate teaching assistants, so that he could "make sense" of the scores. After entering the scores into the computer, Rudy calculated some descriptive statistics. He first calculated the mean and standard deviation. The mean seemed a little low (68 out of 100) and the standard deviation seemed high (28). Therefore, he decided to go back and look at a histogram of the raw scores. Rudy was expecting to see something close to a **normal distribution** of scores. He had always learned that scores on cognitive ability and knowledge tests tend to approximate a normal distribution. Instead, the histogram for the first statistics test seemed to show just the opposite. The distribution of scores was basically a *U*-shaped distribution. That is, there were a bunch of students in the A and high-B range and then a bunch of students in the low-D and F range, with very few in between.

Rudy wasn't sure what to do next. He wanted to show Professor Ullman that he knew the statistics and measurement material, but why was he getting the strange-looking distribution? The course was set up with a 50-student lecture section and two 25-student lab sections. Rudy taught the morning lab session and Lisa taught the afternoon session. "I wonder how the scores for the two lab sections compare?" Rudy thought. Rudy also remembered that on the first day of the lab session students filled out several questionnaires. There were a couple of personality questionnaires, an attitude toward statistics measure, and demographic data, including GPA, year in school, whether the student had transferred from a junior college, gender, ethnicity, and similar items. Could those somehow be useful in understanding what was going on with the test data? Rudy decided he had better present his preliminary results to Professor Ullman and see what she had to say.

Questions to Ponder

1. What additional descriptive statistics should Rudy have run to try to make sense of the exam data?

2. How could Rudy have used the additional questionnaire data to help make sense of the test scores?

3. What statistics could Rudy calculate to determine if there really were any "significant differences" between the two laboratory sections?

4. Professor Ullman has taught the undergraduate statistics class many times. Would it make sense to go back and compare this term's results on the first exam to previous classes' performance on exam 1? Why or why not?

5. What graphical or visual data displays of the data would be appropriate in this situation?

6. Would it be helpful to estimate any population parameters in this situation?

7. Would it make sense to estimate any true scores in this situation?

CASE STUDY 2.2: CHOOSING AND INTERPRETING A CLINICAL TEST

Megan, a second-year clinical psychology graduate student, had just gotten her first assignment in her graduate internship placement in the Community Counseling Center (CCC). Dr. Chavez had given her a set of two standardized psychological tests she was to administer to a CCC client who was referred by a judge from the county's family court system. The client had a history of verbally abusing his wife and children. In addition, he had threatened physical harm against his family on numerous occasions. Fortunately, however, he had never actually followed through on his verbal threats of physical violence. Given the client's history, the judge wanted to refer the client for anger management treatment. In order for the client to qualify for the court-ordered treatment, however, he had to score "sufficiently high" on at least one of two psychological tests. Ultimately, it was up to Dr. Chavez and Megan to determine if he had scored sufficiently high on the tests and to make a recommendation to the judge as to whether the client should be referred to the anger management treatment program.

Megan administered the two psychological tests to the client. She then scored the tests. As it turned out, for both tests the client had fallen just a point or two below the cutoff set by the court to be considered "sufficiently high" to warrant participation in the court-ordered anger management treatment program. However, Megan had just completed her graduate measurement course the term before. She knew that a test taker's observed score is only an estimate of his or her true underlying level on the construct being measured. To her, it seemed wrong to take the test at "face value" in that there is always measurement error associated with any psychological test. What about the other information in this client's history? Feeling a little frustrated, Megan thought it was time to discuss the case further with Dr. Chavez.

Questions to Ponder

1. What statistics should Megan calculate to get an estimate of the client's underlying true score on the psychological measures?

2. If you were Megan, what other information would you want to know about the tests in order to make the best decision possible?

3. Should the nature of the offense have any impact on how Megan determines if the client is "sufficiently high" on the psychological measures? If yes, how so? If no, why not?

4. How should (or could) the other information in the client's file be combined with the test data to make a recommendation to the court?

Exercises

PROLOGUE: The Equal Employment Opportunity Commission (EEOC) has received a complaint about our current Mechanical Comprehension (MC) test from a former job applicant (a female minority) who applied, but was rejected, for our engineering assistant position. As you know, we are in the process of replacing our current MC test with a new one. The EEOC analyst assigned to our case will be here to meet with us in 1 hour so we better have some answers by then. Use the data set "Mechanical Comprehension.sav" described in Appendix B to complete the following exercises.

EXERCISE 2.1: COMPUTING DESCRIPTIVE STATISTICS

OBJECTIVE: To practice computing and interpreting descriptive statistics on test data.

1. What descriptive information can we provide to the EEOC regarding the current MC test being used? How about the proposed one?

2. Create appropriate graphs to describe the current and proposed MC tests.

3. Compute appropriate measures of central tendency, variability, and shape for the current and proposed MC tests.

EXERCISE 2.2: COMPUTING STANDARDIZED SCORES

(*Note:* You will have to refer to the Further Readings for information on how to compute **stanine** and *T* scores, which were not covered in this module because of space limitations.)

OBJECTIVE: To practice creating standardized scores.

1. Create standardized Z scores for both the current and the proposed MC tests.

2. Create stanine scores for both the current and the proposed MC tests.

3. Create standardized T scores (with a mean of 50 and a standard deviation of 10) for both the current and the proposed MC tests.

How do the Z scores, stanine, and T scores compare?

EXERCISE 2.3: COMPUTING BIVARIATE STATISTICS

OBJECTIVE: To practice computing and interpreting inferential statistics.

1. Is the current test related to any other demographic information such as age, education level, or work experience? How about the proposed test?

2. The complainant (with ID #450) is suggesting that the test is biased/unfair. What was her score? What is your best guess of her "true" score? How does her score compare to the scores of the other applicants? To the scores of other female applicants? To the scores of other minority applicants? (Look at this in terms of both the current and the proposed test.)

EXERCISE 2.4: ENTERING AND COMPUTING STATISTICS

OBJECTIVE: To practice entering and computing statistics.

Enter the data in Tables 2.1 and 2.2 into a statistical analysis program (we used SPSS 11.0). You can even use a common spreadsheet program to conduct most of the analyses. Try to replicate the findings presented in the module overview. Compute measures of central tendency, variability, and shape. In addition, try to recreate the figures presented in this module. Finally, create your own figures that you think best represent the data.

Internet Web Site References

2.1. http://www.statsoft.com/textbook/esc1.html

This Web page provides the table of contents for an electronic statistics textbook provided by Statsoft, Inc.

2.2. http://www.socialpsychology.org/methods.htm

This Web page provides links to numerous Web sites related to statistics and research methodology.

2.3. http://huizen.dds.nl/~berrie/

This Web page provides several visual illustrations of common statistical concepts, including the normal distribution.

2.4. http://www.ruf.rice.edu/~lane/rvls.html

This Web page presents Rice University's Virtual Lab in Statistics. It provides an online textbook, case studies, and visual simulations of statistical measurements.

2.5. http://www.wadsworth.com/psychology_d/templates/student_resources/ workshops/stat_workshp/correlation/correlation_01.html

This Web page provides additional information on correlation and regression.

Further Readings

Crocker, L. M., & Algina, J. (1986). *Introduction to classical and modern test theory* (pp. 16–42). Belmont, CA: Wadsworth.

Ghiselli, E. E., Campbell, J. P., & Zedeck, S. (1981). *Measurement theory for the behavioral sciences* (pp. 31–58). New York: W. H. Freeman.

Murphy, K. R., & Davidshofer, C. O. (2001). *Psychological testing: Principles and applications* (5th ed., pp. 67–85). Upper Saddle River, NJ: Prentice Hall.

In addition, most introductory (psychological) statistics books will provide a more detailed description of the descriptive statistics discussed in this module, although not as specific to psychological testing as the preceding references.

Module 3

Psychological Scaling

"*Measurement* essentially is concerned with the methods used to provide quantitative descriptions of the extent to which individuals manifest or possess specified characteristics" (Ghiselli, Campbell, & Zedeck, 1981, p. 2). "*Measurement* is the assigning of numbers to individuals in a systematic way as a means of representing properties of the individuals" (Allen & Yen, 1979, p. 2). "'*Measurement*' consists of rules for assigning symbols to objects so as to (1) represent quantities of attributes numerically (scaling) or (2) define whether the objects fall in the same or different categories with respect to a given attribute (classification)" (Nunnally & Bernstein, 1994, p. 3).

No matter which popular definition of the term **measurement** you choose, several underlying themes emerge. First, we need to be able to quantify the attribute of interest. That is, we need to have numbers to designate how much (or little) of an attribute an individual possesses. Second, we must be able to quantify our attribute of interest in a consistent and systematic way (i.e., standardization). That is, we need to make sure that if someone else wants to replicate our measurement process, it is systematic enough that meaningful replication is possible. Finally, we must remember that we are measuring attributes of individuals (or objects), not the individuals per se. This last point is particularly important when performing high-stakes testing or when dealing with sensitive subject matter. For example, if we disqualify a job candidate because he or she scored below the established cutoff on a preemployment drug test, we want to make sure that the person is not "labeled" as a drug addict. Our tests are not perfect and whenever we set a cutoff on a test, we may be making an error by designating someone as above or below the cutoff. In the previous example, we may be mistakenly classifying someone as a drug user when, in fact, he or she is not.

Levels of Measurement

As the definition of Nunnally and Bernstein (1994) suggests, by systematically measuring the attribute of interest we can either classify or scale individuals with regard to the attribute of interest. Whether we engage in classification or scaling depends in large part on the level of measurement used to assess our **construct**. For example, if our attribute is measured on a **nominal scale** of measurement, then we can only classify individuals as falling into one or another mutually exclusive category. This is because the different categories (e.g., men versus women) represent only **qualitative** differences. Say, for example, we are measuring the demographic variable of race. An individual can fall into one of several possible categories. Hence, we are simply classifying individuals based on self-identified race. Even if we tell the computer that Caucasians should be coded 0, African Americans 1, Hispanics 2, Asian Americans 3, and so on, that does not mean that these values have any quantitative meaning. They are simply labels for our racial categories.

For example, the first author once had an undergraduate student working on a research project with him. She was asked to enter some data and run a few Pearson correlation coefficients. The student came back very excited that she had found a significant relationship between race and our outcome variable of interest (something akin to job performance). Race had a coding scheme similar to that described previously. When the student was asked to interpret the correlation coefficient, she looked dumbfounded, as well she should, because the correlation coefficient was not interpretable in this situation, as the variable race was measured at the nominal level.

On the other hand, we may have a variable such as temperature that we can quantify in a variety of ways. Assume we had 10 objects and we wanted to determine the temperature of each one. If we did not have a thermometer, we could simply touch each one, assuming it was not too hot or too cold, and then rank order the objects based on how hot or cold they felt to the touch. This, of course, is assuming that the objects were all made of material with similar heat transference properties (e.g., metal transfers heat, or cold, much better than wood). This would represent an **ordinal scale** of measurement where objects are simply rank ordered. You would not know how much hotter one object is than another, but you would know that A is hotter than B, if A is ranked higher than B. Is the ordinal level of measurement sufficient? In some cases, it is. For example, if you want to draw a bath for your child, do you need to know the exact temperature? Not really, you just need to be careful not to scald your child.

Alternatively, we may find a thermometer that measures temperature in degrees Celsius and use it to measure the temperature of the 10 items. This device uses an **interval scale** of measurement because we have equal intervals between degrees on the scale. However, the zero point on the scale is arbitrary; 0 degrees Celsius represents the point at which water freezes at sea level. That is, zero on the scale does not represent "true zero," which in this case would mean a complete absence of heat. However, if we were to use a thermometer that used the Kelvin scale, we would be using a **ratio scale** of measurement because zero on the Kelvin scale does represent "true zero" (i.e., no heat).

When we measure our construct of interest at the nominal (i.e., qualitative) level of measurement, we can only classify objects into categories. As a result, we are very limited in the types of data manipulations and statistical analyses we can perform on the data. Referring to the previous module on descriptive statistics, we could compute frequency counts or determine the modal response (i.e., category), but not much else. However, if we were at least able to rank order our objects based on the degree to which they possess our construct of interest (i.e., we have **quantitative** data), then we could actually scale our construct. In addition, higher levels of measurement allow for more in-depth statistical analyses. With ordinal data, for example, we can compute statistics such as the median, range, and interquartile range. When we have interval-level data, we can calculate statistics such as means, standard deviations, variances, and the various statistics of shape (e.g., skew and kurtosis). With interval-level data, it is important to know the shape of the distribution, as different-shaped distributions imply different interpretations for statistics such as the mean and standard deviation.

Unidimensional Scaling Models

In psychological measurement, we are typically most interested in **scaling** some characteristic, trait, or **ability** of a person. That is, we want to know how much of an attribute of interest a given person possesses. This will allow us to estimate the degree of inter-individual and intra-individual differences (as discussed in Module 1) among the subjects on the attribute of interest. This measurement process is usually referred to as **psychometrics** or *psychological measurement*. However, we can also scale the stimuli that we give to individuals, as well as the responses that individuals provide. Scaling of stimuli and responses is typically referred to as *psychological scaling*. Scaling of stimuli is more prominent in the area of psychophysics or sensory/perception psychology that focuses on physical phenomena and whose roots date back to mid–19th century Germany. It was not until the 1920s that Thurstone began to apply the same scaling principles to scaling psychological attitudes. In addition, we can attempt to scale several factors at once. This can get very tricky, however. So more often than not, we hold one factor constant (e.g., responses), collapse across a second (e.g., stimuli), and then scale the third (e.g., individuals) factor.

For example, say we administered a 25-item measure of social anxiety to a group of schoolchildren. We would typically assume all children are interpreting the response scale (e.g., a scale of 1–7) for each question in the same way (i.e., responses are constant), although not necessarily responding with the same value. If they did all respond with exactly the same value, then we would have no variability and thus the scale would be of little interest to us because it would have no predictive value. Next, we would collapse across stimuli (i.e., get a total score for the 25 items). As a result, we would be left with scaling children on the construct of social anxiety.

Many issues (besides which factor we are scaling) arise when performing a scaling study. One important factor is who we select to participate in our study. When we scale people (*psychometrics*), we typically obtain a random sample of individuals from the population that we wish to generalize. In our preceding example, we would want a random sample of school-aged children so that our results generalize to all school-aged children. Conversely, when we scale stimuli (*psychological scaling*), we do not want a random sample of individuals. Rather, the sample of individuals we select should be purposefully and carefully selected based on their respective expertise on the construct being scaled. That is, they should all be **subject matter experts (SMEs)**. In our preceding example, we would want experts on the measurement of social anxiety, particularly as it relates to children in school settings, to serve as our SMEs. Such SMEs would likely include individuals with degrees and expertise in clinical, school, developmental, counseling, or personality psychology.

Another difference between psychometrics and psychological scaling is that with psychometrics we ask our participants to provide their individual feelings, **attitudes,** and/or personal ratings toward a particular topic. In doing so, we will be able to determine how individuals differ on our construct of interest. With psychological scaling, however, we typically ask participants (i.e., SMEs) to provide their professional judgment of the particular stimuli, regardless of their personal feelings or attitudes toward the topic or stimulus. This may include ratings of how well different stimuli represent the construct and at what level of intensity the construct is represented. Thus, with psychometrics, you would sum across items (i.e., stimuli) within an individual respondent in order to obtain his or her score on the construct. With psychological scaling, however, the researcher would sum across raters (SMEs) within a given stimulus (e.g., question) in order to obtain rating(s) of each stimulus. Once the researcher was confident that each stimulus did, in fact, tap into the construct and had some estimate of the level at which it did so, only then should the researcher feel confident in presenting the now scaled stimuli to a random sample of relevant participants for psychometric purposes.

The third category of responses, which we said we typically hold constant, also needs to be identified. That is, we have to decide in what fashion we will have subjects respond to our stimuli. Such response options may include requiring our participants to make comparative judgments (e.g., which is more important, A or B?), subjective evaluations (e.g., strongly agree to strongly disagree), or an absolute judgment (e.g., how hot is this object?). Different response formats may well influence how we write and edit our stimuli. In addition, they may also influence how we evaluate the quality or the "accuracy" of the response. For example, with absolute judgments, we may have a standard of comparison, especially if subjects are being asked to rate physical characteristics such as weight, height, or intensity of sound or light. With attitudes and psychological constructs, such "standards" are hard to come by.

There are a few options (e.g., Guttman's Scalogram and Coomb's unfolding technique) for simultaneously scaling people and stimuli, but more often than not we scale only one dimension at a time. However, we must scale our stimuli first (or seek a well-established measure) before we can have confidence in scaling individuals on the stimuli. Advanced texts such as Nunnally and Bernstein (1994), Ghiselli et al. (1981), and Crocker and Algina (1986) all provide detailed descriptions of different scaling methods for scaling stimuli and response data at a variety of different levels of measurement. We refer you to these advanced texts for more detailed explanations. In the following discussion, we will provide only a general overview of the major unidimensional scaling techniques.

We can scale stimuli at a variety of different measurement levels. At the nominal level of measurement, we have a variety of sorting techniques. In this case, SMEs are asked to sort the stimuli into different categories based on some dimension. For example, our SMEs with expertise in the social anxiety of school-aged children might be asked to sort a variety of questions according to whether the items are measuring school-related social anxiety or not. In doing so, we are able to determine which items to remove and which to keep for further analyses when our goal is to measure school-related social anxiety.

At the ordinal level of measurement, we have the Q-sort method, paired comparisons, Guttman's Scalogram, Coomb's unfolding technique, and a variety of rating scales. The major task of SMEs is to rank order items from highest to lowest or from weakest to strongest. Again, our SMEs with expertise in school-related social anxiety might be asked to sort a variety of questions. However, instead of a simple "yes" and "no" sorting, in terms of whether the questions measure social anxiety or not, the SMEs might be asked to sort the items in terms of the extent to which they measure social anxiety. So, for example, an item that states, "I tend to feel anxious when I am at school" would likely get a higher ranking than an item that states, "I tend to have few friends at school." While both items may be tapping into social anxiety, the first item is clearly more directly assessing school-related social anxiety.

At the interval level of measurement, we have direct estimation, the method of bisection, and Thurstone's methods of comparative and categorical judgments. With these methods, SMEs are asked not only to rank order items but also to actually help determine the magnitude of the differences among items. With Thurstone's method of comparative judgment, SMEs compare every possible pair of stimuli and select the item within the pair that is the better item for assessing the construct. Thurstone's method of categorical judgment, while less tedious for SMEs when there are many stimuli to assess in that they simply rate each stimulus (not each pair of stimuli), does require more cognitive energy for each rating provided. This is because the SME must now estimate the actual value of the stimulus.

Multidimensional Scaling Models

With unidimensional scaling, as described previously, subjects are asked to respond to stimuli with regard to a particular dimension. For example, a consumer psychologist might ask subjects how they would rate the "value" of a particular consumer product. With **multidimensional scaling (MDS)**, however, subjects are typically asked to give just their general impression or broad rating of similarities or differences among stimuli. For example, subjects might be asked to compare several different types of products and simply rate which are similar or which they prefer the best overall. Subsequent analyses, using Euclidean spatial models, would "map" the products in multidimensional space. The different multiple dimensions would then be "discovered" or "extracted" with multivariate statistical techniques, thus establishing which dimensions the consumer is using to distinguish the products. MDS can be particularly useful when subjects are unable to articulate "why" they like a stimulus, yet they are confident that they prefer one stimulus to another.

A Step-by-Step Scaling Example

Let us now work through our earlier example on school-related social anxiety in school-aged children from start to finish. What would be the first step in conducting a study where you wanted to develop a measure to assess school-related social anxiety in school-aged children? Well, our first step is to make sure we have a clear definition of what we mean by our construct of school-related social anxiety. Everyone who hears this term may have a slightly different impression of what we would like to assess. Therefore, we need to be able to present our SMEs with a single definition of what we are trying to assess when we talk about this construct. In this case, we will start with, "School-related social anxiety refers to the uneasiness school-aged children experience when they are in school-related social settings, but that may not be manifested in nonschool social settings such as at home or with friends outside of school. Such uneasiness may include feelings of isolation, physical stressors, and other such psychological and physical symptoms." Okay, it is not great, but it is a start. What next? Now we need to start developing items to assess our construct. Who should do that? Ah, yes, our infamous SMEs. Who should serve as SMEs in this instance and how many do we need? We stated earlier that, ideally, we would want to use school psychologists, clinical psychologists, counseling psychologists, developmental psychologists, and/or personality theorists. It may be difficult, however, to convince such individuals to participate in the item generation stage of the study. Therefore, it may be more practical and realistic for you, the researcher, and some colleagues and/or research assistants to generate potential items and then reserve the SMEs to provide actual ratings on the items you generate.

How many items do we need? Unfortunately, there is no easy answer to this question. The best response is, "The more the better." Ideally, you would want to generate at least twice as many items as you hope to have on your final scale. Therefore, if you want a 25-item scale of school-related social anxiety, you should generate at least 50 items. Now that we have our 50 or more items, it is time to bring in our SMEs. Again, how many SMEs do we need? Ideally, it would be nice to have "lots" of them; in reality, we may be lucky to get four or five. At a minimum, you need to have more than two in order to obtain variability estimates. Any number beyond two will be advantageous, within reason of course. This is also the step where we need to select one of the scaling models. Remember, these "models" are simply standardized procedures that will allow us to attach meaningful numbers to the responses our subjects will ultimately provide. Thus, we need not get too anxious (pardon the pun) over which method we choose to scale social anxiety. One prominent scaling procedure, which we touched on briefly, is Likert scaling, so we will use that.

Before we jump into scaling our stimuli, however, we need to know what type of responses we want our subjects to provide. In fact, this would probably be good to know as we are writing our questions. Remember, we pointed out earlier that these might include evaluative judgments, degree of agreement, frequency of occurrence, and so on. Which one we choose is probably not as critical as the fact that all of our items are consistent with the response scale we choose. For example, we do not want to mix questions with statements. In this case, we will go with the degree of agreement format because this is common with Likert-type scales. With most **Likert scales,** we usually have a four- or five-option response scale ranging from strongly agree to strongly disagree (e.g., 1 = Strongly Disagree, 2 = Disagree, 3 = Undecided, 4 = Agree, and 5 = Strongly Agree). With an odd number of scale values, we have an undecided or neutral option in the middle. With an even number of scale values, we force the respondent to agree or disagree (sometimes called a forced format or choice scale). So should we use four or five options? It is mostly a matter of preference; be aware, however, which one you choose can affect the interpretation of your scores.

So far, we have defined our construct, generated items, and decided on a response scale. Now it is time to let our SMEs loose on the items. Remember, the SMEs are providing their professional judgment as to how well each item represents the construct or to what degree it represents the construct, regardless of their personal feelings. Once we have the SME ratings, how do we use these to decide which items to retain? Well, we could compute statistics such as item-total correlations. That is, we could determine how well a given item correlates with the total score on the scale. If it correlates poorly, then we would likely discard that item. What constitutes "poorly"? There is no hard and fast rule, but you would probably only want to retain items that had at least a .50 or higher correlation with the total scale. You may also want to look at the variability in ratings provided by the SMEs. If the ratings for a given item do not differ much, then the SMEs are being consistent in their ratings, which is a good thing, but from a psychometric standpoint, too little variability leaves us unable to compute certain statistics (i.e., correlation coefficients). Ultimately, which items to keep and which to remove is a professional judgment call. However, in practical terms, remember you wanted a 25-item scale. So why not choose the top 25 items in terms of their item-total correlation and discriminability? Some of these items may, of course, still require further editing before being implemented.

Finally, you are ready to administer your newly developed Likert scale to actual subjects. How many subjects do you need? For the psychometric portion of the study (estimating reliability and validity, as discussed later in the book), the answer is again, "the more the better." Realistically, though, we need to have enough for our statistics to be meaningful. That usually means at least 100 subjects. For evaluating research questions and hypotheses, many factors come into play in determining appropriate sample size. In that instance, most researchers now conduct power and/or precision analyses to determine the most desirable sample size for their particular situation.

An individual's score on the scale will be the sum or mean of his or her responses to the 25 items. Remember that you may have some items that have reverse meaning (e.g., they were really assessing social calmness, not social anxiety). These items will need to be reverse scored. That is, what was a 1 is now a 5, a 2 becomes a 4, 3 stays 3, 4 becomes 2, and 5 becomes 1. This reverse scoring of reversed items should be done before the summated total score is obtained. Now that you have created and evaluated your school-related social anxiety scale, you are ready to carry out the psychometric studies that we discuss in Modules 5 through 8.

Concluding Comments

We began by looking at several definitions of measurement and examining the key elements of psychological measurement. Next, we discussed the different levels of measurement that our psychological scales can assess. Then we talked about key issues distinguishing psychometrics from psychological scaling. We next provided an overview to the different unidimensional scaling models and how they relate to the different levels of measurement. Finally, we worked through a realistic step-by-step example of what an applied scaling project might look like. We also briefly touched on multidimensional scaling. In the final analysis, the key is first to have confidence in your stimuli and responses and then move on to scale individuals. This is the crux of the psychometric process, which is the topic of the remainder of this book.

Practical Questions

1. What is the difference between scaling and classification?

2. What is the difference between psychometrics and psychological scaling?

3. Why do you think it is so difficult to scale more than one dimension (i.e., people, stimuli, and responses) at once?

4. Why is it important to know the level of measurement of our data before we begin the scaling process?

5. How would we scale multiple dimensions at one time?

Case Studies

CASE STUDY 3.1: SCALING STUDY IN CONSUMER PSYCHOLOGY

Benjamin, a senior who had a dual major in psychology and marketing, decided he wanted to do his undergraduate honors thesis in the area of consumer psychology. Specifically, he was interested in determining how well young children were able to recall a series of visual only (e.g., magazine advertisements), auditory only (e.g., radio commercials), and combined visual and auditory (e.g., television commercials) advertisements for Lego® building toys. He had learned in his undergraduate tests and measurements class that most of the time we were interested in looking at individual differences within our subjects. In this case, would it be who was able to remember one type of advertisement better than another? That didn't really seem to be the issue of major concern here. Why would advertisers be interested in the type of preadolescent who remembered one type of advertisement better than others his age? Maybe it would allow advertisers to target their product to specific children (e.g., those who watch PBS programming versus those who watch network or cable programming).

On second thought, Benjamin wondered whether the real issue was which method of advertising was most likely to be remembered by a "typical" child. If so, it seemed as if he should really be more interested in scaling different types of advertising modalities (i.e., stimuli) than in scaling subjects. By doing so, advertisers could determine which modalities would produce the best recall and thus how to most effectively spend their advertising dollars. As Benjamin thought some more, he began to wonder if it was the response that was really of most interest. That is, who cares if the child recalls the advertisement or not, isn't the bigger issue whether the child (or his or her parents) actually buys the toy (i.e., their response)? Maybe he needed to scale the responses children have to the different modes of advertisement, not the subjects or stimuli. Suddenly, it all seemed rather confusing. So, it was off to his advisor's office to get some advice and direction.

Questions to Ponder

1. What type of scaling should Benjamin be most concerned with? Subject, stimulus, or response? Why?

2. Who should Benjamin get to serve as subjects for his study?

3. Would he be better served with a random sample of children or with a relatively homogeneous group of subject matter experts (SMEs) for his scaling study?

4. What level of measurement data is Benjamin dealing with?

5. Will Benjamin actually have to do several scaling projects to get the information he needs?

CASE STUDY 3.2: A CONSULTING PROJECT ON PERFORMANCE ASSESSMENT

Jennifer, a graduate student who had just completed her first year in an industrial and organizational psychology PhD program, was excited because she had just gotten her first consulting job. She was to develop a performance appraisal form to assess workers in her uncle's small domestic cleaning service. There were a total of 15 "maids" and two office supervisors. Her uncle wanted to know which maids should receive a pay raise and how much he should give each of them. He wanted to make sure, however, that their raises were performance based. So, he contracted with Jennifer to create an easy-to-use performance appraisal form that he and his two office supervisors could use to assess each maid and ultimately use that information to determine the size of the raise for each maid.

Jennifer first conducted a literature search to see if she could find an existing performance assessment form that would fit the bill. While some existing forms looked like they might work, it seemed like no matter which one she chose she would have to do some significant modifications. She also noticed that different forms used different points of reference. For example, some performance appraisal forms used an absolute scale (e.g., below standard . . . at standard . . . above standard), while others used a relative scale (e.g., below average . . .

average . . . above average). Some used a paired comparison technique. That is, who is the better performer? Maid A or Maid B? Maid A or Maid C? Also, some scales had three categories or anchors, others five, some seven, and one was on a scale of 1–100. There was even one that had no numbers or words at all; it was simply a series of faces ranging from a deep frown to a very big grin. A bit overwhelmed and a little unsure of how to proceed, Jennifer decided to seek the advice of the professor who would be teaching her performance assessment class next semester.

Questions to Ponder

1. What difference (if any) does it make if Jennifer uses an absolute or a relative rating scale?

2. Should Jennifer just develop her own scale or try to use an existing measure?

3. What issues should Jennifer be concerned with if she modifies an existing scale?

4. Is Jennifer more interested in scaling responses, stimuli, or subjects? Explain.

5. Who should serve as the raters in this case? The supervisors? Her uncle? The respective clients?

6. Would the decision in terms of who will serve as raters affect which type of scale is used (e.g., relative versus absolute versus paired comparison)?

Exercises

EXERCISE 3.1: LEVELS OF MEASUREMENT

OBJECTIVE: To practice defining and identifying different levels of measurement.

Identify two psychological constructs of interest. These could include personality (e.g., anxiety, extraversion), intelligence (e.g., verbal, quantitative, space visualization), or more ephemeral (e.g., infatuation, anger) constructs. Then, identify existing measures of these two constructs and, based on the description of the different levels of measurement discussed in the overview to this module (i.e., nominal, ordinal, interval, and ratio), or your main text, discuss the level of measurement of the constructs. Finally, identify how you would measure the construct at two different alternative levels of measurement.

For example, assume you wanted to look at extraversion and you chose the NEO personality inventory. Most would identify extraversion as being measured at the interval level of measurement using this instrument. Thus, how might you measure extraversion at a nominal, ordinal, or ratio level of measurement?

EXERCISE 3.2: CONDUCTING A SCALING STUDY

OBJECTIVE: To provide practice in conducting a scaling study.

Outline a scaling study similar to the example that is provided at the end of the overview section of the module. Select a construct (other than school-related social anxiety) and answer the following questions:

1. What is the definition of your construct?

2. Who is going to generate items to measure the construct? How many items do they need to generate? Why?

3. What scaling model would be most appropriate for your example?

4. Who is going to serve as SMEs to rate the items?

5. On what basis are you going to select the items to keep for the final version of your scale?

6. Who are going to serve as subjects for your study? How many subjects do you need?

EXERCISE 3.3: SCALING ITEMS

OBJECTIVE: To practice scaling items.

Using the data from the "Bus Driver.sav" data set, scale the 10 task items on the three dimensions of "Frequency," "Relative Time Spent," and "Importance." Use Table 3.1 to fill in the mean task ratings across the three dimensions. In order for an item to be "retained" for further consideration, the task must, on average, be carried out at least "regularly" (i.e., 3.0 or higher) in terms of frequency, fall between "little" and "moderate" (i.e., 2.5 or higher) in terms of relative time spent, and be rated as "very important" (i.e., 4.0 or higher) in terms of importance. Given these criteria, which of the 10 tasks meet all three of these criteria and, thus, should be retained?

Table 3.1   Summary of Task Ratings

Task Number	Average Frequency Rating (≥ 3.0)	Average Relative Time Spent Rating (≥ 2.5)	Average Importance Rating (≥ 4.0)
1			
2			
3			
4			
5			
6			
7			
8			
9			
10			

Internet Web Site References

3.1. http://web.uccs.edu/lbecker/SPSS/scalemeas.htm

This Web page provides information on the nominal, ordinal, interval, and ratio scales of measurement, along with possible arithmetic operations and example statistics for each.

3.2. http://www.fs.fed.us/rm/pubs_rm/rm_rp293.pdf

This Web page displays a paper in PDF format by Thomas Brown and Terry Daniel that provides theoretical and descriptive background on psychological scaling and a specific computer program for psychological scaling called RMRATE. Their paper also provides a detailed description of the application of these procedures to an applied setting.

3.3. http://trochim.human.cornell.edu/kb/measlevl.htm

The Web page also provides information on levels of measurement.

3.4. http://trochim.human.cornell.edu/kb/scaling.htm

This Web page presents an overview of scaling, with links to issues in scaling and explanations of the Thurstone, Likert, and Guttman scaling methods.

Further Readings

Crocker, L. M., & Algina, J. (1986). *Introduction to classical and modern test theory* (pp. 45–66). Belmont, CA: Wadsworth.

Ghiselli, E. E., Campbell, J. P., & Zedeck, S. (1981). *Measurement theory for the behavioral sciences* (pp. 391–420). New York: W. H. Freeman.

Guildford, J. P. (1954). *Psychometric methods.* New York: McGraw-Hill.

Nunnally, J. C., & Bernstein, I. H. (1994). *Psychometric theory* (3rd ed., pp. 31–82). New York: McGraw-Hill.

Torgerson, W. S. (1958). *Theory and methods of scaling.* New York: Wiley.

van der Ven, A. H. G. S. (1980). *Introduction to scaling.* New York: Wiley.

Module 4

Test Preparation
and Specification

I n developing a test from scratch, it might seem that we would begin the
process by writing items. However, test development begins much earlier
than item writing. Indeed, a number of issues must be carefully considered
before creating even a single test item. This module presents these issues as
a number of steps to be conducted during the early phases of test development. These steps, if fully embraced, will facilitate the writing of items and
help ensure the development of a quality test. In many ways, the steps we
take in developing a test prior to item writing are analogous to the steps
a good researcher takes in preparation for conducting a study. Before conducting a study, the researcher must first determine the intended population
to whom he or she would like to generalize the results of the study. Once the
intended population has been determined, the researcher must carefully consider how to design the methodology in order to promote generalizing the
results to the population of interest. In the realm of testing, the test author
must consider a set of related issues.

Step 1: Specify the Type of Measure

Tests can be categorized into measures of maximal performance and measures of typical performance. Measures of maximal performance refer to
aptitude tests or **achievement tests,** including classroom exams and personnel selection tests. Such measures are intended to assess an individual's
all-out effort. Typically, each item on these tests has a known correct

answer. Measures of typical performance, on the other hand, include personality and interest inventories as well as attitude scales. Items on these measures are considered to have no single "correct" response.

While the test development process for these types of measures differs, this module identifies many of the developmental steps these measures share in common. Additional discussion of the development of tests of maximal performance is presented in Module 11, while the development of measures of typical performance is further discussed in Module 15.

Step 2: Define the Domain of the Test

Defining the domain you intend to assess is a crucial step in the test development process. The definition of the domain must be clearly specified in order to determine what limits the test is intended to have. On first blush, providing a definition for the construct may seem easy. After all, you know what you want to measure, right? Or do you? Various researchers define even familiar constructs such as "intelligence" very differently. If you are creating the test, you get to choose the definition that you believe is most appropriate. However, it is important that other experts can express agreement with your definition of the construct.

Some pundits suggest that any good definition of a construct will be relatively brief, perhaps no longer than a couple of sentences. However, there are a multitude of issues to consider in developing the definition. The answers to each of the following questions will have a huge impact on exactly how the construct will be defined.

Step 2a: What Is the Intended Context of the Test?

Is the test intended to assess some trait that applies to all people and is somewhat constant across every context? If so, then this should be specified in the definition. On the other hand, some traits are tied to a particular situation. For example, although conscientiousness is identified as one of the Big Five personality dimensions, a person may be conscientious at work, but not so conscientious in performance of household chores. Thus, we would likely develop a very different scale if we were assessing one's general conscientiousness than if we were merely interested in conscientiousness related to the work environment. By limiting the domain to that context in which we are specifically interested, we will likely reduce the amount of error associated with the test, thus increasing the internal consistency reliability. As an added benefit, test takers might perceive the more specific test as possessing greater face validity than a more general instrument measuring a broader domain.

Step 2b: How Is the Construct to Be Measured Different From Related Constructs?

What is assumed in this question is that you first identify related constructs. Once identified, it is essential to distinguish differences between your construct and related constructs. This will ensure that, once you begin developing items, your test items will not unintentionally stray beyond the limited context to which your test applies. Identification of related but distinct concepts will be important again later on if you choose to collect validity evidence for the newly developed measure using a construct validation approach.

Step 2c: What Is the Dimensionality of the Construct?

Many constructs are fairly broad in nature, but are themselves composed of several related components that must be measured to assess the construct fully. Political conservatism, for instance, is a multidimensional construct. Under the general rubric of political conservatism, one might want to develop specific subscales assessing the dimensions of social, economic, and ecological conservatism. In identifying the dimensionality of a construct, we help ensure that the entire construct is fully assessed.

Step 2d: How Much Emphasis Should Be Placed on Each Dimension or Facet of the Construct?

In identifying that a construct is multidimensional or multifaceted, it becomes imperative to consider how much weight each dimension or facet should have in the final scale. Are all dimensions or facets equally important, or are some more important than others? The number of items per dimension or facet should reflect these decisions.

Although defining the construct may be one of the most underrated steps in test development, there are additional interrelated steps that also deserve increased attention by test developers.

Step 3: Determine Whether a Closed-Ended or Open-Ended Item Format Will Be Used

Should the measure be composed of items that are open ended, as with interview questionnaires, essay exams, and projective tests, or should a limited number of response options be provided for each item, as is the case for multiple-choice exams and scales utilizing Likert-type response options?

Closed-ended items minimize the expertise required for test administration, and responses are far easier to analyze than is typically the case for responses to open-ended items. Because closed-ended items present the response options to test takers, however, they do not allow respondents to clarify their answers. Further, the presence of response options may suggest answers that respondents would not have otherwise considered.

In contrast, test takers can qualify their answers to open-ended items by elaborating upon their responses. Responses tend to reveal that which is most salient to the examinee, and responses are uninfluenced by response options. However, responses to open-ended items can be repetitious, and often provide irrelevant information. Not only must the test administrator be more highly trained than is the case for administration of most closed-ended measures, but individual differences in respondents' abilities to articulate their responses are likely to play a much greater role in testing with open-ended items. Perhaps the greatest concern with open-ended items is the increased difficulty in reliably coding and scoring responses. (See Web Reference 4.2.)

Step 4: Determine the Item Format

Once a decision has been made to use open-ended items, closed-ended items, or some combination of both, the test developer must further choose the type of item format. For an open-ended measure, would a written-response format be acceptable or would additional information be obtained if respondents provided verbal responses? If closed-ended items are to be employed, should multiple-choice, true-false, matching, Likert-scale, or some other closed-ended item format be used?

Once an item format has been selected, additional issues may arise. For example, with multiple-choice items, should each item have four response options, five, or more? Even more thought is required when a Likert-type scale is to be used. Appropriate scale anchors must be determined based on what the respondent is expected to indicate. Agreement with items is typically assessed using anchors ranging from strongly disagree to strongly agree. Frequency is often assessed using anchors ranging from never to always. Many evaluative measures pose statements that are rated using a scale ranging from poor to excellent. Additional Likert-type response options include anchors portraying varying degrees of importance or approval. Thus, it is important that the test construction specialist have a clear understanding of the different types of possible item format options, as well as their advantages and disadvantages.

Step 5: Determine Whether the Exam Will Be Administered Individually or in a Group Setting

Time and resource constraints play a large role in making this determination. While group administration generally has the benefits of greater cost savings and ease of scoring, individual administration of tests allows us to clarify both the items and the test taker's responses, when necessary.

Step 6: Determine the Appropriate Test Length

The inclusion of many high-quality test items allows for better assessment of a testing domain and helps to improve a test's internal consistency reliability by reducing error variance (see Module 5). In many cases, however, considerable time constraints preclude the possibility of a very lengthy exam. Further, a lengthy exam can lead to test-taker fatigue and reduced test-taking motivation. These issues must be considered in relation to the item format and number of items that can be administered. In determining a test's appropriate length, a balance must be struck between practical concerns, such as time constraints, and equally important concerns with the psychometric properties of a test, including reliability. Do keep in mind, however, that because many items are often discarded during the test development process, it is worthwhile to produce as many items as possible in the early stages of test development.

Step 7: Determine the Appropriate Difficulty Level of Items That Will Comprise the Test

The difficulty of items is dependent on the ability of the sample population tested under classical test theory assumptions. Therefore, it is important to have a clear idea of the abilities of potential test takers when developing items to ensure that they are appropriately difficult for this population. For tests of maximal performance, item difficulty can be determined based on the percentage of test takers who get the item correct. Module 12 provides additional information on the process to be employed for item analysis. However, our concerns with item difficulty can be broadened somewhat to apply to measures of typical performance. Identifying the likely population of test takers can assist test developers in creating items that are at the proper level of readability. Items that are written at a level beyond the likely educational attainment of the targeted population of test takers will increase error variance in responses, leading to a less reliable test.

Concluding Comments

Test development begins well before the first item is ever written. Though a novice test developer may be tempted to skip past the steps discussed in this module, such an action will only complicate the process of test development. Careful consideration of the issues presented in this module will help make item writing easier, and have an enormously beneficial impact on the appearance and quality of the finished product.

Practical Questions

1. Why do measures that claim to assess the same construct sometimes appear so vastly different from one another?

2. Some measures of a particular construct are better than others. Discuss what you believe to be the three most important issues that should be considered prior to item writing that may affect the quality of the final measure.

3. To what extent is it likely that two different measures of the same construct that employ the use of distinct item formats will provide similar results?

4. What practical constraints often play a large role in the determination of test specifications?

5. If you were assigned to develop a new measure for a personality construct, what sources might you seek to better inform yourself about the construct prior to defining the construct?

Case Studies

CASE STUDY 4.1: DEVISING A MEASURE OF JOB SATISFACTION

As new interns in the human resource department at SAVECO, Juan and Barbara were excited to receive their first major assignment. The president of the company had just asked them to assess the job satisfaction of the company's 210-person workforce. After returning to a shared office, Barbara was quick to provide the first suggestion. "I think we should work on developing an open-ended questionnaire that we could use to interview employees about their level of satisfaction."

Juan thought for a moment and said, "I'm not so sure. That sounds like a lot of work, not only in developing the interview questions, but also in summarizing the results across employees. I think we should develop a number of opinion statements related to job satisfaction. For each statement, we could ask employees to indicate the degree to which they agree or disagree."

"I don't know if that would work," argued Barbara. "I think the use of open-ended questions presented in an interview format would better capture exactly *what* people are and are not happy about with their jobs, as well as provide some indication as to *why* they feel the way they do. By determining what influences job satisfaction, we might be able to implement some organizational changes to increase job satisfaction."

"Is *why* the employees are happy relevant?" queried Juan. "Our assignment is to determine the degree to which SAVECO's employees are satisfied, not to determine why they are happy or not."

Barbara frowned. "I'm not so certain about that. Just knowing the degree of job satisfaction of the workforce seems silly. I think we need to include some assessment of what influences job satisfaction."

"Well," interjected Juan, "maybe we should be even more concerned with which aspects of their work employees are satisfied. Isn't it possible that employees are satisfied with some aspects of their jobs at SAVECO, and dissatisfied with other parts of their jobs? For example, can't employees be happy with their supervisor, but dissatisfied with their pay?"

"You are right there," Barbara agreed. "Perhaps we need to think this through a bit more before getting started."

Questions to Ponder

1. As an alternative to developing a new measure of job satisfaction, Juan and Barbara might have considered obtaining an existing measure for use at SAVECO. What advantages and disadvantages might there be to

(a) using a preexisting measure versus (b) creating a new measure of job satisfaction?

2. Is job satisfaction a one-dimensional or a multidimensional construct? How might the answer to this question impact the development of the job satisfaction measure?

3. How might the item format chosen to measure job satisfaction impact the
   a. administration of the measure?
   b. analysis of the data?
   c. findings of the investigation?

4. How might the development of clear test specifications help Barbara and Juan avoid their conflict?

5. What sources of additional information regarding the measurement of job satisfaction might Juan and Barbara seek prior to developing test items?

CASE STUDY 4.2: ISSUES IN DEVELOPING A STATISTICS EXAM

The time had come, at last. After countless years as a student, Janie had been teaching her first undergraduate college course—an introductory statistics course—for nearly five weeks. Now the time had finally arrived to create her very first exam. Sure, she'd had plenty of experience on the test-taker side of the table, but now it was her turn to create a test of her own. She had serious criticisms of some of the tests her own professors had administered to her over the years, and she was determined to do better. Janie wanted to ensure that the statistics test was fair by ensuring that the test assessed knowledge proportionate to what was covered in the course. The only trouble was, determining what was actually covered in the course was a little trickier than she had thought it would be.

Because she had only lectured on the first four chapters of the textbook, she thought she'd have a fairly clearly defined domain. The material covered so far included (a) a general introduction to statistics; (b) a chapter on frequency distributions that emphasized the interpretation and development of graphs and tables; (c) a chapter on measures of central tendency, including the mean, median, and mode; and, finally, (d) a chapter on measures of variability, including the range, standard deviation, and variance. The latter two chapters seemed more important than either of the first two chapters. Janie wondered whether it would be best to create more items on these latter chapters, or if students might expect that each chapter would be tested equally. Her stomach began to be tied into knots when she thought about the prospect of having to create a lot of items from the first chapter, which seemed to provide little information of any real substance.

Suddenly, another thought came to her. The test really shouldn't be drawn just from the assigned textbook readings. She recognized that the course content was actually composed of three elements: content that had been presented during lecture only, content that had been part of the assigned textbook readings only, and, finally, content that had been presented in both her lecture and the assigned readings. Each of these components of course content was important, although she recognized an implicit pecking order of importance of the material: the material that she lectured on and was presented in the readings was most crucial to a good understanding of course concepts, while material presented only in lecture would likely come next in importance, and the content that was presented only in the assigned readings was somewhat less important.

Janie was also concerned about the types of items she should use in testing. On the one hand, she wanted to ensure students could apply their learning through use of computational problems, but, on the other hand, she felt that introductory statistics should emphasize understanding of these foundational concepts above anything else. How, then, could she ensure not only that she covered the domain appropriately but also that the right types of items were used to assess exactly the type of learning she hoped to promote? This question was no easier to answer when Janie realized that students would have only about 50 minutes to complete the test.

One thing seemed certain—she was quickly developing a greater respect for the professors who had constructed all those exams she had taken throughout the years.

Questions to Ponder

1. Describe the first few steps you would take in defining the **content domain** that would comprise Janie's statistics exam.

2. Would you recommend that Janie write the same number of items for each of the textbook chapters? Why or why not?

3. What percentage of items should be written for each of the following?
   a. Content presented both in readings and in lecture
   b. Content presented in lecture only
   c. Content presented in the assigned readings only

   On what basis are you making your recommendations?

4. What types of items should Janie use to assess student learning in the statistics class? Should all of the course content be assessed using the same item format?

Exercises

EXERCISE 4.1: DEFINING A PERSONALITY TRAIT

OBJECTIVE: To gain practice in defining a construct as a part of test specification.

There are a large number of personality differences that to date have little or no means of assessment. While some of these constructs are well defined, others suffer the disgrace of poor construct definition. Following is a list of words and phrases that describe propensities that can differ across individuals. Select *one* of the following constructs and develop a clear definition that could serve as the first step toward the operationalization of the construct. Be sure to specify the (a) context and (b) dimensionality of the construct as well as its (c) relationship to, and differentiation from, related constructs.

List of Possible Constructs

1. Jealousy

2. Patience

3. Impulsiveness

4. Street smarts

5. Empathy

6. Selfishness

EXERCISE 4.2: TEST SPECIFICATIONS
FOR A MEASURE OF POTENTIAL FOR VIOLENCE

OBJECTIVE: To illustrate how the purpose of testing influences test specifications.

Assume that you are currently working as a(n)

    a. clinical psychologist for a local parole board, or

    b. industrial/organizational psychologist for the U.S. Postal Service, or

    c. school psychologist for a local high school.

You've recently been asked to create a test to measure "Potential for Violence." Provide a response for each of the following questions related to the test preparation and specification. Be sure to provide a convincing rationale for each response (questions taken from Cohen & Swerdlik, 2002).

1. How would you define the purpose of the test?

2. In what ways will the intended purpose of the test influence your definition of the test?

3. Are there alternatives to developing a new test?

4. What content will the test cover?

5. What is the test's intended dimensionality?

6. What is the ideal format for the test?

7. Who will the test be administered to?

8. What type of responses will be required of test takers?

9. Should more than one form of the test be developed?

10. Who will administer the test?

11. What special training will be required of test users for administering or interpreting the test?

12. How long will the test take to administer?

13. How many items will compose the test?

14. What is the intended difficulty level of the test?

15. How will meaning be attributed to scores on the test?

16. What benefits will result from use of the test?

17. What potential harm could result from use of the test?

EXERCISE 4.3: CBEST TEST SPECIFICATIONS

OBJECTIVE: To gain experience extracting important information about a test from the test specifications.

The California Basic Educational Skills Test (CBEST) is intended to assess and verify acceptable proficiency in reading, writing, and mathematics skills required for teachers. The test specifications for an earlier version of the mathematics section of the CBEST exam were described to prospective test takers as follows:

The Mathematics section of the CBEST assesses basic skills and concepts that are important in performing the job of an educator in California. The 50 questions in this section will require you to solve mathematical problems. Most of the questions will be presented as word problems.

The questions you will be asked come from three major skill areas: estimation, measurement, and statistical principles; computation and problem solving; and numerical and graphic relationships. Approximately 30% of the questions on the test are drawn from the estimation, measurement, and statistical principles area; approximately 45% are drawn from the computation and problem solving area; and approximately 25% are drawn from the numerical and graphic relationships area.

The mathematics skills eligible for testing are listed below.

ESTIMATION, MEASUREMENT, AND STATISTICAL PRINCIPLES

A. Estimation and Measurement

* Understand and use standard units of length, temperature, weight, and capacity in the U.S. measurement system.

* Measure length, perimeter, area, and volume.

* Understand and use estimates of time to plan and achieve work-related objectives.

* Estimate the results of problems involving addition, subtraction, multiplication, and division prior to computation.

B. Statistical Principles

* Perform arithmetic operations with basic statistical data related to test scores (e.g., averages, ratios, proportions, and percentile scores).

* Understand basic principles of probability and predict likely outcomes based on data provided (e.g., estimate the likelihood that an event will occur).

COMPUTATION AND PROBLEM SOLVING

* Add, subtract, multiply, and divide with whole numbers.

* Add, subtract, multiply, and divide with fractions, decimals, and percentages.

* Determine and perform necessary arithmetic operations to solve a practical math problem (e.g., determine the total invoice cost for ordered supplies by multiplying quantity by unit price, summing all items).

* Solve simple algebraic problems (e.g., equations with one unknown).

* Determine whether enough information is given to solve a problem; identify the facts given in a problem.

* Recognize alternative mathematical methods of solving a problem.

NUMERICAL AND GRAPHIC RELATIONSHIPS

* Recognize relationships in numerical data (e.g., compute a percentage change from one year to the next).

* Recognize the position of numbers in relation to each other (e.g., 1/3 is between 1/4 and 1/2; $-7 < -4$).

* Understand and use rounding rules when solving problems.

* Understand and apply the meaning of logical connectives (e.g., and, or, if-then) and quantifiers (e.g., some, all, none).

* Identify or specify a missing entry from a table of data (e.g., subtotal).

* Use numerical information contained in tables and various kinds of graphs (e.g., bar, line, circle) to solve math problems.

Based on the above information, answer each of the following questions.

1. What is the purpose of the CBEST mathematics section?

2. What content is the CBEST mathematics section intended to cover?

3. What is the dimensionality of the CBEST mathematics section?

4. In what ways would viewing these test specifications be useful to a test taker?

5. What additional information might a test taker want?

EXERCISE 4.4: COMPARING TWO
MEASURES OF THE SAME CONSTRUCT

OBJECTIVE: To illustrate the potential impact test specifications can have on the development of measures of the same construct.

For this exercise, identify two different measures of the same construct. For example, you could identify two different measures of the personality construct, agreeableness. Also, obtain the test manual for each measure, if at all possible. (*Note:* Many colleges and universities have test banks in their libraries and psychology and education departments. These test banks may contain many commercially available tests and test manuals.)

After obtaining the two different measures (and test manuals) of the construct, carefully inspect each before answering the following questions.

1. Did both test developers define the construct in the same way? (Be sure to review Step 2 in the module overview before answering this question.) If not, identify the differences in the definitions of the construct used by the test developers.

2. Did each measure use open-ended items, closed-ended items, or both?

3. What item formats were used in each measure of the construct?

4. Is each measure intended to be individually administered, or can it be administered in a group setting?

5. Are the measures of similar length?

6. Who is the intended population of each test? Does the difficulty of the items appear appropriate for this population?

7. Based on your responses to questions 1–6, do you feel one of the two measures might be a better measure of the construct? Explain whether you believe each test developer's decisions regarding test specifications were appropriate for each measure of the construct.

Internet Web Site References

4.1. http://wwwcsteep.bc.edu/CTESTWEB/whatistest/whatistest.html

This Web page provides a simple explanation of testing, with links to explanations of test domains and test inferences.

4.2. http://ag.arizona.edu/classes/aed695a/objectiv1.htm

This Web page provides a brief table intended to demonstrate some of the strengths and weaknesses of objective (i.e., closed-ended) and subjective (i.e., open-ended) test items.

4.3. http://www.isd.uga.edu/teaching_assistant/ta-handbook/testd.html

This Web page provides recommendations regarding basic issues in the development of academic tests, including test format, design, test attributes, and the test form itself. Links to developing and scoring open-ended and closed-ended items are also provided.

4.4. http://www.acenet.edu/calec/ged/specs-A.cfm

This Web page provides a brief sample of test specifications for the General Educational Development (GED) tests.

Further Readings

Ebel, R. L. (1982). Proposed solutions to two problems of test construction. *Journal of Educational Measurement, 19,* 267–278.

Millman, J., & Greene, J. (1989). The specification and development of tests of achievement and ability. In R. L. Linn (Ed.), *Educational measurement* (3rd ed., pp. 335–366). New York: American Council on Education/Macmillan.

Vaughn, K. W. (1951). Planning the objective test. In E. F. Lindquist (Ed.), *Educational measurement* (pp. 159–184). Washington, DC: American Council on Education.

Reliability, Validity, and Test Bias

Module 5

Classical True Score Theory and Reliability

Any phenomenon we decide to "measure" in psychology, whether it is a physical or mental characteristic, will inevitably contain some error. For example, you can step on the same scale three consecutive times to weigh yourself and get three slightly different readings. To deal with this, you might take the average of the three weight measures as the best guess of your current weight. In most field settings, however, we do not have the luxury of administering our measurement instrument multiple times. We get one shot at it and we had better obtain the most accurate estimate possible with that one administration. Therefore, if we have at least some measurement error estimating a physical characteristic such as weight, a construct that everyone pretty much agrees on, imagine how much error is associated with a controversial psychological phenomenon we might want to measure such as intelligence. With classical psychometric true score theory, we can stop "imagining" how much error there is in our measurements and start estimating it.

Classical **true score theory** states that our observed score (X) is equal to the sum of our true score, or true underlying ability (T), plus the measurement error (E) associated with estimating our observed scores, or

$$X = T + E$$

Several assumptions are made about the relationship among these three components. These assumptions are discussed in detail in texts such as Allen and Yen (1979) and Crocker and Algina (1986), so we will not cover them here. Briefly, however, the "true score" is the score we would obtain if we were to take the average score for an infinite number of test administrations. Of course, in practice, one cannot administer a test an infinite number of times, and as noted previously, the vast majority of the time we get only one chance. Therefore, we use **reliability coefficients** to estimate both true and error variance associated with our observed test scores. Theoretically speaking, our reliability estimate is the ratio of the true variance to the total variance:

$$r_{xx} = \frac{\sigma^2_{true}}{\sigma^2_{total}} = \frac{\sigma^2_{true}}{\sigma^2_{true} + \sigma^2_{error}}$$

where r_{xx} is the reliability, σ^2_{true} is the true score variance, σ^2_{total} is the total score variance, and σ^2_{error} is the error variance. Of course, we will never be able to directly estimate the true score and its variance; hence, this particular formula serves merely as a heuristic for understanding the components of reliability. In the following discussion, we will outline several options for estimating test reliability in practice.

Estimating Reliability in Practice

Right about now you are probably saying to yourself, "Okay, that's the theoretical stuff that my textbook talked about, but how do I actually compute a reliability estimate when I need to?" Most of the time, we compute a Pearson product moment correlation coefficient (correlation coefficient for short) or some other appropriate estimate (e.g., a Spearman correlation if we have ordinal data) to estimate the reliability of our measurement scale.

Before we can calculate our reliability estimate, however, we have to decide what type of measurement error we want to focus on. For example, if we want to account for changes in test scores due to time, we calculate the correlation coefficient between a test given at time 1 and the same test given at some later point (i.e., test-retest reliability). Therefore, once we know what source of error we want to focus on, we will know what type of reliability coefficient we are dealing with and thus which correlation coefficient to compute to estimate our reliability.

Looking at the first column of Table 5.1, you will notice three different sources of measurement error that we can estimate with different types of reliability estimates. Notice, however, that one source of measurement error, content sampling, appears twice. Each of these sources can be considered to be tapping into the issue of how consistent our measures are. The first source of error, change in examinees, estimates how consistently our examinees respond from one occasion to another. The next two, content sampling, estimate how consistent items are across test versions or within a given test. Finally, we may estimate the consistency of raters' judgments of examinees or test items.

Table 5.1   Sources of Error and Their Associated Reliability and Statistics

Source of Error	Reliability Coefficient	Reliability Estimate	Statistic
Change in examinees	Stability	Test/retest	r_{12}
Content sampling	Equivalence	Alternate forms	$r_{xx'}$
Content sampling	Internal consistency	Split-half Alpha	r_{x1x2} α
Inter-rater	Rater consistency	Inter-rater	kappa

The second column in Table 5.1 lists the type of reliability coefficient to use when we estimate a given source of measurement error. For example, with changes in examinees our reliability coefficient is an estimate of stability or consistency of examinees' responses over time. With the first form of content sampling measurement error (i.e., row 2 in Table 5.1), we are measuring the equivalence or consistency of different forms of a test. However, with the second form of content sampling measurement error (i.e., row 3 in Table 5.1), we are measuring what is commonly referred to as the **internal consistency** of test items. That is, do all the items in a single test seem to be tapping the same underlying construct? Finally, when we estimate inter-rater sources of measurement error, our reliability coefficient is one of rater consistency. That is, do raters seem to be rating the target in a consistent manner, whether the target is the test itself or individuals taking the test, such as job applicants during an employment interview?

The third column in Table 5.1 presents the name of the reliability estimate we would use to determine the respective sources of measurement error. For example, if we wanted to estimate sources of measurement error associated with changes in examinees over time, we would compute a **test-retest reliability** estimate. Alternatively, if we wanted to examine the first form of content sampling, we would compute what is commonly known as **alternate forms reliability** (also referred to as **parallel forms reliability**). However, for the second form of content sampling, we do not need to have a second form of the test. We would instead compute either a **split-half reliability coefficient** or an alpha reliability coefficient to estimate the internal consistency of a single test. Finally, for estimating sources of error associated with raters, we would compute an inter-rater reliability estimate.

You may remember that in Module 2 we discussed the importance of the correlation coefficient. Why is it so important? As you can see in the last column of Table 5.1, the correlation coefficient is used to compute most forms of reliability estimates. The only difference among the different correlation coefficients is the variables used and the interpretation of the resulting correlation. For example, with a test-retest reliability estimate, we would compute the correlation coefficient between individuals' scores on a given test taken at time 1 and those same individuals' scores on the same test taken at a later date. The higher the correlation coefficient, the more reliable the test or, conversely, the less error attributable to changes in the examinees over time. Of course, many things can affect the test-retest estimate of reliability. One is the nature of the construct being assessed. For example, when we are measuring enduring psychological traits, such as most forms of personality, there should be little change over time. However, if we were measuring transitory psychological states, such as fear, then we would expect to see more change from the first to the second testing. As a result, our test-retest reliability estimates tend to be lower when we are measuring transitory psychological states rather than enduring psychological traits.

In addition, the length of time between testing administrations can affect our estimate of stability. For instance, if we are measuring a cognitive skill such as fluency in a foreign language, and there is a long time period between testing sessions, an individual may be able to practice that language and acquire additional fluency in that language between testing sessions. As a result, individuals will score consistently higher on the second occasion. However, differences in scores from time 1 to time 2 will be interpreted as instability in subjects (i.e., a lot of measurement error) and not learning. On the other hand, if we make the duration between testing sessions too short, examinees may remember their previous responses. There may also be fatigue effects associated with the test-retest if the retest is immediate. So how long should the interval between testing sessions be? Unfortunately, there is no hard-and-fast rule. The key is to make sure that the duration is long enough not to fatigue the examinees or allow them to remember their answers, but not so long that changes may take place (e.g., learning, psychological traumas) that could impact our estimate of reliability. Of course, one way to deal with the possibility of subjects remembering their answers from time 1 to time 2 is to use two different forms of the test.

With alternate forms reliability, we administer examinees one form of the test and then at a later date give them a second form of the test. Because we do not have to worry about the individuals remembering their answers, the intervening time between testing sessions does not need to be as long as with test-retest reliability estimates. In fact, the two testing sessions may even occur on the same day. From a practical standpoint, this may be ideal, in that examinees may be unwilling or simply fail to return for a second testing session. As you have probably surmised, the biggest disadvantage of the alternate forms method is that you need to have two versions of the test. It is hard enough to develop one psychometrically sound form of a test, now you have to create two. Is it possible to just look at content sampling within a single test?

With split-half and alpha reliability estimates, we need only one version of the test. To estimate split-half reliability, we correlate one half of the test with the other half of the test. If we simply correlate the first half with the second half, however, we may have spuriously low reliability estimates due to fatigue effects. In addition, many cognitive ability tests are spiral in nature, meaning they start out easy and get harder as you go along. As a result, correlating the first half of the test with the second half of the test may be misleading. Therefore, to estimate split-half reliability, most researchers correlate scores on the odd-numbered items with scores on the even-numbered items. As you might have guessed by now, we are, in a sense, computing a correlation on only half of our test. Does that in and of itself result in a lower reliability estimate? In fact, it does. Therefore, whenever a split-half reliability estimate is calculated, one should also use the **Spearman-Brown prophecy formula** to correct for the fact that we are cutting the test in half. (*Note:* We demonstrate an alternate use of the formula in Case Study 5.2.)

$$r_{XX'_n} = \frac{n r_{XX'}}{1 + (n - 1)r_{XX'}}$$

where $r_{XX'_n}$ is the Spearman-Brown corrected split-half reliability estimate; n is the factor by which we want to increase the test, which in this case would be 2 (because we are, in a sense, doubling the test back to its original length); and $r_{XX'}$ is the original split-half reliability estimate. Because n is always equal to 2 when correcting our split-half reliability estimate, our formula can be simplified to

$$r_{XX'_n} = \frac{2r_{XX'}}{1 + r_{XX'}}$$

The general form of the Spearman-Brown formula can be used to determine the estimated reliability of a revised version of the test if the number of items on the test is increased (or even decreased) by a specified factor. It is important to note, however, that the formula assumes that the additional items contributed to the test are parallel to the items on the original test. Thus, the new items must be similar to the original items in terms of content, difficulty, correlation with other items, and item variance.

The second, and more common, measure of internal consistency reliability is the alpha reliability estimate. **Coefficient alpha** is sometimes referred to as the average of all possible split-half reliabilities. As a result, the formula for computing alpha is a little more involved than a simple bivariate correlation coefficient:

$$\alpha = \frac{k}{k-1}\left(1 - \frac{\sum \sigma_i^2}{\sigma_x^2}\right)$$

where α is the estimate of the alpha coefficient, k is the number of items on the test, σ_i^2 is the variance of item i, and σ_x^2 is the total variance of the test.

All other things being equal, the more items you have on your test (k) the higher your alpha coefficient will be. Hence, one way to increase the reliability of your test is to increase the number of items on the test. In addition, the alpha coefficient will also increase if we increase the variability of each item. Hence, removing items with very little variability from a test and replacing them with higher-variability items will actually increase your alpha coefficient.

How does one interpret the alpha coefficient? Actually, the interpretation is very similar to that of the other reliability estimates based on correlation coefficients. Zero would indicate no reliability (i.e., all measurement error). A value of one, on the other hand, would indicate perfect reliability (i.e., no measurement error). Thus, the common standard of a reliability estimate of at least .70 or higher holds for alpha as well.

Two precautions should be kept in mind when interpreting alpha reliability estimates. First, many students and practitioners often refer to the alpha coefficient as "the" estimate of reliability. As should be clear by now, based on our discussion of Table 5.1, the alpha coefficient is but one estimate of reliability that focuses on just one form of measurement error.

Therefore, if you are interested in other forms of measurement error (such as stability over time), you will need to compute additional reliability estimates. Second, as Cortina (1993) and Schmitt (1996) pointed out, one common misconception of alpha among naive researchers is that the alpha coefficient is an indication of the unidimensionality of a test. As pointed out previously, if you have a large enough set of items, you will have a high alpha coefficient, but this does not mean your test is unidimensional. The measurement of job satisfaction can serve as a good example of this phenomenon. Most job satisfaction scales measure several different facets of job satisfaction, such as satisfaction with one's job, supervisor, pay, advancement opportunities, and so on. However, the scales can also be combined to create an overall job satisfaction score. Clearly, this overall job satisfaction score is not unidimensional. Because the overall score is typically based on a large number of items, however, the overall scale's alpha coefficient will be large. As a result, it is important for researchers to remember that an alpha coefficient only measures one form of measurement error and is an indication of internal consistency, not unidimensionality.

Finally, to estimate inter-rater agreement, a statistic such as Cohen's kappa can be used. To compute kappa, sometimes referred to as scorer reliability, you would need to set up a cross-tabulation of ratings given by raters, similar to a chi-square contingency table. For example, you might have a group of parents, both the mother and the father (your two raters), rate their children on the children's temperament (e.g., 1 = easygoing, 2 = anxious, 3 = neither). You would want to then determine if the parents agree in terms of their respective perceptions (and ratings) of their children's temperaments. To compute the **kappa statistic,** you would need to set up a 2(raters) × 3(temperament rating) contingency table of the parents' ratings. Then you would compute the kappa statistic as follows:

$$k = \frac{(Oa - Ea)}{(N - Ea)}$$

where k is the kappa statistic, Oa is the observed count of agreement (typically reported in the diagonal of the table), Ea is the expected count of agreement, and N is the total number of respondent pairs. Thus, Cohen's kappa represents the proportion of agreement among raters after chance agreement has been factored out. In this case, zero represents chance ratings, while a score of one represents perfect agreement. (*Note:* Exercise 5.3 provides data for computing Cohen's kappa.)

As with many statistics, however, kappa has not been without its critics (e.g., Maclure & Willett, 1987). One criticism is that kappa is not a good estimate of effect size. Although it will give a pretty good estimate of whether the observed ratings are significantly different from chance (an inferential statistic), using kappa as an estimate of the actual degree of agreement (i.e., as an effect size estimate) should be done cautiously, as the statistic assumes the raters are independent. In our preceding example, it is highly unlikely that the parents will provide independent ratings. Thus, when it can be reasonably assumed that raters are not independent, you would be better off using other estimates of rater agreement, such as the intraclass correlation coefficient.

Thus, we see there are many forms of reliability, each of which estimates a different source of measurement error. In general, immediate test-retest reliability and split-half reliability tend to provide upper-bound estimates of reliability. That is, they tend to provide higher estimates, on average, than other forms of reliability. Coefficient alpha and long-term test-retest tend to provide somewhat lower estimates, on average, while alternate forms reliability, both short and long term, tends to provide lower-bound estimates. Why present this information here? These general trends are important both for interpreting your obtained reliability coefficients and for using your reliability estimates for other purposes, such as determining the standard error of measurement.

What Do We Do With the Reliability Estimates Now That We Have Them?

You are probably asking yourself, "Now that we have an estimate of reliability, what do we do with it?" First, we will need to report our reliability estimate(s) in any manuscripts (e.g., **technical manuals,** conference papers, and articles) that we write. Second, if we have followed sound basic test construction principles, someone who scores high on our test is likely to be higher on the underlying trait than someone who scores low on our test. Often times, this general ranking is all we are really looking for; who is "highest" on a given measure. However, if we want to know how much error is associated with a given test score (such as when we set standards or cutoff scores), we can use our reliability estimate to calculate the **standard error of measurement,** or SEM (of course, we would also need to know the sample standard deviation for the measure). Thus, computing the SEM allows us to build a confidence interval around our observed score so that we can estimate (with a certain level of confidence) someone's underlying true score,

$$SEM = S_x \sqrt{1 - r_{xx}}$$

where S_x is the sample standard deviation and r_{xx} is the reliability estimate.

EXAMPLE: $X = 100$, $S_x = 10$, $r_{xx} = .71$

$$SEM = 10 \sqrt{1 - .71} = 10 \ (.5385) = 5.38$$

$$95\% \ CI = X \pm 1.96*SEM = 100 \pm 1.96*(5.38)$$
$$= 100 \pm 10.54 = 89.46 \le T \le 110.54$$

where X is our test score, 1.96 is the critical z value associated with the 95% confidence interval, SEM is the standard error of measurement value, and T is our estimated underlying true score value.

You can see from the preceding formula that, as our test becomes more reliable, our confidence interval becomes narrower. For example, if we increase the reliability of our test to .80, the SEM in the previous example becomes 4.47 and thus the 95% confidence interval narrows to $91.24 \le T \le$ 108.76. We could even reverse the formula and figure out how reliable our test needs to be if we want a certain width confidence interval for a test with a given standard deviation. For example, if we want to be 95% confident that a given true score is within 5 points (SEM = 2.5, plus or minus in either direction) of someone's observed score, then we would have to have a test with a reliability of .9375:

$$SEM = S_x \sqrt{1 - r_{xx}}, \ becomes \ 1 - \left[\frac{SEM}{S_x}\right]^2 = 1 - \left[\frac{2.5}{10}\right]^2 = 1 - .0625 = .9375$$

Concluding Comments

There will always be some degree of error when we try to measure something. Physical characteristics, however, tend to have less measurement error than psychological phenomena. Therefore, it is critical that we accurately estimate the amount of error associated with any measure, in particular, psychological measures. To estimate the measurement error, we have to first decide what form of error we are most interested in estimating. Once we do that, we can choose an appropriate reliability estimate (see Table 5.1) to estimate the reliability. We can then use the reliability estimate to build confidence intervals around our observed scores to estimate the underlying true scores. In doing so, we will have much more confidence in the interpretation of our measurement instruments.

Practical Questions

1. How much can we shorten an existing measure and still maintain adequate reliability? (See Case Study 5.2.)

2. What are the different sources of error that can be assessed with classical reliability analysis?

3. Does it matter which reliability estimate we put into the standard error of measurement formula?

4. Are some reliability estimates generally higher (or lower) than others? That is, does one tend to serve as an upper- (or lower-) bound reliability estimate?

5. How is Cohen's kappa estimate of reliability different from the other forms of reliability?

6. Why are some authors (e.g., Cortina, 1993; Schmitt, 1996) cautious about the interpretation of coefficient alpha?

Case Studies

CASE STUDY 5.1: DON'T FORGET TO REVERSE SCORE

It didn't make sense. It just didn't. How could the reliability be so low? Chad scratched his head and thought. Chad had agreed to help analyze the data from his graduate advisor's most recent study. Although entering the data into a computer database had not been exciting, it had been relatively easy. Once he had entered each research participant's responses, he spot-checked a few cases to ensure accuracy. He then conducted frequency analyses on each variable to ensure that there were no out-of-bounds responders. In fact, he'd found two cases in which he had incorrectly entered the data. He could tell, because items that were responded to on a five-point Likert-type rating scale had reported scores of 12 and 35, respectively. Sure enough, he'd just made a typo when entering the data. Everything else looked fine.

Or so he thought, until he decided to examine the reliability of one of the scales. Chad's advisor, Dr. John Colman, was primarily interested in troubled adolescents, and over the last several years had investigated adolescent attitudes toward alcoholic beverages. The same measure of adolescent attitudes toward alcohol was routinely used in this research. Respondents indicated on a scale of 1–5 how strongly they agreed with each of the 12 items. Internal consistency reliability estimates for the scale were consistently good, typically around .80. However, not this time, apparently. In computing the reliability estimate for the data he'd just entered, Chad found that alpha was estimated to be −.39.

Chad couldn't remember ever hearing of a negative internal consistency reliability estimate. In addition, he couldn't explain why the scale would have such a different reliability on this sample than it had with the many samples his advisor had previously used. His first thought was that he might have entered the data incorrectly—but he knew he hadn't. After all, he'd checked the data carefully to ensure that the computer data file matched exactly what was on the original surveys. So what could be the problem?

In examining the item-total correlations for each item on the scale, Chad noticed that several items correlated negatively with a composite of the remaining items. Chad grabbed the original survey and reexamined the 12 items that comprised the adolescent attitudes toward alcohol scale. Each item certainly seemed to measure the intended construct. Chad was about to give up and go report the problem to his advisor when he noticed something. Although each of the 12 items measured attitudes toward alcohol, agreement to eight of the items would be indicative of acceptance of alcohol use. In contrast, agreement to the other four items would be indicative of a rejection of alcohol use. That was it. He'd correctly entered the data from the surveys into the computer data file, but had forgotten to recode the reverse-coded items. Because his advisor wanted high scores to be indicative of an acceptance of the use of alcohol, Chad decided he'd recode the four reverse-coded items. To do this, he used the recode command of his statistics program to recode all responses of "5" into "1," "4" into

"2," "2" into "4," and "1" into "5." He did this for each of the four reverse-coded items. Holding his breath, he again computed the alpha. This time, the reliability estimate was $\alpha = .79$, and all of the item-total correlations were positive. Satisfied that he'd been able to resolve the problem on his own, Chad made a mental note to always recode the appropriate items once the entire data file had been completed.

Questions to Ponder

1. In terms of Table 5.1, what type of reliability coefficient did Chad estimate? What source of error is being estimated?

2. Did Chad make the right interpretation of his negative reliability estimate? What else might cause a negative reliability estimate?

3. In practice, how does one know which items to recode and which to keep the same?

4. Both positively and negatively worded items are frequently included on tests. Assuming you recode the negatively worded items before you run your reliability analysis, will the inclusion of negatively worded items affect the test's internal consistency reliability estimate?

CASE STUDY 5.2: LENGTHENING AND SHORTENING PSYCHOLOGICAL SCALES

Sheila was frustrated. Although she was happy with both the topic and the constructs she had chosen to examine in her senior honors thesis, she had hit several roadblocks in determining what measures to use to assess each variable in her proposed study. Now that she had finally identified useful measures to include in her survey, she was concerned that her response rate would suffer because of the rather impressive length of the survey. Reasoning that the sample she hoped to use was unlikely to spend more than a few minutes voluntarily responding to a survey, Sheila considered her options. First, she could eliminate one or more variables. This would make her study simpler and would have the added benefit of reducing the length of the survey. Sheila rejected this option, however, because she felt each variable she had identified was necessary to adequately address her research questions. Second, she considered just mailing the survey to a larger number of people in order to get an adequate number to respond to the lengthy survey. Sheila quickly rejected this option as well. She certainly didn't want to pay for the additional copying and mailing costs. She was also concerned that a lengthy survey would further reduce the possibility of obtaining a sample that was representative of the population. Perhaps those individuals who would not respond to a long survey would be very different from the actual respondents.

Suddenly a grin spread across Sheila's face. "Couldn't I shorten the survey by reducing the number of items used to assess some of the variables?" she thought. Some of the scales she had selected to measure variables were relatively short, while scales to measure other variables were quite long. Some of the scales were publisher-owned measures and thus copyrighted. Others were nonproprietary scales both created and used by researchers. Recognizing the reluctance of publishers to allow unnecessary changes to their scales, Sheila considered the nonproprietary measures. The scale intended to assess optimism was not only nonproprietary but also very long: 66 items. A scale assessing dogmatism was also nonproprietary and, at 50 items, also seemed long. Sheila quickly decided that these would be good scales to target for reduction of the number of items.

In class, Sheila had learned that the Spearman-Brown prophecy formula could be used to estimate the reliability of a scale if the scale was doubled in length. Her instructor also explained that the same formula could be used for either increasing or decreasing the number of items by a certain factor. Sheila knew from her research that the typical internal consistency reliability finding for her optimism scale was .85, and for the dogmatism scale it was .90. Because she wanted to reduce the number of items administered for each scale, she knew the resulting reliability estimates would be lower. But how much lower? Sheila considered reducing the number of items in both scales by one half. Because she was reducing the number of items, the number of times she was increasing the scale was equal to one half, or .5. She used this information to compute the Spearman-Brown reliability estimate as follows:

Optimism Test	Dogmatism Test
$r_{XX'_n} = \dfrac{nr_{XX'}}{1 + (n-1)r_{XX'}}$	$r_{XX'_n} = \dfrac{nr_{XX'}}{1 + (n-1)r_{XX'}}$
$= \dfrac{.5(.85)}{1 + (.5-1).85}$	$= \dfrac{.5(.90)}{1 + (.5-1).90}$
$= .74$	$= .82$

In considering these results, Sheila thought she'd be satisfied with an internal consistency reliability estimate of .82 for the dogmatism scale, but was concerned that too much error would be included in estimates of optimism if the internal consistency reliability estimate were merely .74.

Undeterred, Sheila decided to estimate the reliability if only one third of the optimism items were removed. If one third of the items were dropped, two thirds (or .67) of the original items would remain. Therefore, the Spearman-Brown prophecy estimate could be computed as follows:

$$
\begin{aligned}
\text{Optimism Test} \\
r_{XX'_n} &= \frac{nr_{XX'}}{1 + (n-1)r_{XX'}} \\
&= \frac{.67(.85)}{1 + (.67-1).85} \\
&= .79
\end{aligned}
$$

Sheila decided this reliability would be acceptable for her study. In order to complete her work, Sheila randomly selected 25 (50%) of the items from the dogmatism scale, and 44 (67%) of the items from the optimism scale. She was confident that although her survey form was now shorter, the reliability of the individual variables would be acceptable.

Questions to Ponder

1. In terms of Table 5.1, what type of reliability coefficient did Sheila estimate? What source of error is being estimated?

2. Should Sheila have randomly selected which items to keep and which to delete? What other options did she have?

3. How else might Sheila maintain her reliability levels yet still maintain (or increase) the number of usable responses she obtains?

4. Why do you think Sheila is using .80 as her lower acceptable bound for reliability?

Exercises

EXERCISE 5.1: COMPUTING TEST-RETEST, ALPHA, AND PARALLEL FORMS RELIABILITY VIA COMPUTER

OBJECTIVE: To practice calculating different types of reliability.

Using the data set "Reliability.sav" (see the variable list in Appendix B), perform the reliability analyses outlined below. The scales provided here include a depression scale (14 items, V1–V14), a life satisfaction scale (10 items, V15–V24), a reasons-a-person-retired scale (10 items, V25–V34), a scale with regard to good things about retirement (8 items, V35–V42), and a scale with regard to bad things about retirement (6 items, V43–V48). For your assignment (be sure to do an ocular analysis of all items first, checking for outliers, missing data, etc., before jumping into the reliability analyses):

1. Perform alpha, split-half, and parallel forms reliability analyses for each of the five scales. How do the three different types of reliability compare for each scale listed above? Is one form of reliability more appropriate than another? Discuss for each scale. (*Note:* You may wish to put your results in table form for easy comparison.)

2. Using alpha reliability, with item and scale information, what items should be included in the final versions of each scale in order to maximize the alpha reliability for that scale? (*Note:* You will need to examine the item-total correlations. In addition, once an item is removed, you will need to repeat the process until a final scale is decided upon.)

3. For the life satisfaction and depression scales, determine if the alpha reliabilities are different for men and women (SEX). If yes, any guesses why? (*Note:* This requires using the "split file" option in SPSS or comparable options in other statistics programs.)

4. Based on Cortina (1993), what additional analyses could you conduct to evaluate the reliabilities of each of the scales? (You may perform these analyses if you wish, but it is not required for this assignment.)

EXERCISE 5.2: EXAMINING THE EFFECTS
OF THE SPEARMAN-BROWN PROPHECY FORMULA

OBJECTIVE: To practice using the Spearman-Brown prophecy formula for estimating reliability levels.

Using the Spearman-Brown prophecy formula provided in Case Study 5.2, estimate Sheila's reliability for the dogmatism scale if she used only one third of the number of original items. Is this an "acceptable level" of reliability? Why or why not?

EXERCISE 5.3: ESTIMATING AGREEMENT
COEFFICIENTS (COHEN'S KAPPA)

OBJECTIVE: To practice calculating Cohen's kappa estimate of rater agreement.

Assume you wanted to determine the degree of inter-rater agreement between two forensic psychologists who were each rating 100 potential parolees in terms of their potential for committing additional violent crimes. In general, sociopaths are more likely to commit additional violent crimes than are depressed or normal individuals. Therefore, each psychologist rated each of the 100 potential parolees on a scale of 1–3 in terms of their primary personality category (1 = sociopath, 2 = depressed, 3 = normal). The following results were obtained:

		Forensic Psychologist A		
Forensic		Personality 1	Personality 2	Personality 3
Psychologist B	Personality 1	44	5	1
	Personality 2	7	20	3
	Personality 3	9	5	6

Using the data in the preceding table and the formula for kappa presented in the module overview, determine the level of agreement between the raters.

Internet Web Site References

5.1. http://trochim.human.cornell.edu/kb/reliable.htm

This Web page presents the beginning of the chapter on reliability from Dr. William M. Trochim's electronic textbook.

5.2. http://trochim.human.cornell.edu/tutorial/levell/mazeintr.htm

This Web page provides a 10-item quiz on reliability, along with a rationale for the correct answer to each item.

5.3. http://www.statsoftinc.com/textbook/streliab.html

This Web page presents the beginning of the chapter on reliability from Statsoft, Inc.'s electronic textbook.

5.4. http://www.ruf.rice.edu/~lane/stat_sim/reliability_reg/

This Web page presents a simulation of the effects of the reliability of X and Y on a number of components of regression analysis.

5.5. http://www.unl.edu/BIACO/workshops/reliability%20folder/sld001.htm

This Web page is the start page of a slide presentation by the Buros Institute for Assessment Consultation and Outreach (BIACO) titled "Consistency in Scoring (Reliability) Workshop."

5.6. http://chiron.valdosta.edu/mawhatley/3900/reliablec.htm

This Web page provides a 30-item reliability quiz. Responses are scored immediately. *Note:* Because of the overlap between the concepts presented in Modules 6–8, many of the links listed under a particular module in this section are likely to present additional information relevant to the other modules.

Further Readings

Cortina, J. M. (1993). What is coefficient alpha? An examination of theory and applications. *Journal of Applied Psychology, 78,* 98–104.

Maclure, M., & Willett, W. C. (1987). Misinterpretation and misuse of the kappa statistic. *American Journal of Epidemiology, 126,* 161–169.

Schmidt, F. L., & Hunter, J. E. (1996). Measurement error in psychological research: Lessons from 26 research scenarios. *Psychological Methods, 1,* 199–223.

Schmitt, N. (1996). Uses and abuses of coefficient alpha. *Psychological Assessment, 8,* 350–353.

Traub, R. E. (1994). *Reliability for the social sciences: Theory and application.* Thousand Oaks, CA: Sage.

Module 6

Content Validation

An Important Note

A popular definition of **validity** is whether a test measures what it is intended to measure. More accurately, the process of **validation** does not seek to determine whether the test itself is valid, but rather whether the inferences and conclusions that are made on the basis of test scores are valid (Murphy & Davidshofer, 2001). The traditional concept of validity considered several seemingly independent strategies for establishing the validity of a test, including content validation, criterion-related validation, and construct validation. Today, we recognize that all evidence examined in relation to the inferences and conclusions of test scores contributes to the same process: validation. Although we recognize validity as a unified construct, Modules 6, 7, and 8 each provide a discussion of the issues involved in the various traditional approaches to validation.

The Role of Expert Judgment

The emphasis of the content validation approach is squarely on the judgment of experts. "Experts on what?" you ask. The answer is experts on the domain you are testing. Any single test intended to assess a construct can be potentially composed of an infinite number of items that assess that particular domain. Unfortunately, not a single test taker would ever be able to answer an infinite number of items. Therefore, the test developer must create a limited number of items to assess the domain—these are the items that actually comprise the test. If we have some subset of an infinite number of possible items, it is possible that the items that comprise the test may not be representative of the entire domain the test was intended to assess. The content approach to test validation examines the degree to which the items that comprise the test are representative of the entire theoretical content the test is intended to assess.

The importance of clearly defining a content domain cannot be emphasized enough. During test development, the definition of the content domain determines which items should be written and selected for inclusion in the test. Later, during the content validation process, experts use the definition of the content domain as a basis for judging the degree to which the test has approximated its intended purpose. In Module 4 (see also Web Reference 6.3), we pointed out the importance of adequately defining the domain. Here we see why such a clear specification of the intent of the test is necessary.

Even with the best intentions, however, defining the content domain for some constructs is simply easier than it is for others. Namely, it is easier to describe the content domain of academic achievement and job knowledge than it is to describe the content domains for constructs with less clearly defined boundaries, such as ability and personality. Abstract content domains may defy simple description, making it difficult or impossible to determine whether test items are contained within a particular domain. Content validation is therefore most appropriate for domains that can be concretely described and defined.

Content Validity: A Simple Example

Consider the case in which an instructor develops a midterm exam based on the reading assignments of Chapters 1–6 of the course's textbook. If the midterm exam is composed in such a way that 75% of the questions on the exam come directly from Chapter 5, we might question the **content validity** of the test. Did the exam representatively sample from the entire domain (as defined by Chapters 1–6)? If 75% of the items on the test originate from a single chapter, it is unlikely that the items that comprise the exam are a representative sample of the entire testing domain. Indeed, important topics in Chapters 1–4 and Chapter 6 are likely to have been omitted from the exam. Likewise, topics in Chapter 5 are probably over-represented. Therefore, the test would be considered to have problems in regard to content validity. However, who would be appropriate judges of the content validity of this exam? Certainly, the students would vocally express their opinions. Subject matter experts, such as other instructors of the same course, might be even more useful for providing some indication of the content validity of the exam.

Examination of the content validity of a test relies on accurately defining the domain the test is intended to assess and then making some judgment as to the sufficiency with which that domain has been assessed. The items that comprise the test must be a representative sample of the domain. That does not mean that all content areas within a domain need be assessed equally. Rather, more important topics should be assessed proportionate to their relative importance to other topics in the domain.

Formalizing Content Validity With the Content Validity Ratio

Although a correlation coefficient is not used to assess content validity, several approaches have been suggested to help quantify content validity through the summary of raters' judgments. For example, Lawshe (1975) proposed the **content validity ratio (CVR)**. In assessing the CVR, a panel of subject matter experts (SMEs) is asked to examine each item on a test. For each item, each SME rates whether the item is "essential," "useful," or "not necessary" to the operationalization of the construct. Across raters, the CVR for an item is determined as follows:

$$CVR = \frac{n_e - \frac{N}{2}}{\frac{N}{2}}$$

where n_e is the number of SMEs rating the item as essential and N is the total number of SMEs making a rating.

Acceptable Size of the Content Validity Ratio

The CVR can range from +1 to −1 for a particular item, with higher scores indicating greater content validity for the item. A CVR of 0 indicates that half the SMEs rated the item as essential. Thus, any positive value indicates that over half of the SMEs rated the item as essential. Items that are deemed to have too low a CVR value would be deleted from the test before administration. But what exactly is a low CVR value? Lawshe (1975) suggested that appropriate CVR values would exceed statistical levels of chance. To operationalize this suggestion, Lawshe (1975) presented a table of the minimum CVR values based on a one-tailed significance test with $p = .05$. Because the CVR value is dependent on the number of SMEs in the sample, a minimally statistically significant CVR value will be highly dependent on the number of SMEs used to provide ratings. For example, Lawshe concluded that a CVR value of .29 would be fine when 40 SMEs were used, a CVR of .51 would be sufficient with 14 SMEs, but a CVR of at least .99 would be necessary with seven or fewer SMEs. Obviously, following Lawshe's recommendations strictly would require a substantial number of SMEs. Note that, in practice, positive CVR values that are considerably lower in magnitude than required using Lawshe's criterion have sometimes been used as the basis to argue for evidence of content validity when a relatively small number of SMEs are used to provide ratings (e.g., Schmitt & Ostroff, 1986).

A Content Validity Ratio Computational Example

Let's try a computational example. Consider the case in which a test developer has developed a 30-item job knowledge test. Wanting to know the content validity ratio of each item, our test developer asks 12 job incumbents to act as SMEs and rate each item on a three-point scale. The degree to which each item is an essential element of job knowledge is rated on a scale with anchors ranging from 0 (not necessary) to 1 (useful) to 2 (essential). Item 14 on the 30-item scale receives nine ratings of "essential," two ratings of "useful," and one rating of "not necessary." What is the CVR of item 14?

$$ \text{CVR} = \frac{n_e - \frac{N}{2}}{\frac{N}{2}} $$

$$ = \frac{9 - \frac{12}{2}}{\frac{12}{2}} = \frac{9 - 6}{6} = \frac{3}{6} = .50 $$

Although 9 out of the 12 SMEs provided a rating of "essential," the CVR value is only .50. According to Lawshe, when 12 SMEs are used a CVR of at least .56 would be required to retain the item. Thus, item 14 would be discarded (unless additional SMEs could be found to rate the item, and the CVR recomputed).

The Content Validity Index

It is important to note that the CVR provides an item-level analysis of validity, while our concern is often with the validity of the test as a whole. To determine an index of the content validity for the test as a whole, the mean CVR across all retained items is computed, resulting in the **content validity index (CVI)**. It should be noted that reliance on the CVI alone could be problematic in determining the validity of a test. After all, consider the example discussed earlier in which an instructor developed a midterm exam that was heavily weighted on a single chapter from the textbook. Individually, each item might receive a high CVR rating. By computing the average CVR rating across all retained items, we would determine that our test's CVI was impressively high. However, few would claim that the test was truly content valid because it fails to assess many important aspects of the entire domain tested. Therefore, Lammlein (1987, as cited in DuBois & DuBois, 2000) suggested that it is important to obtain additional judgments from the SMEs regarding whether the number of items proportionately represent the relative importance of each knowledge category the test is intended to measure.

A Second Approach to Formalizing Content Validity

Barrett (1992, 1996) proposed quantifying content validity through use of a content validation form (CVF). This approach employs a series of 18 questions posed to SMEs. Each question assesses one of three aspects of the test: (1) the test as a whole, (2) an item-by-item analysis, and (3) symptoms of questionable tests. Questions regarding the test as a whole include judgments on the need for and appropriateness of the test. The item-by-item analysis assesses each item individually, such as the correctness of the scoring key. Finally, symptoms of questionable tests pose questions that are not crucial to establishing content validity, but that are characteristic indicators of a test that is content valid. For example, would SMEs be expected to be able to pass the test?

Face Validity

Content validity is based on judgment, particularly the judgment of SMEs. However, test takers themselves often make judgments as to whether the test appears valid. Such judgments are referred to as **face validity**. This judgment is based less on the technical components of content validity, and more on what "looks" valid (Anastasi & Urbina, 1997). While the veracity of the content validity judgments typically relies heavily on the competence of the SMEs, Bornstein (1996) asserted that face validity is an essential element in understanding the concept of validity (see also Web Reference 6.2). Further, research has indicated that test takers' perceptions regarding a test, including perceptions of face validity, can have an important impact on test-taking motivation and performance (Chan, Schmitt, DeShon, & Clause, 1997). Therefore, the judgments of both SMEs and test takers should be taken into consideration in any assessment of the content validity evidence for a test.

Concluding Comments

The content approach to test validation is one of several traditional strategies for determining whether a test measures what it purports to measure. The content approach relies heavily on expert judgments of whether test items representatively sample the entire content domain. The selection of appropriate test experts (i.e., SMEs) is key to ensuring a proper assessment of content validity. These SMEs then provide importance ratings for each item, which can be summarized quantitatively with the CVR and CVI statistics.

Practical Questions

1. Validity is a unified construct. In what ways does content validity provide evidence that a test measures what it purports to measure?

2. Would it be more appropriate to adopt a content validation approach to examine a final exam in a personality psychology course or to examine a measure of conscientiousness? Explain.

3. The content approach to test validation relies heavily on expert judgment. Discuss the degree to which you feel it is appropriate to rely on judgment to provide evidence of validity.

4. Would content validity alone provide sufficient evidence for validity for a(n) (a) employment exam? (b) extraversion inventory? (c) test to determine the need for major surgery? In each case, provide an argument for your reasoning.

5. Does face validity establish content validity? Explain your answer.

6. What could a student do if he or she thought a classroom exam was not content valid?

7. What could an instructor do if a student asserted that a classroom exam was not content valid?

8. Consider a test or inventory of your choosing. If you wanted to examine the content validity of this measure, how would you go about choosing experts to provide judgments?

9. Is quantifying content validity through the use of the CVI, CVF, or other similar method necessary to establishing content validity? Explain.

10. Imagine the case in which 14 SMEs were asked to provide CVR ratings for a five-item test. Compute the CVR for each of the items based on the following ratings:

Item	Not necessary	Useful	Essential
1	1	3	10
2	6	6	2
3	0	0	14
4	0	2	12
5	0	5	9

11. Given that 14 SMEs were used to provide the ratings in question 10, which items do you feel have received a CVR so low that you would recommend deleting the item? Justify your response.

12. What is the CVI for the five-item test in question 10 prior to deletion of any items due to low CVR?

Case Studies

CASE STUDY 6.1: WHAT IS SUFFICIENT CONTENT VALIDATION?

In her years of experience as a clinical therapist, Juanita had come to suspect that some of her clients seemed to share a common trait. Specifically, a significant portion of her clients expressed great loneliness. Juanita found that different therapeutic approaches had varying success with these clients, depending on the degree of loneliness experienced. To help match the correct therapeutic approach to the client, Juanita sought a self-report paper-and-pencil scale of loneliness. Unfortunately, she was unable to locate a scale with established reliability and validity. Undaunted, Juanita began development of a paper-and-pencil measure that would assess the degree of loneliness experienced by the respondent.

Juanita began by reading scientific journals and book chapters on the construct of loneliness. Based on her understanding of the research and her own clinical experience, Juanita defined the trait of loneliness as a persistent, painful awareness of not being connected to others. Juanita then used her knowledge of test construction to develop a measure of 33 items intended to assess the trait of loneliness.

Upon completion of the development of her scale, Juanita wondered whether her new creation was indeed content valid. Therefore, before administering the scale to any clients, she asked four other experienced therapists to scrutinize the items. Each of these clinicians provided positive assurance that the scale seemed to capture the concept of loneliness quite well. Satisfied, Juanita set out to begin using her scale.

Questions to Ponder

1. Are Juanita's efforts sufficient to provide evidence of content validity? Explain.

2. To what degree does Juanita's purpose for the test influence your response to question 1?

3. What additional sources might Juanita seek to help define the trait of loneliness?

4. Is Juanita's choice of individuals to serve as SMEs appropriate? Explain.

5. Has Juanita used an appropriate number of SMEs? Explain.

6. How might Juanita identify other SMEs who would be useful in the content validation of her scale?

7. Is it possible that 33 items could capture the complexity of a construct such as the trait of loneliness?

CASE STUDY 6.2: CONTENT VALIDATION OF A PERSONNEL SELECTION INSTRUMENT

Reflecting for a moment on the results of his ambitious undertaking, Lester smiled. His boss at the Testing and Personnel Services Division of this large midwestern city had assigned him the task of validating the selection test for the job of *Supervisor—Children's Social Worker* only two weeks ago, and he had just completed the task. Lester was quite satisfied with the method he'd used to validate the test, and happier still with the results of the effort.

Upon his first inspection of the newly created test, the 145 items seemed to make sense for assessing the behavioral dimensions identified in the job description—knowledge of federal and state laws related to child welfare, supervisory skills, skill in data analytic techniques; skill in reading comprehension, and so on. Still, Lester knew little about the job of a social work supervisor. However, he did have access to the city's database that contained names of individuals who actually held this position. Through repeated efforts, Lester was able to persuade seven long-time incumbents in the position of *Supervisor—Children's Social Worker* to serve as expert raters for assessing the content validity of the new test.

Lester arranged for each of the seven subject matter experts (SMEs) to attend a one-day session. At the beginning of the day, Lester carefully explained the importance of assessing the content validity of the test, and then explained the process that was to be used to review each item on the test. Each rater was to make several independent judgments about each and every item on the test. Specifically, SMEs were asked to consider several dimensions of item QUALITY, including (a) the appropriate level of difficulty, (b) the plausibility of item distracters, and (c) the veracity of the answer key. Each SME was then asked to indicate whether he or she was satisfied with all three of these indicators of quality, or not satisfied, if any one of the three characteristics needed improvement. If the latter choice was indicated, the SME was asked to provide additional comments for how the item might be improved.

In addition to the QUALITY rating for an item, each SME provided a second rating based on RELEVANCE. For the relevance ratings, each SME was asked to rate the extent to which the knowledge area or ability assessed by the item was essential to correctly performing the critical functions of the job of *Supervisor—Children's Social Worker*. SMEs rated each item as 2 (Essential), 1 (Useful, but not essential), or 0 (Not useful).

Lester then used both the QUALITY and RELEVANCE ratings to determine which items might be kept in the test and which might be deleted or revised. Specifically, Lester decided that items would be retained if the QUALITY rating was "satisfied" by at least 57% of the raters (i.e., four of the seven SMEs) and if the mean RELEVANCE rating for that particular item was at least 1.5. Using these criteria, Lester eliminated 30 items from the original test. The resulting content-validated test retained 115 items.

As a final step, Lester computed the content validity ratio (CVR) for each of the retained 115 items based on the SMEs' RELEVANCE ratings. Once the CVR was computed for each item, he then computed the mean CVR across all 115 of the retained items. It was this result that pleased Lester the most—the mean CVR score was .78. Reflecting on his work, Lester began to wonder whether now was a good time to ask his boss for a raise.

Questions to Ponder

1. Would seven SMEs serve as a sufficient number of expert raters to provide adequate evidence of content validity for this employment selection test? Why or why not?

2. Do the criteria Lester used for inclusion of an item seem appropriate? Defend your response.

3. Why would Lester be happy with a mean CVR rating of .78?

4. What other validation strategies might Lester have employed? What additional information would be needed to adopt a different validation strategy?

Exercises

EXERCISE 6.1: IDENTIFYING SMES

OBJECTIVE: To gain practice identifying appropriate samples to provide content validation ratings.

For each of the following tests, identify two different samples of people who would have the expertise to serve as subject matter experts (SMEs) for providing judgments regarding the content validity of the test.

1. A knowledge test of local residential electrical codes

2. A measure of political predisposition along the liberalism/conservatism continuum

3. A midterm exam for a high school algebra course

4. A structured interview used to select salespersons

5. A survey of the electorate's preferences for major political office in the upcoming election

EXERCISE 6.2: ENSURING REPRESENTATIVE ASSESSMENT OF TEST DIMENSIONS

OBJECTIVE: To consider the relative importance of various dimensions of a test.

Given the limited number of items that can be included on a test or inventory, test developers must often make difficult decisions regarding the proportion of items that can be used to assess each dimension of a construct. For each of the following multidimensional tests, determine the proportion of items you would choose to assess each of the specified dimensions. For each test, ensure the total proportion of items sums to 100% across dimensions. Justify your determination for each test.

1. A knowledge test of local residential electrical codes assesses knowledge of (a) municipal, (b) county, and (c) state electrical codes.

2. A midterm exam for a high school algebra course assesses each of the following topics:
   a. Working with variables
   b. Solving equations
   c. Solving word problems
   d. Polynomial operations
   e. Factoring polynomials
   f. Quadratic equations
   g. Graphing linear equations
   h. Inequalities

3. A structured interview used to select salespersons is intended to assess each of the following characteristics of the applicant:
   a. Ability to communicate verbally
   b. Planning and organization
   c. Persuasiveness
   d. Anxiety in social situations

4. A measure of religiosity is composed of the following dimensions:
   a. Religious beliefs
   b. Religious practices
   c. Religious knowledge
   d. Religious feelings (mystical experiences, sense of well being, etc.)
   e. Religious effects on personal behaviors

EXERCISE 6.3: DETERMINING THE CVI OF A MEASURE OF UNDERGRADUATE ACADEMIC WORK ETHIC

OBJECTIVE: To gain experience obtaining and computing content validity ratings.

INSTRUCTIONS: Below you will find a description of a measure intended to assess the construct Undergraduate Academic Work Ethic. Following this brief description are the items initially written to compose the scale.

For this exercise, choose an appropriate sample of at least 10 individuals to act as SMEs for this scale. Ask these SMEs to familiarize themselves with the proposed dimensions of the scale. Then ask each SME to rate each item on the scale as "essential," "useful," or "not necessary." Remind the SMEs that negatively worded items can be just as useful in assessing the construct as positively worded items. Finally, provide a response for each of the following:

1. Compute the CVR for each item on the scale.

2. Compute the CVI for the entire set of 20 items that comprise the initial scale.

3. Based on statistical significance, Lawshe (1975) recommended that with 10 raters the CVR should be at least .62 to retain an item. Which items would be deleted using this criterion?

4. If the items identified in the preceding item were deleted, what would be the CVI of the remaining items?

The Undergraduate Academic Work Ethic Measure

The Undergraduate Academic Work Ethic scale is a 20-item measure of the academic work ethic of undergraduate college students. Undergraduate academic work ethic is defined as an undergraduate student's academic work habits, including:

    a. class-related attendance and participation
    b. study habits
    c. procrastination tendencies
    d. dedication to schoolwork
    e. academic honesty

Respondents are asked to indicate the degree to which they agree with each item using a five-point Likert-type scale ranging from 1 (Strongly Disagree) to 5 (Strongly Agree).

1. I make an effort to come to every class, even when I don't feel like attending.

2. I am NOT overly concerned with being in class at the beginning of the lecture.

3. I enjoy participating in class discussions.

4. I would go to my professor's office hours if I needed help in the class.

5. When working in a group, I rarely attend all the group meetings.

6. When writing a paper, I usually wait until the last minute to start it.

7. I usually do NOT procrastinate when it comes to my homework.

8. I have a tendency to cram for tests.

9. I do the least amount of work required in order to pass.

10. I consider myself to have good time management skills when it comes to my schoolwork.

11. I rarely take advantage of extra-credit opportunities.

12. I would turn down an appealing offer to go out if I had to study.

13. During finals week, I rarely have any free time because I am so busy studying.

14. If I don't understand something in class, I will ask the professor or a classmate to explain it.

15. It would NOT bother me to receive a poor grade in a course.

16. I try to be one of the top-ranked students in the class.

17. Doing well in school is NOT a priority in my life.

18. I set high academic goals for myself.

19. I would cheat on a test if I knew I could get away with it.

20. I would allow a classmate to copy my homework.

Internet Web Site References

6.1. http://www.burns.com/wcbugesp.htm

This Web page by William C. Burns attempts to relate information on content validity from the Uniform Guidelines on Employee Selection Procedures (UGESP) in an easy-to-understand manner. This Web page presents excerpts from the UGESP along with commentary to facilitate understanding. Compare the "classic" and "extended" views of content validity presented in the guidelines.

6.2. http://www.jalt.org/test/rob_1.htm

This Web page presents an interesting opinion piece by Dennis M. Roberts who argues that face validity has a legitimate place in assessment.

6.3. http://www.rci.rutgers.edu/~judithjf/validityofODs.htm

This Web page presents a list of questions to ask regarding the measurement validity of an operationalization of a construct.

Further Readings

Burns, R. S. (1996). Content validity, face validity, and quantitative face validity. In R. S. Barrett (Ed.), *Fair employment strategies in human resource management* (pp. 38–46). Westport, CT: Quorum Books/Greenwood.

Chan, D., Schmitt, N., DeShon, R. P., & Clause, C. S. (1997). Reactions to cognitive ability tests: The relationships between race, test performance, face validity perceptions, and test-taking motivation. *Journal of Applied Psychology, 82*, 300–310.

Guion, R. M. (1978). "Content validity" in moderation. *Personnel Psychology, 31*, 205–213.

Messick, S. (1995a). Validity of psychological assessment: Validation of inferences from persons' responses and performances as scientific inquiry into score meaning. *American Psychologist, 50*, 741–749.

Tenopyr, M. L. (1977). Content-construct confusion. *Personnel Psychology, 30*, 47–54.

Module 7

Criterion-Related Validation

I f the purpose of validation is to examine whether the inferences and conclusions based on test scores are defensible, just how does the criterion-related approach provide this information? The answer is relatively straightforward. The criterion-related approach to test validation involves examining the empirical relationship between scores on a test and a criterion of interest, typically by use of a correlation coefficient. The appropriate choice of a criterion will depend on what inferences we hope to make. Thus, in determining the validity of a college entrance exam, we would desire a criterion of college success. In determining the validity of an employment selection exam, we would want a criterion of successful job performance. Moreover, in examining the success of a new type of psychiatric therapy, we would select a criterion that captured psychological health.

In everyday language, it is common to inquire *whether* a test is valid. Criterion-related validation strategies remind us to inquire about *what* exactly the test is valid *for*. In fact, test scores may validly predict scores on one criterion, but not another. For example, intelligence may serve as a good **predictor** of college grade point average (GPA), but serve as a poor predictor of morality. Thus, when using the criterion-related approach to validation, it is essential that the criterion choice be relevant to the intended purpose of testing.

Criterion-Related Validation Research Designs

Three research designs can be employed in the examination of **criterion-related validity** (see Web Reference 7.1). Although these designs differ in the order in which test scores and criterion scores are collected, a more important issue revolves around the selection of the sample used in the validation study. **Predictive validity** studies correlate test scores with criterion scores collected at some future date. Here, the desire is to examine how well test scores predict future criterion scores. Predictive criterion-related research designs allow random samples to be obtained for the study. **Concurrent validity** studies collect test and criterion scores at about the same time. Because there is no lag in time between collection of test scores and collection of criterion scores, the validity of the test can be determined much more quickly than is the case for most predictive designs. However, because the sample is typically predetermined (i.e., limited to those individuals for whom we can immediately collect criterion data) in concurrent criterion-related research, the sample on which the validation study is conducted is rarely randomly selected. A third research design that can be used for criterion-related validation is somewhat less well known: **postdictive validity** designs. With postdictive designs, criterion scores are collected prior to obtaining test scores. As is the case for the concurrent design, postdictive criterion-related validation studies use a predetermined sample. In this case, the sample is limited to those individuals for whom we already have criterion data.

Independent of the research design, examining the empirical relationship between the test and the criterion provides validity evidence. However, the design of the study often has important implications for the possible conclusions that can be drawn from the data. With concurrent criterion-related validity, for example, we are interested in how well test scores are indicative of one's current standing on a criterion. Because individuals can change considerably over time due to a number of factors, the concurrent and postdictive research designs are not as well suited to prediction of future criterion performance as the predictive criterion-related approach.

Examples of Criterion-Related Validation

Industrial/organizational psychologists frequently use criterion-related validity to demonstrate the job relatedness of a proposed employment selection test. A predictive criterion-related validity approach would require the administration of an experimental selection test to job applicants. Selection of new employees is then made either completely randomly or on some basis unrelated to scores on the experimental selection test. Those applicants that are hired are then provided an adequate amount of time to learn the new job—perhaps 6 months to a year. At the end of this time period, criterion information is collected, such as supervisor ratings of employee performance.

A correlation between scores on the experimental selection test and the job performance criterion provides the estimate of predictive criterion-related validity.

An estimate of the concurrent criterion-related validity for a new selection test is typically derived by administering the experimental selection test to current employees. Simultaneously, job performance criterion scores are obtained for these individuals. A correlation between scores on the experimental selection test and the job performance criterion provides the estimate of concurrent criterion-related validity.

A postdictive design to examine the criterion-related validity of an employment test might be conducted to examine whether a newly developed test of conscientiousness might relate to employees' absenteeism records (i.e., a job performance criterion). The measure of conscientiousness would be administered to employees. The absenteeism record for each of these same employees would be accessed for some specified amount of time, such as the last two-year period. A correlation between scores on the measure of conscientiousness and absenteeism would provide the estimate of the postdictive criterion-related validity.

Although the concurrent and postdictive approaches have the obvious advantage of requiring considerably less time to evaluate the experimental selection test than does the predictive approach, traditionally concerns have been raised about the degree to which the sample used to validate the test (e.g., current employees) differs from the population the test is actually intended for (e.g., job applicants). For example, job applicants would be much more motivated to use an impression management response strategy on a job selection test than would current employees. Interestingly, however, research provides evidence that the validity estimates yielded by predictive and concurrent designs are nearly identical (Barrett, Phillips, & Alexander, 1981; Schmitt, Gooding, Noe, & Kirsch, 1984).

Interpreting the Validity Coefficient

Because the criterion-related approach to validation correlates test scores with criterion scores, an easily interpretable measure of effect size is provided that will range from −1 to 0 to +1. Because most tests are constructed such that higher scores on the test are intended to be associated with higher scores on a criterion (e.g., we typically assert the relationship between intelligence and performance, not stupidity and performance), a **validity coefficient** will typically range from 0 to 1. Still, many individuals are surprised to learn that the magnitude of a validity coefficient rarely exceeds .50. While the purpose of testing will determine what magnitude of correlation will be considered sufficient for a given situation, Cohen's (1988) suggestions for the interpretation of the magnitude of correlation-based effect sizes might be useful. Cohen suggested that correlations of .1 are small, .3 are moderate, and .5 can be considered to be large. It is important to keep in mind that even relatively small validity coefficients can improve prediction significantly over random selection.

A criterion-related validity estimate can be used to determine the percentage of variance accounted for in the criterion by use of the predictor. The **coefficient of determination** is a simple formula to compute:

$$r_{xy}^2 * 100\%$$

where r_{xy} is the validity coefficient.

As an example, a validity coefficient of $r_{xy} = .4$ would indicate that, by using our test, we could explain 16% of the variability in the criterion. In the case of a selection exam with a validity of $r_{xy} = .4$, we would be able to predict 16% of the variability in job performance by using the test in our selection system. Of course, that would also mean that $100\% - 16\% = 84\%$ of the variability in the criterion remained unexplained. Although we could add more tests to increase our prediction of the criterion, that solution is not without its problems (see Module 17).

Attenuation and Inflation of Observed Validity Coefficients

Although it is easy to grasp a basic understanding of the criterion-related approach to test validation, a number of issues should be considered when employing use of this validation strategy. The magnitude of an observed validity coefficient can be affected by a number of factors. These problems are discussed below, along with suggested corrections that may provide a more accurate (and often larger) criterion-related validity estimate.

Inadequate Sample Size

Due to ignorance, convenience, or practical limitations, criterion-related validation studies often employ use of samples that are too small. Because of sampling error, criterion-related validation studies that employ very small samples may produce spurious results regarding the estimated magnitude of the population correlation. Further, because statistical power relies heavily on sample size, use of an inadequate sample size often results in a failure to detect an authentic relationship between the test and the criterion in the population. Such a finding may lead to the unnecessary rejection of the use of the test under consideration.

The clear recommendation to avoid these problems is simple, if not always practical: increase the size of the sample used in the criterion-related validation study. How large should the sample be? Schmidt, Hunter, and Urry (1976) suggested use of sample sizes in excess of 200 individuals for criterion-related validation studies. Unfortunately, samples of this size are not always possible to obtain. What other options exist? The concept of *synthetic validity* suggests that the validity of a test can be generalized from one context to another similar context (Guion, 1965; Lawshe, 1952). For example, a small organization may wish to use a selection test to hire a new office assistant. Because the organization currently employs only eight office assistants, a full-blown criterion-related validation study would be out of the question. However, if the organization can identify a number of job duties that are performed by its office assistants that are similar to those job duties performed by office assistants in larger organizations, then employment tests that have been shown to be highly related to job performance for office assistants in the larger organizations should validly predict the job performance of office assistants in the small organization. Further, meta-analytic reports of the relationship between predictors and a specific criterion could also be sought out to determine the feasibility of use of a predictor (see Module 9).

Criterion Contamination

Another concern in criterion-related validation is **criterion contamination.** Criterion contamination is present when a criterion measure includes aspects unrelated to the intended criterion construct. Put another way, criterion contamination occurs when the criterion measure is affected by construct-irrelevant factors that are not part of the criterion construct (Messick, 1989). Criterion contamination often results in an inflated observed validity coefficient. A common source of criterion contamination occurs when an individual with knowledge of test scores also assigns criterion scores.

Many organizations employ the use of assessment centers in which employees participate in a number of exercises intended to assess management potential. Indeed, many organizations have used these assessment center scores as a basis for determining future promotion. Criterion contamination would result if the organization later decided to examine the relationship between assessment center scores and promotion. Obviously, a strong positive correlation would exist, because the assessment center scores were used as the basis for determining who would be promoted and who would not.

The problem of criterion contamination can only be addressed through appropriate measurement of the criterion and by minimizing construct-irrelevant variance in the measurement of both the predictor and the criterion.

Attenuation Due to Unreliability

Because a test is judged based on its relationship to a criterion in criterion-related validation, we had better ensure that the criterion itself is appropriate, and is measured accurately. All too often, however, this is not the case. A criterion-related validity coefficient will be attenuated (i.e., reduced) if the criterion is not perfectly reliable. As a result, we might erroneously conclude that our test fails to demonstrate criterion-related validity. Unfortunately, most psychological constructs—including criteria—are measured with some amount of error (see Module 5). Because our focus in validation is the test, we can ethically perform a statistical correction for unreliability in the criterion (Spearman, 1904) in order to provide a more accurate assessment of the validity of the test:

$$r_{xyc} = \frac{r_{xy}}{\sqrt{r_{yy}}}$$

where r_{xyc} is the validity of the test, corrected for unreliability in the criterion; r_{xy} is the original observed validity of the test; and r_{yy} is the reliability of the criterion.

For example, let us consider the case in which a measure of general cognitive ability was being considered for use in hiring retail sales clerks at a popular clothing store. A consultant conducted a concurrent criterion-related validation study and correlated job incumbent scores on the cognitive ability test with supervisor ratings of job performance. The consultant determined that cognitive ability was indeed related to supervisor ratings of job performance, $r_{xy} = .37$. However, the consultant was able to determine that the reliability of supervisor ratings of job performance was only .70. What would be the validity of the test of cognitive ability following correction of the criterion due to unreliability?

$$r_{xyc} = \frac{r_{xy}}{\sqrt{r_{yy}}} = \frac{.37}{\sqrt{.70}} = \frac{.37}{.84} = .44$$

Obviously, the validity coefficient is more impressive following **correction for attenuation** due to unreliability in the criterion.

Note that *mathematically* we could also correct for attenuation due to unreliability in the test at the same time we correct for attenuation in the criterion. This can be done by slightly modifying the preceding formula

$$r_{xyc'} = \frac{r_{xy}}{\sqrt{r_{xx'}r_{yy}}}$$

where $r_{xyc'}$ is the validity of the test, corrected for unreliability in the test and the criterion, and r_{xx} is the reliability of the test.

If the consultant decided to further correct for unreliability in the test, we could extend the preceding example. Assuming the reliability of cognitive ability scores on this test was found to be .88, we could perform the following analysis:

$$r_{xyc'} = \frac{r_{xy}}{\sqrt{r_{xx'}r_{yy}}} = \frac{.37}{\sqrt{.88(.70)}} = \frac{.37}{\sqrt{.62}} = \frac{.37}{.79} = .47$$

Correction for attenuation due to unreliability in both the criterion and the predictor would further increase our estimate of criterion-related validity. Unfortunately, this last analysis should *not* be performed to provide an estimate of the validity of our test, because the error associated with unreliability in our predictor will be present whenever we administer the test. If, on the other hand, we wish to know the true population correlation between our test and our criterion (as is often the case in meta-analysis), then correction for unreliability in both the predictor and the criterion is ethically permissible. Web Reference 7.2 demonstrates the effect of unreliability on observed predictor-criterion relationships.

Restriction of Range

Restriction of range is another important concern with criterion-related validation. The variability in test scores in our sample may be considerably smaller than that in the actual population. Unfortunately, it is typically the case that when we reduce the variability in test scores, we reduce the magnitude of the observed correlation. We would then erroneously conclude that our test is less valid than it actually is. This, in fact, is a major concern when using concurrent criterion-related validity rather than predictive designs. Fortunately, there is a formula (Pearson, 1903) to statistically correct for the effects of restriction of range in the test, assuming we can estimate the variability of scores in the population:

$$r_{xyu} = \frac{r_{xy}\dfrac{S_u}{S_r}}{\sqrt{1 - r_{xy}^2 + r_{xy}^2 \dfrac{S_u^2}{S_r^2}}}$$

where r_{xyu} is the unrestricted validity, r_{xy} is the obtained validity, s_u is the population (i.e., unrestricted) predictor standard deviation, and s_r is the restricted predictor standard deviation.

As an example, let us once again consider the case described previously, in which a consultant has determined the criterion-related validity estimate of a cognitive ability test for predicting the job performance of retail sales clerks is $r_{xy} = .44$ (following correction for attenuation due to unreliability in the criterion). However, this consultant learns that the standard deviation of cognitive ability test scores among job incumbents is only $s_r = 9$, whereas the standard deviation of cognitive ability test scores among applicants for the position of clerk in this retail store is $s_u = 13$. Here, there is clear evidence that score variability in the job incumbent sample is restricted in comparison to the variability of scores among applicants. Thus, we would expect that our unrestricted validity estimate would be greater than our current estimate of .44. Let us work through the example:

$$r_{xyu} = \frac{r_{xy}\dfrac{S_u}{S_r}}{\sqrt{1 - r_{xy}^2 + r_{xy}^2 \dfrac{S_u^2}{S_r^2}}} = \frac{.44\dfrac{13}{9}}{\sqrt{1 - (.44)^2 + (.44)^2 \dfrac{13^2}{9^2}}}$$

$$= \frac{.44(1.44)}{\sqrt{1 - .19 + .19\dfrac{169}{81}}} = \frac{.63}{\sqrt{1 - .19 + .19(2.09)}}$$

$$= \frac{.63}{\sqrt{1 - .19 + .40}} = \frac{.63}{\sqrt{1.21}} = \frac{.63}{1.10} = .57$$

Thus, after the additional correction of attenuation due to restriction in range of the predictor, we find that the criterion-related validity of our test of cognitive ability is quite impressive. For an interactive example of the impact of restriction of range on the relationship between X and Y, see Web Reference 7.2.

Additional Considerations

The criterion-related approach to test validation discussed in this module assumes that we consider the sample of test takers as a single group. Some-times, however, we might be concerned whether a test is valid for one sub-group of our sample and not for another. The subgroups can be determined on the basis of whatever is relevant to the researcher, including those based on age, sex, or ethnicity. *Differential validity* examines whether there exist separate test validities for these groups. This topic is considered in Module 10.

Further, our discussion in this module has been limited to the case in which we are examining the relationship between a criterion and a single test. Module 17 addresses additional concerns that arise when more than one predictor is utilized in relation to a criterion.

Concluding Comments

The criterion-related approach to validation attempts to provide evidence of the accuracy of test scores by empirically relating test scores to criterion scores. Despite the seemingly simplistic nature of this endeavor, a number of issues must be considered regarding the research design, the sample, and the criterion employed.

Practical Questions

1. In what ways does the criterion-related approach to test validation help estab-lish that a test "measures what it purports to measure"?

2. What are the differences among predictive, concurrent, and postdictive criterion-related validity designs?

3. The various criterion-related validity research designs might not be equally appropriate for a given situation. For each of the following criterion-related

validity designs, provide an example situation in which that design might be preferred:
   a. Predictive
   b. Concurrent
   c. Postdictive

4. What factors would you consider to ensure that you have an appropriate criterion?

5. What factors might attenuate an observed correlation between test scores and criterion scores? Explain.

6. What might inflate an observed correlation between test scores and criterion scores? Explain.

7. For each of the following, explain how the correction formula provides a more accurate estimate of the true relationship between the predictor and the criterion:
   a. Correction for unreliability in the criterion
   b. Correction for range restriction in the predictor

8. Although it is empirically possible to correct for attenuation due to unreliability in a predictor, this is a violation of ethics if we intend to use the predictor for applied purposes. Explain why we can ethically correct for unreliability in the criterion but cannot ethically correct for unreliability in a predictor.

9. How could a small organization determine which selection tests might be appropriate for use in selection of new employees?

Case Studies

CASE STUDY 7.1: USING MECHANICAL ABILITY TO PREDICT JOB PERFORMANCE

"This will be a cinch," Cecilia had thought when she first received the assignment to conduct a criterion-related validity study. She'd been a human resource (HR) specialist at Joyco for only three weeks, and she relished the thought of tackling her first major project independently. In fact, she had jumped at the opportunity when her boss asked her to conduct a criterion-related validation study to determine whether a newly created test of mechanical ability would be useful in selecting production workers. She thought it would be relatively easy to collect test scores and correlate them with some measure of job performance.

Only slowly did she realize how much thought and hard work would actually take place to complete the task properly.

She soon realized the first major issue she'd have to tackle was identifying an appropriate criterion. Clearly, job performance was appropriate, but how should job performance be measured? Supervisors formally appraised each production worker's performance annually, and the HR office seemed pleased with the quality of the process. Still, Cecilia knew the supervisor ratings were far from perfect assessments of an employee's job performance.

Cecilia's thoughts suddenly leaped to another concern—when her boss had asked her to determine the criterion-related validity of the new test, she had provided a two-week deadline. Such a tight deadline clearly precluded use of a predictive design. Unfortunately, the current production workers were likely very different from job applicants. In comparison to applicants, current production workers tended to be older, they were more similar to one another ethnically, and they also had much more job experience. Given the timeline provided by her boss, however, Cecilia thought that it was the current production workers that she'd need to use to validate the proposed selection tests.

Undeterred, Cecilia went ahead with the project. Cecilia administered the new mechanical ability test to a sample of Joyco's production workers. In an effort to ensure she'd done a complete job, Cecilia also collected information on everything she thought *might* be relevant. Nonetheless, she knew she had collected an impressive amount of information regarding the new test of mechanical ability and the criterion, including the following:

Sample size for the validation study $= N = 178$ job incumbents

Observed validity $= r_{xy} = .24$

Reliability of the new mechanical ability test $= r_{xx} = .85$

Reliability of supervisor ratings of job performance $= r_{yy} = .78$

Standard deviation of mechanical ability tests scores for current employee sample $= 9$

Standard deviation of mechanical ability test scores for applicant sample $= 14$

Although the completion deadline was quickly approaching, Cecilia still had a ways to go before producing an accurate criterion-related validity estimate for the new mechanical ability test. Cecilia slumped back into her chair. "This is definitely going to take some work," she thought.

Questions to Ponder

1. What research design did Cecilia use to conduct her criterion-related validation study? What was the major determinant of this decision?

2. Why might Cecilia have preferred another research design for her criterion-related validation study?

3. Would Cecilia have to be concerned with criterion contamination in conducting this validation study? Explain.

4. Identify three alternate criteria Cecilia might have used to assess job performance, rather than supervisor ratings. What concerns do you have with each possible criterion?

5. Given the sample used to validate the proposed selection tests, which correction formulas would be most important to use?

6. Given the data Cecilia collected, compute each of the following:
   a. Correction for attenuation in the criterion
   b. Correction for predictor range restriction (*Note:* Use the corrected validity estimate from part a.)

7. Examining the corrected validity coefficient produced in question 6b, how impressed would you be with this test of mechanical ability for use in selection of new employees? Would you recommend use of the test? Explain.

CASE STUDY 7.2: AN INVESTIGATION OF STUDENT DROPOUT RATES

Principal Andrew Dickerson of Mountain Central High School had a hunch. Actually, it was more like a strong suspicion. At nearly 15%, the student dropout rate in his high school was well above the statewide average. Upon assuming his position, Principal Dickerson had pledged that he would change things for the better. Although he knew it would be impossible to eliminate dropouts altogether, he intended to do everything in his power to curb the problem. To begin, he intended to identify factors that put students most at risk for dropping out. The usual socioeconomic factors helped identify some individuals who might be at risk for dropping out, but combined, these factors accounted for only a modest amount of the variance in dropout rates at his school.

In reviewing the academic files of the six latest students to drop out, Principal Dickersón noticed that most of these students had experienced behavior problems in the very early years of their formal education. Principal Dickerson began to wonder whether this was also true of other students who had dropped out of high school. He knew enough about research methods to acknowledge that you couldn't conclude anything on such a small sample. Further, he felt it was necessary to examine the files of those students who hadn't dropped out of school, in order to determine their record of discipline in early education as well.

Principal Dickerson decided to examine a sample of all students who had entered his high school in the years 1995–1999. This five-year block would provide him with a total sample of about 1,500 students who entered as freshmen. Because the dropout rate at his school averaged roughly 15% during this time period, he knew about 225 of these students dropped out of school without graduating. Committed to thoroughly testing his hunch, Principal Dickerson assigned three members of his staff to scan the grade school academic records of all 1,500 students who had entered Mountain Central High School between 1995 and 1999. These staff members were told to inspect each student's grade school records and to record the number of behavioral problems noted while the student was in grades 1 through 5. Principal Dickerson planned to correlate these records of behavior problems with whether or not the student graduated. Given the vast amount of work involved, Principal Dickerson sure hoped his hunch was right.

Questions to Ponder

1. Why must we examine those individuals who graduated from high school if our real concern is with those students who dropped out of high school?

2. What type of criterion-related validity design did Principal Dickerson employ? Explain.

3. Principal Dickerson developed his hunch after reviewing the files of six recent dropouts. Would the files of six dropouts be sufficient to identify a potentially useful trend that should be followed up with an empirical investigation? What minimum number of files do you feel could be used to initially form a hypothesis worthy of empirical testing?

4. What other methods might Principal Dickerson have employed to identify possible correlates of high school dropout rates?

5. Principal Dickerson is planning to investigate the relationship between early education behavioral problems and high school dropout rate. If the study reveals a significant relationship between these variables, how might this information be used to combat the problem of high school dropouts?

Exercises

EXERCISE 7.1: IDENTIFYING POSSIBLE PREDICTORS AND CRITERIA

OBJECTIVE: To gain practice identifying relevant predictors and criteria for validation.

For each of the criteria presented in items 1–3, identify at least two psychological or cognitive measures that might serve as useful predictors in a criterion-related validation study.

1. Grades in an educational psychology doctoral program

2. A medical student's "bedside manner" as a doctor

3. Success in a retail sales position

For each of the scenarios presented in items 4–6, recommend at least two relevant, practical measures that could serve as criteria.

4. A state in the Southeast would like to determine the usefulness of requiring road tests for drivers older than 70 years of age.

5. A supervisor wishes to determine the job performance of her factory workers.

6. A researcher wishes to determine whether regular consumption of a certain vitamin supplement influences cardiovascular health in men aged 50–75.

EXERCISE 7.2: DETECTING VALID PREDICTORS

OBJECTIVE: To gain experience identifying valid predictors in a data set.

PROLOGUE: The data set "Bus driver.sav" contains a number of variables that assess job performance. Because several independent measures are also included in this data set, we might be tempted to identify variables that might be useful for predicting the performance of future bus drivers. Following are descriptions of several potential predictors and measures of bus driver job performance.

Possible predictors

Variable name	Description
so_hpi	Hogan Personality Inventory service orientation subscale
st_hpi	Hogan Personality Inventory stress tolerance subscale
r_hpi	Hogan Personality Inventory reliability (e.g., integrity) subscale
age	Age of bus driver, in years
sex	Sex of bus driver, coded 0 = male, 1 = female
tenure	Tenure on the job, in years

Job performance measures

Variable name	Description
sickdays	Number of sick personal days in last year
srti	Number of self-reported traffic incidents in last year
drivetst	Score on driving performance test
pescore	Overall performance evaluation score

Use the data set "Bus driver.sav" to correlate the possible predictors with the job performance measures and then answer the following questions. (*Note:* For this exercise, examine the predictors individually using correlation. An opportunity to examine combinations of these predictors using multiple regression is provided in Exercise 17.1.)

1. Overall, how highly are the possible predictors intercorrelated?

2. Overall, how highly are the job performance measures intercorrelated?

3. Overall, how useful would the personality measures be in predicting job performance?

4. Overall, how useful would the demographic variables be in predicting job performance?

5. Inspecting only the significant correlations, interpret the findings for tenure across the job performance criteria.

6. If you were examining the validity of a set of variables you hoped to use for prediction, and you found validity coefficients similar to those in this analysis, what would you do?

EXERCISE 7.3: PREDICTING SALES JOB PERFORMANCE USING ZERO-ORDER CORRELATIONS

OBJECTIVE: To practice computation of a validity coefficient using statistical software.

PROLOGUE: A sales manager hoping to improve the selection process for the position of product sales compiled the data file "Sales.sav." The manager administered several tests to her current employees and also collected basic demographic information. Simultaneously, the manager collected performance data in the form of quantity of products sold by each employee in the past month. The variables in the data file include the following:

Variable name	Description
sex	Sex of employee, coded 0 = female, 1 = male
ethnic	Ethnicity of employee, coded 0 = Caucasian, 1 = African American
w1–w50	Each indicates the employee's score on a separate item on the test of cognitive ability, coded 0 = incorrect, 1 = correct
cogab	Employee's total cognitive ability score
sde	Employee's score on a test assessing one's level of self-deception
impress	Employee's score on a test of impression management
selling	Number of products employee sold in the past month

1. What type of validation study is the manager conducting? Explain.

2. Examining the zero-order correlations, what variables are significantly related to selling?

3. What percentage of variance in selling is accounted for by impression management?

4. If impression management were measured with an $\alpha = .80$, what would be the validity estimate of this variable following correction for attenuation due to unreliability?

5. Cognitive ability has little relationship to performance in these employees.
   a. Is this finding likely due to poor reliability in the measure of cognitive ability? Explain.
   b. Is this finding likely due to very poor reliability in the measure of "selling"? Explain.
   c. Even if cognitive ability were highly related to selling, what other information provided in this data set would make you wary of using cognitive ability for selection of new employees?

Internet Web Site References

7.1. http://www-class.unl.edu/psycrs/451/e4/crvalidity.PDF

This Web page presents an overview of many criterion-related validity issues, including predictive versus concurrent designs, **incremental validity,** and the relationship between reliability and validity.

7.2. http://www.ruf.rice.edu/~lane/stat_sim/reliability_reg/index.html

This Web page, from Rice University, allows users to examine the effects of changing the reliability of a predictor (X) or criterion (Y) on the observed correlation between X and Y. A link is also provided to exercises that question users about the effects of variable reliability on the correlation between X and Y.

7.3. http://www.ruf.rice.edu/~lane/stat_sim/restricted_range/

This Web page, from Rice University, allows users to examine the effects of restricting the range of a predictor variable (X) on the observed correlation between X and Y. A link is also provided to useful exercises that question users about the effects of restriction of range.

Further Readings

Barrett, G. V., Phillips, J. S., & Alexander, R. A. (1981). Concurrent and predictive validity designs: A critical reanalysis. *Journal of Applied Psychology, 66,* 1–6.

Bryant, F. B. (2000). Assessing the validity of measurement. In L. G. Grimm & P. R. Yarnold (Eds.), *Reading and understanding more multivariate statistics* (pp. 99–146). Washington, DC: American Psychological Association.

Schmidt, F. L., & Hunter, J. E. (1980). The future of criterion-related validity. *Personnel Psychology, 33,* 41–60.

Society for Industrial & Organizational Psychology, Inc. (2003). *Principles for the validation and use of personnel selection procedures* (4th ed.). Bowling Green, OH: Author.

Sussmann, M. (1986). The validity of validity: An analysis of validation study designs. *Journal of Applied Psychology, 71,* 461–468.

Module 8

Construct Validation

I n the two previous modules examining validation, we discussed the role of expert judgment and the use of a correlation between test scores and a relevant criterion as methods for providing evidence of the meaningfulness of test scores. Cronbach and Meehl (1955) discussed a third validation strategy that they felt was best suited to the many instances when test scores assess an attribute or a quality (i.e., a construct) that is not readily operationalized. Their arguments were so powerful that today **psychometricians** view all validation efforts as evidence regarding construct validation.

"Psychology works with crude, half-explicit formulations" (Cronbach & Meehl, 1955, p. 294). Although this is an astonishing declaration, Cronbach and Meehl used this assertion not to urge the abandonment of psychological inquiry, but rather to argue for the necessity of establishing explicit, testable theories about the constructs psychologists investigate, and the test scores arising from the operationalization of these constructs. It is a fact that psychologists often study constructs that are only indirectly observable, such as intelligence, personality, and ability. Therefore, each psychological test is created to measure a specific construct of interest. To define a construct, we specify a sort of theory regarding that construct. This theory defines our construct, and it specifies our expectations regarding the relationship between our construct and other constructs, between our construct and other measures (i.e., tests), and between our test and other measures. Cronbach and Meehl (1955) referred to this as a *nomological network* (see Web Reference 8.1d). The explication of this theory allows for both empirical investigation and rational discussion of the theory's propositions. Such undertakings are the work of construct validation.

According to Cronbach and Meehl (1955), various studies can be conducted to produce evidence regarding the **construct validity** of test scores. Such studies include the following:

Studies of group differences: If two groups are expected to differ on a construct, do they indeed differ as expected?

Studies of internal structure: If a test is put forth as measuring a particular construct, then the items on the test should generally be interrelated. Thus, analysis of the internal consistency of items, such as coefficient alpha, can provide evidence of construct validation.

Studies of the stability of test scores: We would expect measures of enduring traits to remain stable over time, whereas measures of other constructs are expected to change over time, such as following an intervention or experimental treatment. Construct validation evidence can be garnered based on whether test scores reflect the expected stability (or lack thereof) over time.

Studies of process: Unfortunately, differences in test scores are sometimes determined by more than just the construct the researcher intended to assess. A test intended to assess one's mathematical ability may unintentionally assess one's verbal ability, for example, if many of the items involve word problems. Examination of the process by which a test taker derives a response may thus provide important evidence challenging the construct validity of a test.

Correlation matrices and factor analysis: Frequently, more than one test claims to measure the same construct. If two tests do measure the same construct, we would expect to find a correlation between the tests. If such a correlation is not found, we do not know which of the two tests is problematic, or even whether the fault lies in the conceptualization of the construct itself.

Because construct validation does not put forward a single premise regarding the construct and test scores, but rather refers to the process of examining the entire "nomological network," there is no single validity coefficient that will "prove" construct validity. Rather, construct validation represents an ongoing examination of the propositions set forth in the nomological network. Therefore, while evidence can be garnered in support of the propositions in the network, no single study can be conducted that definitively proves the construct validity of a measure. However, research evidence contrary to the proposed network may provide convincing evidence of the need to question either the interpretation of test scores or our understanding of the construct itself.

Examining Patterns of Relationships

Each of Cronbach and Meehl's (1955) suggestions for examining construct validation is very useful. Still, correlation matrices and factor analysis have frequently been used to provide evidence for the construct validity of test scores. This is because researchers often wish to examine the expected patterns of relationships between various measures of a construct, as well as between a measure of the construct and other measured variables.

As an example, let us assume that a researcher has recently developed a scale to assess extraversion—the so-called New Extraversion Measure (NEM). As you probably know, extraversion is a construct intended to represent the degree to which an individual is outgoing, social, and outer directed. Although commercially available scales to assess extraversion already exist, perhaps the researcher was motivated to create a new measure in order to avoid paying to use proprietary measures in his research, or maybe he was dissatisfied with other research measures of extraversion. Although the researcher no doubt took careful steps during the development of the scale, how certain can we be that the newly developed NEM actually assesses the construct of extraversion? One way to provide construct validity evidence for the new scale is to correlate scores on the NEM with scores from preexisting measures that assess related constructs. For example, we would expect scores on the NEM to be correlated with scores on the extraversion scale of the NEO Personality Inventory (NEO PI) and the sociability scale from the Hogan Personality Inventory. If scores on the NEM correlated highly with scores on these preexisting measures of extraversion, then we would have some evidence for the construct validity of the scale. This evidence is referred to as **convergent validity.** Scores on the new measure should correlate highly with scores on preexisting measures of theoretically similar constructs.

Further evidence could be provided if the researcher was able to demonstrate that scores on the NEM were uncorrelated with scores on measures assessing theoretically dissimilar constructs, such as conscientiousness and locus of control. If scores on the NEM were unrelated to scores on measures assessing theoretically dissimilar constructs, the researcher would have evidence of **divergent (or discriminant) validity.**

Multitrait-Multimethod Matrices

In proposing the concept of a **multitrait-multimethod (MTMM) matrix,** Campbell and Fiske (1959) introduced a method for examining the expected patterns of relationships between alternative measures of a variety of constructs. Using an MTMM matrix, we can systematically assess the relationships between two or more constructs (i.e., traits), each of which is measured using two or more methods. Data are collected from a single sample of individuals. The MTMM matrix is the resulting correlation matrix between all pairs of measures (see Web Reference 8.1e for an example).

Evidence of convergent validity for a measure of interest is provided in an MTMM matrix when our measure of a trait of interest correlates highly with traits that are theoretically similar to it (regardless of the methods used to assess these other traits). Evidence of discriminant validity occurs when our measure of a trait of interest has a low correlation with traits that are theoretically dissimilar from it (again, regardless of the methods used to assess these other traits).

An MTMM matrix has the additional benefit of examining the effect of method of measurement on observed correlations. Common method variance (CMV) refers to a problem in which correlations between constructs are artificially inflated because the data were obtained using the same method of data collection for each variable. Thus, CMV results in correlations between studied variables due not to some underlying relationship between constructs (i.e., traits), but rather to the use of the same method of measurement in each of our tests. In psychology, our concern is often with the overuse of self-reports. For example, a personality researcher may employ use of Likert-type rating scales to assess a number of self-report variables in a study. Because the same method of measurement is used to assess each of these variables, observed correlations between variables may be inflated due to the tendency of research participants to respond similarly across items assessed in this manner. CMV, therefore, would be a potential concern.

An MTMM matrix is capable of examining the degree to which CMV influences the observed correlations between variables. To build an MTMM matrix, multiple methods (e.g., self-reports, peer ratings, observations) of assessment must be used to assess each included trait. To produce evidence of construct validity in this way, the pattern of correlations within an MTMM matrix must provide evidence that our measure of a trait of interest correlates higher with theoretically similar constructs that are measured by different methods than our measure of interest correlates with measures of theoretically dissimilar constructs, whether measured using the same method of measurement or not. When variables that are theoretically distinct but measured using the same method are found to correlate highly, we would suspect the influence of CMV.

Let us consider a brief concrete illustration, based on the earlier example. Let us assume that we administered several scales and obtained the following correlations:

	NEO PI Extraversion (peer report)	NEO PI Conscientiousness (peer report)	LOC (self-report)
NEM (self-report)	.57	.18	.37

Here, scores on the NEM and NEO PI extraversion scale represent theoretically similar constructs—indeed, both scales are intended to measure the same trait. The NEO PI conscientiousness subscale and locus of control (LOC) subscale are theoretically dissimilar from extraversion. Further, the data were collected using two different methods. The NEM and the LOC are measured by self-report, whereas peer reports were used for both of the NEO PI subscales. Here, the researcher asked peers to complete the NEO PI subscales as they saw the target individual (the person completing the self-report scales).

Inspection of these scores suggests evidence of convergent validity. NEM scores do, in fact, correlate well with scores on the NEO PI extraversion subscale. There is also evidence of discriminant validity, in that scores on the NEM correlate less highly with either the LOC or the NEO PI conscientiousness subscale than NEM scores correlate with the NEO PI extraversion subscale. Note that the correlation between scores on the NEM and the LOC are moderate, however. This unexpected correlation between variables may be due to an actual relationship between the constructs, or it may be attributable to CMV.

Confirmatory Factor Analysis

Although visual inspection of an MTMM matrix provides some evidence of the construct validity of a measure, research has found that intuitive interpretations of these matrices can yield erroneous conclusions (Cole, 1987). Rather, today confirmatory factor analysis (CFA) is the preferred method for examining the convergent and discriminant validity of MTMM matrices (e.g., Schmitt & Stults, 1986; Widaman, 1985). Using CFA to examine a complete MTMM model, each measured variable is considered to be derived from trait, method, and unique factors. If a researcher were measuring three traits with three different methods, there would be a total of nine variables. The three distinct measures of a single trait are expected to load on a single trait factor. Variables that share a particular method of measurement are expected to load on a single method factor. Thus, three trait and three measurement factors would be predicted. Theoretically, correlations between trait and method factors, along with estimates of trait and measurement variance, can be used to assess convergent and discriminant validity. Kenny and Kashy (1992), however, pointed out that estimation problems are nearly universal in the application of CFA to complete MTMM matrices. These authors provided two alternate CFA models for analyzing MTMM data. Confirmatory factor analysis is discussed in more detail in Module 18.

A Contemporary Conception
of Construct Validation

It may have occurred to you that Cronbach and Meehl's (1955) assertions regarding construct validation can be applied to all test validation efforts. Indeed, contemporary thinking on validation views any evidence regarding the interpretation of test scores as construct validation (Messick, 1995a). This includes each of the types of research studies suggested by Cronbach and Meehl, as well as the validation efforts we previously referred to as content validation and criterion-related validation. After all, each of these validation strategies is intended to do the same thing: provide "a compelling argument that the available evidence justifies the test interpretation and use" (Messick, 1995a, p. 744).

In the development of such an argument, we should carefully consider exactly what threats exist to construct validity (Messick, 1995a). The first threat, *construct underrepresentation,* refers to measurement that fails to capture the full dimensionality of the intended construct. Thus, construct underrepresentation occurs when important elements of the construct are not measured. The second major threat to construct validity is *construct-irrelevant variance.* This refers to the measurement of reliable variance that is not part of the construct of interest. That is, something is measured that is not part of the intended construct. Construct-irrelevant variance can include the measurement of other constructs or the assessment of method variance. Unfortunately, both threats to construct validity may be committed simultaneously whenever measuring a construct. Thus, as Messick pointed out, validation is concerned with examining the extent to which our measurement both underrepresents the intended construct *and* assesses construct-irrelevant variance.

If all validation efforts can be viewed as providing construct validation evidence, then we have developed a *unified* vision of test validation. As

Messick (1995a) cautioned, however, there are many important, and often entangled, issues related to construct validation. To increase awareness of these many issues, Messick distinguished six important aspects of construct validity. Each of these aspects is briefly presented below.

Content: The content aspect of construct validity specifies the boundaries of the construct domain to be assessed. It is concerned with both the relevance and the representativeness of the measure. In this way, the content aspect is reminiscent of the issues presented in Module 6 on content validation.

Substantive: The substantive aspect of construct validity expands on the concerns of the content aspect by suggesting the need to include "empirical evidence of response consistencies or performance regularities reflective of domain processes" (Messick, 1995a, p. 745). In the assessment of the construct, assessment tasks should be included that are relevant to the construct domain, and the processes required to respond to these assessment tasks should be empirically examined.

Structural: The structural aspect reminds us of the importance of ensuring that the construct domain determines the rational development of construct-relevant scoring criteria and scoring rubrics. This aspect of construct validity emphasizes the importance of score comparability across different tasks and different settings.

Generalizability: The generalizability aspect of construct validity asserts that the meaning of the test scores should not be limited merely to the sample of tasks that comprise the test, but rather should be generalizable to the construct domain intended to be assessed. Evidence regarding the generalizability of test scores would help determine the boundaries of the meaning of the test scores.

External: The external aspect of construct validity refers to the empirical relationships between the test scores and scores on other measures. The external aspect examines whether the empirical relationships between test scores and other measures is consistent with our expectations. This aspect includes the elements of convergent, discriminant, and criterion-related validities introduced earlier.

Consequential: The consequential aspect of construct validity encourages the examination of evidence regarding the consequences of score interpretation. Messick recommended that such examination be conducted not only in the short term but also over longer periods of time. The primary concern is to ensure that any negative consequences of test usage are unrelated to sources of test invalidity.

Concluding Comments

Construct validation is concerned with any and all evidence regarding the meaningfulness of test scores. Rather than examining various "types" of validity, we now recognize that the interpretation and use of test scores requires an ongoing process of validation. Many issues related to the meaning of test scores have been routinely ignored by researchers and test developers. The contemporary conceptualization of construct validity promotes awareness of many of these long-neglected issues.

Practical Questions

1. The unified view of test validation regards all aspects of validation as reaching for the same goal. What is the overall goal of test validation?

2. Identify at least three measures of intelligence. In what ways do these operationalizations of this construct differ? In what ways are they similar? Do you think each is as good a measure of intelligence as the others? What makes some better (or worse) than the others?

3. What did Cronbach and Meehl (1955) mean by the term "nomological network"?

4. Can reliability estimates be used to provide evidence of the construct validity of test scores? Explain.

5. Explain how a researcher could conduct a "study of process" to provide evidence of the construct validity of test scores.

6. a. Identify two established measures that could be used (other than those discussed previously) to examine the convergent validity of the NEM.
   b. Identify two established measures that could be used to examine the discriminant validity of the NEM.

7. Why is common method variance (CMV) a concern in construct validation studies that involve correlation matrices?

8. Correlations between what elements of an MTMM matrix would provide the best assessment of CMV?

9. How does use of an MTMM matrix provide evidence of the construct validity of test scores?

10. Why would CFA produce better evidence of construct validity than visual inspection of an MTMM matrix?

11. Messick (1995a) identified six aspects of construct validation. Choose any three of these aspects to discuss how Messick's conceptualization has extended your awareness of the meaning of construct validation.

Case Studies

CASE STUDY 8.1: LOCATING A
MEASURE OF EMOTIONAL INTELLIGENCE

Ever since learning about the concept in her psychology class, Khatera had known that she would complete her thesis on the construct of emotional intelligence. Since her initial introduction to the term, she learned that emotional intelligence represented a complex construct consisting of multiple dimensions, including self-awareness, empathy, and an ability to manage emotions. Khatera was proud that, despite the complexity of the construct, she was among the first students in her entire graduate class to clearly specify her research hypotheses. Further, Khatera secretly reveled in her advisor's praise for developing such a great research idea and for doing it so quickly.

There was just one problem. Because the construct of emotional intelligence was relatively new, few measures had been developed to assess the construct. Further, those that were commercially available were unaffordable, at least on a graduate student's salary. The vast majority of research on the topic, however, seemed to use one of these commercially available measures of emotional intelligence. Khatera had spent a considerable amount of time investigating ways to measure emotional intelligence at little or no cost to her, and she was beginning to fear that she'd soon face a difficult decision: either pay a considerable amount of money for commercially available measures of emotional intelligence or abandon her thesis idea altogether and start from scratch.

Just yesterday, however, she'd gotten a lucky break. In reviewing research articles, she stumbled across one article that used a measure of emotional intelligence she hadn't heard of before. Much to her glee, Khatera discovered that the items of the scale were actually printed in the article itself. Khatera sent an e-mail to the author of the article and was ecstatic to receive an immediate response from the author giving her permission to use the scale.

Unfortunately, Khatera's thesis advisor, Dr. Jennifer Bachelor, seemed far less enthusiastic about the newly discovered scale of emotional intelligence. Indeed, Dr. Bachelor insisted that Khatera produce some evidence of the psychometric properties of the scale before using it in her thesis research. Determined not to delay progress on her thesis any longer, Khatera set out to find that evidence. If she closed her eyes, she could almost see her name emblazoned on the spine of her bound thesis.

Questions to Ponder

1. What role should cost play in determining an appropriate measure for research?

2. Why would Dr. Bachelor be skeptical of the scale of emotional intelligence that Khatera found?

3. What information in the article should Khatera search for to help address some of her advisor's concerns?

4. What other steps could Khatera take to gather information regarding the validity of the newly found scale of emotional intelligence?

5. What evidence of validity for a measure is most frequently provided by (a) publishers of commercially available tests and (b) authors of research scales?

6. What validity evidence would you consider sufficient to use in an important research study such as a graduate thesis?

CASE STUDY 8.2: EXPLAINING THE CONCEPT OF VALIDITY

DiAnn wasn't too surprised to see Edgar arrive shortly after her office hours began. The material recently presented by the instructor in the psychological testing course for which she served as the graduate teaching assistant was challenging for many of the students in the class. "How can I help you, Edgar?" she inquired.

Edgar, his usual affable persona replaced by a serious tone, replied, "I can't get this topic of validity. I knew I'd better come in and see you after I threw the textbook down in frustration."

"Wow, I'm glad you did. What seems to be the trouble?" DiAnn asked.

"Well, in class I thought I understood the definition of validity. *Validity refers to whether the test measures what it purports to measure.* Fine. But after class the more I read the textbook's explanation of validity, the more I got confused."

Interrupting, DiAnn asked, "How so?"

Edgar was ready. "I was reading about content validity, criterion-related validity, and construct validity. Are these all related? Or are they different? Initially, as I was reading, there seemed to be three distinct types of validity. But then it seemed that I couldn't tell the difference among the three."

DiAnn smiled. "Perhaps you are smarter than you give yourself credit for Edgar. In many ways, you are correct." As DiAnn explained what she meant by her rather cryptic initial response, Edgar began to feel more and more comfortable with the material.

Questions to Ponder

1. In what ways does "content validity" provide evidence of the meaningfulness of test scores?

2. In what ways does "criterion-related validity" provide evidence of the meaningfulness of test scores?

3. Is Edgar's concern over not being able to distinguish among the various validation strategies warranted? Explain.

4. Explain why the trinitarian view of validity (content, criterion-related, construct) is inappropriate.

5. Explain how Messick's (1995a) aspects of construct validation incorporate each of the following "outdated" terms under the umbrella of construct validity:
   a. Content validity
   b. Criterion-related validity
   c. Convergent and discriminant validity

Exercises

EXERCISE 8.1: IDENTIFYING
MEASURES FOR CONSTRUCT VALIDATION

OBJECTIVE: To gain experience in identifying relevant measures for examining convergent and discriminant validity.

PROLOGUE: Imagine that you have recently developed the following construct measures. For each of these newly developed instruments, identify two actual measures that could be used to examine the new instrument's convergent validity, and two actual measures that could be used to examine the new instrument's discriminant validity. When possible, propose measures that use different methods of measurement (e.g., self-report for one proposed measure, and observer ratings for the other measure).

1. A newly developed paper-and-pencil intelligence test intended to assess academic giftedness among sixth graders

2. An interview evaluating an adult's personal integrity

3. A self-report form assessing one's interpersonal assertiveness

4. A peer rating form measuring an individual's general optimism

5. A supervisor's rating form of an employee's career achievement motivation

EXERCISE 8.2: TRADITIONAL ANALYSIS OF AN MTMM MATRIX

OBJECTIVE: To identify relevant elements of an MTMM matrix and provide a correct interpretation of the data.

PROLOGUE: Following is a multitrait-multimethod matrix containing three traits, each of which has been assessed by three measures. A letter labels each trait. A number labels each method. The list of traits and methods is as follows:

Traits	*Methods*
A. Conscientiousness	1. Self-report paper-and-pencil measure
B. Integrity	2. Spousal rating
C. Extraversion	3. Rater observation

Assume that you have recently developed a new self-report paper-and-pencil measure of conscientiousness (A_1). You have obtained the data shown in Table 8.1.

Note: Although the data in Table 8.1 were obtained from Campbell and Fiske (1959), variable labels have been fabricated.

Table 8.1   Example of an MTMM Matrix

		Method 1			Method 2			Method 3		
		A_1	B_1	C_1	A_2	B_2	C_2	A_3	B_3	C_3
Method	A_1	.89								
1	B_1	.51	.89							
	C_1	.38	.37	.76						
Method	A_2	.57	.22	.09	.93					
2	B_2	.22	.57	.10	.68	.94				
	C_2	.11	.11	.46	.59	.58	.84			
Method	A_3	.56	.22	.11	.67	.42	.33	.94		
3	B_3	.23	.58	.12	.42	.66	.34	.67	.92	
	C_3	.11	.11	.45	.34	.32	.58	.58	.60	.85

Scale reliabilities are presented in bold across the diagonal.

1. Underline all the validity diagonals in the matrix.

2. Using a pencil (or dashed lines), identify each of the heterotrait-heteromethod triangles in the matrix.

3. Using a blue pen (or solid lines), identify the heterotrait-monomethod triangles in the matrix.

4. Examine the pattern of correlations within the comparable triangles you have identified. Is the pattern of correlations similar?

5. Examining the correlations you have identified that are relevant to the construct validity of your self-report paper-and-pencil measure of conscientiousness, thoroughly discuss the evidence you have concerning convergent and discriminant validity.

EXERCISE 8.3: PROPOSING VALIDATION STUDIES

OBJECTIVE: To consider methods for providing evidence of construct validity for a new measure.

Messick (1995a) identified six distinct aspects of construct validity, each of which addresses a distinct issue or set of issues. In Exercise 8.2, we introduced a newly developed pencil-and-paper self-report scale of the personality construct conscientiousness. For each of the six aspects of construct validity, briefly describe a research study that could provide evidence regarding the construct validity of the test scores produced by our newly developed measure of conscientiousness. Be sure to identify the issue that each proposed study is intended to address.

1. Content

2. Substantive

3. Structural

4. Generalizability

5. External

6. Consequential

EXERCISE 8.4: EXAMINING ELEMENTS OF A NOMOLOGICAL NETWORK

OBJECTIVE: To determine whether empirical evidence provides support for expected relationships between measures.

An industrial/organizational psychologist developed a personality-based measure to assess the integrity of potential job applicants. The measure she developed was intended to mask the purpose of the test from test takers. To examine the validity of the personality-based integrity measure, the psychologist administered the measure to a group of $N = 255$ individuals. She also administered two additional measures to this same group of individuals: an overt measure of integrity, in which individuals are queried about their actual involvement in theft and dishonest behaviors; and a measure of general cognitive ability. The data are presented in the data file "nomonet.sav."

1. What is the expected pattern of relationships among these three measures? Explain.

2. Is there evidence of convergent validity for the personality-based integrity measure?

3. Is there evidence of discriminant validity for the personality-based integrity measure?

4. Based on the obtained results, can the psychologist claim that she has established the construct validity of the measure? Explain.

Internet Web Site References

8.1. http://trochim.human.cornell.edu/kb/constval.htm

This Web page, from William M. Trochim's electronic textbook, presents construct validity as the overarching category for all forms of measurement validity. The following links from Trochim's electronic textbook provide additional examination of construct validity:

8.1a. http://trochim.human.cornell.edu/kb/considea.htm

This Web page provides an expanded definition of construct validity. The Web page provides a graphic to help students visualize the role of theory and observation in construct validation.

8.1b. http://trochim.human.cornell.edu/kb/convdisc.htm

This Web page provides detailed explanations and illustrations of the terms convergent validity and discriminant validity.

8.1c. http://trochim.human.cornell.edu/kb/consthre.htm

This Web page identifies and discusses common threats to construct validity.

8.1d. http://trochim.human.cornell.edu/kb/nomonet.htm

This Web page provides a clear explanation of Cronbach and Meehl's (1955) conception of a nomological network.

8.1e. http://trochim.human.cornell.edu/kb/mtmmmat.htm

This Web page presents an excellent visual depiction of the examination of construct validity using a multitrait-multimethod (MTMM) matrix.

8.1f. http://trochim.human.cornell.edu/kb/pmconval.htm

This Web page presents Trochim's approach to construct validation using "pattern matching."

8.2. http://chiron.valdosta.edu/mawhatley/3900/validc.htm

This Web page presents a 25-item quiz on measurement validity. Responses are scored immediately.

Further Readings

Cronbach, L. J., & Meehl, P. E. (1955). Construct validity in psychological tests. *Psychological Bulletin, 52,* 281–302.

Eid, M. (2000). A multitrait-multimethod model with minimal assumptions. *Psychometrika, 65,* 241–261.

Landy, F. J. (1986). Stamp collecting versus science: Validation as hypothesis testing. *American Psychologist, 41,* 1183–1192.

Marsh, H. W. (1991). Confirmatory factor analysis of multitrait-multimethod data: A comparison of alternative models. *Applied Psychological Measurement, 15,* 47–70.

Messick, S. (1995b). Standards of validity and the validity of standards in performance assessment. *Educational Measurement: Issues and Practice, 14,* 5–8.

Pedhazur, E. J., & Schmelkin, L. P. (1991). *Measurement, design, and analysis: An integrated approach* (pp. 52–80). Hillsdale, NJ: Erlbaum.

Trochim, W. (2000). *The research methods knowledge base* (2nd ed.). Cincinnati, OH: Atomic Dog.

Trochim, W. M. (2003). *The research methods knowledge base* (2nd ed.) [On-line]. Retrieved from http://trochim.human.cornell.edu/kb/index.htm

Module 9

Validity Generalization
and Meta-Analysis

S chmidt and Hunter (2001) discussed the myth of the "perfect study." That is, if we could somehow get a large enough sample with perfectly reliable and valid measures we could definitively answer the key and nagging questions plaguing the social and behavioral sciences. Although some large-scale studies have been conducted with thousands of participants, most individual empirical studies, particularly in psychology, tend to average in the hundreds (or less) of participants, not thousands. As a result, sampling error is a major source of error in estimating population relationships and parameters within any given empirical investigation. In addition, a variety of factors (i.e., methodological artifacts), such as unreliable measures, restriction of range, and artificial dichotomization of continuous variables, are an undeniable part of any individual empirical investigation. In the end, such artifacts cloud our observed relationships and ultimately our ability to estimate population relationships based on sample data. Therefore, it is simply unrealistic to believe that any single study is going to be able to definitively explain the complex relationships found among key variables in the social and behavioral sciences. So, what is a budding social and behavioral scientist to do?

Well, if we could somehow cull individual empirical studies examining similar phenomenon conducted by different researchers, we could drastically reduce the effects of sampling error. In addition, if we could somehow correct for the artifacts noted previously (e.g., unreliability, restriction of range), we could also reduce the effects of these sources of error and as a result would have much better estimates of our population parameters. Up until the late

1970s, however, most reviews of the extant empirical research on a given topic were narrative in fashion. The inevitable conclusion of almost every narrative review seemed to be that the empirical research was contradictory and inconclusive and as a result more research was needed. As granting agencies and policymakers became more and more frustrated with consistently predictable inconclusive findings, researchers in the social and behavioral sciences began to seek ways to quantify the cumulative findings in a given research area. In the mid- to late 1970s, several researchers (e.g., Glass, 1976; Schmidt & Hunter, 1977) proposed analytic procedures that would allow researchers interested in summarizing a body of empirical literature to do so in a quantitative fashion. Thus, the concept of **meta-analysis** (the analysis of analyses) was born—or at least "discovered" by social and behavioral scientists.

Validity Generalization

Early work on quantitatively summarizing previous empirical studies by Schmidt and Hunter (1977) focused specifically on criterion-related validity coefficients (as discussed in Module 7), examining how cognitive ability tests, for example, could predict job performance for a variety of jobs across organizations. That is, they were interested in generalizing empirical validity estimates from one situation to another. The conventional wisdom up to that point in time was that all validity coefficients were situation specific (i.e., the situational specificity hypothesis), meaning that validity coefficients were expected to differ from one situation or organization to another due to differences in jobs and/or the context of the job. However, Schmidt and Hunter demonstrated that most of the differences that were observed in empirical criterion-related validity estimates from one job or organization to another were simply the result of sampling error and other artifacts such as unreliable measures and restriction of range. Obtaining a weighted (based on sample size) average validity coefficient and correcting the weighted estimate for sampling error was recommended by Schmidt and Hunter as a more precise way of estimating validity coefficients. Correcting for only sampling error associated with studies is known as performing a "bare bones" **validity generalization** (VG) study. Such studies provide stronger and more realistic estimates of the average observed validity coefficients across studies than is possible in any single study.

In addition, if other corrections beyond sampling error are also made (e.g., for unreliability or restriction of range), then this is referred to as psychometric VG. Performing these additional corrections for psychometric shortcomings in the studies used to compute the VG estimates allows researchers to better estimate the latent relationship among constructs. Thus, performing these additional (psychometric) corrections allows researchers to move beyond simply documenting observed relationships to formulating and testing relationships among latent constructs. If, subsequent to making the additional corrections, substantial variability in the observed validity coefficients were still unaccounted for, a search for potential moderators would be initiated. What constitutes "substantial variability" remaining? Schmidt and Hunter used the 75% rule. That is, if sampling error and various other **statistical artifacts** account for less than 75% of the variability in observed validity coefficients, nonartifact (true) variability likely exists and so moderator analyses should be performed. Such moderators might include the type of organization or job, when the study was conducted, the type of criterion used in the validation study, and so forth.

From Validity Generalization to Psychometric Meta-Analysis

Schmidt and Hunter (1977) soon realized, however, that their procedures could be applied not just to validity coefficients but also to any estimate of association (or effect size) between key variables. Hence, they (Hunter, Schmidt, & Jackson, 1982) independently proposed a much broader set of procedures similar to the meta-analytic strategies of Glass, McGaw, and Smith's (1981). The first of two major goals of most meta-analyses is to obtain the most accurate and best possible point estimate of the population effect size. For example, if you wanted to know the relationship between the Premarital Compatibility Index (X) and how long couples stay married (Y), you would need to obtain all available correlation coefficients between these two variables from previous empirical studies. You would then compute a weighted-average observed correlation (validity coefficient) across all studies obtained. This weighted-average statistic would be your point estimate of the population correlation (ρ_{xy}) between the compatibility index and the length of marriage. Other statistical indexes (e.g., t, Z, and d) can also be used within the same meta-analytic study, and formulas are available to convert such estimates from one statistic to another so that all the studies will be on the same metric. For example (see also Web Reference 9.2):

$$\text{For } t_{df} : r = \sqrt{\frac{t^2}{t^2 + df}} \text{ or for } Z : r = \sqrt{\frac{z^2}{N}} \text{ or for } \chi^2 : r = \sqrt{\frac{\chi^2}{N}}$$

where t is the obtained Student t statistic, df is the degrees of freedom associated with that t statistic, z is the obtained Z statistic, N is the sample size, and χ^2 is the obtained chi-square statistic. Formulas are also available for the standardized difference (d) statistic and the F statistic. Scores in various formats can also be converted to a common standardized difference d statistic when one is more interested in group differences as opposed to simple bivariate associations as with the r statistic.

Your next question hopefully is, "So how good is this point estimate?" Hence, the second key goal of most meta-analytic procedures is to determine the variability around the estimated effect size, or what is commonly called a confidence interval (CI). The CI tells us how much confidence we have in the population parameter we estimated initially. Sometimes, however, we are more interested not in the population parameter but rather in the value we would obtain if we were to conduct the study again. To answer this question, we would instead calculate a credibility interval (CRI). To obtain either the CI or the CRI, we would need to know the standard error of the average correlation coefficient. This statistic will be presented later.

Conducting a Meta-Analysis

Schmitt and Klimoski (1991) presented a flow chart of seven steps to be carried out in conducting a meta-analysis (see Table 9.1). Before we even begin any meta-analytic work, however, we must clearly and precisely identify what it is we hope to accomplish by conducting a meta-analysis. Continuing with our earlier example, it may be to determine how useful the Premarital Compatibility Index (PCI) is in predicting marriage longevity. Once this is clear, the first step is to compile a list of relevant published and unpublished studies using a variety of sources and computerized search options. Next, we must then read all of the papers obtained and formulate hypotheses about potential **moderator variables**. For example, maybe the age of the couple, whether it is their first marriage, or their religious beliefs could all serve as potential moderators. Third, we need to develop a coding scheme and rules of inclusion and exclusion of studies. Should, for example, only studies that used version 1 of the PCI be included? Fourth, we need to train those who will be doing the coding, and after coding a few studies, we should check for inter-coder consistency. Once we are satisfied the raters are consistent (and accurate), then step 5 is to code all studies pulling out the key data (e.g., sample size, effect size) to conduct our meta-analysis, as well as essential information regarding potential moderators. In step 6, we actually analyze the data. Finally, in step 7, we draw appropriate conclusions about the effect of interest and potential moderators.

Table 9.1   Flow Chart for Meta-Analysis

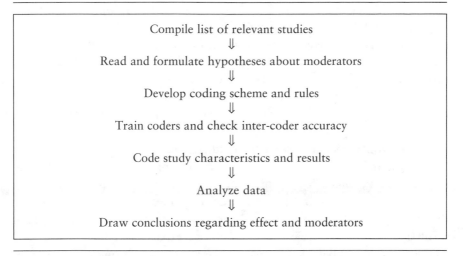

Compile list of relevant studies
⇓
Read and formulate hypotheses about moderators
⇓
Develop coding scheme and rules
⇓
Train coders and check inter-coder accuracy
⇓
Code study characteristics and results
⇓
Analyze data
⇓
Draw conclusions regarding effect and moderators

SOURCE: Adapted by permission from Schmitt, N., & Klimoski, R. (1991). *Research Methods in Human Resource Management*. Cincinnati, OH: Southwest Publishing.

Although, at first glance, the process of conducting a meta-analysis may seem straightforward, Wanous, Sullivan, and Malinak (1989) noted numerous judgment calls that need to be made in the process of conducting a meta-analysis. The judgment calls start at the very beginning when we must first define the domain of research to be studied. They continue through establishing the criteria for deciding which studies to include, how to search for them, and how studies are ultimately selected for inclusion. The judgment calls continue when we must decide which data to extract, how to code the data, whether to group similar variables, the actual calculations to perform, and the subsequent search for moderators. How these judgment calls go can dramatically impact what gets studied, how it gets studied, and the interpretation of the resulting analyses. Thus, if nothing else, one needs to be detailed and explicit in reporting any meta-analytic procedures.

A Step-by-Step Meta-Analysis Example[1]

Previous research has indicated that the age at which individuals retire affects their subsequent retirement satisfaction and adjustment (e.g., Kim & Moen,

---

[1] This example is based in part (and very loosely) on a meta-analysis conducted by Shultz and Taylor (2001). Please note that several creative liberties have been taken for pedagogical purposes.

2001; Shultz, Morton, & Weckerle, 1998). As a result, it would be informative to know what factors seem to be predictive of the age at which individuals retire. Beehr (1986), however, suggested that individuals first have certain preferences regarding retirement, which, in turn, influence their intentions with regard to retirement. It is these intentions that ultimately lead to actual retirement decisions. Thus, to understand the retirement process, one must first understand the prospective preferences and intentions toward retirement that older individuals have, not simply document (in a retrospective fashion) the actual retirement age and it predictors. Therefore, Shultz and Taylor (2001) set out to perform a meta-analysis of the predictors of planned retirement age.

Shultz and Taylor's (2001) first task was to compile a list of relevant studies that had examined the factors that predict planned retirement age (see Table 9.1). Therefore, Shultz and Taylor performed an extensive review of the interdisciplinary research literature on the predictors of planned retirement age using several electronic database search engines, including the AgeLine database, EBSCOhost, ERIC, General Science Abstracts, Humanities Abstracts, JSTOR, PsycINFO, ScienceDirect, Sociological Abstracts, and Wilson Omnifile. In addition, they performed a manual search of relevant journals (*The Gerontologist, International Journal of Aging and Human Development, Journals of Gerontology, Journal of Vocational Behavior, Personnel Psychology, Psychology and Aging, Research on Aging*) from 1980 to 2000 and reviewed the reference sections of review articles and book chapters to locate relevant empirical studies reporting correlation coefficients (i.e., effect size estimates) between a variety of potential predictors and planned retirement age. Studies that did not measure planned retirement age and/or did not report zero-order bivariate correlation coefficients were excluded.

As is unfortunately true of many meta-analytic studies, the vast majority of the empirical studies did not provide individual effect size estimates (e.g., bivariate correlation coefficients or t, F, or χ^2 values that could be converted to correlation coefficients) in the papers themselves. Instead, most papers, particularly the older studies, reported only results of multivariate analyses (e.g., logistic regression coefficients, beta-weights in hierarchical ordinary least squares regressions). In all, 16 different studies (one study had two samples) that provided individual effect size estimates were coded for the variables that are hypothesized to influence planned retirement age. Because of the small number of studies, no specific moderator hypotheses were put forth. Cohen's kappa statistic, which measures inter-rater reliability (see Module 5), was computed. Somewhat surprisingly, perfect reliability was obtained with regard to whether the raters agreed on which variables were measured in each of the coded studies.

Meta-Analytical Procedure and Results

The bivariate correlation coefficients were subjected to the meta-analytic procedures outlined in Hunter and Schmidt (1990) using the MetaWin 16 meta-analysis program (see Web References 9.1 and 9.2). Study correlation coefficients were weighted by sample size, and corrections were made for sampling error and, when data were available, for measurement error (i.e., unreliability in the predictor and/or criterion variables) using the artifact distribution method (Hunter & Schmidt, 1990).

Table 9.2 summarizes the number of studies (k); the pooled sample size (N); the unweighted-average effect size (r_{ave}); the sample weighted-average effect size (r_{wa}); the corrected sample weighted-average effect size (r_{wc}), which has been corrected for unreliability of the predictor and/or criterion variable when the information was available; the percentage of variance attributable to sampling error; and, finally, the 95% confidence interval for the uncorrected sample weighted-average effect size estimate indicating whether the estimated population correlation coefficients are significantly different from zero. Thus, Table 9.2 summarizes the results obtained for the predictors of planned retirement age. Only predictor variables with effect size estimates from at least two different studies with different authors were included (see Exercise 9.2 for an example of how to compute by hand many of the statistics reported in Table 9.2).

As can be seen in Table 9.2, the average weighted effect size estimates are generally small. In fact, sex had an unweighted-average correlation of zero. Age was clearly the strongest predictor of planned retirement age, with a weighted-average correlation of .29 (considered a medium to large effect size—see Web Reference 9.2). Education (.21), expected retirement adjustment (–.17), and job satisfaction (.13) demonstrated small to medium effect sizes. All others variables estimated were below .10.

Interpretation of Meta-Analysis Results and Limitations

The major goal of the meta-analytic study described here was to summarize the relationships among a number of variables (including demographic, financial, health, psychosocial, and organizational) that have a suggested and/or demonstrated association with planned retirement age. The limited evidence that was summarized supports past research that indicates that age is a strong predictor of anticipated retirement age, and that education level, household income, job satisfaction, and expected retirement adjustment are also predictive, albeit less so than age, of planned age of retirement.

Table 9.2 Meta-Analysis of the Correlates of Planned Retirement Age (From Shultz & Taylor, 2001)

| Factor | k | N | Average Correlations | | | % Total Variance | 95% Confidence Interval | |
			r_{ave}	r_{wa}	r_{wc}		Lower Bound	Upper Bound
Demographics								
Age	10	4039	.3285	.2927	.3103	13.59	.2645	.3210
Education	6	3154	.1417	.2087	.2087	57.50	.1753	.2421
Sex	5	1391	.0000	-.0068	-.0068	28.74	-.0595	.0458
Financial								
Pay satisfaction	4	821	-.0050	.0017	.0020	100+	-.0669	.0703
Household income	4	1039	-.1425	-.0984	-.0984	9.80	-.1587	-.0381
Health								
Self-rated health	5	1244	.0100	-.0040	-.0054	23.80	-.0597	.0517
Health satisfaction	4	690	.0100	.0302	.0337	64.52	-.0446	.1049
Psychosocial								
Job satisfaction	9	5307	.1322	.1346	.1563	81.84	.1081	.1610
Expected ret. adj.	2	475	-.1350	-.1669	-.1968	32.73	-.2545	-.0793

NOTE: k = the number of studies, N = the pooled sample size, r_{ave} = the average correlation coefficient without correction or weighting, r_{wa} = the uncorrected sample weighted-average correlation coefficient, r_{wc} = the sample weighted-average correlation coefficient corrected for unreliability of measurement, and % Total Variance = the percentage of total variance in the effect sizes that is accounted for by sampling error only. Confidence intervals were computed from weighted-average correlation coefficients (uncorrected).

These results serve as a starting point for both larger-scale meta-analytic investigations on the topic and future theoretical model-testing studies. As for future, large-scale meta-analyses, it may be difficult to obtain correlation coefficients from studies carried out decades ago and to track down unpublished conference papers and technical reports on the topic. Continued diligence in obtaining such information may prove fruitful in the end, in that not only will more reliable and stable estimates of population values of central tendency and dispersion be obtained, but if the estimates do, in fact, demonstrate heterogeneity, then moderators can also be assessed. In terms of future model-testing studies, while most effect sizes were considered small in the Shultz-Taylor (2001) study, they may still prove useful in future theory testing as they provide the best quantitative summary of past studies. Also, as more variables are assessed, the total variance accounted for should increase as well.

Several major limitations with regard to the Shultz-Taylor (2001) study should be mentioned. First, it was disappointing how few empirical studies report the effect size estimates (e.g., bivariate correlation coefficients) needed to complete a meta-analysis in this area. Dozens of published studies have been conducted looking at the predictors of planned retirement age, retirement intentions, and the actual retirement decision. Most, however, report only multivariate results and not the basic descriptive statistics of individual effect sizes needed for meta-analyses. For example, an earlier qualitative review of the area by Doering, Rhodes, and Schuster (1983) turned up 34 studies that examined a variety of predictors of the retirement decision-making process. However, only 3 of the 34 studies reviewed by Doering et al. reported bivariate correlation coefficients (or similar effect size estimates), with most reporting results of multivariate analysis of variance (MANOVA), logistic regression, or discriminant function analyses. Consequently, the results of Shultz and Taylor's (2001) attempted meta-analysis are limited in their generalizability to a broad range of studies.

Second, because of the small number of studies, moderator analyses were not attempted. As indicated in Table 9.2, however, only two of the nine estimated relationships exceeded Hunter and Schmidt's (1990) 75% criterion. That is, sampling error accounted for more than 75% of the variance in observed effect size estimates in less than one quarter of the relationships examined. Therefore, if these relationships hold for large samples of effect sizes, moderator analyses should be conducted in future meta-analytic studies in order to determine what factors, beyond sampling error and other psychometric artifacts, account for the observed differences in empirical effect size estimates across studies.

Concluding Comments

No single study will ever be able to definitively answer the meaningful and complex questions typically addressed in social and behavioral science research. However, meta-analytic procedures allow us to cull data from numerous studies on a given topic, thus drastically reducing sampling error. In addition, most meta-analytic procedures also allow for correction of a variety of study artifacts, thus further helping to clarify the relationships we study in the social and behavioral sciences. However, as noted in the example study provided, the process of conducting a meta-analysis can be a daunting one, with many judgment calls along the way, sometimes with little reward.

Practical Questions

1. Assume you wanted to carry out a meta-analysis to determine how effective typing software is in improving typing speed and accuracy. What is the best way to get started in conducting such a meta-analysis?

2. Most papers and books on meta-analysis say one should include both published and unpublished studies on a given topic. How does one go about getting unpublished studies?

3. How do I decide which studies to include or exclude? What information to code?

4. Can a single person conduct a meta-analysis or does it take a team of researchers? Why?

5. There are several options with regard to which analytical approach to use. How do I decide which one to use?

6. How do I decide which moderators to examine?

Case Studies

CASE STUDY 9.1: THE REALITIES OF CONDUCTING A META-ANALYSIS

Raul, a second-year master's student, was very excited that his thesis committee had just approved his proposal to conduct a meta-analysis looking at what predicts employees' satisfaction with their supervisor. His committee wisely suggested that he focus on only three key predictors of supervisor satisfaction: the managerial style of the supervisor, the perceived competence of the supervisor, and the degree of warmth exhibited by the supervisor. Raul was excited in that he was the first master's student in his program ever approved to conduct a meta-analysis for his thesis. In addition, he was glad he didn't have to go beg other students to fill out a lengthy questionnaire to collect his data or have to go out to organizations to collect data. Raul figured all he had to do was "go find" the data that were already out there and (re)analyze them.

In Raul's original search of the literature for his thesis proposal using PsychLit, he obtained almost a thousand "hits" on the words "supervisor satisfaction," so he figured it would be just a matter of narrowing it down a little. However, as Raul began to examine the abstracts of these papers, he realized a large portion of them were not empirical studies. In fact, most were short articles in popular magazines on how to increase one's satisfaction with one's supervisor. So, after days, and then weeks, of sifting through abstracts, he was finally able to narrow down his list to 150 or so articles in the last 40 years that were empirical investigations of supervisor satisfaction.

Upon closer inspection, however, he realized that less than half the studies investigated managerial style, perceived competence, and warmth in relation to employees' current supervisor satisfaction. Well, that didn't seem so bad. In fact, he was relieved he had a more manageable number of articles to work with. As he delved further into the studies, however, it seemed every study was using a different measure of supervisor satisfaction. The same seemed to be true for managerial style and the perceived competence measures. About the only consistently measured variable seemed to be the perceived warmth of the supervisor. In addition, most of the studies conducted prior to 1980 reported multivariate results (e.g., R^2) but didn't provide actual correlation coefficients—the exact "data" he needed for his study. Frustrated and a bit overwhelmed, Raul decided it was time to go see his thesis advisor for some help.

Questions to Ponder

1. What other databases or outlets should Raul have used to obtain a more complete set of studies on supervisor satisfaction?

2. If you were Raul, what criteria would you use to decide which studies to include and which to exclude?

3. How should Raul go about deciding which factors in the studies to code to investigate possible moderators later on?

4. Is it possible for Raul to use the studies that don't provide correlations? What are his options?

5. How many studies do you think Raul will ultimately need in order to satisfy his thesis committee? In order to obtain "accurate" results?

CASE STUDY 9.2: HOW TO CONDUCT A META-ANALYSIS

Ming-Yu, a new PhD student, was just given her first assignment as a graduate research assistant for Professor Riggs. Professor Riggs was a quantitative psychologist who studied the effects of sport fishing on a variety of psychological outcomes. Ming-Yu was to take a stack of 60 studies obtained by the previous research assistant for a meta-analytic study examining the varying effects of lake (e.g., bass), stream (e.g., trout), and deep-sea (e.g., marlin) fishing on stress levels of the participants. She was asked to "code" each study, and when she was done with that, she was to enter the relevant data and "analyze them."

Ming-Yu had never fished in her life so she did not have a clue as to what she should be coding in the studies. Undaunted, however, she read each study and eventually was able to come up with what she thought was a reasonable coding scheme. She then coded each study and extracted the relevant data to be entered into the meta-analysis program. She coded for year of study, size of sample, type of journal, type of design, and reported effect size. She also pulled out the relevant information to examine possible moderators. For example, she looked at where the fishing took place (river vs. lake/ocean) and the type of rod used (cheap vs. expensive). Thus, her next assignment was to enter the data and begin the preliminary analyses. However, Professor Riggs, being a quantitative psychologist, had six different meta-analysis programs. She tried to contact Professor Riggs to see which program he wanted her to use but he was not available, as he was out doing "field work" on his next fishing study. So, it was up to her to select an appropriate software option, enter the data, and obtain initial results.

Ultimately, she chose one of the more popular meta-analysis programs and carried out the initial analysis. The preliminary analysis, however, seemed to indicate that the type of fishing made very little difference in the stress levels of participants. However, Professor Riggs had spent nearly his entire career demonstrating the superior stress-reducing effects of stream fishing over other types of fishing. Ming-Yu was not looking forward to her next meeting with Professor Riggs.

Questions to Ponder

1. If you were Ming-Yu, would you have coded for any other variables?

2. What factors should Ming-Yu have considered in choosing which software package to use to analyze the data?

3. What do you think could have led to Ming-Yu getting results contradictory to the results Professor Riggs had found in most of his individual studies?

4. Should Ming-Yu have "updated" the previous literature search? If so, how?

5. Because Ming-Yu didn't find any difference, does she need to conduct moderator analyses?

Exercises

EXERCISE 9.1: OUTLINING A META-ANALYTIC STUDY

OBJECTIVE: To practice outlining a meta-analytic study.

Individually or in small groups of three to five, students will select a topic on which to perform a meta-analysis. They will then outline, in detail, the steps to be taken if they were to actually carry out this study. In particular, they need to address the stages of meta-analysis outlined by Schmitt and Klimoski (1991) in Table 9.1. For example:

- Where can we find studies on this topic?
- How do we locate unpublished studies?
- What moderator hypotheses might be appropriate for this topic?
- How should we code studies? Who should code the studies?
- How will we assess inter-coder accuracy?
- What statistical artifacts should be corrected for when running the studies?

EXERCISE 9.2: ALBEMARLE
SUPREME COURT CASE

OBJECTIVE: To calculate meta-analytic estimates by hand.

BACKGROUND: In Table 9.3, you will find data from the *Albemarle Paper Co. v. Moody* (1975) Supreme Court case. The case involved looking at the use of meta-analysis (more specifically, validity generalization) to "validate" several tests across a series of jobs. Albemarle lost the case, not because it used meta-analysis, but rather because it failed to perform adequate job analyses to show that the jobs were sufficiently similar and required comparable knowledge, skills, and abilities (KSAs) to apply the tests for all jobs investigated (really more of an issue of transportability). In addition, Albemarle's initial validation efforts were criticized because of the use of only older experienced white male workers (the new job applicants were younger, largely inexperienced, and more ethnically and gender diverse) and the use of deficient job performance measures.

ASSIGNMENT: Table 9.3 displays the data for the Beta, W-A, and W-B tests that the Albemarle Paper Company used for personnel selection purposes for a variety of jobs. An example of how to perform a "bare bones" meta-analysis for the Beta exam is provided. Perform similar analyses for the W-A and W-B exams. Specifically, calculate the weighted average r, the s_r^2, and the σ_e^2, and perform a χ^2 analysis for each exam. Also, determine the percentage of total variance accounted for by sampling error and the 90% credibility and 95% confidence intervals for both scales/exams.

Provide a brief, less than one typed page or so, interpretation and explanation of what all of this means.

Table 9.3   Data for Exercise 9.2

| | | | Test | |
Job Group	N	Beta	W-A	W-B
Caustic Operator	8	.25	1.00	.47
CE Recovery Operator	12	.64	.32	.17
Wood Yard	14	.00	1.00	.72
Technical Services	12	.50	.75	.64
B Paper Mill	16	.00	.50	.34
B Paper Mill	8	−.50	.00	.00
B Paper Mill	21	.43	.81	.60
Wood Yard	6	.76	−.25	1.00
Pulp Mill	8	.50	.80	.76
Power Plant	12	.34	.75	.66

| | | Beta Test Example | | |
Job Group	N	r	N^*r	$N^*(r-\bar{r})^2$
Caustic Operator	8	.25	2.00	.0098
CE Recovery Operator	12	.64	7.68	1.5123
Wood Yard	14	.00	0.00	1.1372
Technical Services	12	.50	6.00	.5547
B Paper Mill	16	.00	0.00	1.2996
B Paper Mill	8	−.50	−4.00	4.9298
B Paper Mill	21	.43	9.03	.4415
Wood Yard	6	.76	4.56	1.3538
Pulp Mill	8	.50	4.00	.3698
Power Plant	12	.34	4.08	.0363
Total	117		33.35	11.6447

(Continued)

Table 9.3 (Continued)

$$\bar{r} = \frac{\sum Nr}{\sum N} = \frac{33.35}{117} = .2850 \qquad\qquad K = \text{number of studies (here 10)}$$

$$s_r^2 = \frac{\sum [N\,(r - \bar{r})^2]}{\sum N} = \frac{11.6447}{117} = .0995 \qquad \sigma_e^2 = \frac{(1 - \bar{r}^2)^2 k}{\sum N} = \frac{(.8441)(10)}{117} = .0721$$

$$\sigma_\rho = \sqrt{s_r^2 - \sigma_e^2} = \sqrt{.0995 - .0721} = .1655 \quad \chi_9^2 = \frac{Ns_r^2}{(1 - \bar{r}^2)^2} = \frac{(117)(.0995)}{.8441} = 13.8ns$$

$$\text{Percentage of variance accounted for by sampling error} = \frac{\sigma_2^2}{s_r^2} = \frac{.0721}{.0995} = 72.5\%$$

$$95\% \text{ Confidence Interval} = \bar{r} \pm Z_{\alpha/2} * \frac{\sigma_e}{\sqrt{k}} = .2850 \pm 1.96 * \frac{\sqrt{.0721}}{\sqrt{10}} = .119 \le \rho \le .451$$

$$90\% \text{ Credibility Interval} = \bar{r} \pm Z_{\alpha/2} * \sigma_\rho = .2850 \pm 1.645 * .1655 = .0128 \le \bar{r} \le .5572$$

Internet Web Site References

9.1. http://mirror.eschina.bnu.edu.cn/Mirror1/accesseric/ericae.net/meta/index.html

This Web page includes links to multiple manuscripts on the topic of meta-analysis, as well as links to download meta-analytic software.

9.2. http://www.lyonsmorris.com/MetaAnalysis.htm

This Web page by Larry C. Lyons provides an introduction to Hunter and Schmidt's meta-analysis.

9.3. http://www.pitt.edu/~super1/lecture/lec1171/

This Web page presents a slide show by Arindam Basu titled "How to Conduct a Meta-Analysis." Additional links are embedded in selected slides.

9.4. http://bmj.com/collections/ma.htm

This Web page presents seven papers examining the procedures to be used to conduct a reliable meta-analysis in medical research.

Further Readings

Lipsey, M. W., & Wilson, D. B. (2001). *Practical meta-analysis*. Thousand Oaks, CA: Sage.

Rothstein, H. R., McDaniel, M. A., & Borenstein, M. (2002). Meta-analysis: A review of quantitative cumulation methods. In F. Drasgow & N. Schmitt (Eds.), *Measuring and analyzing behavior in organizations: Advances in measurement and data analysis*. San Francisco: Jossey-Bass.

Schmidt, F. L., & Hunter, J. E. (2001). Meta-analysis. In N. Anderson, D. S. Ones, H. K. Sinangil, & C. Viswesvaran (Eds.), *Handbook of industrial, work and organizational psychology* (Vol. 1, pp. 51–70). Thousand Oaks, CA: Sage.

Schmitt, N., & Klimoski, R. (1991). *Research methods in human resource management* (pp. 403–426). Cincinnati, OH: Southwest.

Module 10

Test Bias and Unfairness

A s we noted in Module 1, applied psychological testing is as much a political process as it is a psychometric one. Not surprisingly, then, accusations of test bias and unfairness surface on a predictable basis whenever a test is used to make an important decision affecting people's lives. Some laypeople have used the terms *test bias* and *test fairness* interchangeably. However, a series of articles from the professional testing literature of the late 1960s and early 1970s clearly distinguish the two concepts. Test **bias** is a technical psychometric issue that focuses on statistical prediction, while test **fairness** is a sociopolitical issue that focuses on test outcomes. The concept of test bias has been operationalized in several ways (including differences in subgroup test means or validity coefficients); however, the consensus definition or current standard is what is known as the Cleary model (AERA/APA/NCME, 1999; see also Web Reference 10.1). Namely, one determines if a test has differential prediction for one group versus another by means of moderated multiple regression (MMR) analysis. Specifically, we are looking for possible subgroup differences in either regression slopes or y intercepts. It is up to us, as evaluators of the test, to determine what subgroups are relevant. However, it is most common to examine so-called "protected" subgroups of test takers. These are typically demographically determined subgroups that receive protection by law. Thus, test bias is most commonly examined in subgroups formed on such factors as age, sex, or ethnicity.

Establishing Test Bias

For example, we may use a test to predict which clinical patients are most likely to commit suicide. We may find that the test is a very good predictor of suicide for young (younger than 18 years old) and old (older than 70 years old) patients, but not a very good predictor for those in between (see Figure 10.1). As a result, the two extreme age groups may have a different slope from the middle age group when we try to predict suicide risk based on the test score. In addition, although the two extreme age groups may have approximately the same slope, they may have very different y intercepts. For example, younger clients who obtain a test score of zero may have a much lower predicted likelihood of committing suicide (i.e., a lower y intercept) than elderly clients, yet the rate of increase in the likelihood of committing suicide (i.e., the slope) is approximately equal (see Figure 10.1 for an illustration of these biases).

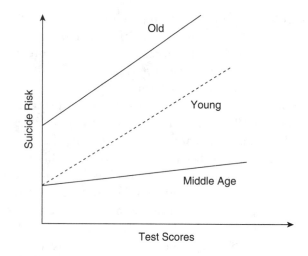

Figure 10.1   Hypothetical Regression Lines for Three Age Groups

To demonstrate intercept and slope bias empirically in our preceding example, we would first enter the test score and age group variables into a multiple regression prediction equation to predict suicide risk. If the **regression coefficient** for the age group variable were significant, possible **intercept bias** would be indicated. To test for possible **slope bias**, the interaction between age group and test performance (i.e., their cross product) would be entered in the second step of the regression equation. If the regression coefficient for the interaction term were significant, that would indicate possible slope bias.

There is typically little evidence of test bias in terms of slope bias in most applied settings. When a particular group scores lower on average on the test, they also tend to score lower on average on the criterion, resulting more often in intercept bias rather than slope bias. For example, in Figure 10.1, the young group scored lower on average on the test than the old group; however, the young test takers also have a lower predicted chance of committing suicide. Thus, the real problem would come in if we used a common (i.e., single) regression line for the young group and the old group. If, in fact, a single regression equation were used for both groups, for any given score on the test we would overpredict the risk of suicide in young clients, while underpredicting the risk of suicide in older patients. Thus, we must make sure that subgroup differences are not present before a test is administered.

Sackett, Laczo, and Lippe (2003) recently revisited the issue of test bias (or what they referred to as differential prediction), focusing on the so-called omitted-variable problem. That is, they wanted to see if omitting a variable from the analysis that was related to the criterion and the grouping variable, but not the other predictor (i.e., the test scores), caused the predictor variable to appear to be biased against certain subgroups when, in fact, it was not. Sackett et al. provided convincing evidence for the need to search for such omitted variables using data from the U.S. Army's Project A. They were able to show that a personality test of conscientiousness appeared to be biased against African Americans when it was the only variable used to predict job performance. However, when the Armed Services Vocational Aptitude Battery (ASVAB), a cognitive test, was also added to the prediction equation, the test was no longer biased. Thus, researchers must be continually aware of potential omitted variables that may be the "real culprits" in terms of test bias.

Test Fairness

The concept of test fairness, unlike test bias, is not a psychometric concept. It is a sociopolitical concept. As a result, there tends to be little consensus in regard to what constitutes test (un)fairness. In some ways, then, test fairness is similar to beauty—it tends to be "in the eye of the beholder." As a result, two individuals can take the same test, at the same time, under identical circumstances, yet one may claim the test is unfair while the other thinks it completely fair. Many accusations of test unfairness really stem from the testing process rather than the test per se. For example, some individuals may be allowed extra time or provided clues or assistance during the exam while other are not afforded such advantages. Thus, an important first step to heading off complaints of test unfairness is to standardize the testing process to every extent possible. That is, everyone is treated exactly the same, unless, of course, an individual requests and is granted a "reasonable accommodation" under laws such as the Americans with Disabilities Act (ADA).

Even if you are able to completely standardize the testing process, however, some individuals (i.e., stakeholders in the testing process) may still claim unfairness. For example, a parent who desperately wants his or her child to be admitted to a highly selective private school may claim unfairness if the child does not obtain a high enough score to be admitted into the school. In the vast majority of cases, it is the individual who does not obtain the favorable outcome as a result of using the test who is most likely to complain that the test is unfair. Thus, most accusations of unfairness tend to be more about the outcome of the testing process than the test per se. As a result, much of the debate that occurred in the professional literature in the late 1960s and early 1970s revolved around how best to define the outcomes of testing.

Figure 10.2 displays four quadrants (or possible outcomes) when a test is given and a cutoff score is set. Quadrant A would represent a correct decision (i.e., a positive hit). The persons falling in this quadrant passed the test and are subsequently successful on the criterion (e.g., job performance). Similarly, Quadrant C also represents a correct decision (i.e., a negative hit). Quadrant C individuals failed the test but also would be unsuccessful on the criterion. Quadrants A and C together thus represent the **hit rate.** In Quadrant B, however, these individuals passed the test but would not be successful on the outcome. These individuals represent a decision error and thus they are labeled **false positives.** Quadrant D individuals were unsuccessful on the test but would have been successful on the criterion. These individuals are referred to as **false negatives.** Minority group members are often overrepresented in Quadrant D. You will notice that as the cutoff score is moved to the right (e.g., it is more difficult to pass the test) the size of Quadrants C and D grows much larger in comparison to that of Quadrants A and B. If we have a situation where having a large number of false positives (Quadrant B individuals) would be particularly detrimental, then moving the cutoff score higher to reduce Quadrant B may be justified. For example, who wants a surgeon who might be a false positive (i.e., Quadrant B individual)?

In reference to the professional testing debate of the late 1960s and early 1970s mentioned earlier, several models were put forth regarding how the outcomes should be distributed in order for the test to be considered "fair." For example, advocates of the **constant ratio model** argued that there should

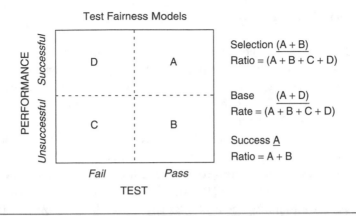

Figure 10.2   Distinguishing Different Forms of Test Unfairness

be a *constant ratio* for each subgroup in terms of who is "successful" (on the criterion) and who passes the test. That is, the ratio $(A + D) / (A + B)$ in Figure 10.2 should be the same for all subgroups (e.g., men versus women, or Caucasian versus African American versus Hispanic versus Asian). Alternatively, others argued that the *conditional probability* of the proportion of individuals selected versus those who would be successful on the criterion should be the same for each subgroup. That is, the ratio of $A / (A + D)$ in Figure 10.2 should be the same for all subgroups. Another argument put forth suggested that there should be an *equal probability* of the proportion selected versus those who pass the test for each subgroup. That is, the ratio of $A / (A + B)$ in Figure 10.2 should be the same for all subgroups. Finally, some argued that a *culture-free* test would have an equal **selection ratio** for each group. That is, the ratio of $(A + B) / (A + B + C + D)$ in Figure 10.2 should be the same for all subgroups.

Many other possibilities exist; however, the common thread through all the definitions debated in the professional literature was that, in order for the test to be "fair," the outcomes (however variously defined) should be approximately the same for each subgroup. However, the only way to obtain most of these comparable outcomes is to have different cutoff scores and/or performance standards for each subgroup. The Civil Rights Act of 1991, however, prohibits differential treatment of different subgroups. Thus, the test fairness debate has been somewhat of a moot issue in recent years within the professional testing arena. However, as you might imagine, the test fairness debate has not ebbed in the practice setting. Tests are still being used to make life-altering decisions, and as a result, test fairness continues to be a hot issue.

A Step-by-Step Example of Estimating Test Bias

As noted previously, Sackett et al. (2003) initially found that a measure of conscientiousness was biased against African Americans when predicting job performance. Once a cognitive ability test was added into the regression equation, however, the conscientiousness test was no longer biased against African Americans. Saad and Sackett (2002) found gender differences on the conscientiousness variable as well. Therefore, we decided to look closer at the conscientiousness construct to see whether there might be gender differences in using conscientiousness to predict a few different outcomes. Using data from Mersman and Shultz (1998), with a sample size of approximately 320 subjects, we found women ($N = 221$, $M = 6.78$, $s = 1.02$) to have significantly higher conscientiousness scores (using Saucier's, 1994, Mini-Markers measure of the Big Five personality constructs) than men ($N = 91$, $M = 6.48$, $s = .97$) for a sample of working students ($t_{310} = 2.46$, $p = .015$, $\eta^2 = .019$). Thus, the two groups do differ in their level of conscientiousness, with women scoring significantly higher on conscientiousness.

As noted earlier, mean differences on a test typically are not considered an indication of test bias. Instead, we need to determine if the mean differences are associated with differential prediction of a criterion variable. Another factor looked at in the Mersman-Shultz (1998) study was whether the subjects engaged in socially desirable responding. That is, do subjects tend to provide answers that are viewed as more socially acceptable than their "honest" answers? In the Mersman-Shultz data set, the conscientiousness scores and the social desirability scores correlated at .405. That is, those who scored high on conscientiousness also tended to score high on social desirability. Therefore, while conscientiousness is typically considered a good thing (e.g., being dependable and trustworthy), responding in a socially desirable way is considered a bad thing in that the respondents who have high social desirability scores may not be providing completely accurate or truthful answers.

If we were to try to predict social desirability based on the conscientiousness scores, given we know that they are associated, we would want to know whether there is any bias in doing so. As already noted, women scored significantly higher on conscientiousness than men. They also scored higher on the social desirability scale although these differences were not statistically significant. To determine test bias, however, we must move beyond looking at mean differences and instead look at differences in prediction. Examining Figure 10.3, we can see that the slopes and intercepts appear to be the same for men and women when using conscientiousness scores to predict scores on the social desirability measure (see Web Reference 10.2 for other graphical techniques for assessing test bias). In fact, the regression equation for men when using conscientiousness to predict social desirability was $\hat{y} = 87.31 + 10.39*$Conscientiousness, whereas the regression equation for women was $\hat{y} = 87.24 + 10.57*$Conscientiousness. As you can see, the slopes (10.39 vs. 10.57, difference = .18) and intercepts (87.31 vs. 87.24, difference = .07) are virtually the same. In addition, when conscientiousness and gender were used in a prediction equation to predict social desirability, only the conscientiousness regression weight was significant (another indication of a lack of intercept bias). The addition of the cross-product term between conscientiousness and gender (i.e., moderated multiple regression) did not significantly improve the prediction equation. This lack of significance demonstrates a lack of slope bias.

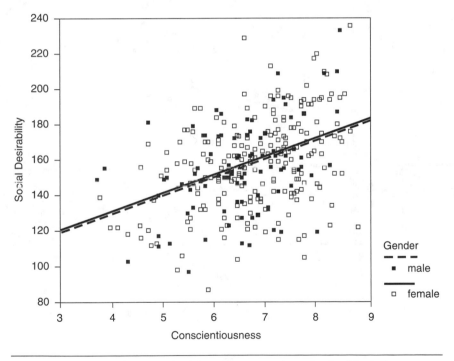

Figure 10.3   Actual Regression Lines Demonstrating a Lack of Both Intercept and Slope Bias

Next, we wanted to see if conscientiousness was related to intellect (sometimes referred to as "openness to experience"), another measure of the Big Five personality traits. In fact, conscientiousness and intellect correlate at .286. Thus, we wanted to determine if there is any bias in using conscientiousness to predict intellect. Remember, women scored significantly higher than men on conscientiousness; however, men ($N = 91$, $M = 6.74$, $s = 1.17$) scored significantly higher than women ($N = 225$, $M = 6.37$, $s = 1.16$) on the intellect scale ($t_{310} = -2.54$, $p = .012$, $\eta^2 = .020$). Looking at Figure 10.4, it appears we may have intercept bias, but probably no slope bias. The regression equation for women using conscientiousness to predict intellect was $\hat{y} = 3.98 + .35*$Conscientiousness, whereas the regression equation for men was $\hat{y} = 4.28 + .38*$Conscientiousness. Thus, we see a difference of .30 in the y intercepts, but only .03 in the slopes.

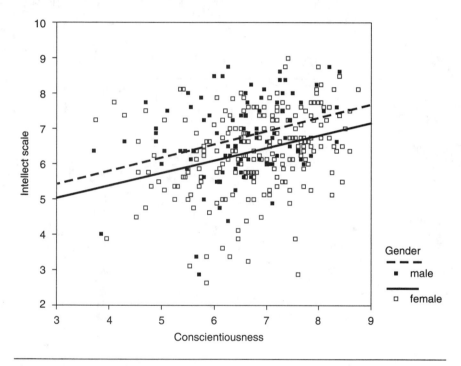

Figure 10.4   Actual Regression Lines Showing No Slope but Intercept Bias

We must be careful, however, not to overinterpret the differences in slopes intercepts, or both, as they are based on unstandardized regression values. Thus, the size of the observed differences is highly dependent on the scale used to measure both the predictor and the criterion variables. Therefore, we again need to compute a moderated multiple regression, adding in conscientiousness and gender in the first step and their cross product in the second step. As anticipated, gender was a significant predictor of intellect in the first step, thus indicating intercept bias. However, there was not a significant increase in prediction when the cross product of conscientiousness and gender was added into the regression equation in the second step, thus demonstrating a lack of slope bias. As noted earlier, instances of slope bias are relatively rare. In fact, we were unable to find any demonstration of slope bias in the Mersman-Shultz (1998) data set.

Concluding Comments

Test bias and test fairness are separate, although potentially related, concepts. Test bias (also referred to as prediction bias) is a technical psychometric issue that can be investigated empirically through procedures such as moderated multiple regression. Slope bias tends to be relatively rare, while intercept bias is somewhat more common. However, researchers must be aware of potential omitted variables that can change one's conclusions regarding test bias. In addition, researchers must also investigate possible criterion problems (i.e., maybe it is not the test but the criterion being used), differing sample size issues (i.e., we tend to have drastically smaller sample sizes for minority groups), and also the influence of individual items versus the entire test (to be discussed in more detail in Module 20). In addition, moderated multiple regression analysis assumes homogeneity of error variances. If this assumption is not met, alternative procedures should be used to estimate slope and/or intercept biases (see Web Reference 10.3). Finally, it should be noted that we have focused in this overview on test bias in terms of bias in prediction. Test bias can also be conceptualized in terms of bias of measurement. That is, our test is actually measuring a different trait than we said it was. Test bias in the form of bias in measurement will be discussed in Module 20.

Test fairness, conversely, is more of a sociopolitical concept. As a result, there is no standardized way of determining if a test is fair or not. We presented several conceptual models for defining test fairness; however, many others are possible. Standardizing the testing process and treating everyone the same can, however, go a long way toward heading off claims of test unfairness. In the end, though, adequately addressing test unfairness would require treating different subgroups differently on either the test or the criterion variable. This is unacceptable in many instances, and, as a result, you may well be left to search for another test that does not demonstrate test unfairness.

Practical Questions

1. Based on the data in Figure 10.1, what would have happened if we had used a common regression line to predict suicide risk in all three age groups?

2. Assuming we did use the same regression line for all three groups, which group would be most likely to raise claims of test bias? Unfairness?

3. How does one go about narrowing down the seemingly endless list of potential "omitted variables" in moderated regression analysis used to determine test bias?

4. Why do you think that intercept bias is much more common than slope bias?

5. What other factors (besides a truly biased test or an omitted variable) might be falsely suggesting test bias when, in fact, the test is not biased?

6. Which stakeholders in the testing process (see Module 1) are responsible for determining whether test bias actually exists or not?

7. Can a test that is determined to be biased still be a fair test? Alternatively, can a test that is determined to be unfair still be an unbiased test?

Case Studies

CASE STUDY 10.1: ESTIMATING TEST BIAS IN A PHYSICAL ABILITY TEST

Larry had just completed his master's degree in industrial and organizational (I/O) psychology and obtained his first job with the human resources department of a large local school district. The school district had just had an EEOC (Equal Employment Opportunity Commission) complaint filed against it regarding its physical ability test used to select school security officers (SSOs). In particular, both women and older (i.e., those age 40 and older) applicants had complained that the dynamometer test (a test of hand grip strength) was biased against both groups. Therefore, one of Larry's first projects was to determine if, in fact, the dynamometer test was biased against these two groups.

Fortunately for Larry, the school district tested a very large number of applicants each year for the SSO job. In addition, because the dynamometer test had been used for almost two decades, he had data going back almost 20 years and thus had a sufficiently large sample of female and older job candidates who had subsequently been hired, thus allowing him to examine for possible test bias on sex and age. Looking back on his notes from his graduate applied psychological measurement class, Larry remembered that he had to perform a moderated multiple regression analysis to examine for possible test bias. Larry first looked at possible test bias based on gender by entering all the dynamometer test scores in the database for those who had been hired and the gender variable (0 = women, 1 = men) into the regression equation to predict those who successfully completed a 12-month probationary period. Both the dynamometer and the gender variables had significant regression coefficients (i.e., they significantly predicted who passed probation). Therefore, in a second step, Larry entered the interaction term (i.e., gender × test score) into the regression equation. Lo and behold, the regression coefficient for the interaction term was also significant in predicting who successfully completed probation.

Next, Larry reran the multiple regression equation. This time, however, Larry entered the dynamometer test score and age (less than age 40 = 0, age 40 and older = 1) in the first step to predict successful completion of probation. Again, both regression weights were significantly related to who completed probation. However, when Larry entered the interaction term (test score × dichotomous age group) in step 2 of the regression equation, the regression coefficient for the interaction term was not significant. Now, it was time to sit down and look at the results more carefully and try to figure out what was going on with this dynamometer test.

Questions to Ponder

1. Does there appear to be any test bias in terms of gender? If so, what kind of predictor bias seems to be evident?

2. Does there appear to be any test bias in terms of age? If so, what kind of predictor bias seems to be evident?

3. If you were Larry, what omitted variables would you investigate? Would you look for different potential omitted variables for gender and age? Why or why not?

4. What other factors besides the omitted-variable concern might be impacting Larry's results?

5. Would drawing a scatterplot (similar to Figures 10.3 and 10.4) help in determining what is happening with the data or is the moderated multiple regression analysis sufficient?

6. Does the criterion variable that Larry used (i.e., whether a new hire passed probation) make a difference in whether we are likely to find test bias?

CASE STUDY 10.2: BIAS IN MEASURING ACTIVITIES OF DAILY LIVING

Joelle, a life span developmental psychology graduate student, recently completed an internship at an adult day care facility. The majority of the facility's clientele were elderly individuals who were living with their adult children and needed assistance with their activities of daily living (ADLs, i.e., eating, toileting, ambulating, bathing). The adult children typically worked during the day and could not afford a full-time home nurse. In addition, most adult children were concerned that even if they could afford a home nurse, the inability of their parent to interact with others their own age would lead to a feeling of social isolation and eventually to depression. Therefore, while most of these elderly individuals used walkers or were in wheelchairs, they were still able to get around somewhat and interact with others their own age at the facility. However, at some point in the near future, most of the clients would probably have to be referred to a full-time care facility (i.e., a nursing home).

In the past, each decision to refer a client to a full-time care facility was made on a case-by-case basis. However, a major determinant of whether a client was referred to a full-time care facility was how he or she scored on the standardized ADL scale. This scale measured how much difficulty (from 1 = none at all to 7 = a great extent) the client had performing personal functions such as bathing, ambulating, and eating. Those who scored beyond an established cutoff score were typically referred to nursing homes. However, the adult day care facility had received several complaints from the adult children of several clients that the test was somehow unfair or biased against minority clients. To the adult children, it appeared that minority clients were much more likely to be referred to a nursing home than were Caucasian clients. Therefore, the director of the center, knowing that Joelle had just completed an applied psychometrics course, asked her if she could somehow "determine" if, in fact, the ADL test was biased or unfair to minority clients. Joelle was unsure of where to start. She knew that the predictor was the ADL test, but what was the criterion? In addition, the adult day care facility wasn't all that big and hadn't been using the ADL test all that long, so there weren't many data available on who had and had not been referred, particularly for minority clients. A little unsure of where to even start, Joelle decided it was time to e-mail her psychometrics professor to see if he had any suggestions for her.

Questions to Ponder

1. If you were Joelle, where would you start? What key factors would you want to consider?

2. What information would you want to know from the test publisher or from reviews conducted of the test?

3. Does this appear to be more of a test bias or test fairness issue? Why?

4. If Joelle wanted to examine for test bias, what data would she need?

5. Which of the models of test fairness presented in the module overview would be most applicable here? Why?

6. Assuming Joelle actually found the test to be "unfair," what could she do to make the test fair?

Exercises

EXERCISE 10.1: EXAMINING TEST BIAS

OBJECTIVE: To practice computing moderated multiple regression analyses and drawing scatterplots to examine test bias issues.

Using the data set of Mersman and Shultz (1998) ("Personality.sav" in Appendix B), recreate the results presented in Figures 10.3 and 10.4. In addition, recreate the regression equations presented in the module overview. Finally, run the moderated multiple regression procedure for both the social desirability and the intellect criterion variables. What are your final regression equations? (*Note*: Be sure to use the honest condition responses when computing these regressions, i.e., conmean1 and intmean1.)

EXERCISE 10.2: EXAMINING DIFFERENT MODELS OF TEST BIAS/FAIRNESS (EEOC REQUEST FOR INFORMATION AND ANALYSIS—PART 2)

OBJECTIVE: To practice running and interpreting data to investigate several forms of test bias.

BACKGROUND: In Exercise 2.1, you performed some analyses for two mechanical comprehension tests in regard to an Equal Employment Opportunity Commission (EEOC) complaint using the "Mechanical Comprehension.sav" data set (see Appendix B for a description of the data). Well, *they're back*. The EEOC is requesting additional information/analyses regarding the complaint about our current mechanical comprehension (MC) test from a former job applicant (an older [more than 40 years of age] female minority, case ID # 450) for a clerical position. As you might remember, we are in the process of replacing our current MC test with a new one. The EEOC analyst assigned to our case will be here to meet with me tomorrow so we better have some answers by then. Specifically, they want us to look for test bias in our current MC measure using the four "models" outlined in Arvey and Faley (1988). Are any of these present and to what extent? (You probably should review your previous notes and analyses from Exercise 2.1 first if you have completed that exercise.)

1. **Model I**: *Mean difference between subgroups* (described on pages 122–123 of Arvey & Faley, 1988). Specifically, examine the group differences between minority and majority group applicants. Also, examine the differences between male and female applicants. Tests these group means for statistical significance using independent groups *t* tests. What did you find?

2. **Model II**: *Difference in validities* (described on pages 123–130 of Arvey & Faley, 1988). Specifically, compute the criterion-related validity coefficients separately for majority and minority groups and also for men and women. Perform separate analyses using both the current and the proposed mechanical comprehension tests as the predictor variables, respectively, and the job performance ratings as the criterion variable.

3. **Model III:** *Difference in regression lines* (described on pages 130–138 of Arvey & Faley, 1988, and pages 274–275 of Crocker & Algina, 1986). Specifically, compute separate regression analyses for men and women, as well as for minority and majority groups. Use the same predictor and criterion variables as in Model II. To perform the moderated multiple regression, however, you will also need to enter the demographic term (i.e., minority or sex) as well as the cross product of the demographic term and the appropriate mechanical comprehension test into the regression equation. In addition, create four scatterplots, one each for both the current and the proposed MC test as well as for sex and ethnicity. Be sure to plot separate regression lines for the respective demographic groups.

4. **Model IV:** *Thorndike's "quota" model* (described on pages 138–141 of Arvey & Faley, 1988). To perform this analysis, you will have to set a cutoff on both the mechanical comprehension test and the job performance rating (similar to Figure 10.2). We recommend using the median value for the job performance measure (i.e., a 50% base rate) to make things a little easier. Now adjust the cutoffs for the mechanical comprehension exams for each group in order meet the requirements of the model. This model is similar to the equal probability model discussed in the module overview (i.e., the proportion $A / [A + B]$ is the same for each group). What final cutoffs should be used for each group on each of the two mechanical comprehension tests in order to meet the requirements of the model?

5. Are there any other analyses we should carry out to be comprehensive and fully prepared?

Internet Web Site References

10.1. http://www.ou.edu/russell/whitepapers/Cleary_model.pdf

This PDF file presents a portion of the EEOC Uniform Guidelines on Employee Selection Procedures relevant to test bias.

10.2. http://www.damosaviation.com/detection%200f%20bias.doc

This MS Word file titled "How Can I Detect Bias in a Test?" presents several graphical depictions of bias.

10.3. http://members.aol.com/IMSAP/api.html

This Web site provides an online calculator of alternative statistics (e.g., the James-Alexander statistics) to the typical moderated multiple regression (MMR)

procedure for determining test bias when one violates the assumption of homogeneity of error variances across groups. You will need to input summary statistics for each group (i.e., the N, S for the test, S for the criterion, and the correlation between the test and criterion for each subgroup).

Further Readings

Arvey, R. D., & Faley, R. H. (1988). *Fairness in selecting employees* (2nd ed.). New York: Addison-Wesley.

Berk, R. A. (Ed.). (1982). *Handbook of methods for detecting test bias.* Baltimore: Johns Hopkins University Press.

Camilli, G., & Shepard, L. A. (1994). *Methods for identifying biased test items.* Thousand Oaks, CA: Sage.

Practical Issues in
Test Construction

Module 11

Developing Tests
of Maximal Performance

Given that students are administered possibly hundreds of tests throughout their academic careers, it should not be surprising to find that most students equate the term "testing" with educational assessment. This module is concerned with the development of the sorts of psychological tests with which students are most familiar—tests of knowledge, achievement, and ability. What distinguishes these tests from other psychological measures (such as those discussed in Module 15) is that tests of maximal performance are intended to assess an individual's performance at his or her maximum level of effort (Cronbach, 1970). Further, the items that comprise tests of maximal performance typically have a single correct answer.

Despite their familiarity with taking these types of tests, few students have considered the process that is required to develop tests of maximal performance. Unfortunately, it may also be true that, in many cases, little thought actually did go into the development of these tests. Module 4 discusses the preparatory steps required to develop any psychological test—it would be a good idea to review these steps before proceeding with the current module.

Getting Started

Initially, the developer of a test of maximal performance must clearly specify the domain the test is intended to assess. In developing a classroom knowledge test, this is likely to be a fairly straightforward process. The domain is often limited by the reading assignments, lectures, and class discussions. Still, the relative weighting or emphasis on various topics must be determined. For the development of a job knowledge test, however, specification of the domain may be considerably more complex. For example, for the job of human resource worker what exactly does "Knowledge of Equal Employment Opportunity (EEO) law" mean? Does this include knowledge of executive orders and court decisions, or is it limited to legislation? Would the test assess knowledge at the federal level only, or should state and local statutes also be assessed? These issues need to be specified in order to guide subsequent item writing, as well as to serve as a basis for evaluating the test once initial development is complete. Hopefully, you recognize that these issues relate to the content aspect of test validation (see Modules 6 and 8).

Speed Versus Power Tests

An important issue for the construction of tests of maximal performance is whether the test will be a pure speed test, a pure power test, or some combination of both. Tests can differ in the emphasis on time provided for completion during administration. Pure **speed tests** provide a large number of relatively easy items. How someone performs is determined by the number of items that can be completed in a relatively short period of time. Alternatively, **power tests** provide an ample amount of time for completion. Here, how someone performs is assumed to result from differences in understanding or ability. Many tests use some combination of both speed and power. The Wonderlic Personnel Test (WPT) (Wonderlic, Inc., 2002), for example, is a measure of cognitive ability often used in personnel selection. Test takers are provided exactly 12 minutes to complete the 50 items that comprise the test. Although the time provided is brief, it is unlikely that many test takers would get all items correct even if given an unlimited amount of time to complete the test.

Murphy and Davidshofer (2001) pointed out that computation of an internal consistency method for estimating reliability is inappropriate for speed tests. Because any items that are completed by a test taker on a pure speed test are likely to be correct, and all items that are not completed are necessarily incorrect, an internal consistency reliability estimate will be greatly inflated. Indeed, such a value is likely to approach 1.0. Test-retest or equivalent forms are more appropriate methods to assess reliability of pure speed tests (Crocker & Algina, 1986).

Level of Cognitive Objective

The items that comprise a test can assess various levels of cognitive objectives. While some items are intended to assess whether a test taker has retained basic facts, others are intended to assess a test taker's ability to perform more complex tasks, such as develop rational arguments based on evaluation of information. Bloom (1956) proposed a useful taxonomy for categorizing the level of abstraction assessed by test items. Bloom's taxonomy includes the following six levels, ordered in terms of increasing abstraction (see also Web Reference 11.8):

- *Knowledge:* These items are the most concrete and include memorization of fact.
- *Comprehension:* These items assess understanding and interpretation of information.
- *Application:* These items measure the test taker's ability to use information to solve novel problems.
- *Analysis:* These items assess the test taker's ability to see patterns and organize components of a whole.
- *Synthesis:* These items assess the test taker's ability to draw appropriate conclusions from information and to use old ideas to create new ones.
- *Evaluation:* These items at the highest level of abstraction require test takers to compare and discriminate between ideas. Test takers are required to substantiate their choices based on rational argument.

The intended purpose of the testing will determine the appropriate mix of items assessing various levels of abstraction. Those tests of maximal performance that are intended to assess higher-order cognitive objectives should be composed of more items that assess higher levels of abstraction than tests that are intended to assess lower-order cognitive objectives.

Item Format

The test specifications for tests of maximal performance must consider the appropriate format for items. Constructed-response (i.e., closed-ended) items include multiple-choice, true-false, and matching. These items provide test takers with a number of possible options from which to select the correct choice. Free-response (i.e., open-ended) items, including short-answer and essay items, require test takers to provide an answer varying in length from a few words to several pages. Free-response items may also require the solution of mathematical or other problems in which no set of possible solutions is provided. Although constructed-response options have been criticized in some educational quarters (e.g., Resnick & Resnick, 1992; Wiggens, 1989), it is important to recognize that both constructed- and free-response item formats have benefits and shortcomings.

For tests of maximal performance, free-response items are generally easier to create than constructed-response items. Some test developers prefer free-response items because they more readily allow for the testing of higher-order cognitive objectives. Because test takers produce their own response, free-response items also allow test takers to provide evidence of the depth of their knowledge. Whereas free-response items assessing maximal performance are relatively easy to create, they can be difficult and time-consuming to score. A certain degree of subjectivity is hard to avoid in scoring the responses of test takers. Further, because free-response items frequently take greater time to administer, these tests typically contain fewer items than their constructed-response counterparts. The inclusion of fewer items raises concerns over whether the test assesses a truly representative sample of the entire content domain. Another practical concern is whether test takers interpret the free-response items in the way the test developer intended. Invariably, some test takers fail to focus their response on the question asked. Finally, a test taker's language ability may have a significant influence on his or her responses to free-response items. The degree to which language ability is an important component of the testing domain must be considered.

Maximal performance tests composed of constructed-response items are typically easy to score objectively. These tests are therefore suitable for administration whenever a large number of individuals will be tested. Further, these tests can include a large number of items, which provides a more representative assessment of the content domain. However, constructed-response items can be much more difficult to construct than free-response items, particularly if the test developer's goal is to assess higher-order cognitive objectives. Constructed-response items that are poorly written can be either unintentionally difficult, as is the case with the inclusion of double negatives in item stems, or too easy, when either the item stem or a previous item suggests the correct response. Due in part to the difficulty of constructing quality constructed-response items, test developers are likely to retain items for administration to additional groups of test takers. Such practices raise concerns with test security.

It is wrong to decry the perceived weaknesses of one format while trumpeting the virtues of another format as appropriate for all testing situations. However, choice of item format is an important consideration, as it will impact a variety of factors, including the level of knowledge assessment, the test's efficiency of assessment, objectivity of scoring, and even the strategies employed by examinees in preparation for the test. The test developer must carefully consider the intent of the testing and carefully select an item format (or combination of item formats) useful for that purpose.

Item Writing

Once the test specifications are complete, item writing can begin. Many sources provide recommendations regarding the construction of specific item formats. Following are brief descriptions of several specific item formats and a sample of item-writing recommendations taken from Ebel and Frisbie (1986), McKeachie (1994), Tuckman (1988), and Wiersma and Jurs (1990). These or other similar sources (such as Web References 11.1–11.5) should be consulted for more complete recommendations on item writing.

True-False Items

True-false items require a test taker to determine whether a statement is valid. These items tend to be easily created and require little time to administer. Unfortunately, the apparent simplicity of creating true-false items makes these items popular with unskilled test developers. Further, because each item has only two possible response options (i.e., true or false), item discrimination is often low. Tips for writing quality true-false items include the following:

- Express the item as clearly, concisely, and simply as possible.
- Assess only important knowledge; avoid assessment of trivia.
- Create items that assess understanding—not just memory.
- Avoid double negatives.
- Use more false statements than true statements in the test.
- Word the item so that superficial logic suggests a wrong answer.
- Ensure that the intended correct answer is obvious only to those who have good command of the knowledge being tested.
- Make the wrong answer consistent with a popular misconception or a popular belief irrelevant to the question.

Matching Items

Matching items typically present a number of stems in one column and response options in a separate column. These items are useful for determining whether a test taker can distinguish between similar ideas, facts, or concepts. Because of the required brevity of matching items, they typically assess lower-order cognitive objectives, thus encouraging rote memorization. Tips for writing quality matching items include the following:

- Denote each item stem with a number, and each possible response option with a letter.
- Choose item stems and response options that demonstrate the test taker's ability to distinguish between similar things.
- Keep response options short.
- Provide additional plausible response options to avoid a "process of elimination" approach.
- Provide clear instructions regarding what the test taker is intended to do. For example, specify whether response options can be used more than once.

Multiple-Choice Items

Multiple-choice items are used extensively in many testing contexts; thus, test takers are very familiar with this testing format. Multiple-choice items present a statement or question in an item stem, followed by a choice among several possible response options. These items can be used to assess both lower- and higher-order cognitive objectives, although greater expertise is required to develop the latter. Tips for writing quality multiple-choice *item stems* include the following:

- Make sure that items assess important, significant ideas.
- Pose a question (or statement) that has a definitive answer.
- Avoid giveaways as to the correct answer.
- When using a negative in the item stem (e.g., *not*), use capitalization or underlining to ensure the word is read.
- Consider using two sentences in the stem, one to present necessary background information, and one to ask the question.
- Use gender and ethnicity in an inclusive fashion. Alternate between "she" and "he." Proper names should reflect ethnic diversity.

Tips for writing quality *response options* for multiple-choice items include the following:

- Place words that appear in every response option in the stem.
- Arrange response options in a logical order.
- Include plausible distracters.
- Include some true statements in the distracters that do not correctly answer the question posed in the stem.
- Ensure that response options are parallel—that is, of approximately equal length and of equal complexity.
- Write brief response options, rather than long ones.
- Across the test, ensure that the correct response is balanced roughly equally across the possible response options (i.e., A, B, C, D, and E).

- Create distracters that include familiar-sounding phrases that would be attractive to those with only superficial knowledge.
- Avoid use of "all of the above." Once a test taker has determined that at least two response options are correct, the correct response must be "all of the above."
- Use "none of the above" only if this is sometimes the correct response option. Further, avoid the common mistake of including the option "none of the above" *only* in items for which it is the correct response.
- Avoid use of "A & C"–type response options. While item difficulty increases, item discrimination does not improve.

Short-Answer and Essay Items

Short-answer and essay items are free-response items that are typically used to assess higher-order cognitive objectives. These items differ in the length of response required. Tips for *writing* quality short-answer and essay items include the following:

- Ask only questions that produce responses that can be verified as better than other responses.
- Provide terminology in the questions that limit and clarify the required response.
- Provide multiple specific questions rather than a very limited number of long questions.
- Do not provide test takers a choice among several questions. This, in effect, is providing different exams to different students. The equivalency of alternative essay items is highly suspect.
- Specify the amount of points for each part of an essay item.
- Test each item by writing an ideal answer prior to administration.

The following tips are provided to help improve the quality of *scoring* short-answer and essay items:

- When you are familiar with the test takers, ask test takers to record a confidential code rather than names on the test.
- Develop a set of criteria for the scoring of each item.
- Read several responses before assigning grades.
- Select papers to serve as excellent, good, nominal, and poor models of the standards by which you are grading.
- Assign global, holistic grades to each question rather than multiple grades on such elements as content, originality, grammar, and organization.

Test-Wise Test Takers

Item-writing recommendations are intended to clarify the item for test takers, avoid unnecessary assessment of language capabilities, assist in ensuring good test psychometrics, and ward against test-wiseness. Test-wiseness refers to the ability to answer items correctly based not on knowledge of the subject matter tested, but rather on clues presented by the item itself or elsewhere in the test. A classic example is the recommendation that if you have no idea as to the correct answer on a multiple-choice item, simply select the longest response option (see Web Reference 11.6 for additional examples, and Web Reference 11.7 to test your own level of test-wiseness). You may notice in the lists of sample recommendations given previously that some tips are intended to "trip up" those who would seek to practice their test-wise skills on the test.

The Process of Item Modification

The remaining steps in the development of a maximal performance test include (a) having subject matter experts (SMEs) review the items, (b) pretesting the items, and (c) making any necessary modifications. For large-scale applications, SMEs are asked to provide confirmation that items assess the intended construct. When SMEs question the relevance of an item, it is dropped from further consideration. Pretesting is often initially conducted on a small sample to determine whether items are interpreted as intended. This is then followed by large-scale piloting that allows the examination of the test's factor structure and internal consistency reliability, along with computation of item statistics. In classroom settings, these steps are typically undertaken less formally. The instructor will often attempt to critically evaluate any newly written items. Another instructor or a teaching assistant may also be asked to provide feedback. Unfortunately, classroom exams are rarely pretested. Rather, students themselves typically serve as both the pilot and the implementation sample. Of course, once the test is administered those items with poor item statistics can be subsequently discarded.

Concluding Comments

Creation of a test of maximal performance proceeds through a series of important steps. Prior to development of test items, the test developer must make a number of important decisions regarding the test's content, item format, test length, and so on. A number of recommendations exist for the development of good items. Once initially developed, pretesting, examination by experts, and other steps should be taken to modify items prior to administration.

The construction of a knowledge test is a deliberate process intended to ensure the reliability and validity of the test. However, what may not be quite as obvious in this module is that test developers must make a large number of choices throughout this process. It is this considerable flexibility that allows test developers to engage their creative juices as well.

Practical Questions

1. Why is test-wiseness a problem in tests of maximal performance?

2. What do you think of intentionally incorporating test-wise characteristics into item distracters? Defend your position.

3. What are the advantages and disadvantages of constructed-response items?

4. What are the advantages and disadvantages of free-response items?

5. Why shouldn't use of "all of the above" be included in multiple-choice response options?

6. Why shouldn't test takers be given a choice among several different essay items?

7. Why are multiple short-answer items preferable to one long essay question?

8. Why is pretesting of items important in test construction?

9. Who would be appropriate to fulfill the role of SME for a test designed to assess knowledge of:
   a. 12th-grade mathematics?
   b. modern automotive repair?
   c. American pop culture?

Case Studies

CASE STUDY 11.1: ESSAY SCORING AND WRITING ABILITY

Jaime was rightly proud of the midterm exam he created for the course in which he served as teaching assistant, PSY 451: Introduction to Forensic Psychology. The instructor, Dr. Dan Kellemen, had asked him to create a free-response test that could be completed within the 1.5-hour class session. Jaime had given a lot of thought to proper test construction techniques in the creation of the test. He carefully went over the topics Dr. Dan wanted covered, and he considered the relative importance of these various topics. Jaime considered a variety of free-response options for the test, but in the end decided to modify Dr. Dan's usual approach of two to three essay questions. Similar to the midterm exam Dr. Dan had used the previous semester, Jaime's test was organized around three large "questions." However, Jaime used these broad questions only to introduce the topic and to help students focus on the subitems that followed. Under each of the three broad questions, Jaime created between three and four subitems labeled a, b, c, and so on. It was the responses to these items that were to be graded for the exam. Following each of these subitems, Jaime recorded the number of points that a student could possibly receive for that item. Items on more important topics received a higher number of points. Overall, the exam contained 10 items.

Before showing the test to Dr. Dan, Jaime produced responses to each item to ensure that the questions were, in fact, capable of being answered. Based on this exercise, Jaime had to revise a couple of the items. Much to Jaime's delight, Dr. Dan had been noticeably impressed with the quality of the exam and had not made a single modification. During the administration of the exam, a few students asked for the usual types of clarification, but no one indicated any major difficulties in understanding the items on the exam. Now that the students had completed their midterm, Jaime's next responsibility was to score them.

When it came to scoring, Jaime was once again a man with a plan. To be fair to everyone, he had asked students to record only their student identification numbers on their blue books, rather than their names. He also planned on scoring every student's response to the first item, before scoring even a single response to the second item. Jaime also decided to assign a single, holistic score to each item, rather than assigning separate scores based on content, clarity, originality, and so forth. Even so, Jaime was surprised how long it took to score all of the exams in the class.

Back in class the next day, Jaime was excited to return the exams to the students. It was, in many ways, the final step in the lifespan of his first exam. Later that day during office hours, he received a visit from Juan, a student in the class. Juan demanded to know why he received a much lower score than another student who, he claimed, had provided similar correct answers. As evidence, Juan produced both his own and another student's blue books. On question after question, the content of each response was similar, yet Jaime had given the other student a higher score. "How could that be?" Jaime nearly wondered aloud. Stalling, Jaime informed Juan that he'd examine both blue books and would provide a decision at the next class session.

In reviewing both blue books more carefully, Jaime realized that he had to agree with Juan on one point—both blue books contained similar quality of information in response to the items. However, Juan's responses were characterized by poor grammar, spelling, and a general lack of organization. Still, the answers were there, if one searched for them sufficiently. "What role should writing ability play in determination of this grade?" wondered Jaime. On the one hand, it seemed irrelevant to knowledge of forensics. On the other hand, wouldn't clear communication play a major role in the job of forensic psychologist? Luckily, perhaps, he was "just" the TA—he'd need to seek the advice of Dr. Dan on this one.

Questions to Ponder

1. Jaime followed a number of recommended steps for test development. For each of the following, explain how it assists in the development of a quality test of maximal performance:
   a. Consideration of the various weighting of topics
   b. Consideration of appropriate response formats
   c. Creation of subitems, rather than fewer, larger essay questions
   d. Specification of the number of points assigned to an item
   e. Creation of ideal responses to items prior to test administration

2. Jaime also followed a number of recommended steps to score this essay test. For each of the following, explain how it helps improve reliability:
   a. Recording of student identification numbers rather than names on blue books
   b. Scoring one item at a time for all respondents, before proceeding to the next item
   c. Using holistic scores for an item, rather than using multiple subscores for an item

3. Jaime unwittingly included writing ability in his scoring. Is writing ability an appropriate test component for a university class in forensic psychology? Explain.

CASE STUDY 11.2: EASY MONEY?

"It'll be easy money." So said the director of faculty development, when trying to convince Dr. Patricia Lonergan to present a brief overview on test development to a group of interested faculty. She'd earn $200 for delivering a two-hour lecture. The words still rang in her ears. "It'll be easy money." So then, what could have gone so wrong?

Patricia had taught a graduate-level course in test construction for several years, but she knew it would be a challenge to condense a semester's worth of material into a two-hour faculty seminar. Recognizing that most faculty were interested primarily in how to improve the development of their own tests, Patricia decided to limit her lecture to a quick overview of the concepts of reliability and validity, followed by a lengthy discussion of item-writing tips, and ending with simple procedures for computing item statistics.

Though she had lectured many times before on these subjects, Patricia realized she was more than a little anxious about presenting before a group of her peers. She had only been out of graduate school for three years, and she knew that her colleagues at her university had reputations as great teachers. Perhaps it was for this reason that she decided to bring along a lengthy handout that would help the faculty participants remember her main points. Reflecting back on the experience, Patricia was grateful that she'd brought the handout—otherwise, most of her points would never have been heard at all.

The talk had gotten off to a fairly good start. The conference room in which she gave the presentation was surprisingly full—nearly 20 faculty members were in attendance, most of whom she had never met. These faculty members seemed to follow most of what she reviewed about the importance of developing reliable and valid exams. Most of the participants nodded in agreement to her points, and she noticed that several jotted down a few notes. Somewhat disappointingly, however, no one seemed to contribute his or her own thoughts about these topics.

Then came what Patricia considered the "meat" of her presentation—a discussion of item-writing tips. In referring to the handout, she asked the faculty participants to alternate taking turns reading aloud the recommendations for writing the first type of items she planned on discussing, multiple-choice questions. A few tips were read. Then Patricia noticed that, simultaneously, several faculty members raised their hands to contribute to the discussion. "Great," thought Patricia, "now we'll get some insights into people's own approaches to creation of these items." But no. Instead, that's when things started to go terribly wrong.

Patricia first selected a faculty member from the philosophy department. Clearing his throat, he asked, "Why should we waste our time discussing these so-called objective items. Everyone knows they serve no good academic purpose." A professor across from him concurred, saying, "Unless we abandon our dependence on these types of items, we'll never prepare our students for the real world. Life doesn't provide multiple-choice options." Looking at Patricia, a third faculty member accusatorily asked, "If you call these constructed-response items 'objective,' what does that say about your opinion of essays? Are you saying they are subjective?" Several other faculty members added their own comments in support of these individuals.

Just when Patricia was trying to formulate a response—any response—several other faculty members began taking issue with the comments of their colleagues. "I'm tired of this rhetoric about the importance of testing through writing," quipped a member of the chemistry department. Actually, now that Patricia thought about it, he hadn't used the word "rhetoric," but something a bit more colorful. At any rate, several other faculty members then chimed in their agreement with the chemist. A few complained about the large size of their classes and the perceived difficulty in using free-response exams. The next few minutes were something of a blur to her. Suffice it to say, however, that a heated discussion erupted, and little of her talk went as planned. Try as she might, her colleagues seemed a lot more interested in airing their opinions about the appropriateness of certain item formats rather than her recommendations for writing better test items.

Returning to her office, Patricia reflected once more on those words that had got her into this in the first place. "It'll be easy money."

Questions to Ponder

1. Do certain item formats prepare students for the "real world" better than others? Why or why not?

2. What are likely some of the arguments put forth by those who reject constructed-response testing in universities? To what degree do you feel these arguments are valid?

3. In a university setting, why might some departments likely champion free-response item formats while other departments prefer constructed-response formats?

4. What role does politics play in the choice of adoption of item formats in a college classroom?

5. What role should practical concerns (such as class size) play in the determination of item formats?

6. Can constructed-response items assess higher-level cognitive objectives?

7. What item formats do you prefer to be tested with? Why?

8. Based on your own personal experience and observations, in what ways does the choice of item format influence student test preparation?

Exercises

EXERCISE 11.1: USING BLOOM'S TAXONOMY TO RATE ITEMS

OBJECTIVE: To identify an item's level of abstraction using Bloom's (1956) taxonomy.

Match each item with its correct level of abstraction. Use each possible response option no more than once. You may refer to the following Web site for expanded definitions of each of the possible levels of item abstraction in Bloom's (1956) taxonomy:

http://www.coun.uvic. ca/learn/program/hndouts/bloom.html

Item	Level of Abstraction
1. Identify the six levels of item abstraction in Bloom's (1956) taxonomy.	A. Knowledge
2. Compare and contrast the goal-setting and expectancy theories of work motivation.	B. Comprehension
3. Critique the effectiveness of trickle-down economics.	C. Application
4. Given the symptoms expressed by the patient, recommend a course of treatment.	D. Analysis
5. Explain the major principles of the term "selection of the fittest."	E. Synthesis
	F. Evaluation

EXERCISE 11.2: DETERMINATION OF TEST COMPOSITION

OBJECTIVE: To gain practice developing test specifications for knowledge tests.

In developing knowledge tests, many important decisions must be made to ensure that test objectives are achieved. Although unlimited time and resources might allow for creation of a near-perfect knowledge test, almost all exams must be developed with practical considerations in mind. For each of the tests described below, complete the following:

A. Determine the item format.

Select one or more item formats that will appropriately measure the test objectives.

B. Determine the number of points per format.

Assuming the test will be scored out of 100 points, determine the total number of points that will be used for each item format chosen. For example, if you choose to create a test with multiple-choice and essay questions, assign the total number of points to be assessed by multiple-choice format and the total number of points to be assessed by essay format. (*Note:* The total number of points must sum to 100.)

C. Determine the number of items per format and the number of points per item for each format.

For each item format selected, determine the number of items that will be written. The number of points assigned to each individual item (within a particular format) will be determined by dividing the number of points for this item format by the number of items using this format.

D. Provide justification.

Explain and justify why you believe your decisions will lead to the development of a practical, reliable, and content-valid exam.

1. Test Description:

Midterm exam for an entry-level statistics course for the behavioral sciences

Number of students: 30

Class period: 60 minutes, plus 40-minute lab

Students would be expected to:

- Summarize, display, and interpret sets of data.
- Understand the logic of statistical analysis, probability, and hypothesis testing.
- Conduct descriptive statistical analyses and probability problems with the use of a calculator.

2. Test Description:

Final exam for an introductory psychology course

Number of students: 200

Class period: 1.5 hours

Students would be expected to:

- Define basic psychological terminology.
- Comprehend the role of research in the field of psychology.
- Understand major psychological theories and research findings.
- Identify leading contributors to the field of psychology.
- Critically apply the principles and theories of psychology to contemporary daily life.

3. Test Description:

Final exam in a college-level history course entitled History of Western Civilization

Number of students: 25

Class period: 3 hours

Students would be expected to:

- Demonstrate factual knowledge of the history of Western civilization.
- Understand how various conditions, social structures, and ideas shape the development of society.
- Identify the historical roots of current practices and debates.

4. Test Description:

Final exam for a graduate-level educational measurement course

Number of students: 12

Class period: 3 hours

Students would be expected to:
- Discuss the purposes, utility, and limitations of various psychometric concepts.
- Compare and contrast classical test theory with item response theory.
- Identify and compute appropriate psychometrics for a given testing situation.

EXERCISE 11.3: WRITING ITEMS TO ASSESS KNOWLEDGE

OBJECTIVE: To develop high-quality items to assess knowledge of a specific domain.

Students sometimes complain that items on a test are vague, exceedingly difficult, or even unrelated to the topics presented in the course. Here's your opportunity to see what it's like to create those items yourself.

For this exercise, you will develop a knowledge test that contains a minimum of 25 constructed-response (e.g., matching, multiple-choice, and true-false) items and three short-answer essay items. In completing this exercise, heed the following instructions:

A. Carefully define the domain that you are seeking to test.
- Perhaps consider a course that you have recently taken, or a course for which you may have served as a teaching assistant. However, any domain of knowledge that can be clearly defined is acceptable, from knowledge of basic photography to knowledge of plot and character development on the *Buffy the Vampire Slayer* television series.

B. For the constructed-response items, choose a format (or formats) that is appropriate to assess the level of abstraction for the domain you are assessing.
- Justify your selection of each item format chosen.

C. Attempt to write items that will representatively sample the entire content domain.

D. Avoid all common pitfalls in item writing.

E. Identify the appropriate response to each constructed-response item.

Internet Web Site References

11.1. http://testing.byu.edu/faculty/handbooks.asp

This Web page, hosted by Brigham Young University, provides faculty with information for the development of better tests. Links to several pdf files are provided on such topics as how to prepare better tests, how to prepare better multiple-choice items, research studies about multiple-choice writing, and preparing effective essay questions.

11.2. http://www.ed.gov/databases/ERIC_Digests/ed398236.html

This Web page, provided by ERIC, gives some recommendations on writing multiple-choice stems and response options.

11.3. http://caacentre.lboro.ac.uk/resources/objective_tests/index.shtml

This Web page provides definitions and examples of a number of different types of constructed-response items.

11.4. http://ucs1.ucs.umn.edu/oms/truefalse.htmlx

This Web page, developed by the University of Minnesota Office of Measurement Services, provides a discussion of the advantages and disadvantages of true-false items, along with true-false item-writing guidelines.

11.5. http://www.pitt.edu/~ciddeweb/faculty-development/fds/testing2.html

This Web page, from the University of Pittsburgh, provides advice to faculty on how to develop and score essay questions. A chart is included indicating the approximate length of time, per item, that should be allotted for completion of various types of items.

11.6. http://ucs1.ucs.umn.edu/lasc/onlinecourses/c456.htmlx

This Web page, from the University of Minnesota Learning and Academic Skills Center, provides an example of test coaching. The utility of such coaching can be minimized by proper test construction.

11.7. http://www.nald.ca/fulltext/hudson/iytrans/page88.htm

This Web page provides a quiz to test your test-wise skills. By clicking "next" at the bottom of the page, the answer to each item is explained.

11.8. http://www.coun.uvic.ca/learn/program/hndouts/bloom.html

This Web site identifies and explains each of the categories of Bloom's taxonomy for categorizing an item's level of abstraction.

Further Readings

Linn, R. L. (Ed.). (1989). *Educational measurement* (3rd ed.). New York: American Council on Education/Macmillan.

Ory, J. C., & Ryan, K. E. (1993). *Tips for improving testing and grading.* Newbury Park, CA: Sage.

Osterlind, S. J. (1998). *Constructing test items: Multiple-choice, constructed-response, performance, and other formats.* Boston: Kluwer.

Rodriguez, M. C. (2002). Choosing an item format. In G. Tindal & T. M. Haladyna (Eds.), *Large-scale assessment programs for all students: Validity, technical adequacy, and implementation* (pp. 213–231). Mahwah, NJ: Erlbaum.

Module 12

Classical Test Theory Item Analysis

In Module 11, we discussed how best to construct maximal performance (i.e., knowledge) tests. After you put in hours and hours (if not days and days or weeks and weeks) constructing such a test, the day will finally come when you actually have to give the test to someone. Once you administer the test to a designated group of test takers, you will want to evaluate it. That is, you will want to know if the test worked the way you hoped it would and if it is accomplishing what you set out to accomplish. If the test is not up to your high standards, are you going to simply throw out the entire test? We hope not. Instead, you will want to determine which specific items may be causing problems (i.e., you will want to perform an **item analysis**). You can then eliminate and/or replace the lackluster items or, better yet, revise and reuse the problematic items. Think about it, you just spent a lot of time and painstaking effort writing items to create your test, so you do not want to be throwing out items needlessly or, worse yet, indiscriminately. Thus, the questions become "Which items do I keep unchanged?" "Which do I throw out?" "Which do I try to salvage with some well-placed revisions?" The answers can be found in your favorite classical test theory item analysis statistics. (See Web References 12.1 and 12.2 for a more detailed overview of the item revision statistics discussed in this module.)

Item Difficulty

Once you have the data following administration of your test, you will want to look at two key statistics. The first is the *item response distribution*. In particular, you will want to know how difficult the group of test takers found each item to be (i.e., the **item difficulty**). This statistic is typically referred to as the *p value* (for percentage correct), indicating what percentage of test takers answered a given item correctly. While ideally we strive to obtain an average *p* value of 50% correct in order to maximize the variability of the entire test and thus the reliability, in practice, issues such as guessing on multiple-choice items and more than half the students failing a class usually prohibit such a low average *p* value. The typical range of *p* values for educational and employment knowledge tests is somewhere between approximately 50% and 90% correct per item. In particular, we want to have easier items at the beginning of the test in order to allow the test taker to get "warmed up." However, if our *p* value is too extreme (i.e., near 0%, all test takers answering it incorrectly; or 100%, all answering it correctly), then that item is of little use to us, because the lack of variability results in minimal differentiation among test takers. It should be noted, however, that these are assumptions under **classical test theory** (CTT) models. Modern test theory models (i.e., item response theory, IRT) make somewhat different assumptions (see Module 19 for a discussion of the differing assumptions between CTT and IRT).

We must keep in mind, however, that an item is not good or bad in and of itself; rather, the real question is whether it is helping us to differentiate among test takers. Therefore, for example, you may have a job knowledge question that all senior computer programmers could easily answer, but only about 70% of entry-level computer programmers could answer. Hence, that item might serve us well in an employment exam to select entry-level computer programmers, but would be of little use to us in the promotional exam for senior computer programmer.

Item Discrimination

Our second key item analysis statistic is an index of item discriminability. Analogous to the concept of reliability being a necessary but not sufficient condition for validity, variability in a group of test takers is a necessary but not sufficient condition for **item discrimination**. That is, we want to obtain items that allow us to discriminate, in the psychometric, not legal, sense, among test takers. However, if test takers do not vary in their responses, then the item will be of little use to us. For example, if we are using a test we developed to decide which students should be placed in remedial reading classes versus normal classes versus accelerated classes, then we need to have a test—more specifically, test items—that allow us to differentiate these three levels of students. The more precise our need to discriminate among test takers, the more items of varying difficulty we will need to make those fine distinctions. In addition, each item should predict some internal (e.g., total test score) or external (e.g., grade point average, GPA) criterion of interest. These are evaluated with item discrimination statistics.

There are several item discrimination indexes we can compute. One of the earliest and most basic approaches was to examine contrasting groups. Here we break the test takers into the highest-scoring one third, the middle one third, and the lowest-scoring one third of the distribution of scores. Alternatively, some item analysis programs compare the upper and lower 27% of the distribution of test takers (see Web References 12.3 and 12.5). We then examine each item to see what percentage of each extreme group correctly answered a particular item and compute the difference between those two percentages. We hope that the upper group will answer the item correctly more often than the lower group. Hence, we are looking for positive difference scores. In fact, we are basically doing the same thing we did with item difficulty (i.e., looking at p values), the difference being that we are now examining them within each of these extreme subgroups. While this approach provides only a crude estimate of item discrimination, it does provide some valuable information. For example, assume we see that the overall p value for an item is about 70%. At first blush, that might appear to be a good item. If we looked at contrasting groups, however, we might notice that only 50% of the top-scoring group answered the item correctly, while 90% of the bottom-scoring group answered the item correctly. Clearly this is an item we would want to look at more closely in that those who did worse on the test overall are actually doing better on this particular item. The down side of this procedure is that we end up ignoring a significant portion of test scores in the middle of the test score distribution. Why not use the entire set of test scores? That is exactly what our next set of item analysis statistics does.

More precise and complete indicators of item discrimination are the biserial and point-biserial correlation coefficients between how the test takers answered a given item (i.e., correct or incorrect) and overall test performance. Thus, these indexes use all the available test data to compute an index of discrimination. These indexes are typically referred to as the *item-total correlations*. Ideally, we hope to have a positive and strong (i.e., close to 1.0) item-total correlation. In practice, a positive low-to-moderate (i.e., .10–.50) correlation typically suffices as an indicator of an acceptable item. Of the two factors, direction and strength, direction is the more critical concern. A positive item-total correlation (assuming the items are scored 0 for incorrect and 1 for correct) would indicate that those who correctly answer a particular item also tend to do well on the test overall. This is what we are hoping for. Conversely, a negative item-total correlation would indicate that those test takers who answer a particular item correctly tend to do worse on the test overall. That would not be a good thing. We do not want items that the knowledgeable test takers answer incorrectly, while those lacking in sufficient knowledge of the subject matter answer them correctly. Thus, a negative item-total correlation would be an indication that something is problematic with a given item. This would require going back and examining the item carefully. Maybe this is a "trick" question where one of the nonkeyed alternatives (distracters) is being selected more frequently by the more knowledgeable test takers. Thus, simply replacing that one distracter may be enough of a revision to remedy the problem.

In addition, we need to have acceptable test-taker-to-item ratios in order to obtain stable item-total correlation coefficients. Ideally we would like to have at least 5–10 test takers per item. However, in many situations (e.g., the class-room), this ratio is rarely achieved. Thus, we have to work with whatever data we have. We also need to be cautious in computing item-total correlations when the number of items on the test is small (e.g., less than 20). This is because the total test score includes the item we are correlating it with. Thus, the fewer the number of items on the test, the more weight that item will have in the compu-tation of the total test score. Crocker and Algina (1986) provided a correction formula that can be used when the number of items on the test is small. When the number of items is larger, there is no need for such a correction.

You are probably asking yourself what the difference is between the biser-ial correlation and the point-biserial correlation. The **point-biserial correlation coefficient** is an index of the association (a Pearson product moment correla-tion coefficient) between the dichotomous item response and the overall test score. Thus, it is an index of how well the item differentiates candidates in terms of the knowledge or trait being measured by the test. The biserial corre-lation coefficient, however, corrects for the often-artificial dichotomy created by scoring an item as correct or incorrect. That is, all those test takers who answer an item correctly most likely do not have the exact same level of knowledge or trait being measured by the test. Similarly, all those who answer the item incorrectly are not equally deficient in the knowledge or trait. Thus, there is an underlying continuum of knowledge or trait, assumed to be nor-mally distributed, that is measured by each item on the test. However, this continuum is masked to a large extent by dichotomizing the item. The biserial correlation corrects for this artifact. As a result, the biserial correlation is always somewhat larger than the point-biserial correlation. The difference between the two values for any item becomes more extreme as the p value becomes more extreme (see Crocker & Algina, 1986, pp. 315–320, for a more detailed discussion of the difference between the two indexes). Linear poly-chotomous item scoring more directly addresses the problem of artificially dichotomizing item scores by providing partial credit for "incorrect" alterna-tives based on how "reasonable" the alternative response options are. Linear polychotomous scoring, however, requires specialty software that is much harder to come by than classical test theory item analysis software for dichoto-mously scored tests (Shultz, 1995).

We may also correlate each item with some external criterion instead of the total test score. For example, early development of biographical data (i.e., biodata) used in employment situations correlated how job applicants performed on a given item with an external criterion of interest. A classic example is that during World War II there was a question on a biographical data form that asked fighter pilot trainees if they had ever built model airplanes that flew as a child. According to lore, this item was the single best predictor of how many "kills" (i.e., enemy planes shot down) a fighter pilot had. However, you might have surmised that if all the items are selected based on their level of association with their respective criteria, then it is unlikely you will have an internally consistent test. As a result, using item-criterion correlations as the primary basis for constructing tests is less common today.

Norm-Referenced Versus Criterion-Referenced Tests

Up to this point, we have assumed that we are interested primarily in **norm-referenced testing.** That is, we want to be able to maximally differentiate among test takers. Thus, we want average p values close to .50 in order to maximize the variability and thus increase the reliability of our test. This is the case in many employment situations, for example, where we have more applicants than openings and we need to narrow down our potential employee pool. Hence, being able to differentiate among test takers is a key concern, and thus we wish to maximize the variability among test takers.

Alternatively, in educational and state licensing scenarios, the goal is not to maximize variability among test takers. Instead, we are interested in determining if the test takers have achieved a certain level of competence. Thus, content validity of the test is of paramount importance. In these scenarios, item discrimination statistics are of little use. Item difficulty statistics, on the other hand, may be of use in evaluating test items. However, the goal in using item difficulty statistics is not to maximize variance among test takers. Instead, the primary objective is to assess if the test takers have achieved a given level of competence (as in a licensing exam) and/or whether the primary objectives of an instructional process were successfully conveyed (i.e., the effectiveness of classroom instruction). A problem is that we may not know why a p value is low. It could be that the instructor did not cover the educational objective assessed by a given item or it may be that the students were not paying attention when it was covered or the objective was confused with another concept or the item itself is technically flawed. Thus, more detective work is needed to assess *why* a given item is not performing as expected when we are interested in **criterion-referenced testing** as opposed to norm-referenced testing.

This additional detective work might include examining the difference between p values for items given before (pretest) and after (posttest) instruction. In addition, we might enlist subject matter experts (SMEs) to review our items to see if the troublesome items are indeed assessing our objective and doing so appropriately. We may also conduct focus groups with some test takers after they take the test to determine why they selected the responses they did. Doing so may allow for immediate remedial instruction or, at the very least, improve future instruction and evaluation.

Overall Test Statistics

In addition to analyzing each individual test item, test developers and users need to evaluate the overall test statistics as well. For example, what is the average p value across the entire test? How about the average item-total correlation? What is the alpha reliability of the test? The variability? The minimum and maximum values? The standard error of measurement? The shape (i.e., skewness and kurtosis) of the distribution of exam scores? Such statistics can prove valuable in making revisions to the test. While they may not help in revising specific items, they will provide hints on where to focus your revision efforts. For example, if the average p value on a classroom test is only 55% correct, you will want to determine if revising particularly attractive item distracter alternatives might make them less attractive and thus increase the average p value on the test. Alternatively, you may notice that the test is highly negatively skewed and leptokurtic (very peaked). That is, test takers are concentrated at the upper end of the score distribution, with only a few doing poorly. Thus, you may want to look at the distracters that no one is choosing for the high p-value items and make those distracters somewhat more attractive in order to lower the average p value, thus reducing the skewness of the test.

A Step-by-Step Example of an Item Analysis

Table 12.1 displays eight items taken from a test recently administered to students in an undergraduate tests and measurements class. There were actually 74 items on the test and 35 students took the test. The values presented in Table 12.2 are based on all 74 items and 35 students, even though only eight items are displayed in the table. Remember we stated earlier that ideally we would want 5–10 test takers per item. In this case, we have a little more than two items per test taker. Obviously, the ratio of items to students leaves a lot to be desired. Thus, we must be cautious not to read too much into the statistics we obtained from our classical test theory item analysis. It would be foolish, however, to simply ignore valuable test item analysis statistics because we failed to reach some ideal ratio of test takers to items. Basically, we have to work with whatever we have. Welcome to the reality of classroom testing.

Table 12.1   Example of Undergraduate Tests and Measurements Exam Questions

---

1. Testing is to assessment as _____ is to _____.
   A. blood test:physical exam   C. mechanic:automobile
   B. blood test:X-ray   D. selection:placement

2. In everyday practice, responsibility for appropriate test administration, scoring, and interpretation lies with
   A. test users.   C. elected representatives.
   B. test developers.   D. test publishers.

3. Which of the following best describes norms?
   A. They give meaning to a behavior sample.
   B. They provide a parallel form for comparison.
   C. They indicate whether a test is reliable.
   D. They tell whether a distribution of scores is normally distributed.

4. Which is true of a psychologist who is relying on a single test score to make an important decision about an individual? The psychologist is
   A. acting responsibly if the test is reliable and valid for the purpose for which it is being used.
   B. violating a basic guideline in psychological assessment.
   C. utilizing a case-study approach to assessment.
   D. acting in a perfectly legal and ethical way.

5. Of the following, which best characterizes what "validity" refers to?
   A. How a test is used   C. How a scale is scaled
   B. How a test is scored   D. How a test is normed

6. Much of 19th-century psychological measurement focused on
   A. intelligence.   C. sensory abilities.
   B. ethics and values.   D. personality traits.

7. Which of the following is the most important reason why translating a test into another language is not recommended?
   A. It can be extremely costly.
   B. It can be extremely time-consuming.
   C. Meanings and difficulty levels of the items may change.
   D. Precise translation is never possible.

8. Test-retest reliability estimates would be least appropriate for
   A. intelligence tests.
   B. tests that measure moment-to-moment mood.
   C. academic achievement tests on topics such as ancient history.
   D. tests that measure art aptitude.

Table 12.2   Item Analysis Results for Example Tests and Measurements
Questions

	Item Statistics					Alternative Statistics				
								Endorsing		
Seq. No.	Scale Item	Prop. Correct	Disc. Index	Point Biser.	Alt.	Prop. Total	Low	High	Point Biser.	Key
1	0–1	.51	.48	.38	A	.51	.22	.70	.38	*
					B	.03	.00	.00	−.08	
					C	.17	.22	.00	−.26	
					D	.29	.56	.30	−.17	
					Other	.00	.00	.00		
2	0–3	.86	.44	.52	A	.86	.56	1.00	.52	*
					B	.14	.44	.00	−.52	
					C	.00	.00	.00		
					D	.00	.00	.00		
					Other	.00	.00	.00		
3	0–4	.14	−.12	.00	A	.14	.22	.10	.00	*
					B	.80	.67	.90	.09	?
		CHECK THE KEY			C	.03	.00	.00	.05	
		A was specified, but B works better			D	.03	.11	.00	−.26	
					Other	.00	.00	.00		
4	0–9	.54	.47	.36	A	.46	.67	.20	−.36	
					B	.54	.33	.80	.36	*
					C	.00	.00	.00		
					D	.00	.00	.00		
					Other	.00	.00	.00		
5	0–11	.71	.44	.42	A	.71	.56	1.00	.42	*
					B	.06	.00	.00	−.08	
					C	.11	.33	.00	−.37	

	Item Statistics					Alternative Statistics				
							Endorsing			
Seq. No.	Scale Item	Prop. Correct	Disc. Index	Point Biser.	Alt.	Prop. Total	Low	High	Point Biser.	Key
					D	.11	.11	.00	−.17	
					Other	.00	.00	.00		
6	0–13	.23	.50	.56	A	.49	.78	.40	−.31	
					B	.03	.11	.00	−.20	
					C	.23	.00	.50	.56	*
					D	.26	.11	.10	−.11	
					Other	.00	.00	.00		
7	0–22	.69	−.09	−.11	A	.00	.00	.00		
					B	.00	.00	.00		
	CHECK THE KEY				C	.69	.89	.80	−.11	*
	C was specified, but D works better				D	.31	.11	.20	.11	?
					Other	.00	.00	.00		
8	0–48	.89	.33	.44	A	.06	.22	.00	−.43	
					B	.89	.67	1.00	.44	*
					C	.03	.00	.00	−.08	
					D	.03	.11	.00	−.18	
					Other	.00	.00	.00		

Test statistics:

Number of items	74	Median	40.00
Number of examinees	35	Alpha	0.81
Mean	39.74	SEM	3.75
Variance	72.48	Mean P	0.54
Standard deviation	8.51	Mean item-total	0.26
Skew	0.27	Mean biserial	0.35
Kurtosis	−0.35	Max score (low)	34
Minimum	24.00	N (low group)	9
Maximum	59.00	Min score (high)	44
		N (high group)	10

Table 12.2 displays the item analysis statistics generated from a commercially available item analysis program (ITEMAN for Windows, Version 3.5, Assessment Systems Corp.; see Web Reference 12.5). The ITE-MAN program provides several important pieces of item analysis information. In the first column is the "sequence number." This number matches the number of the corresponding question in Table 12.1. In the second column is the "scale-item" number. This feature allows you to look at subtests within the overall test. Here we did not have any subtests, so the first number for all items is zero. The number after the hyphen is the number of the question from the original test. For example, the fifth question listed here was actually question 11 on the complete 74-item version of the test.

The next three columns provide the item analysis statistics for the keyed response. Column 3 displays the item difficulty statistic of proportion correct. For example, for sequence item 1, just over half the students answered this item correctly, while 54% answered question 4 correctly. While these p values are ideal from a variability standpoint, they are at the lower end of the acceptable range for a classroom test for two reasons. First, these items are from a four-option multiple-choice test, so by answering randomly the student has a 25% chance of getting the item correct just by chance. Therefore, we would expect p values even for ideal items to be somewhat higher than 50%. Second, this is more of a criterion-referenced test than a norm-referenced test. Therefore, we would expect (hope) that the typical p value would be higher than 50%, indicating that a larger portion of the students have learned the material.

Items 2, 5, 7, and 8 have p values between .69 and .89. These are much more typical of the level of difficulty instructors should strive for in creating classroom tests. However, we still need to examine the item discrimination indexes before we can put our stamp of approval on these items. At the other end of the difficulty continuum, only 14% of students answered question 3 correctly, while only 23% answered question 6 correctly. Both of these items need to be examined carefully to determine how they may be revised or edited to make them easier. Again, because the focus is more on criterion-referenced than norm-referenced standards, we may also investigate whether the item was covered in class or somehow caused confusion among the students. Thus, based on the item difficulty statistics, at least initially, it appears that items 2, 5, 7, and 8 are acceptable. Items 1 and 4 are somewhat low, but may serve to balance out some other easier items (with 90% plus p values) on the test. Items 3 and 6 will command the bulk of our attention as they have extremely low p values.

Column 4 displays the discrimination index: Disc. Index $= P_{\text{High}} - P_{\text{Low}}$, where P_{High} is the percentage of students in the highest 27% of the score distribution who answered the item correctly and P_{Low} is the percentage of students in the lowest 27% of the score distribution who answered the item correctly. Hence, the discrimination index values in Table 12.2 represent the difference in p values for these two groups. As noted earlier, we want a discrimination index that is moderate to large and positive. All but items 3 and 7 appear to meet these criteria. Hence, we would want to look at items 3 and 7 more closely. In fact, note that the ITEMAN program prints a message to "CHECK THE KEY __ is specified - __ works better," indicating that an alternative option has a higher discrimination index, point-biserial value, or both than the keyed option. Remember that a disadvantage of the discrimination index is that it ignores the middle 46% of the distribution of test scores. Thus, we should also examine column 5, which displays the point-biserial correlation coefficient. Again, we are seeking moderate to large, as well as positive, point-biserial correlation coefficients. In this case, the point-biserial correlation appears to confirm the results of the discrimination index. That is, items 3 and 7 should be examined more closely, given that the former has a point-biserial correlation coefficient of zero and the latter is negative. Thus, the item difficulty statistics lead us to focus on items 3 and 6, while the item discrimination indexes suggest we focus on items 3 and 7. In order to do so, we must next look at the response alternative statistics in columns 7 through 10.

First, let us turn our attention to the most offending question, item 3. It has an extremely low p value (.14) and a small negative discrimination index. Inspecting column 7, we see that most individuals (80%) chose option B (option A was the keyed response). Looking at Table 12.1, item 3 dealt with the issue of norms. Thinking back as the instructor, we might remember that we talked about z scores and norms on the same day. As a result, students may have assumed that, similar to z scores, norms "provide a parallel form for comparison." Is this question salvageable? Possibly, by simply replacing option B with another option, for example, "They provide evidence of content validity," fewer individuals will choose option B in favor of the keyed response, option A.

The second troublesome item is item 6. The p value for item 6 was very low (.23); however, the two discrimination indexes are quite favorable. What is going on here? It appears option A (which 49% of students chose) was too attractive. Looking at Table 12.1, we see this item dealt with the topic of historical issues in measurement. We may find out from asking students afterward that they chose option A because many of them read the question too quickly and when they read "19th century" they thought 1900s instead of 1800s. Therefore, replacing the "19th century" with "1800s" in the stem of the question may well be all that is needed to raise the p value for this item.

The third item of concern is item 7. Although almost 70% of the students answered this item correctly, those students actually did worse on the test overall (i.e., they had a negative item-total correlation). Looking at the alternative statistics in Table 12.2, we see that no students chose alternative A or B. The keyed answer was option C, which 69% chose, while 31% selected option D. In addition, those who did choose option D also did better on the test overall. Looking at Table 12.1, we see that this item dealt with translating a test into another language. It may have been that the stem uses the term "translating" and option D uses "translation." Hence, changing option D to something such as "It is difficult to accommodate different dialects in other languages" may make it less attractive to the high scorers. In addition, you would want to make options A and B at least a little more attractive. Removing the term "extremely" from options A and B would make them somewhat more attractive. A student who is "test-wise" will know that terms such as "extremely" are more likely to be used in distracters than in keyed alternatives.

Finally, it was noted earlier that it is wise to look at not only individual item statistics but also statistics for the entire test. Several informative statistics were obtained for this 74-item test, and they can be found at the end of Table 12.2. First, the average p value was .54. That is probably too low a figure for a classroom examination. However, from a practical standpoint, we would rather have a test that is a little too hard than too easy. It would be difficult to justify taking points away from the test takers under the rationale that the test was too easy, but few test takers will complain about a hard test having bonus points added. The mean point-biserial correlation of .26, while a little low, is positive. The alpha reliability for the test was .81. While this is clearly an acceptable level of reliability, this may be due to simply having 74 items on the test. It is unlikely that the 74 items represent a single trait or dimension. The distribution of test scores was also positively skewed (skew = .27) and somewhat flat (i.e., platykurtic, kurtosis = −.34). Most classroom tests tend to have a slight negative skew or close-to-normal distribution. Thus, the positive skew in this sample is yet another indication that the test is probably too hard and the items with lower p values are in need of revision.

Concluding Comments

We need to examine both item difficulty and item discrimination indexes to determine whether we should keep an item as is, revise it, or throw it out. In addition, examining the overall test statistics will provide guidance on which items to focus our efforts. In order to have confidence in our statistics, we need to have adequate sample sizes, both in terms of absolute numbers (e.g., more than 25 subjects) and in terms of subject-to-item ratios (ideally at least 5–10 subjects per item). In most instances, at least minor revisions will be required to the stem, the alternative responses, or both. For example, your item difficulty index might be .70 and your item discrimination index .50. Both would indicate a useful item. However, inspection of the item analysis might indicate that none of the test takers chose option B. Hence, you would want to revise or replace option B to make it more attractive, especially to those with little knowledge of the concept being examined. Thus, every attempt should be made to revise an item before it is tossed out. In the end, you should have very few instances where an entire item needs to be thrown out. Instead, a few well-placed revisions (sometimes a single word change) can go a long way in improving the quality and usefulness of future uses of the revised items.

Practical Questions

1. What is the difference between an item difficulty index and an item discrimination index?

2. How do you know whether to calculate the discrimination index (which contrasts extreme groups), the biserial correlation, or the point-biserial correlation coefficient as your item discrimination statistic?

3. How do you decide which external criterion to use when computing an item-criterion index?

4. Is there ever a time when a .25 p value is good? How about a 1.00 p value?

5. Will your criteria for evaluating your item difficulty and discrimination indexes change if a test is norm referenced versus criterion referenced?

6. Will your criteria for evaluating your item difficulty and discrimination indexes change as the format of the item changes (e.g., true-false; three-, four-, or five-option multiple choice; Likert scaling)?

7. Oftentimes in a classroom environment, you might have more students (subjects) than you have items. Does this pose a problem for interpreting your item analysis statistics?

8. What corrections, if any, might you make to items 1, 2, 4, 5, and 8 in Table 12.2?

Case Studies

CASE STUDY 12.1: ITEM ANALYSIS IN AN APPLIED SETTING

Andrew, a third-year graduate student, was enrolled in a PhD program in quantitative psychology. He had recently obtained a highly competitive summer internship with a Fortune 500 company in its employment testing section. As one of his first assignments, his new supervisor asked Andrew to review the item analysis statistics for a short 25-item timed test of **general mental ability (GMA)** that the company administers to thousands of job candidates every year. Test scoring is conducted and processed within four regional centers (East, South, West, and Midwest). Therefore, before combining all the regions, Andrew decided to first examine the item statistics within each region by each of five broad job classifications (i.e., administrative/professional, clerical, skilled craft, semiskilled, and unskilled/laborer).

After completing and reviewing the initial set of item analyses, Andrew noticed an interesting pattern. The first 10 items had very good item analysis statistics for the clerical and semiskilled positions, but not very good statistics for the other job classifications. In particular, he noticed an extremely high percentage (more than 98%) of the administrative/professional candidates and 88% of the skilled craft candidates answered the first 10 questions correctly, while very few (less than 10%) of the unskilled/laborer job candidates answered the first 10 questions correctly. As a result, the item discrimination indexes for these job classes were near zero. For items 11–19, the item analysis statistics were still unfavorable for the administrative/professional candidates and unskilled/laborer candidates, but were much more favorable for the skilled craft candidates. Finally, for items 20–25 the item analysis statistics were favorable for the administrative/professional candidates, but very few of the other candidates were even able to attempt these items. As a result, their p values were extremely low and their item discrimination indexes were near zero. To top it all off, this pattern seemed to hold for three of the four regions, but the midwestern region seemed to be getting very different results. In particular, the unskilled and semiskilled job candidates appeared to be doing significantly better on the early items than their counterparts in other regions of the country. Somewhat perplexed, it seemed time for Andrew to discuss things with his new supervisor.

Questions to Ponder

1. What might explain the pattern of results that Andrew observed for the different job classifications?

2. Given the differing results by job classification, should the same test still be used for all the job classifications? What key issues should Andrew consider?

3. What might be unique about the unskilled and semiskilled job candidates in the Midwest as compared to their counterparts in the West, South, and East?

4. What do you think would have happened if Andrew had not separated the data by job classification and region?

5. Andrew focused primarily on the difficulty index. What other item-level statistics should he compute? What unique information would they provide?

CASE STUDY 12.2: ITEM ANALYSIS FOR AN OUTCOMES ASSESSMENT MEASURE

Linda, a second-year master's student, had agreed to help out the department of psychology with its outcomes assessment process. In exchange for her work on the project, the department chair agreed to let Linda use some of the data collected for the outcomes assessment project for her master's thesis. Linda had decided to investigate whether students' attitudes toward statistics were related to performance on a comprehensive statistics exam. Therefore, Linda needed to construct a 100-item statistical knowledge test. She gathered old exams, study guides, and items from professors in the department who taught undergraduate and graduate statistics classes. She went through piles of statistics books, study guides, and test banks of test items to draft items for the test. Some professors had even agreed to write items for her.

After several months of pulling together items and going through multiple revisions from the department outcomes assessment committee, Linda was finally ready to pilot test her assessment device. She was able to get 21 current graduate students in the program to take her 100-item statistics knowledge test. Some of the items seemed to be working for her, while others clearly needed revision. Table 12.3 displays the item analysis results for the first five items from her assessment device. Answer the questions that follow, based on the item analysis results reported in Table 12.3.

Table 12.3   Item Analysis Results for the First Five Items of a 100-Item Statistics Knowledge Test

	Item Statistics				Alternative Statistics			
Quest. No.	Prop. Correct	Biser.	Point Biser.	Alt.	Prop. Endorsing	Biser.	Point Biser.	Key
1	0.381	0.238	0.187	A	0.238	−0.106	−0.077	
				B	0.143	−0.227	−0.146	
				C	0.381	0.238	0.187	*
				D	0.238	−0.022	−0.016	
2	0.667	0.353	0.272	A	0.238	−0.615	−0.447	
				B	0.000	0.000	0.000	
				C	0.095	0.366	0.211	
				D	0.667	0.353	0.272	*
3	0.143	0.238	0.153	A	0.810	−0.392	−0.271	
				B	0.143	0.238	0.153	*
				C	0.048	0.533	0.248	
				D	0.000	0.000	0.000	
4	0.857	0.614	0.396	A	0.857	0.614	0.396	*
				B	0.095	−0.770	−0.444	
				C	0.048	−0.084	−0.039	
				D	0.000	0.000	0.000	
5	1.000	0.000	0.000	A	0.000	0.000	0.000	
				B	1.000	0.000	0.000	*
				C	0.000	0.000	0.000	
				D	0.000	0.000	0.000	

Questions to Ponder

1. How did students seem to do based on the five items presented in Table 12.3?

2. Based only on the information presented in Table 12.3, what revisions should Linda make to each item?

3. Do you have a concern that Linda had 100 items but only 21 subjects? What problems might this cause in interpreting her item analysis results?

4. Why do you think 0.000s are printed for all the entries in item 5, as well as for some options in the other items?

5. Which item would you say is the "best" item? Why?

6. Are there any items Linda should simply just throw out (i.e., they are just not worth spending the time revising)?

7. What additional information would be helpful in evaluating the test items?

8. Is there a problem with using graduate students during the pilot-testing phase if the test will eventually be used as an outcomes assessment device for undergraduates?

Exercises

EXERCISE 12.1: ITEM ANALYSIS
OF AN ORGANIZATIONAL BEHAVIOR TEST

OBJECTIVE: To practice evaluating items using item analysis statistics.

Selected items (13 to be exact) from a 50-item multiple-choice test given to an undergraduate organizational behavior class are presented in Table 12.4. Look through the test to get a sense of the item types and content and then proceed to the actual assignment outlined below. (*Note:* You will need to have access to the Internet to complete this assignment.)

Assignment

Part 1—Working alone or in small teams, perform an item analysis of the data at the end of Table 12.4. You will do this by going to Web Reference 12.4. Once at the Web site, enter the data at the end of Table 12.4 in the boxes as appropriate and select "compute" (i.e., run the program). The results will come up on the screen. You should have access to a printer at this point because you cannot "save" the output (at least as far as we can tell). Once the output is printed, you are ready for Part 2 (the fun stuff).

Part 2—Working alone, interpret the results of your item analysis. That is, go through each item and see what the statistics (e.g., proportion correct, biserial correlations, and point-biserial correlations) look like for each item and each response option for each item. Discuss if the item is "okay" (i.e., no recommended changes) or if changes are needed to improve the item. As you might guess, there should be very few (if any) questions that are without room for improvement. Perhaps a single option needs to be reworded or the stem needs wording changes. Perhaps the item as a whole is just too complex for an undergraduate class and should be thrown out. However, this option should be extremely rare given how difficult it is to come up with sufficient questions. Therefore, what you need to do is (1) discuss what should be done to improve the item/question (e.g., reword the stem, reword a distracter) and (2) discuss why you think that should be done, based on the information from the item analysis and your general understanding of good item writing and editing principles discussed in Module 11. Please annotate your item analysis printout directly and hand it in with your critique of the test (one to two pages).

EXERCISE 12.2: ITEM ANALYSIS OF A TESTS AND MEASUREMENTS CLASS EXAMINATION

OBJECTIVE: To re-create the item analysis results found in the step-by-step example in the module overview.

Working alone or in small teams, perform an item analysis of the data at the end of Table 12.5. The data from Table 12.5 are also available at www.sagepub.com/shultzdatasets or from your instructor, allowing you to cut and paste the data into the appropriate box at the Web site listed under Web Reference 12.4. Once at the Web site, enter (or cut and paste)

Table 12.4   Questions and Data for Exercise 12.1

Organizational Behavior Questions

General Instructions: There are two parts to Exam I. In part I, there are 50 multiple-choice questions worth 1 point each (50 points, part I). In part II, you will complete five of six short-answer essay questions worth 5 points each (25 points, part II). Therefore, work at a steady pace and do not spend too much time on any given question.

Multiple-Choice Instructions: *Read each question carefully. Mark your answers on the answer sheet provided.*
Name: _____   Date: _____

1. Joe doesn't like his job very much, but does it quite well. By contrast, Sam likes his job a great deal, but doesn't do it very well. To help explain the underlying reasons why this might occur at the individual level of analysis, an OB scientist would be most likely to conduct research that
   A. attempts to prove Theory X and disprove Theory Y.
   *B. measures Joe and Sam's individual behavior and attitudes.
   C. examines the interpersonal dynamics between Joe and Sam.
   D. focuses on the structure of the organization within which Joe and Sam work.

2. You are working as an assistant to an OB scientist on a research project. She is trying to find out when people are motivated by pay and when they are motivated by recognition. By examining the connection between motivation and incentives, she appears to be using which one of the following approaches in her research?
   A. the open-systems approach
   B. the human resources approach
   C. the Hawthorne approach
   *D. the contingency approach

3. A proponent of scientific management is most likely to be interested in
   A. treating people in a humane way.
   B. using the contingency approach.
   C. conceiving of people using an open-systems perspective.
   *D. learning ways to improve productivity on the job.

4. The Hawthorne studies were important because they
   A. provided support for scientific management.
   B. demonstrated that human behavior in organizational settings is highly predictable.
   *C. called attention to the complex factors that influence behavior in organizational settings.
   D. established that the study of human behavior was not particularly relevant in organizational settings.

(Continued)

Table 12.4 (Continued)

(9) 5. Suppose an OB scientist wants to learn how the employees of a certain company responded to a massive downsizing plan that was recently implemented. To find out, he or she conducts careful interviews with many of the different people involved and then summarizes the results in a narrative account describing all the details. This scientist appears to be using
   A. participant observation.
   *B. the case method.
   C. survey research.
   D. the experimental method.

(10) 6. Once we form a favorable impression of someone, we tend to see that person in favorable terms. This is known as
   A. the similar-to-me effect.
   B. the attribution effect.
   *C. the halo effect.
   D. a stereotype.

(14) 7. Suppose an Army major inspects his troops' barracks on the average of once a month, although at no predetermined times. The major could be said to be using a _____ schedule of reinforcement.
   A. fixed ratio
   *B. variable interval
   C. fixed interval
   D. variable ratio

(22) 8. Personality exerts strong influences on behavior in
   A. personal life more than in organizations.
   B. organizations more than in personal life.
   C. situations in which external forces encourage certain actions.
   *D. situations where external pressures to behave a certain way are not strong.

(25) 9. Compared to Maslow's need hierarchy theory, Alderfer's ERG theory
   *A. is less restrictive.
   B. is more poorly supported by existing research.
   C. proposes a higher number of needs.
   D. all of the above.

(27) 10. To help strengthen employee commitment to goals, an organization should
   A. provide feedback about performance.
   B. set very difficult goals.
   *C. involve employees in the goal-setting process.
   D. provide monetary incentives along with specific goals.

(33) 11. Which of the following is *not* a technique typically used to assess people's satisfaction with their jobs?
    A. critical incidents
    B. interviews
    C. questionnaires
    *D. participant observation

(34) 12. According to Herzberg's two-factor motivator-hygiene theory, which of the following factors is most likely to be associated with job satisfaction?
    A. high pay
    B. pleasant working conditions
    *C. opportunities for promotion
    D. social relations with coworkers

(45) 13. We see a coworker totally screw up a major project. If we perceive that this is an unusual (unstable) behavior and that this event was due to external pressures (an external locus of control), we are likely to attribute our colleague's actions to
    *A. bad luck.
    B. a difficult task.
    C. a lack of effort.
    D. a lack of ability

ANSWER KEY: 2443232413431

NUMBER OF ITEMS: 13

RESPONSES OFFSET BY: 3

NUMBER OF ALTERNATIVES: 4444444444444

RESPONSES:
01 2413334313144
02 4443212333411
03 2443334313144
04 4143344314123
05 2443331413431
06 2223234431131
07 4213133413422
08 4243332411122
09 2343233211133
10 2443332413432
11 2443234413431
12 2243322313432

NOTE: Column 3 should be left blank for all subjects. Once the data are entered at the Web site, go to the top left of the page and click on "compute." The resulting data output should look similar to Table 12.3.

the data in Table 12.5 in the boxes as appropriate and select "compute" (i.e., run the program). The results will come up on the screen. Next, see if you get the same results as were presented in Table 12.2.

Table 12.5   Data for Step-by-Step Example

```
Key AAAAAABCBCAACCBDCDDDBCCBBCAABBBDBCCBAACCBACABBABDBCDBBBBCBCAABAAACBADCCBDC
Number of items: 74
Items offset by: 03
No. of Alts
4444444444444444444444444444444444444444444444444444444444444444444444444444
01 DABBCAADADAAACBAADDDACABABBBBDBBCDAAAACDACACADADBBCCCBBAAABAAABCAACDCAABBDD
02 CAAAAABDACADDDBACBDCBCAEBAAACBADBCDADACDBDAADBCBDACDABAACABAABDAACCDABBBDD
03 CDABAAACBCAAACCDCDDCBDDDBADABBBDDAADBAACBCCABBBBDCDDBBDCDCCAABBBACBCABBBDD
04 DDAAABBDACAAACBACDCAADDCDADABBBDBAAABBCABAAACADBDADDABDBCBAADBACDADADABDDD
05 A-AAAAACBDDACCBACDCDACDDACAADDDDDADABBCABADABBDBDACADABBDDAAABADACDDACCBDD
06 ADABBABDBCACACBACDCDADBDDADABABDDDCAAACDABAACBDBADCDBBABCCBAABBAACCDBCCDDD
07 ADABAAACBDAADCBBCDDDACCBBCAABBAADDABABCCCCAABBDBAADADBBBCBCAABDDACBDBDBBDD
08 BCABBABAACBCDACCCDDDBCBDCCCABBCBBABAAAADBACABBDBDACDDBDBDCBBDBABBCBABCBDDD
09 ADABACADACABDCBACDCAACBDBCABBBBDBCBAAAACBACABBABACCABBCACDAAABBAACCDDACDCD
10 CAABCADCBDCAACDDCDDCACDCDDBAAADDBAAABACABCCADBADAADCABACBAAADBAAACDCBCCACD
11 AAABAADCACABCCCBCCCDBDBBCCCABBCBBDCAADCCBACADBABDADCBBDBBDDAADBAABBACCBDDC
12 CAABAAABADABDABABBDDBCDDCAABBBBADACBBACABDAABBBCDACDBAAACDAAADBAACDBDCBDDC
13 ADABBABDACDAADBCBDCDBDBDBCAABCCDBAAACBACBABACBDBDCCAABABABDADBCAACACDBBDDD
14 AAABACBDADAAACCCDAABCBBCAAABBBDBCADDACCBACBBBDBDBDBABDBADBAABAAACBADABBCD
15 ACBBABDDACCAACBABDCDBCBDBDAABAAADBADAADCADBCCACDAADBDBCCBADBADDCBABDDCBBBDA
16 CCABAAABCBDBAACCDCDCCBDBDBCAABBBDBDCADACDACCADCCBAADDBCCBADDAADCAACACDCBDDD
17 ADABABBCBCACACBACBCCBCABCCABABCDDAAABCACBDAACBDBAABDBBBCACBAAABBACCAACBADD
18 DDAAAADDADCAACBACADDACBDDABBABACDADABACDDBAAABCBADBDDDBABCCBADBCABBBDCBBBDD
19 DAABBBABDBBCADCBACDDDADDDDCAABABDCDCDBACDCACACBDBDACDDBAACBBAABCBACBAAABDDD
20 ABABAABDBAAACCBDCDCCBCABCADABBBDBCADAACABAAABBABDACDBBBBCBAADBDBACBACBBBDD
21 ACBBAABAACACDBBACDDDBCCDDCAABBCDBAAADDCDABDADADBDDDADBDDCBBAABCAACBCACBABC
22 ACABACADBCAADCBBCDDDBCDDCAAABBCDDACACADCBBAADBDBDDDABBABCBBAABDBACBCDCBDDD
23 DAABAABCBCAAAABDCDCDBCDCAAABBCDBCDABACDDCAABBDBDDCDBBBACBBAABABDCBCDABBDD
24 AAABACDCACDACCBACDDDBDDDDBAABBAADDDAAACDBCAADBDBDBDDDBABCABADBAAACDDCCCDDD
25 DCABAAADBCAAACBBDDCDACDDCCAAABDDBADBDACDBACACBDBDCBBBDACCBAABAAACDADCCDDD
26 DABDAADDADDBDABACDCDACCCADBBDCBBBAADADCAAACADAABDCCDBCAADABCDAABBBDADCDBCD
27 DAABBABABCAAACBACDDCBDCDDDBABABCDADADACCBCDADBDBACDDDCABCDBAABDBACDDDCBDDD
28 DAAAABCBCAACCBDCDBDADCDCCAABBBBBCCBAACCAADABBABDACBBBBBCBBAABAAACBADCBADD
29 AAACACACBDAAABBACDCCACDBCAAABDBDBDAADACCAAAABBCBDACBBBAACBCADBCABCBDDCBDDD
30 AAABAAAABDAACCBACDCDACBDBCCABACDBCDABACDBACABBAACADDDDCDBCBCBCAABBAACBBBCCDDD
31 AAABAABABCAAACBACBDDACDBBCAABBBDBACBAACABDCADBABABCBBBBCDAAABBAACBADCCDDD
32 AAABAAAADBCAACCBBCADDBCCDDCAABBBADCAABACCBDDABBABDACDBBBBCDCBABCAACADDABDDD
33 CDBBACADBCAAADBADADCBCCDABBACADBDCBACDCCBDDACCCACBDDBAAADDADBDBBBCDACBBBD
34 DDABAABAADAABBCCCDDDACDDADDBAACDBACABDCDAABACCDBAADDDBBBCABADCDAACCDDABDDC
35 AAABAADAADAACCCDCDCACDDBAABBBCDBCCBAACCBACABBCBDBCDBBDBCDAAABABACBBBCCBDC
```

NOTE: Column 3 should be left blank for all subjects. Once the data are entered at the Web site, go to the top left of the page and click on "compute." The resulting data output should look similar to those provided in the module overview.

Internet Web Site References

12.1. http://pareonline.net/getvn.asp?v=4&n=10

This Web page presents an article by Jerard Kehoe titled "Basic Item Analysis for Multiple-Choice Tests," which provides suggestions for improving multiple-choice tests using basic item statistics.

12.2. http://www.ntlf.com/html/pi/9811/exams_1.htm

This Web page presents an article by Raymond M. Zurawski titled "Making the Most of Exams: Procedures for Item Analysis." Item difficulty and item discrimination are discussed.

12.3. http://www.msu.edu/dept/soweb/itanhand.html

This Web page, from Michigan State University's Scoring Office, provides a basic tutorial on the use of item analysis for improving academic tests.

12.4. http://www.hr-software.net/cgi/ItemAnalysis.cgi

This Web site allows you to enter raw test data and calculate item analysis statistics.

12.5. http://www.assess.com/Software/iteman.htm

This Web site provides a description of the ITEMAN classical test theory item analysis software. It also includes a downloadable demo version of the ITEMAN program.

Further Readings

Crocker, L. M., & Algina, J. (1986). *Introduction to classical and modern test theory* (pp. 311–338). Belmont, CA: Wadsworth.

Haladyna, T. M. (1999). *Developing and validating multiple-choice test items* (2nd ed.). Mahwah, NJ: Erlbaum.

Module 13

Scoring Tests

U p to this point in the book, we have focused on proper techniques for developing and evaluating tests. We have talked about establishing evidence for the reliability and validity of our tests. We have even talked about performing item analyses to evaluate individual items on a test. Essentially, we have been recommending you perform certain analyses to make sure you would have confidence in any decisions that resulted from use of the test. At some point, however, you will have to do something with the test. That is, as noted in Module 1, you are most likely administering the test to help you make an important decision. As a result, you will have to score the test and most likely set a cutoff or pass point for the test to decide who "passes" and who "fails." In the rest of this overview, we present several of the more common methods for scoring tests, thus allowing us to actually use our test data to help us make important, even life-altering, psychometrically sound decisions with confidence.

Berk (1986) presented a self-described "consumer's guide" to setting pass points on criterion-referenced tests. He presented a continuum from purely judgmental procedures to purely empirical procedures. At the purely judgmental end of the continuum are procedures that rely heavily on the use of opinions from subject matter experts (SMEs) such as the Angoff, Ebel, and Nedelsky methods of setting passing scores. These procedures are often used in setting **cutoff scores** for employment knowledge testing as well as professional licensing exams where those scoring above the cutoff score qualify for the job or appropriate license (see Web References 13.1–13.3 for an overview of these three judgmental procedures for setting cutoff scores).

Judgmental Methods

The most common judgmental method of setting passing scores is the Angoff method. The Angoff method of setting passing scores asks SMEs to determine the probability (0%–100%) of a "minimally competent person" (MCP) answering a given multiple-choice item correctly. These probabilities are averaged across SMEs for each item and then summed across all items to get the final cutoff score. For example, on a five-item test, several SMEs may assign probabilities of passing for the five items that average to .70, .75, .80, .85, and .90, respectively, for each of the five items. Summing these average probabilities across the five items gives us a cutoff score of four out of five (or 80%) for this example. Thus, one of the reasons for the popularity of the Angoff method is its simplicity.

For the Nedelsky method, each SME examines each multiple-choice question and decides which alternatives an MCP could eliminate (e.g., option D really isn't feasible). As a result, for a four-option (one correct response and three distracters) multiple-choice question, the only values possible are 25% if no distracters can be eliminated, 33% if one distracter can be eliminated, 50% if two distracters can be eliminated, or 100% if all three distracters can be eliminated. Again, these ratings (or judgments) are averaged across all SMEs for each question and then summed across items in order to set the pass point.

A third, more involved, method is the Ebel method. For the Ebel method, the SMEs set up a 3 × 4 table. Across the top of the table is the difficulty level of each item (easy, moderate, and difficult) and down the side is the relevance of each item (essential, important, acceptable, and questionable). Then, similar to the previous two methods, the SMEs determine the likelihood that an MCP would correctly answer items that fall within each of the 12 cells in the 3 × 4 table. For example, the minimally competent test taker should have a very high probability of answering an easy and essential item correctly, whereas such a person would have a very low probability of getting a questionable and difficult item correct. Once this classification table is complete, all items on the test are placed into one of the 12 cells in the 3 × 4 table. Then, the number of items in the cell is multiplied by the probability of answering the items in the cell correctly, and the totals for each cell are then summed across all 12 cells to establish the pass point. Note that when there are few items on the test, there may be some cells that have no items. In addition, from a content validity standpoint, we would hope to have more essential and important items than those rated merely as acceptable or, worse yet, questionable. Thus, the distribution of items across cells can vary dramatically from test to test.

A persistent problem with these three judgmental methods of setting cutoff scores is how the "minimally competent person" (MCP) is defined. While all the individuals performing the scoring are SMEs, they may not be using the same standard or have the same ideal person in mind when they think of an MCP. Maurer and Alexander (1992) provided some helpful hints on how to deal with this issue. For example, the SMEs could discuss, as a group, what constitutes an MCP and develop a common written description. SMEs would then have the written description to refer to when they make their independent ratings. In addition, if the MCP refers to someone who is applying for a certain job or licensing in a particular occupation, detailed job analysis information could be used to develop the written MCP description.

Once the MCP is adequately defined, frame-of-reference training could be provided to SMEs. Such training allows SMEs to rate a series of items that have predetermined standards in terms of the probability of success for MCPs on such items. A facilitator can then discuss any discrepancies that occur between the sample ratings provided by SMEs during the training and the predetermined standards. Alternatively, SMEs could be provided with actual item analysis statistics (e.g., p values) to give them a sense of the difficulty of the item for all test takers. This would then provide some context for providing item ratings with regard to the MCPs. No matter which procedures are used to improve the definition and ratings of MCPs, it must be remembered that SMEs are selected because they are subject matter experts. Thus, we expect them to share and use their respective expertise when making their ratings. Therefore, we must be careful not to be too prescriptive in the rating process provided to SMEs. Hopefully, we have selected a diverse group of SMEs in terms of sex, age, race, experience, specialty, geographical location, and other relevant characteristics. As such, differences in the conceptualization of the MCP may be inevitable and even desirable, to some extent.

Maurer and Alexander (1992) also suggested adding several procedural and psychometric techniques to the standard judgmental methods, thus allowing one to assess the quality of the ratings provided by SMEs. A procedural technique would be the inclusion of bogus items in the test. These might include items that could easily be answered by all respondents or by none at all. Thus, the SMEs who rated such items with other than 0% and 100%, respectively, may be providing questionable responses for other items as well.

An example psychometric technique to assess the quality of SME ratings would include identifying idiosyncratic raters by looking at rater-total correlations, which are analogous to the item-total correlations discussed in Module 12. Such correlations will allow you to identify SMEs whose ratings are out of line with the other SMEs. Of course, such correlations do not tell us why the aberrant SMEs' ratings are out of line with those of the other SMEs. It could be due to a variety of factors, including flawed reasoning, inattentiveness, or a host of other reasons. The question, of course, becomes what to do with such aberrant ratings. Should they be deleted? Given less weight? Maurer and Alexander (1992) suggested other, more advanced and complicated psychometric techniques, such as item response theory and **generalizability theory,** to assess the quality of SME ratings. Please consult their paper for a complete discussion of these and other similar techniques for improving and evaluating Angoff ratings in particular.

Judgmental/Empirical Methods

The preceding methods for setting pass points rely entirely on the independent judgment of SMEs. That is, with the Angoff, Nedelsky, and Ebel methods, the SMEs typically make their respective ratings independently, and their results are simply averaged. Thus, each SME does not have access or knowledge of the other SMEs' ratings. Other methods, however, such as the Delphi technique, use informed judgments. That is, each SME makes his or her initial independent ratings, but then a moderator summarizes the initial ratings and these data are then shared with all SMEs (usually only summary data with no individual SME names attached). Each SME is then allowed to make changes to his or her ratings based on the summary data provided by the moderator. No one *has* to change his or her ratings, however; they are simply afforded the opportunity to do so. In some instances, there may be several rounds of ratings and summary data before ratings are finalized.

You may be thinking, couldn't you accomplish the same thing by simply letting the SMEs talk about their ratings? Why go through such a potentially time-consuming and arduous process? Those of you who have taken a social psychology class probably already know the answer to this question, as it has to do with group dynamics. Not all group members, particularly new or younger group members, may feel comfortable disagreeing in public with other "more senior" SMEs. Thus, having a moderator and allowing for "anonymous" data feedback can be a good way to counteract certain group dynamics while still allowing SMEs to have feedback on the group's ratings.

Empirical/Judgmental Methods

While empirical/judgmental methods are more "data driven" than the preceding methods, purely empirical methods for setting cutoff scores are relatively rare. Some test users have applied rules of thumb such as setting the pass point 1 standard deviation below the mean for the entire group, but these can be very difficult to justify in court. An example that combines empirical data with SME judgments is the contrasting groups method. In this method, SMEs identify two groups of individuals (e.g., proficient versus nonproficient; successful versus unsuccessful; masters versus nonmasters). You then plot the distribution of scores for the two groups and set the cut-off score where the two distributions intersect (see Figure 13.1). The advantage of this method is that it equalizes the chance of making a false positive and a false negative decision. That is, once you set a pass point, you run the risk of mistakenly classifying someone as "passing" (false positive) or mistakenly classifying someone as "failing" (false negative). The contrasting groups method of setting pass points typically equalizes both errors.

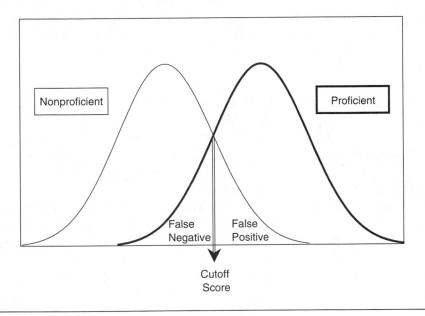

Figure 13.1   Setting Pass Points With Contrasting Groups

However, there may be occasions when it is important to minimize one form of error over the other. For example, when selecting for positions that pose a substantial potential risk to the public, such as nuclear power plant operators or air traffic controllers, we tend to minimize false positives (hiring unqualified candidates) at the risk of increasing false negatives (not hiring potentially qualified candidates). Thus, the cutoff score in Figure 13.1 would be moved to the right in order to minimize the number of false positives, but, of course, resulting in an increasing number of false-negative decisions. As you might have guessed, your data will most likely not be as "clear cut" as those depicted in Figure 13.1. For example, the proficient and nonproficient groups might substantially (or completely) overlap. As a result, it may be difficult to set a cutoff score using the contrasting groups method. In such cases, other procedures may be needed to establish a passing score.

Subgroup Norming and Banding

Before the 1991 Civil Rights Act (CRA), it was fairly common to have different norms (or cutoff scores) for different groups. For example, a municipality may have established that an applicant had to score at the 85th percentile on a physical strength test to be hired as a firefighter. However, that was not the 85th percentile for the entire applicant pool; rather, it was within a given subgroup. Therefore, if you were a man, the 85th percentile may have translated to a raw score of 90 out of 100. The 85th percentile for a woman, however, may have equated to a raw score of 80 out of 100. Thus, while both male and female firefighter applicants had to score at the same percentile within their respective subgroup, those cutoff scores actually equated to different raw scores. This was done in order to reduce the **adverse impact** of the test on women. The 1991 CRA, however, bans the use of **subgroup norming.** Instead, everyone must be judged on the same absolute standard. Brown (1994), Gottfredson (1994), and Sackett and Wilk (1994) provided some interesting discussion on this controversial topic.

A second procedure sometimes used to deal with subgroup differences in the test is to set up "bands" of scores. For example, all scores are rank ordered from highest to lowest and bandwidths are typically established using some psychometric (e.g., two standard errors of measurement) or logical (e.g., every five points) rationale. With fixed bands, the band must be exhausted before one moves on to the next band. For example, if the band goes from 96 to 100 (a bandwidth of 5) and there are seven people in that band, all seven individuals must be selected or disqualified before you can select an individual with a score less than 96. Assume we have the same scenario but now are using sliding bands. The person with a score of 100 is chosen and so the next highest score is 98. The band would slide down and now range from 94 to 98. The advantage of using either **banding** method is that it allows you to take "other things" into consideration for individuals within a given band. However, this issue, similar to within-group norming, has been controversial on psychometric, legal, and ethical grounds (see Web Reference 13.6).

Campion et al. (2001) provided a nice summary of some of the more salient issues involved in using banding as an alternative to setting a single pass point, particularly with regard to personnel selection. In particular, they addressed issues such as how wide the bandwidths should be, the psychometric and practical rationales for establishing bands and legal issues with regard to the use of banding, as well as practical issues on whether and how to use banding. Their commentary, which includes the perspectives of advocates, opponents, and neutral observers, appears to reach a consensus that banding can serve legitimate organizational purposes of allowing other factors, such as diversity issues, to be incorporated into the decisions that result from the use of tests. However, there is still disagreement on the legitimacy of using psychometric rationales for establishing bands and on the potential legal implications of using bands. All the commentators appear to agree that additional research is needed that compares the actual outcomes of using banding with the outcomes that would be obtained from other procedures such as strict top-down selection or setting a single pass point (which, in a sense, is a banding procedure that has only two bands: pass and fail).

A Step-by-Step Example of Setting Cutoff Scores

In the step-by-step example provided in Module 12, we looked at the abridged results from a 74-item multiple-choice exam used in a tests and measurements class. Eight items were selected as examples for detailed psychometric examination. Assume a local private-sector employer that was interested in hiring an intern who had a specialization in test development and administration contacted us. The company has asked us to provide the names of at least five "technically qualified" candidates from whom they will make a selection decision. Thus, it will be up to us to determine who would be a "minimally competent person" (MCP) in this instance. Because the position requires technical knowledge regarding developing and administering both psychological and knowledge tests, we could use the 74-item tests and measurements exam, assuming it meets our standards for reliability and validity. Thus, we would need to administer the test and then identify those students who would be considered MCPs.

We could use one of the judgmental methods, such as the Angoff, Nedelsky, or Ebel method, for establishing the cutoff score. For these procedures, we would need to assemble a group of SMEs to provide ratings for all 74 items. How many SMEs do we need? As we discussed in Module 5 on reliability, other things being equal, the inter-rater reliability will increase the more raters we have. "More is better" is not much guidance, however. In this instance, three to five raters may be sufficient given the nature of the project. In practical terms, we may be lucky to get just one other person to provide ratings. Hopefully, at least some diversity (in terms of both demographics and technical competence) will be evident in however many raters we end up using. We should also incorporate some of the suggestions of Maurer and Alexander (1992) that we discussed previously such as providing the SMEs with feedback and developing an agreed-upon single definition of the MCP. We may also want to provide raters with frame-of-reference training so that they have some practice providing such ratings. Such training also provides the SMEs with immediate feedback on how they are performing in the rating task. After the ratings are complete, we would also want to perform rater-total correlations to identify aberrant SMEs and potentially eliminate their responses. This all assumes, of course, that we have more than two SMEs.

Alternatively, we could use an empirical procedure such as the contrasting groups method discussed earlier to set the pass point. Here we would have to identify "proficient" and "nonproficient" students in order to set the cutoff score. We could have SMEs identify each student as proficient or nonproficient; however, from a practical standpoint, that may be difficult. Alternatively, we could use some other standard to distinguish students on proficiency. In this case, we may choose to use the standard that those students who received a B or higher in the class were deemed proficient, while those who received a B⁻ or lower were deemed nonproficient. Figure 13.2 displays the actual data from a class from which we had complete data on 33 students; one student dropped out before she received her final grade, so she could not be classified on proficiency. As we warned earlier, "real data" (such as the data in Figure 13.2) will not be as straightforward as the ideal data shown in Figure 13.1.

We said earlier to set the cutoff score where the two distributions (proficient and nonproficient) intersect. It appears, however, that the two distributions intersect several times in Figure 13.2. Which intersecting point should we use? Part of the problem is the small sample sizes for the two groups. Using the preceding criterion, we have 18 students in the proficient group and 15 students in the nonproficient group. Thus, within either group, most scores have only one person within each group, with only three scores (72, 89, and 107) having two individuals. No score had more than two students for either group. Thus, the shape of the curve may be somewhat deceptive given the small sample sizes. Again, welcome to the reality of applied testing. Based on the data in Figure 13.2, we would recommend setting the cutoff score at either 82 or 85 because that is where the lines for the two groups

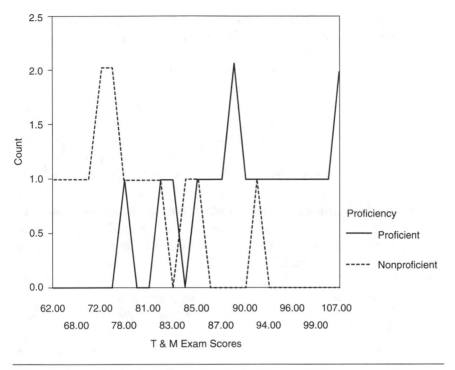

Figure 13.2   Contrasting Groups Results for Tests and Measurements Exam

cross. One practical constraint might be that with a higher cutoff score we may not have enough students to recommend. Alternatively, we may have too many to recommend with the lower cutoff score. Thus, other practical realities may also come into play when setting the cutoff score in this situation.

Concluding Comments

Both judgmental and empirical methods can be used to establish cutoff scores. Most of the time, it is best to use some combination of informed, expert judgment and empirical data to make this critical decision. Keep in mind, however, that setting cutoff scores is a very controversial issue with many practical and legal implications. For example, where we set the cutoff score will affect both the validity and the **utility** of our test. If we have an extreme cutoff score (i.e., almost no one passes), then we will have a highly restricted sample, and scores on the test will be unlikely to correlate with other variables due to the restriction of range. On the other hand, if almost everyone passes, then the utility of the test will be diminished, as we are not taking advantage of the fact that higher scores on the test are associated with higher criterion scores. In addition, the lack of variability will mean our test scores will not correlate with other variables of interest.

Another practical issue is that we often use more than one test when making important decisions. How does the placement of a cutoff score on an early test hurdle influence how we make later cutoff score decisions? For example, if we are using several tests in a multiple-hurdle fashion and very few individuals are able to pass our first test, then we may have to set the cutoff score on later tests extremely low. As a result, we may end up hiring individuals who are "not proficient" on factors assessed by later measures simply because we do not have enough individuals left in the pool due to overly restrictive early cutoff scores.

Finally, when we set the pass point, we make the decision of who "passes" (i.e., obtains a valued outcome) and who "fails" (i.e., does not obtain the valued outcome). As a result, some people may like our decision and others may not. Therefore, we need to be able to defend and justify whatever procedure we ultimately end up using. Cascio, Alexander, and Barrett (1988) provided a comprehensive review of the legal, psychometric, and professional issues involved in establishing cutoff scores.

Practical Questions

1. How do we best define the "minimally competent person" when using judgmental methods such as the Angoff, Nedelsky, and Ebel methods?

2. When does a method for setting pass points go from being judgmental/empirical to empirical/judgmental? Does it really matter?

3. What legal issues do we need to be concerned with when setting cutoff scores?

4. Does where we set the cutoff score affect the validity of the test? The utility?

5. How do we know whether we should minimize false-positive or false-negative decisions? Will that decision impact the procedure we use to make the cutoff score decision?

6. Do we really even need to set cutoff scores? Why not just rank order all the test scores from highest to lowest and provide the valued outcome until it runs out?

7. What if we set a cutoff score and no one passes?

Case Studies

CASE STUDY 13.1: SETTING A CUTOFF SCORE ON A COMPREHENSIVE EXAMINATION

Alexius, a fifth-year doctoral student, had agreed to sit on the committee that was restructuring the doctoral comprehensive exams for his department. It seemed every year students complained about the long essays they had to write and professors complained about having to read and grade the essays with little guidance. Therefore, a committee of mostly full professors in the department was formed to explore the possibility of having a new two-part multiple-choice comprehensive exam. The first part would be a 250-question multiple-choice exam covering several general areas (e.g., history and systems, statistics, and research methods). The second part of the test would also have 250 multiple-choice questions but in the student's area of concentration (e.g., social, cognitive, clinical, or I/O psychology). Thus, the test would consist of 500 multiple-choice questions in all. While a common standard of 80% correct or 90% correct could be used to set the pass point, the committee did not feel that was wise, as they knew the questions on the test would change each year. In addition, while all students in a given year took the same general portion of the test, students in different concentrations took different area-specific tests. Thus, it was felt a new pass point should be established each year for each test segment. Several of the counseling professors on the committee sat on the state licensing board for counseling psychology, and they used a similar procedure to set the pass point for the professional licensing exam for counseling psychologists in their state for the written multiple-choice portion of the exam.

Because the number of students who took the comprehensive exams in a given year was relatively small (i.e., usually less than 20 students), an empirical strategy for setting the cutoff score did not seem feasible. However, the committee was uncomfortable with using a purely judgmental procedure for setting the cutoff score. In addition, multiple cutoff scores had to be set, one for the general portion of the test and a separate cutoff score for each specific test. The committee chair, who also happened to be the department chairperson, asked Alexius to provide the committee with a proposal of how best to set the cutoff scores for each portion of the test. Alexius felt a bit over-whelmed. Here were all these professors in the department, many who had been there 30 years or more, and they were asking him for recommendations on how to set cutoff scores for the tests. Yes, he had just taken his comprehensive exams the year before, but that was under the old system when you had to write six or eight long essays, not this multiple-choice format. In some ways, he thought this was probably better than having to write all those questions. Therefore, Alexius went back to his notes from his applied psychological measurement class and started a literature search on the "best practices" for setting cutoff scores in such situations.

Questions to Ponder

1. If you were Alexius, where would you start your search for "best practices" for setting cutoff scores on a graduate comprehensive examination?

2. While a purely empirical method for setting the cutoff scores seems unrealistic given the small sample sizes, what things could Alexius do to make his judgmental procedures more empirical?

3. Who are the likely SMEs for setting the cutoff scores for the general test? The area-specific tests?

4. Is there a problem with the same individuals writing the questions and also helping to set the cutoff scores on the test they created?

5. Would information from past "pass rates" be of any use to the committee given that the format is being changed?

CASE STUDY 13.2: SETTING A CUTOFF SCORE ON A COLLEGE ENTRANCE EXAM

Lui-Ping (most people just called her Jasmin), a recent master's graduate, had decided to return home to Malaysia after graduation. After a short job search, she obtained a job with the ministry of education. One of Jasmin's first assignments was to help set the cutoff score for the national entrance exam for the three most sought-after public universities in Kuala Lumpur (the capital city of Malaysia). The three universities received tens of thousands of applications every year. It was no wonder; anyone who was admitted received free tuition. In addition, the top employers from across Malaysia (all of Southeast Asia, in fact) seemed to focus much of their recruitment effort for new employees at these three top public universities. Therefore, if a student were able to get into one of these three universities, he or she would be "set for life."

The ministry of education, however, had just recently reformatted the entrance exam to cover several new topics. As a result, a new cutoff score had to be "recommended" to the universities. Ultimately, the universities were free to choose their own cutoff scores, but they relied heavily on the expertise provided by the ministry of education, as that is where much of their funding came from. Therefore, Jasmin was asked to help determine the appropriate cutoff score for the three universities. This could be difficult, she thought, as the three universities seemed to be so different. The first was a technical university, focusing on engineering and the physical sciences. The second university was a more traditional liberal arts university, with a wide breadth of offerings and a much smaller student body. The third university had a strong focus on the professional degrees, with emphases in business, social work, medicine, law, and education. These all seemed so different. How could she set a single cutoff score for all three universities? It was time to sit down with her new boss and get more clarification on what she should do next.

Questions to Ponder

1. Should Jasmin recommend the same cutoff score for each university or should different cutoff scores be recommended?

2. Instead of having one overall cutoff score, might it be better to have separate cutoff scores for different portions of the exam?

3. Should Jasmin take into consideration the other criteria used by each of the universities to select its students? If so, how?

4. Given the large sample of data Jasmin will have to work with, how might she incorporate some empirical data into the cutoff score decision?

5. Who should be the SMEs for Jasmin in helping her to set the cutoff score(s)?

Exercises

EXERCISE 13.1: JUDGMENTAL
PROCEDURES FOR SETTING CUTOFF SCORES

OBJECTIVE: To practice setting cutoff scores using the Angoff and Nedelsky methods.

SCENARIO: The psychology department has decided to begin using graduate students to teach the lab portion of Psychology 210, Psychological Statistics. To ensure students wishing to be graduate teaching assistants (GTAs) are "minimally competent," we will give the graduate statistics final exam from last year to those students wishing to be GTAs. The exam can be found in Table 13.1. Those "passing" the test will be allowed to interview for the GTA positions. Therefore, we must determine who is "minimally competent" in statistics by setting an appropriate cutoff score on the exam.

EXERCISE: Half the class will use the Angoff method to set the cutoff score on the test. A rating sheet for the Angoff method can be found in Table 13.2. The other half of the class will use the Nedelsky method to set the cutoff score on the exam. A rating sheet for the Nedelsky method can be found in Table 13.3. If time permits, have the groups switch and use the other method they did not use the first time. Compare the cutoffs from the two separate groups of raters.

1. How do the two methods compare? Discuss possible reasons for the likely differences obtained.

2. Discuss issues surrounding the use of different methods and different groups of raters.

EXERCISE 13.2: DELPHI METHOD
FOR SETTING CUTOFF SCORES

OBJECTIVE: To practice using a judgmental/empirical method for setting cutoff scores.

(Text continues on page 239)

Table 13.1   Graduate Psychological Statistics Final Exam (* indicates the keyed answer)

---

1. A bivariate distribution is represented in the most complete fashion by a
   A. Pearson r_{xy}.   *C. scatterplot.
   B. straight line.   D. line, whether curved or straight.

2. A causal relationship between X and Y can be inferred
   A. any time r_{xy} is other than zero.
   B. only for values of r_{xy} close to 1.00.
   C. whenever we use a test of group differences (e.g., t, F).
   *D. only on grounds that go beyond the statistics used to analyze the data.

3. Which, if any, statistic below is NOT subject to the influence of sampling variation (error)?
   A. the mean   C. the standard deviation
   B. the correlation coefficient   *D. all of these are subject to sampling variation

4. The correlation between job aptitude scores and job success ratings is computed to be +.29 for employees hired in the last 6 months. Which of the following is a legitimate guess as to the value of r_{xy} had all, rather than just the best qualified applicants, been hired?
   A. < +.29   *C. > +.29
   B. +.29   D. insufficient information to even guess

5. Which of the following types of scores do NOT provide equal intervals when moving away from the center of the distribution by standard deviation units?
   A. z scores   C. raw scores
   B. T scores   *D. percentiles

6. The fundamental condition that permits proper statistical inference is
   *A. random sampling.   C. a normal distribution of scores.
   B. having large sample sizes.   D. knowledge of the population parameters.

7. "Degrees of freedom" refers to the number of
   A. samples in the sampling distribution.   C. tests we are free to use.
   *B. data points that are free to vary.   D. days to spring break.

(Continued)

Table 13.1 (Continued)

---

8. In statistical work, a significant difference is one that is large enough
    - A. that chance cannot affect it.
    - B. to be meaningful to the experimenter.
    - C. that it leads to retention of the null hypothesis.
    - *D. that it would rarely be expected to occur by chance if H_0 is true.

9. When samples are dependent, the standard error of the difference between two means will be
    - *A. larger than when samples are independent.
    - B. smaller than when samples are independent.
    - C. smaller or larger depending on the situation.
    - D. unaffected by the degree of dependence of the samples.

10. Using paired observations (dependent observations) is most advantageous when
    - A. sample sizes are equal.
    - B. standard deviations must be estimated from samples.
    - *C. the association between pairs of scores is high (e.g., large individual differences).
    - D. actually, it is never advantageous to have paired observations versus independent ones.

11. Interval estimates are generally preferred over point estimates because interval estimates
    - A. have a firmer statistical basis.
    - B. result in greater statistical precision.
    - *C. account for sampling error.
    - D. are based on more degrees of freedom.

12. We construct a 99% confidence interval for P, the population proportion of freshmen able to pass an English placement exam. The sample interval ranges from .43 to .49. This tells us that
    - A. there is a 99% probability that P falls between .43 and .49.
    - *B. there is a 99% probability that an interval so constructed will include P.
    - C. 99% of the time, P will fall between .43 and .49.
    - D. 99% of intervals so constructed will fall between .43 and .49.

13. Suppose a 95% confidence interval for $\mu_x - \mu_y$ ranges from −5 to +2. If H_0: $\mu_x - \mu_y = 0$ were tested against a two-tailed alternative hypothesis using $\alpha = .05$, our decision about H_0 would be that we
    - A. made a type I error.
    - B. should reject H_0.
    - *C. should retain H_0.
    - D. cannot determine from the information provided.

14. In general, reducing the risk of committing a Type I error
    A. reduces the risk of committing a Type II error.
    *B. reduces the power of the test statistic used.
    C. increases the power of the test statistic used.
    D. has no effect on any of these issues.

15. In a one-way ANOVA, the following results are obtained: SSb = 83.7, SStot=102.6. Thus, the SSw =
    A. 186.3.   C. 51.3.
    *B. 18.9.   D. none of these.

16. The assumption of homogeneity of variance in ANOVA designs means that
    *A. group population variance should be the same for all groups.
    B. within-group variance should be the same as total variance.
    C. between-group variance should be the same as total group variance.
    D. within-group variance should be the same as between-group variance.

17. In ANOVA for repeated measures, SSw is partitioned into
    A. SSb and Sssubj.   C. SSsubj and Sstot.
    B. SSb and Sserror.   *D. SSsubj and Sserror.

18. A standard score regression equation reads: $Z_{\_} = \beta Z_x$. If the correlation coefficient is +.5 and Johnny is 2 standard deviations above the mean on X, what standard score position will Johnny be predicted to have on Y?
    *A. +1.0   C. +2.0
    B. +1.5   D. none of these

19. In a one-way ANOVA involving three groups, the alternative hypothesis would be considered supported if, in the population,
    1. all means were equal.
    2. two means were equal but the third was different.
    3. all three means have different values.
    A. 1   C. 3
    B. 2   *D. Either 2 or 3 is true

20. The purpose of the Fisher's r to z transformation is to correct for
    *A. varying shape of the sampling distribution of r.
    B. differing values of n (particularly when $n < 30$).
    C. an unknown mean of the sampling distribution of r.
    D. an unknown standard deviation of the sampling distribution of r.

21. A Z score in a given distribution is 1.5. If the mean = 140 and $s = 20$, then the equivalent raw score is
    A. 95.   C. 165.
    B. 160.   *D. 170.

(Continued)

Table 13.1 (Continued)

22. Suppose that a distribution of test scores is very negatively skewed. Mary obtains a raw score equal to the mean of the distribution. She proclaims, "I scored at the 50th percentile." You smile and calmly tell her that she
    - A. has indeed scored at the 50th percentile.
    - *B. actually scored below the 50th percentile.
    - C. actually scored above the 50th percentile.
    - D. actually scored at the 25th percentile.

23. If the distribution of raw scores above (in Q22) were transformed to Z scores, the new distribution will be
    - A. normally distributed.
    - B. symmetrical but not normal.
    - *C. negatively skewed.
    - D. positively skewed.

24. ρ is to the sampling distribution of r as _____ is to the sampling distribution of the mean.
    - A. S_x
    - *B. μ_x
    - C. σ_x
    - D. η_x

25. An interval estimate for the population parameter (e.g., ρ, σ, μ) is highly preferable to a point estimate when
    - *A. N is small.
    - B. N is large.
    - C. the sample statistic is small.
    - D. the sample statistic is large.

26. A 95% confidence interval for ρ is computed and is found to be $-.75$ to $+.25$. This suggests that
    - A. ρ is probably negative.
    - *B. a small sample size was used.
    - C. a computational error was made.
    - D. r is significantly different from zero.

27. The size of the standard error of the distribution of sample means will _____ the population standard deviation.
    - A. always be the same as
    - B. always be larger than or equal to
    - *C. always be smaller than or equal to
    - D. sometimes be larger and sometimes be smaller than

28. Which of the following represents a Type II error?
    - A. no effect when there really is an effect
    - B. no effect when there really is no effect
    - C. an effect when there really is an effect
    - *D. an effect when there really is not an effect

29. Which combination below is most likely to lead to the most powerful study?
   A. small N, $\alpha = .01$, two-tailed test
   C. small N, $\alpha = .01$, one-tailed test
   B. large N, $\alpha = .05$, two-tailed test
   *D. large N, $\alpha = .05$, one-tailed test

30. The power of any statistical test can be represented as
   *A. $1 - \beta$.
   C. $\alpha + \beta$.
   B. $1 - \alpha$.
   D. $\alpha - \beta$.

31. Sample size affects the power of a statistical test because of its influence on the
   *A. standard error of the sampling distribution.
   C. effect size "d."
   B. skewness of the sampling distribution.
   D. sample standard deviations.

32. Multiple regression and factorial ANOVA are similar conceptually in that
   A. all variables are continuous.
   C. we have both multiple IVs and DVs.
   B. the IVs are independent of one another.
   *D. you end up partitioning variance into explained and error.

33. I ran my analyses and got an ω^2 value that was negative. What likely happened?
   A. My F value must have been negative.
   B. Treatment effects were reversed.
   C. I had more error variance than treatment variance.
   *D. I must have made a calculational error because ω^2 can never be negative.

34. Which of the following is NOT an advantage of multiple regression over factorial ANOVA.
   A. I can use continuous and/or nominal IVs with MR.
   B. I can test for nonlinear relationships with MR but not with ANOVA.
   C. MR takes into account correlations among IVs.
   *D. All are advantages of MR over factorial ANOVA.

35. Correlations are to covariance as _____ are to raw scores.
   *A. Z scores
   C. percentiles
   B. standard deviations
   D. means

36. The reason we should thoroughly describe our data before jumping into inferential statistics is because we
   A. have to see if our DV is normally distributed.
   B. need to find out if we have any outliers in our data.

(Continued)

Table 13.1 (Continued)

    C. should get an ocular feel for our data to help us better explain our results.

  *D. all of the above are pretty legitimate reasons to do descriptive analyses before inferential ones.

37. The importance of sampling distributions of our statistics to statistical inference is that they

  *A. have known properties based on the central limit theorem.

    B. allow us to determine the probability of obtaining our statistic.

    C. guide us to which statistic will best answer our question of interest.

    D. tend to always reject the null hypothesis when we have very large sample sizes.

38. Which statement is true?

  *A. Any problem in hypothesis testing could be handled through estimation.

    B. Any problem in estimation could be handled through hypothesis testing.

    C. Hypothesis testing and estimation are mutually interchangeable.

    D. Hypothesis testing and estimation are never interchangeable.

For the following four examples, indicate whether we should use an independent- or dependent-group design statistic to analyze data from the experiment described.

39. Thirty-three (33) Republicans were compared to 33 Democrats for signs of depression on November 4, 1992.

  *A. independent   B. dependent

40. A psychologist gave a pretest and matched each subject with another subject. Half the subjects were given a gin and tonic and half were given plain tonic. All 40 subjects then learned statistics.

    A. independent   *B. dependent

41. The first 10 subjects to sign up for an experiment were asked to fill out a questionnaire. Then the next 10 subjects to sign up filled out a similar questionnaire and the two groups were compared.

  *A. independent   B. dependent

42. The attitudes of 21 students toward statistics were compared to those of each one's "favorite professor."

    A. independent   *B. dependent

43. The chairperson of the psychology department has asked you to determine whether the number of men who select psychology as their major differs significantly from that of women. The most appropriate way to answer the chair's question would be by doing a(n)

A. independent-groups *t* test.

B. dependent-groups *t* test.

C. preplanned contrast of men and women.

*D. *z* test for differences between proportions.

44. The chair of the psychology department recommended you to the vice president for student affairs who wants to find out if there is a relationship between how far a student drives to school and his or her GPA. He has divided the students into five groups (< 15-minute commute, 15- to 30-minute commute, 31- to 45-minute commute, 46- to 60-minute commute, and > 60-minute commute). The most appropriate way to answer the VP's question would be to calculate

*A. an *F* statistic for an independent-groups one-way ANOVA.

B. an *F* statistic for a dependent-groups one-way ANOVA.

C. a tetrachoric correlation coefficient.

D. Tukey HSD statistics comparing the group means.

45. Harper and Wacker (1983) wished to examine the relationship between scores on the Denver Developmental Screening Test and scores on an individually administered intellectual measure for 555 three- to four-year-old children (with both measures having interval scales). Which of the following would best assess the relationship between the two measures?

A. Kendall's Tau correlation

B. an η^2 or ω^2 statistic to assess association

C. a tetrachoric correlation coefficient

*D. Pearson's *r* statistic (assuming the relationship is linear)

46. Franklin, Janoff-Bulman, and Roberts (1990) looked at the long-term impact of divorce on college student's levels of optimism and trust. They compared students from divorced families and students from intact families. They found no differences on generalized trust, but children from divorced families showed less optimism about the future of their own marriages. In order to state the results as they did, they must have performed _____ to analyze their data.

*A. an independent-groups *t* test

B. an η^2 or ω^2 statistic to assess association

C. a tetrachoric correlation coefficient

D. Pearson's *r* statistic (assuming the relationship is linear)

47. Olson and Shultz (1994) studied the influence of sex and source of social support (supervisor, friend, coworker, or spouse) on the degree of overall social support reported being received by a sample of 314 employees from a large automotive manufacturer. Employees rated the amount of support they received from each of the above sources. This study is best represented by a

(Continued)

Table 13.1 (Continued)

A. 2 × 4 factorial ANOVA.
*B. 2 × (4) mixed-design ANOVA.
C. (2) × 4 mixed-design ANOVA.
D. two repeated-measures ANOVAs, one for men and one
   for women.

48. Cochran and Urbancyzk (1982) were concerned with the effect of height
of a room on the desired personal space of subjects. They tested 48
subjects in both a high-ceiling (10 feet) and a low-ceiling (7 feet) room.
Subjects stood with their backs to a wall while a stranger approached.
Subjects were told to say, "Stop," when the approaching stranger's
nearness made them feel uncomfortable. The dependent variable was the
distance at which the subject said, "Stop." Which of the following would
be most appropriate to properly analyze the researchers' data?

A. independent-groups t test   C. preplanned contrast of men
                                            and women

*B. dependent-groups t test   D. z test for differences
                                            between proportions

49. The right side of a person's face is said to resemble the whole face more
than does the left side. Kennedy, Beard, and Carr (1982) asked 91 subjects
to view full-faced pictures of six different faces. Testing for recall was
conducted one week later, when subjects were presented with pictures of
12 faces and were asked to identify the ones they had seen earlier. At
testing, subjects were divided into three groups of roughly equal size. One
group was presented with full-faced photographs, one group saw only the
right side of the face in the photograph, and one group saw only the left
side. The dependent variable was the number of errors. Which of the
following would be most appropriate to properly analyze the researchers'
data?

*A. an F statistic for an independent-groups one-way ANOVA
 B. an F statistic for a repeated-measures one-way ANOVA
 C. an η^2 or ω^2 statistic to assess association in factorial designs
 D. dependent-groups t tests with follow-up ω^2s

50. I ran a one-way ANOVA and calculated $\eta^2 = .34$ (eta square). If I dummy
coded my IVs and ran a multiple regression, I would need to look at the
_____ to get the equivalent measure in multiple regression.

*A. R^2 C. Wherry-corrected R^2
 B. Adj R^2 D. Lord-Nicholson–corrected R^2

Table 13.2   SME Rating Sheet for the Angoff Method

Think of a group of "minimally competent students." Now, for each item, estimate the probability that a student from this minimally competent group could answer the given question correctly. Write this probability in the space provided for that question.

1. _____	18. _____	35. _____
2. _____	19. _____	36. _____
3. _____	20. _____	37. _____
4. _____	21. _____	38. _____
5. _____	22. _____	39. _____
6. _____	23. _____	40. _____
7. _____	24. _____	41. _____
8. _____	25. _____	42. _____
9. _____	26. _____	43. _____
10. _____	27. _____	44. _____
11. _____	28. _____	45. _____
12. _____	29. _____	46. _____
13. _____	30. _____	47. _____
14. _____	31. _____	48. _____
15. _____	32. _____	49. _____
16. _____	33. _____	50. _____
17. _____	34. _____	Σp = _____

Table 13.3   SME Rating Sheet for the Nedelsky Method

For each item, cross out the alternatives that you believe a minimally competent student should be able to eliminate. Then, in the space provided for each question, write the p value for that item (i.e., 4 alts. = .25, 3 alts. = .33, 2 alts. = .50, 1 alt. = 1.00).

1. _____	18. _____	35. _____
2. _____	19. _____	36. _____
3. _____	20. _____	37. _____
4. _____	21. _____	38. _____
5. _____	22. _____	39. _____
6. _____	23. _____	40. _____
7. _____	24. _____	41. _____
8. _____	25. _____	42. _____
9. _____	26. _____	43. _____
10. _____	27. _____	44. _____
11. _____	28. _____	45. _____
12. _____	29. _____	46. _____
13. _____	30. _____	47. _____
14. _____	31. _____	48. _____
15. _____	32. _____	49. _____
16. _____	33. _____	50. _____
17. _____	34. _____	Σp = _____

This exercise requires that you first complete the steps in Exercise 13.1. Next, the professor or some other "moderator" will summarize the initial set of ratings for the class. You will then be provided with the results and be allowed to make changes to your initial ratings based on your review of the summary results. However, you need not make any changes if you believe your initial ratings are still an accurate assessment of your evaluation of each of the items. The moderator will then compute a second set of summary statistics based on the second set of ratings.

1. Did you find the summary ratings helpful to you as you reviewed your initial set of ratings?

2. If you changed some of your ratings, why did you make changes?

3. Did you notice any patterns in your ratings compared to the summary ratings? For example, did you tend to be more stringent or lenient in your ratings than the other raters?

4. Do you feel that frame-of-reference training would have helped you provide more "accurate" ratings? Why or why not?

5. How do the two sets of summary ratings compare?

EXERCISE 13.3: CONTRASTING GROUPS METHOD FOR SETTING CUTOFF SCORES

OBJECTIVE: To practice using empirical procedures to make passing score decisions.

The data set "passing scores.sav" has fictitious data for 200 students' scores on the graduate statistics exam in Table 13.1. Using the data set, create a line graph that compares the proficient group and the nonproficient group (DESIG) in terms of their respective scores on the graduate statistics final exam (FINAL).

1. Based on your line graph, where would you set the passing score?

2. Can a case be made for more than one passing score (similar to the step-by-step example)?

Internet Web Site References

13.1. http://www.afte.org/AssociationInfo/certification/Files/Appendix%20G.pdf

This PDF file presents a brief explanation of the Angoff procedure, along with example instructions to raters.

13.2. http://www.ipmaac.org/conf97/donnoe.pdf

This PDF file presents a conference paper comparing the Angoff, Ebel, and Nedelsky cutoff score methods.

13.3. http://www.aami.org/certification/download/PassScoreGuide.pdf

This PDF file, from the Professional Testing Corporation, titled "Guide to Setting Passing Scores," discusses the Angoff, Ebel, Nedelsky, and other methods of setting cut scores.

13.4. http://www.ucc.uconn.edu/~wwwiopsy/banding.htm

This Web page, presented by Kristen Haggis, discusses the use of banding in employee selection decision making.

13.5. http://www.psc-cfp.gc.ca/ppc/assessment_cp6_e.htm

This Web page, from the Public Service Commission of Canada, presents an overview of general issues related to setting cutoff scores.

13.6. http://siop.org/tip/backissues/tipju197/Gutman.html

This Web page presents an article by Gutman and Christiansen titled "Further Clarification of the Judicial Status of Banding."

Further Readings

Biddle, R. E. (1993). How to set cutoff scores for knowledge tests used in promotion, training, certification, and licensing. *Public Personnel Management, 22,* 63–79.

Campion, M. A., Outtz, J. L., Zedeck, S., Schmidt, F. L., Kehoe, J. F., Murphy, K. R., & Guion, R. M. (2001). The controversy over score banding in personnel selection: Answers to 10 key questions. *Personnel Psychology, 54,* 149–185.

Impara, J. C., & Plake, B. S. (1997). Standard setting: An alternative approach. *Journal of Educational Measurement, 34,* 353–366.

Module 14

Diversity Issues

One major purpose of testing is to assess individual differences. It is ironic, then, that a major criticism of testing is that it too often fails to consider issues of diversity. As used here, diversity issues refer to concerns that arise when testing specific populations categorized on the basis of ethnicity, gender, age, linguistic ability, or physical disability. Although test creators often attempt to use a diverse sample during test development, most tests are based on white middle-class individuals (Padilla, 2001). According to Fouad and Chan (1999),

> The most widely used tests were conceived by White psychologists working within a White mainstream culture for the purpose of assessing psychological traits in men. Yet, tests that were initially developed for men are routinely given to women, and those intended for White U.S. citizens are administered to members of minority groups or are used in other countries. (p. 32)

In essence, the primary concern in testing diverse populations is whether the psychometric properties of the test (e.g., reliability and validity) change when the test is used on a population that differs from that used during test development and standardization. The ability of a typical test to produce reliable and accurate scores for members of other diverse groups is suspect.

Testing is most pervasive in educational settings. Indeed, Haney, Madaus, and Lyons (1993) estimated that the average U.S. public school student is administered between three and eight standardized tests each year. As Samuda (1998) pointed out, however, as a group, minority children have always scored lower on standardized tests—whether the minority group was the Irish at the turn of the 20th century, southern and eastern Europeans a few decades later, or blacks and Spanish-speaking groups later in the 20th century. Given the influence testing has in determining educational and work opportunities, the inappropriate use of tests can have serious long-term effects on individuals, groups, and American society as a whole.

Reasons for Concern

The potential reasons for differential performance across diverse groups are as different as the groups themselves, including differences in experience, beliefs, test-taking motivations, familiarity with testing, English language ability, and values. These factors may lead minorities to score considerably lower than white middle-class Americans (Padilla, 2001). If test performance is dependent on a certain degree of common experience, then tests will be problematic to the degree that all test takers do not fully share in that common experience.

Sternberg and Grigorenko (2001) argued that, to perform well on an ability test, the test taker must possess a certain test-taking expertise. If this same expertise is correlated with outcomes considered valuable in society (such as performance in school or on the job), then the test is considered useful. However, test-taking expertise may not be as highly developed for individuals in different cultures. Unfortunately, such cultural differences in test-taking expertise may obscure the true capabilities of members of a group. As an example, Sternberg and Grigorenko pointed out that while Western assessment of intelligence often emphasizes speed of mental processing, other cultures emphasize depth of mental processing, even to the extent of suspicion of work that is done too quickly. Perhaps an even more startling example used by these authors is based on a study reported by Cole, Gay, Glick, and Sharp (1971). The researchers asked adults of the Kpelle tribe in Africa to sort names of various objects. The Kpelle sorted the names functionally (e.g., banana–eat), much in the same way very young children might in the West. Reflecting unanimity of cognitive theory, however, Western tests of intellect consider functional sorting to be inferior to taxonomic sorting (e.g., banana–type of fruit). Attempts to cajole the Kpelle into sorting the names in a different manner were unsuccessful until a researcher finally asked how a stupid person might sort the names. Immediately, a member of the tribe provided a taxonomic sorting of the names. Clearly, then, cultural differences do exert important influences on the way respondents view what is "correct."

Test Equivalence

Although issues of diversity are clearly important considerations in testing, the appropriate methods for addressing these concerns are significantly less clear (Frisby, 1998). One commonly encountered problem is how to administer a test developed in English to a non–English-speaking sample. **Back translation** refers to tests that have been translated by bilingual individuals from English to the target language, and then retranslated back into English by other bilingual individuals. The idea is that if the retranslated English version of the test is highly similar to the original English version, then the target language test version must be acceptable. Unfortunately, this process falls far short of ensuring equivalent test versions (Sperber, Devellis, & Boehlecke, 1994; see also Web References 14.2 and 14.3).

A number of ways of conceptualizing test equivalence have been proposed (e.g., Lonner, 1990; Marsella & Kameoka, 1989; Steenkamp & Baumgartner, 1987). Lonner (1990), for example, identified four issues to consider regarding equivalence of tests that are translated for use in a culture other than that in which it was initially developed.

Content equivalence refers to whether items are relevant to the new group of test takers. In 1972, Robert Williams created the Black Intelligence Test of Cultural Homogeneity, or BITCH. This test is composed of words, terms, and expressions particular to black culture. An example item is, "If a judge finds you guilty of holding wood [in California], what's the most he can give you?" A member of any other ethnic group is virtually certain to perform poorly on the test. Williams's point is that many of the items on commonly used tests of intelligence are similarly irrelevant for members of nonwhite groups.

Conceptual equivalence examines whether, across cultures, the same meaning is attached to the terms used in the items. To describe something as "wicked," for example, can have either very positive or very negative attributions, depending on the audience. Conceptual equivalence is concerned with the degree to which test takers share a common understanding of the terms used in the items.

An examination of *functional equivalence* determines the degree to which behavioral assessments function similarly across cultures. Interest inventories are often used to illustrate this form of equivalence. In the United States, for example, there exists an expectation that career choice is a personal decision. Thus, the assessment of career interests is quite popular. Such inventories would be far less useful in societies in which one's family largely determines the career one pursues.

Reid (1995) pointed out a second example relevant to functional equivalence. Whereas Americans have a negative connotation of the concept of "dependency," the high value placed on interdependence in Japanese society leads to positive regard for the concept of dependency. Given the cross-cultural differences in understanding of the concept, use of American measures of dependency would be inappropriate for use in a Japanese population.

Scalar equivalence assesses the degree to which different cultural groups produce similar means and standard deviations of scores. Clearly, this form of equivalence is difficult to obtain given true between-group differences. Fouad and Chan (1999) recommended interpretation of an individual's score on a psychological test within the cultural context of the test taker, rather than in comparison to a mainstream norm.

Testing Individuals With Disabilities

Issues of test equivalence can also be raised when testing individuals with disabilities. While the validity of test scores may change when a test is adapted for an individual with a disability, failing to adapt the test for a disability will likely be even more detrimental to the validity of test scores. The Americans with Disabilities Act (ADA) requires test administrators to provide individuals with disabilities a reasonable **accommodation.** Exam administrators are encouraged to provide test takers with a description of each test well in advance of test administration, in order to allow test takers with disabilities the opportunity to request a needed accommodation. Unfortunately, it is virtually impossible to provide guidelines as to exactly what accommodations or test adaptations will be necessary to ensure test equivalence across all possible disabilities. Therefore, decisions regarding what constitutes a reasonable accommodation are determined on a case-by-case basis. Ways in which tests might be adapted, or in which an accommodation might be provided, include increasing the amount of time given to take the test, increasing the font size used on the test, translation into Braille, verbal administration of a test, allowing verbal responses to test items, and so on. Additional information regarding reasonable accommodations required by the ADA is presented in Web Reference 14.4.

In Module 11, we introduced the Wonderlic Personnel Test (WPT) as a measure of cognitive ability. This test is composed of 50 constructed-response items administered with a 12-minute time limit. The WPT test manual suggests a number of possible test accommodations for individuals with specified disabilities (Wonderlic, Inc., 2002). For example, in testing individuals with learning disabilities, the WPT is initially administered by means of the usual timed procedure. The WPT is then administered a second time, but the individual is allowed to complete the exam without a time limit. The number of items correct on each of the two test administrations is then compared. If the difference in number of items correct between the two administrations is less than nine, the test administrator is encouraged to use the test taker's original timed score as representative of the test taker's ability. Using the regular test administration procedure, an individual's test score is determined simply by summing the number of items correct. On the other hand, if the difference between the two testing administrations is nine points or more, then the untimed administration is thought to serve as a better representation of the learning-disabled individual's ability. In this latter case, the individual's test score is determined by subtracting a value of six from the number of items the individual got correct on the untimed administration of the test. While the recommendations of the WPT test manual suggest that this accommodation is reasonable, some test administrators may take issue with this recommended adjustment. For example, a test administrator may be concerned with the impact of practice effects on test performance when using this accommodation, particularly given the likely brief interval between testing and retesting.

The WPT is also available in a Braille version. This version is administered untimed, and the test score is again determined by subtracting a value of six from the number of items correct.

Levels of Accommodation

Styers and Shultz (2002) suggested that researchers typically categorize accommodations into three levels. Level I accommodations, called "Change in Medium" accommodations, present disabled individuals with the same test items presented to other test takers, but the items are presented in a different manner, such as by providing a reader or a Braille version of a test to a blind individual. Level II accommodations, "Time Limits," provide additional time for individuals with disabilities when completing power tests. Level III, or "Change in Content," accommodations include item revision, deletion of items on the test, and change in item format. Any modification of typical administration procedures should be noted in the reporting of test scores.

It is important to note that accommodations should not be provided if the disability is directly relevant to the construct being assessed. For example, sign language interpretation should not be provided for a test assessing hearing ability. Professional judgment plays an important role in determining whether, and to what degree, a reasonable accommodation is necessary.

Concluding Comments

Test users must be aware that the psychometric properties of a test may change when used on a population different from that for which the test was originally developed. Concerns with testing diverse populations remain at the forefront of debate in American society. This area of testing is currently experiencing significant theoretical and empirical development that will no doubt greatly improve our understanding of the true meaning of test scores.

Practical Questions

1. Why can't we assume that test psychometrics will be the same for different groups of people?

2. What cultural factors might impinge upon a test's ability to transfer to different test populations?

3. How might differences in experience with testing influence test scores?

4. Describe the process of back translation.

5. Why is back translation insufficient to guarantee equivalence?

6. Provide an example of each of the four types of test equivalence identified by Lonner (1990).

7. If you had recently translated a test into a different cultural context, how would you assess each of the four types of equivalence?

8. What factors should be considered when determining whether a requested test accommodation is reasonable?

Case Studies

CASE STUDY 14.1: CULTURAL DIFFERENCES IN MARITAL SATISFACTION

"Will she ever be happy?" grumbled Chin, mostly to herself. Chin was, of course, referring to her thesis advisor. Everything, it seemed, revolved around her thesis right now. She and her fiancé had even arranged their wedding date so that it would come after her planned graduation date. Unfortunately, Chin had struggled mightily to develop a thesis topic before stumbling across a topic at the dinner table. Her parents, who had emigrated from China over two decades ago, maintained close ties with their extended family—including those who remained in China and those who had similarly immigrated to the

United States. At dinner three weeks ago, Chin's mother was talking about how unhappily married several of Chin's cousins were. Indeed, more than one of her older cousins had already been divorced. The cousins her mother was referring to were all, like Chin herself, born and raised in the United States. But then her mother said something that got Chin thinking, "I don't remember people being unhappy in their marriages in China. I wonder what it is with kids these days." That was it. Exactly what Chin was looking for. Her mind whirled. Wouldn't it be interesting to compare marital satisfaction between the United States and China?

Chin had always been interested in her heritage. Perhaps because of this, she'd also been an avid reader of the psychological literature on cultural value differences. Thus, by combining this interest with her other major life interest right now—marriage—Chin knew this would be a perfect starting point for her thesis. She couldn't imagine being more motivated by another topic.

Over the next few weeks, Chin pored over relevant literature, and she even developed a proposed model of the relationships between specific cultural values and their impact on marital satisfaction. She then began to think of methodological issues. She had already planned on visiting her grandmother in China this summer, so it seemed that she could collect data from a Chinese sample while she was there. She had even identified an often-used scale called the Marital Satisfaction Index that seemed perfect for her research. Much to her pleasant surprise, she learned that two research studies had already developed and used a Chinese-language version of the very same scale. Armed with her information, she scheduled a meeting with her thesis advisor.

Never had a meeting been so deflating. Her thesis advisor, Dr. Michelle Wordes, had initially seemed very interested in the project. Indeed, she approved of Chin's proposed research model, and even seemed to agree with the hypotheses. However, when it came time to discuss methodology, Dr. Wordes became more and more negative about the idea. Dr. Wordes had focused most of her criticism on the Chinese version of the scale. "How do you know if the item wording is truly equivalent to the original?" she inquired. She didn't seem all that impressed that two other researchers had used the scale—and gotten their results published. Finally, Chin thought of a brilliant idea. She argued that since her parents were bilingual, she could have them help determine whether the items on the English and Chinese versions expressed the same ideas.

But was Dr. Wordes satisfied by this suggestion? Oh, no. Dr. Wordes then asserted that even if the wording were the same on the two versions, that maybe the items would be interpreted differently in the two cultures, or even that "marital satisfaction" as conceived in the United States might be a completely different concept in China.

Finally, Dr. Wordes asked the question that Chin could not get out of her mind: "So if you find differences in marital satisfaction between those in the United States and those in China, would the results be attributable to differences in cultural values or differences in versions of the test?" Even now, an hour after the meeting, Chin had yet to formulate a satisfactory response.

Questions to Ponder

1. Would Chin's parents serve as appropriate interpreters of the accuracy of the translation of the Marital Satisfaction Index? Why or why not?

2. What form of test equivalence is Dr. Wordes concerned about when she questions whether:
   a. the items are worded equivalently?
   b. the items would be interpreted similarly by the two groups?
   c. marital satisfaction is an equivalent construct across the two groups?

3. How could Chin respond to the final question posed by Dr. Wordes?

4. Should Chin abandon her research idea, or is there some way of addressing Dr. Wordes's concerns?

CASE STUDY 14.2: A FAILURE TO CONSIDER TEST EQUIVALENCE

In his *History of Psychology,* Hothersall (1990) provided a dramatic example of how failure to consider issues of test equivalence can have very serious consequences. In the late 1800s and early 1900s, the United States experienced significant immigration from countries in

Southern and Eastern Europe. As occurs still today, those who were born in the United States viewed much of this immigration as a serious threat. Indeed, there was widespread concern that the country was unable to bear the burden of the influx of socially and mentally defective immigrants. Such concerns led to federal legislation forbidding the immigration of lunatics and idiots.

Of course, identification of such individuals was a rather daunting task. Prominent psychologist Henry H. Goddard was invited to Ellis Island to examine immigrant-screening procedures. On his initial visit, Goddard used his visual judgment to select one individual that he believed to be mentally defective out of a group of 100 new immigrants. Using an interpreter, Goddard administered the Binet Intelligence Test to the man. Consistent with Goddard's expectations, the man's score indicated a mental age of only eight years. Over the objections of the interpreter that the test was unfair due to the immigrant's unfamiliarity with the questions, Goddard concluded that the Binet test confirmed his suspicions of the immigrant's mental status.

The initial visit was followed by a second, in which Goddard stationed an assistant to visually inspect immigrants as they walked by. The assistant selected nine immigrants whom she suspected of mental deficiency. Again, the Binet test was administered to all nine, and all nine were found to be of below-normal intelligence. Based on this and some additional work, Goddard recommended the use of psychological tests to screen immigrants for mental deficiency.

Hothersall (1990) reported that immigration inspectors took Goddard's advice and began to use psychological methods of screening, resulting in dramatic increases in deportation rates due to mental deficiency over the next several years. After obtaining additional funding, three members of Goddard's staff spent three months at Ellis Island, administering a number of psychological tests. Some of these tests included questions such as "What is Crisco?" and "Who are the New York Giants?" A large number of immigrants performed poorly on these tests, leading Goddard to conclude that more than 75% of a number of immigrant groups (including Italians, Jews, Hungarians, and Russians) were mentally deficient. Goddard's work, along with that of other psychologists at the time, was later used to justify the adoption of restrictive immigration policies.

Questions to Ponder

1. Identify the interdependence of testing and societal values portrayed in the case study.
   a. How do societal values influence testing today?
   b. How does testing influence societal values?

2. What type(s) of test equivalence did Goddard fail to consider?

3. In Goddard's time, as it is today, immigrants come from multiple countries and speak many different languages. Could a single intelligence test be devised for use on all of these groups? Why or why not?

4. One possible response to question 3 is to argue that a single test could not be developed to assess all immigrant groups. If this were the case, how could the intelligence of immigrants be assessed?

5. Why would Goddard reject the objections of the language interpreter? In your opinion, were his actions intentionally malicious or inadvertently oblivious?

6. Hindsight is 20/20. That is, it is often easy to criticize those in the past for making serious errors of judgment. How can we be sure that today's test users are not committing similar errors?

Exercises

EXERCISE 14.1: BACK TRANSLATION OF TEST ITEMS

OBJECTIVE: To examine the equivalence of the back translation of test items.

For this exercise, select at least 15 items from a psychological measure of your choice (some items are presented in other modules within this book). Follow the instructions under one of the following two options and then answer the questions below.

Option 1: Identify two individuals who are proficient in reading and writing the same foreign language as well as English. Present the items you have selected in English to the first individual and ask him or her to translate the items into the foreign language. Once that person has completed the task, present the translated items to the second individual. Ask this person to retranslate the items into English.

Option 2: Visit a Web site (see the sample list that follows) that translates from English to a foreign language of your choice. Using the Web site, translate the English items into the foreign language. Next, visit a second Web site that also translates languages and retranslate the (translated) items from the foreign language back into English.

http://www.freetranslation.com/

http://world.altavista.com/

http://www.systransoft.com/

http://www.translation.langenberg.com/

http://translation2.paralink.com/

1. Compare the retranslated items to the original set of items. Are the retranslated items equivalent to the original English items?

2. What difficulties were encountered in translating items from one language to another?

3. Did problems arise in the translation of idiomatic expressions? To what degree would you be concerned with conceptual equivalence of the translated items?

4. Would you feel confident that the foreign language translation could be used with native speakers of that language? Why or why not?

EXERCISE 14.2: A SAMPLE OF ITEMS FROM THE CHITLING TEST

OBJECTIVE: To gain awareness of the importance of cultural sensitivity in testing.

PROLOGUE: Sociologist Adrian Dove (1971) created the Chitling Test to demonstrate the impact of culture on cognitive test performance. The following Web site (http://ccins.camosun.bc.ca/~tonks/courses/psyc110/ chitling.htm) further explains the purpose of the test and provides a link to 15 sample items. First, try to answer the items correctly and then score your performance using the key provided at the bottom of the page containing the test items. Then consider the following questions.

1. What was your score on these 15 items? Do you feel this score is reflective of your cognitive ability?

2. To what extent do you believe commonly used measures of cognitive ability are culturally biased?

3. For each of the following pairs of groups, consider how cultural and experiential differences might affect test scores. Why might one group in each pair outperform the other on a typical standardized test of achievement or cognitive ability?
   a. Recent Latino immigrants versus American-born Caucasians
   b. Young adults versus senior citizens
   c. Upper-middle-class adults versus economically disadvantaged adults

4. What can be done to eliminate or at least minimize the influence of culture in testing?

5. Are there certain aspects of culture in a nation that should be universally known or recognized by all individuals living in that country? Why or why not?

6. In Module 10, we learned that test bias is detected by examining subgroup differences in regression lines when relating test scores to important criteria. However, society often equates the issue of cultural bias to test fairness. Why should test developers be concerned with societal perceptions of fairness in addition to actual test bias?

EXERCISE 14.3: REASONABLE ACCOMMODATIONS IN TESTING

OBJECTIVE: To consider appropriate accommodations for testing individuals with disabilities.

For each of the following scenarios, propose a reasonable test accommodation if you feel the accommodation is justified.

For each accommodation you recommend,

   a. identify the level of accommodation you are proposing,
   b. explain why you believe your proposed accommodation is appropriate for the given situation, and
   c. discuss any concerns you might have about the equivalence of the resulting test score in comparison to the scores of nondisabled test takers who did not receive an accommodation.

If you do not feel a test accommodation is justified,

   a. explain why and
   b. discuss any concerns you might have in comparing the disabled individual's test score to that of nondisabled test takers.

1. A college student with dyslexia requests an accommodation for an upcoming essay-based midterm exam in a course with 90-minute class sessions.

2. For the job of customer service representative, an applicant with minor hearing loss requests an accommodation on a selection test assessing skill in attentive listening.

3. A blind college student requests an accommodation for an upcoming multiple-choice exam.

4. An individual with a medical history of back pain requests an accommodation on a physical abilities test when applying for the job of police officer.

Internet Web Site References

14.1. http://www.intestcom.org/test_adaptation.htm

This Web page from the International Test Commission (ITC) presents guidelines for adapting psychological and educational tests for use in different linguistic and cultural contexts. The guidelines address the context of the testing, test development and adaptation, administration, and score interpretation.

14.2. http://spansig.org/Translation/articles/art.v019n04.backtranslation.htm

This Web page, authored by a translator, provides commentary on some issues involved in back translation. Similar issues are relevant to linguistic translations of test items.

14.3. http://www.soc.surrey.ac.uk/sru/SRU31.html

This Web page, from the quarterly publication *Social Research Update*, presents an article authored by Maria Birbili titled "Translating from One Language to Another." The article discusses concerns with equivalence, idiomatic expressions, and grammar.

14.4. http://www.eeoc.gov/policy/docs/accommodation.html

This Web page, provided by the U.S. Equal Employment Opportunity Commission, presents a document titled *Enforcement Guidance: Reasonable Accommodation and Undue Hardship under the Americans with Disabilities Act*. The Web page is intended to clarify "the rights and responsibilities of employers and individuals with disabilities regarding reasonable accommodation and undue hardship."

14.5. http://www.multiculturalcenter.org

This Web page of the Multicultural Center for Research and Practice of the Antioch New England Graduate School provides links to information on multicultural test titles, multicultural topics in psychology, and multicultural experiential exercises.

Further Readings

Arnold, B. R., & Matus, Y. E. (2000). Test translation and cultural equivalence methodologies for use with diverse populations. In I. Cuellar & F. A. Paniagua (Eds.), *Handbook of multicultural mental health: Assessment and treatment of diverse populations* (pp. 121–136). San Diego, CA: Academic Press.

Ekstrom, R. B., & Smith, D. K. (Eds.) (2002). *Assessing individuals with disabilities in educational, employment, and counseling settings.* Washington, DC: American Psychological Association.

Sandoval, J., Scheuneman, J. D., Ramos-Grenier, J., Geisinger, K. F., & Frisby, C. (Eds.). (1998). *Test interpretation and diversity: Achieving equity in assessment.* Washington, DC: American Psychological Association.

Module 15

Developing Measures of Typical Performance

This module is concerned with the development of measures of typical performance. Measures of typical performance are concerned with assessing an individual's typical preferences, or how he or she normally behaves or performs (Cronbach, 1970). Examples of these sorts of measures include personality inventories, attitude surveys, and self-reports of behavior.

A Necessary Forewarning

Did you know that even minor changes in question wording, format, response options, or the ordering of questions can result in major changes in the responses obtained to measures of typical performance? Schwarz (1999) reviewed troubling examples of problems that can occur in survey research. For example, Schuman and Presser (1996) reported that when asked, "What is the most important thing for children to prepare them for life?" a little more than 61% of respondents to a constructed-response survey chose the response option, "To think for themselves." When this same question was asked using a free-response format, however, less than 5% of the sample provided this response. Perhaps even more disconcerting is the finding that respondents who hold no opinion on a topic will often construct one when queried by a researcher (Feldman & Lynch, 1988). Bishop, Oldendick, Tuchfarber, and Bennett (1980), for example, found that roughly a third of respondents expressed an opinion on whether the 1975 Public Affairs Act should be repealed, even though no such act existed. Schwarz (1999) argued that respondents make tacit assumptions about the pragmatic—not the literal—meaning of a question. Thus, respondents provide answers that use rules of "cooperative conversational conduct" to try to make sense of questions that are posed to them.

Such findings serve as crucial reminders of both the imperfection of psychological measures and the importance of assessing constructs that are truly meaningful to the sample of respondents. Still, there is no denying the importance of assessment of opinions, attitudes, and traits in today's society. The question, then, is how do we develop good measures of typical performance? Fortunately, you've come to the right place.

Test Specifications

At the risk of repeating ourselves, have you read Module 4 yet? As was the case for tests of maximal performance (see Module 11), the first step in the construction of a measure of typical performance is the careful development of test specifications. In developing these measures, the primary activity of the test specifications is to clearly define the construct of interest and to delineate it from related (but distinct) constructs. By painstakingly defining our construct, the process of writing items becomes far simpler (as do our later efforts in providing evidence of construct validity).

Free-Response Versus Constructed-Response Items

Of course, test specifications will also help us to determine the appropriate item format. In constructing a measure of typical performance, test developers may choose between free-response items and constructed-response items. Free-response items on measures of typical performance present a question or prompt and allow respondents to provide any answer they feel is appropriate. While the most common mode of response to these items is verbal, theoretically respondents could be asked to provide written responses. Written responses, however, are typically much shorter in length and may not reveal sufficient information about the respondent's beliefs or actions.

In providing answers to free-response items, respondents use their own frame of reference. Respondents are much less likely to be influenced by the researcher's preexisting expectations, which can be a concern with use of constructed-response items. Further, by providing respondents the option to respond in their own words, we are more likely to determine their most salient thoughts. Free-response items also allow respondents to qualify both their answers and their understanding of the item.

Unfortunately, when given the opportunity to provide a response in their own words, respondents may provide information that is largely irrelevant to the item. A single respondent may also tend to repeat answers across a number of questions. Another concern with use of free-response items on a test of typical performance is that respondents are likely to differ in their ability to articulate answers. Differences in language and/or cognitive abilities may exert a large influence on the quality and depth of responses provided. Respondents may also use terms that have different meanings to them than to the researcher, leading the researcher to misinterpret an individual's response. A practical concern with the use of free-response items is that the variability of responses can be very difficult to code into a finite number of usable categories. Analyzing such qualitative data can be quite difficult.

This is not to say that the alternative, constructed-response items, is a panacea. While constructed-response items can often be administered and analyzed more easily, these items do not allow respondents to qualify their answers. Thus, pilot testing of constructed-response items is even more necessary than with free-response items in order to determine whether respondents interpret the items in the way the researcher intended. Even when the item is interpreted correctly, the presentation of response options often suggests answers to respondents that they otherwise would not have come up with on their own (Schwarz, 1999).

Additional Test Specification Issues

In a unique and intriguing book, Schuman and Presser (1996) explored a number of important issues regarding the development of a specific type of measure of typical performance: attitude surveys. Chapter by chapter, these authors present a single issue and then provide suggestions for scale development based on a combination of their own research and a review of the extant literature. Among the many issues addressed in their book are the following:

- *Does the ordering of items influence responses?* Sometimes. When order effects do occur, however, they can exert a large influence on the responses provided by test takers. Order effects do not always result in greater consistency in responses to items. Rather, they can result in heightening differences in responses to items as well. Unfortunately, it is difficult to predict when the ordering of items will influence responses. Order effects appear most likely to occur when multiple items assess the same (or very similar) issue and when respondents provide overall summary evaluations rather than more specific evaluations. Web Reference 15.1 presents additional information on the effects of multiple aspects of item context—including ordering—on responses.

- *Should items include a "don't know" response option?* A corollary question might ask, "To what degree should respondents be pushed to provide a response?" Because researchers are typically after information from a respondent, some hesitation in the acceptance of a "don't know" response is understandable. After all, the researcher would want to communicate to the respondent that his or her opinions, attitudes, or beliefs are important. However, what if the individual really hasn't ever considered the issue assessed by the question? Encouraging respondents to provide a response would only increase error variance in the obtained data. Schuman and Presser (1996) reported that when a "don't know" response is explicitly provided, an average of 22% more respondents will take this option. Some individuals will provide meaningful responses when the "don't know" response option is omitted, but will respond, "don't know" when the response option is presented as a possibility. The effect of provision of a "don't know" response option on the correlation between attitude variables is somewhat murky at this point. There is some evidence that correlations between attitude variables can be stronger when a "don't know" response option is presented to test takers. However, this effect is not always the case, in that sometimes correlations are stronger between items when the "don't know" response option is omitted.

- *Will respondents make up a response if they know nothing about the question posed?* Perhaps. In their research, Schuman and Presser (1996) found that about 30% of respondents will provide an opinion on a law they know nothing about if a "don't know" option is omitted. However, their research also found that a number of those respondents providing a "fictitious" response couched their responses in terms of great uncertainty, such as asserting, I "favor—though I really don't know what it is" (p. 159). It is likely that, in the absence of the "don't know" response option, respondents attempt to figure out what the obscure topic of the question is about and then provide a reasonable answer based on their interpretation of the item.

- *Does acquiescence influence responses in attitude measurement?* **Acquiescence** refers to the tendency of respondents to agree with an attitude statement. Given the ubiquitous use of Likert-type response scales with anchors ranging from "strongly disagree" to "strongly agree," the possibility of an acquiescence bias is a very real concern. However, does research indicate that acquiescence actually has a serious effect on survey responses? Quite simply, yes. In a study conducted by Schuman and Presser (1996), the percentage of acquiescent responses was somewhere in the range of 16%–26%.

Further, evidence suggested that acquiescence could change the magnitude of the observed relationships between variables. Because acquiescence can occur whenever items are posed in a one-sided fashion, we might wonder whether acquiescence is also a concern for items that ask a one-sided question to which an individual might be required to respond "yes" or "no." For example, "Do you believe that liberals are more likely to fan the flames of partisanship than conservatives?" Again, the available research indicates that these sorts of one-sided questions are just as susceptible to acquiescence as are items that require respondents to indicate their level of agreement with a statement. Despite our awareness of concerns with acquiescence, the causes and effects of acquiescence are not yet fully understood. (See Module 16 for additional discussion of acquiescence as a response bias.)

These are but a sampling of the issues that Schuman and Presser (1996) explored. Anyone hoping to develop expertise in the area would be wise to read Schuman and Presser's entire book.

Item Writing

Once the issues related to test specification have been considered, it is time to draft the initial pool of items. Generally, the more items that can be initially generated the better, as a good portion of items will undoubtedly be discarded during subsequent steps in the test development process. Still, we should never sacrifice item quality for quantity. In drafting items, consider the following guidelines:

- *Keep items as simple as possible.* Respondents are likely to differ in educational level, as well as in vocabulary and language abilities.

- *Define ambiguous terms.* Respondents are often unfamiliar with terms that may be considered commonplace to the test developer. This concern speaks once again to the importance of pilot testing both items and instructions.

- *Ensure that response options (if provided) are logically ordered and mutually exclusive.*

- *Assess choices respondents would make today, not what they plan to do in the future.* For example, inquire whom an individual would vote for if the election were held today, not whom they plan on voting for in an upcoming election. While individuals are notoriously poor at predicting their own future behavior, they can report what they would do now.

- *In an effort to guard against acquiescence and random responding, ensure that about half of the items are worded such that a favorable attitude requires respondents to disagree with the item.*

Just as important, be sure to *avoid* the following:

- *Double-barreled items.* These are items that assess more than one thing. For example, "My favorite classes in high school were math and science."

- *Double negatives.* Respondents required to respond on an agreement scale often experience difficulty interpreting items that include the word "not."

- *False premises.* These are items that make a statement and then ask respondents to indicate their level of agreement with a second statement. For example, "Although dogs make terrific pets, some dogs just don't belong in urban areas." If a respondent does not agree with the initial statement, how should he or she respond? Notice that this item has the further complication of including a double negative.

- *Leading or loaded items.* These items implicitly communicate what the "right" answer should be. For example, "Do you support or oppose restrictions on the sale of cancer-causing tobacco products to our state's precious youth?" The use of these items is sometimes appropriate, however, when respondents might otherwise be uncomfortable in reporting a certain attitude or behavior that might be considered socially deviant (e.g., self-reports of sexual practices).

Rational or Empirical Test Development?

The use of the terms "rational" and "empirical" to identify the developmental process of a measure of typical performance is misleading, in that rational *and* empirical methods of test development involve both logic and empiricism (Gough & Bradley, 1992). However, the "rational" and "empirical" labels perhaps capture the emphasis of each of these developmental methods. Rational test development refers to a process that practically ensures the internal consistency of the test. With this approach, items are initially drafted to closely match the definition of the construct the test is intended to assess. Once the original pool of items is drafted, subject matter experts (SMEs) are used to confirm that these items are, indeed, relevant to the intended construct. For each item, each SME uses a rating scale to indicate how closely the item corresponds to the conceptualization of the construct. Items that are rated by SMEs as irrelevant to the construct are discarded.

The emphasis in empirically derived tests is on the relationship between test scores and an external criterion of interest, not on the internal consistency of items per se. In drafting items for an empirically derived test, less concern is placed on whether the items closely assess the underlying theoretical construct. Thus, it is often the case that the initial pool of items is much larger for an empirically devised measure than for a rationally developed measure. Using the empirical method, items that might be even tangentially related to the researcher's conception of the construct assessed are often included in the original pool of items. The pool of developed items is not subjected to the judgment of SMEs. Rather, the researcher identifies an external criterion of interest for which the items are intended to distinguish between various levels or categories. In a personnel selection test, for example, the criterion might be supervisor ratings of job performance. In a measure of psychopathology, the criterion might be the individual's psychiatric history (or lack thereof). After administering the items to a sample and collecting criterion information from the sample, item responses are correlated with the external criterion. Those items that distinguish between different levels of the criterion are retained for further pilot testing, while those items that do not differ across criterion levels are deleted.

Pilot Testing and Analysis

Whichever method is used to develop a measure of typical performance, the importance of **pilot testing** the measure cannot be overstated. The sample selected for the pilot test should be as representative as possible of the eventual targeted population, and, as is always the case, larger samples provide more stable estimates.

In a rationally developed measure, data from the pilot test are factor analyzed (see Module 18) to examine the underlying dimensionality of the measure. Reliability analysis (see Module 5) is then conducted on emergent subdimensions of the scale (if any), as well as on the overall scale. An item may be discarded following either the factor analysis or the reliability analysis if it fails to demonstrate strong relationships with other items.

As discussed previously, the first step in pilot testing an empirically derived measure is the collection of data on both the newly developed measure and the criterion. Each item is then individually correlated with the criterion. Those items that are strongly related to the criterion are retained, while the remaining items are discarded. Due to concerns regarding the capitalization on chance, data are collected on the remaining items and the criterion using a second sample, and again the relationship between individual items and the criterion is examined. Items that again demonstrate a strong relationship with the criterion are retained for the final scale.

Concluding Comments

Well, there you have it. Using the procedures outlined in this module, you are now ready to go out and create your own measure of typical performance. What? You don't think you're ready yet? Nonsense! Of course, you are. However, if you feel you're not quite ready for prime-time test construction, maybe it's best to first find an example or two. Gough and Bradley (1992) provided excellent examples of both empirical and rational methods of developing measures of typical performance, so you might want to start there.

Practical Questions

1. This module begins by discussing serious concerns with self-report measures. Do such concerns indicate we should abandon this type of inquiry?

2. Why is defining the intended construct so essential to the development of a measure of typical performance?

3. What can a developer of a measure of typical performance do to ensure that respondents will understand the items on the measure correctly?

4. In assessing someone's opinion, when might you prefer to use a free-response item format? When might you prefer to use a constructed-response item format?

5. Why is it sometimes appropriate to use loaded items when assessing self-report of a person's behavior?

6. What is acquiescence? What can a test developer do to reduce our concern with acquiescence?

7. Why shouldn't we ask respondents what they plan to do in the future?

8. What is the major difference between rational and empirical methods of test development?

9. Is rational test development unempirical?

10. Is empirical test development irrational?

Case Studies

CASE STUDY 15.1: DEVELOPMENT OF THE MINNESOTA MULTIPHASIC PERSONALITY INVENTORY

The Minnesota Multiphasic Personality Inventory (MMPI) is one of the earliest and best-known empirically derived tests. Graham (1977, 1999) presented a detailed description of the development of the original version of the MMPI, based largely on the writings of the initial test developers, Starke Hathaway and J. Charnley McKinley.

Dissatisfied with the inefficiency and unreliability of individual interviews and mental exams, Hathaway and McKinley sought to develop a paper-and-pencil personality inventory that could be used for psychological diagnostic assessments. The test developers identified approximately 1,000 personality-type statements from a wide variety of sources, including published attitude scales, psychiatric case histories, and textbooks. These 1,000 items were then reduced to 504 relatively independent items.

As with any empirically derived test, the choice of a criterion was crucial. Hathaway and McKinley obtained two groups, whom Graham (1997, 1999) referred to as the Minnesota normals and the clinical participants. The Minnesota normals were composed of 1,508 individuals, including visitors of hospital patients, recent high school graduates who attended precollege conferences at the University of Minnesota, hospital workers, and others. The clinical sample was composed of 221 psychiatric patients from the University of Minnesota Hospitals. These individuals were further divided into eight subgroups based on their clinical diagnosis.

The 504 potential items were administered to both the Minnesota normals and the specific clinical subgroups. Responses to each item were examined to determine whether an item differentiated between groups. Items that did differentiate between normal and clinical subgroup samples were retained and considered for inclusion in the MMPI scale for that particular diagnosis.

The test developers then cross-validated the clinical scales by administering retained items to new samples of normal and clinically diagnosed individuals. Items that were again able to differentiate between groups were subsequently included in the MMPI. The MMPI was then used to assist in the diagnosis of new patients.

Interestingly, the revision of the MMPI, which began in the early 1980s, adopted a somewhat more theoretical approach in that items were added to assess specific content areas (such as suicide potential and drug abuse) that subject matter experts deemed were underrepresented in the earlier version.

Questions to Ponder

1. Why did Hathaway and McKinley begin with such a large pool of potential items?

2. In what ways would item selection have differed if the original MMPI had been rationally developed?

3. Discuss the degree to which you feel the choice of criterion was appropriate for the MMPI.

4. Why did Hathaway and McKinley cross-validate the clinical scales?

5. Why would the process used to develop the MMPI be advantageous for diagnosing clinical patients?

6. Why would the revision of the MMPI include a somewhat more theoretical approach to test development?

7. The MMPI has sometimes been used in the selection of new employees. Is this an appropriate use of the test? Why or why not?

CASE STUDY 15.2: IDENTIFYING THE DIMENSIONALITY OF JOINERSHIP

"I knew this topic wasn't any good, but none of you listened to me, did you?" asked Doug, half in jest.

He and four other students in his graduate test construction seminar had recently begun working on a semester-long test construction project. Their assignment was to select a psychological trait, clearly define the domain, write items, and then conduct the usual steps for rational test development. Unfortunately, the semester was passing by quickly, and the students had just now begun to define the trait they had selected. Today, the group had decided to meet to hammer out a definition of the construct. Even so, there obviously remained some dissension as to whether the selected trait was really worth measuring at all.

"What sort of trait is *joinership* anyway?" continued Doug.

"You know, I really like the idea of this construct," retorted Kandice. "It seems to me that some people are more likely to join a lot of community groups and organizations, whereas others are never willing to join such organizations. As far as I know, there is no other scale intended to distinguish between these sorts of people."

Although she enjoyed this friendly bickering, Sangeeta was determined to get down to business. "Does anyone have any ideas as to how we should define the construct?"

Kristin had been waiting for this opportunity. "How about 'The number of groups a person joins'?"

"That's not bad," said Akira, "but does that mean we'll just measure how many groups a person is a member of? We could measure that with a single self-report item."

"No," protested Kristin, "I meant that we'd view the construct as a trait . . . more like someone's propensity for joining multiple groups."

"Would that mean that we are just interested in whether people *join* organizations? Or should we also measure their actual level of involvement in those organizations that they do join?" asked Akira.

Doug smiled. "Sorry, folks, but I see another problem. Without specifically saying so, I think we all have been thinking about the groups we're referring to as sort of social clubs and community organizations that generally have positive connotations. Are we also interested in a person's propensity for joining negative groups like gangs and cults?"

Sangeeta was ready to add her thoughts. "That's good, Doug, but maybe that's part of the dimensionality of the construct that we haven't talked about yet. Maybe there are different factors that would influence an individual to be attracted to different types of community groups. For example, maybe there exist different tendencies for people to join social groups versus religious groups versus violent groups."

Seeing an opening, Kandice jumped in, "You know, I did a little research last night in preparation for our meeting. I found a theory by Forsyth (1998) of why people join groups. According to Forsyth, people join groups to meet one of five functional needs, namely, Belongingness, Intimacy and Support, Generativity, Influence, and Exploration."

"Oh my," said Akira, obviously impressed. "Those needs sound like the dimensions of joinership we've been searching for. Wouldn't it make sense for us to write items that assess an individual's desire to join groups to satisfy those needs?"

"You bet," added Kristin. "And how's this for a formal definition? 'An individual's propensity to join multiple groups in order to satisfy each of Forsyth's (1998) needs.'"

"I think we're on to something big," said Sangeeta.

"Finally," added Doug.

Questions to Ponder

1. What special challenges might there be for defining a newly conceptualized construct such as joinership?

2. How would measurement of a personality trait differ from self-reported behavior? What implications would this have for the development of the scale?

3. A thorough test specification would likely discuss constructs that were similar, but distinct, from the construct assessed by the measure. What constructs might be used to compare and contrast joinership?

4. How important is it to define the context in which the scale is to be used? For what purposes could the joinership scale be used?

5. Explain how theory provided assistance in the development of the *joinership* scale. What role should theory play in the development of a psychological measure?

6. Now that the group has decided on the dimensionality of the construct, how should item writing proceed?

Exercises

EXERCISE 15.1: IMPROVING SURVEY ITEMS

OBJECTIVE: To identify and correct poorly written survey items.

Each of the items below share the following five-point Likert-type response scale:

1	2	3	4	5
Strongly Disagree	Disagree	Neither Agree nor Disagree	Agree	Strongly Agree

For each item, determine whether the item is clearly written or in need of improvement. If the item is in need of improvement, rewrite the item to eliminate the problem.

1. Many people fail to realize that the U.S. government is secretly run by a little-known, small group of individuals.

2. Advances in CAT and IRT have had a profound effect on the field of testing.

3. I will vote for Senator Wilson in the upcoming election.

4. The best times of my life were in high school and college.

5. I am in favor of our city council's revitalization plan.

6. Although the Christian Bible has revealed many essential truths, there are some passages of the Bible that we will never understand.

7. I tend to be shy.

8. Twenty-five pages of reading per week is an appropriate amount for a lower-division college course.

9. Doctors should never assist in a person's suicide.

10. I've volunteered in my community on many occasions.

PROLOGUE to Exercises 15.2–15.4: The following three exercises ask you to enact a number of steps required in scale construction. Items were developed to assess the fabricated construct of joinership. This construct can be defined as the propensity for an individual to join multiple groups. The scale is based loosely on the functional perspective, proposed by Forsyth (1998). The functional perspective assumes that the tendency for people to gather in groups reflects the usefulness of the groups to their members. The model proposes that individuals join groups to satisfy several functional needs. Although Forsyth originally proposed more than five needs, items were developed to assess an individual's drive to satisfy only the following functional needs:

1. *Belongingness:* The need for contact and inclusion with others

2. *Intimacy and Support:* The need for loving and supportive relationships

3. *Generativity:* The desire for goal achievement

4. *Influence:* The need for exertion of power

5. *Exploration:* The desire for personal growth

In accordance with the rational method of test development, specific items were written to assess each of these possible subdimensions of joinership. Care was taken to ensure that on the completed 42-item scale each subdimension of joinership was represented by a roughly equal number of items (approximately eight or nine). Furthermore, a third of the items were negatively worded (i.e., required reverse coding), to help guard against acquiescence bias. The following 42 items resulted from this development process.

1. I would rather listen to others' instructions than get up and take command myself.

2. When problems arise, I look to others for support.

3. When working with people, I achieve more goals than I could on my own.

4. I think it is important to support community activities.

5. I don't feel a particular desire to try new things or learn new skills.

6. I feel that belonging to multiple organizations inhibits my personal growth.

7. Before making a decision, I ask for the advice of other people.

8. I am most happy when I am included in a group of my peers.

9. I am more likely to join groups when I can occupy a position of leadership.

10. In a group discussion, I am the person who talks the least.

11. I take advantage of opportunities to influence others.

12. Establishing caring relationships with others is a priority for me.

13. I like to work with others to reach the goals I have set for myself.

14. I like interacting with people who have similar interests.

15. I like to engage in a variety of new activities.

16. I take advantage of opportunities that increase my social status.

17. I prefer to solve problems by myself.

18. I can take care of myself, so I have little need for others.

19. Every person should have a cause or belief that they work towards.

20. I am open to new ideas and perspectives on life.

21. Sharing tasks decreases the amount of work I have to do.

22. I feel left out when I see others involved in a group.

23. The search for personal growth is done best when it is approached as a solitary endeavor.

24. I like to organize and lead the group.

25. Personal growth is a priority for me.

26. In general, I like being in charge of things.

27. I feel most satisfied when the goals I accomplish are achieved through my own efforts.

28. A goal-oriented person is less likely to join groups.

29. When I am having trouble, I count on others for support.

30. Exploring new ideas provides me with opportunities for personal growth.

31. Interaction with others motivates me to achieve my goals.

32. Forming supportive relationships with others is important to me.

33. I enjoy spending most of my free time doing activities that involve others.

34. I avoid organizations/groups because of pressures to conform.

35. Interacting with others helps me to develop my creativity.

36. I prefer being alone rather than being with others.

37. I feel uncomfortable sharing my problems with others.

38. In order to achieve my goals, I need the help of others.

39. Being with other people provides me with a sense of security.

40. I don't like being responsible for making important decisions.

41. I thrive on constant contact with other people.

42. I do not feel comfortable leading other individuals.

Thirty-five individuals served as subject matter experts (SMEs) to provide rational ratings of the items. Each rater was given detailed written and verbal instructions on how to complete the ratings. SMEs were provided with the definition of each of the five functional needs subdimensions and asked to rate the degree to which each item assessed its particular functional need. A five-point Likert-type scale was provided, with response options ranging from 0 for "No relevance" in assessing the defined functional need to 4 for "Highly relevant" to assessing the defined functional need. The resulting data file is titled "Joinership rational ratings.sav."

A sample of 230 respondents was then administered the items. These individuals were asked to indicate how much they agreed with each item using the following scale:

1	2	3	4	5
Strongly Disagree	Disagree	Neither Agree nor Disagree	Agree	Strongly Agree

Data were entered into a file, and negatively worded items were reverse coded. The resulting data are included in the data file "Joinership data recoded.sav."

EXERCISE 15.2: EXAMINING SME
RATINGS OF THE JOINERSHIP ITEMS

OBJECTIVE: To refine the draft joinership scale using information provided by SME ratings.

Use the data file "Joinership rational ratings.sav" to do the following:

1. Compute the mean and standard deviation of each item.

2. Determine a single cut score that you believe reflects SMEs' judgments that the item is too low in relevance to be included for further consideration. There are no rules of thumb here—you'll have to rely on your own judgment. However, don't set your cut score so high that you have too few items for the remaining steps.

3. Justify your choice of a cut score in item 2. Why should items that receive a rating at the cut score or above be retained for further analysis? Why should items below this cut score be discarded from further analysis?

EXERCISE 15.3: FACTOR
ANALYZING THE JOINERSHIP ITEMS

OBJECTIVE: To examine the dimensionality of the remaining joinership scale items. (*Note:* If you have not yet covered Module 18, your instructor may ask you to skip Exercise 15.3 and proceed directly to Exercise 15.4.)

1. Using the data file "Joinership data recoded.sav," conduct an exploratory factor analysis of those items that were retained following examination of the SME ratings. Use the following options found within your data analysis software:
   • Choose principal axis factoring as the method of extraction.
   • Request a scree plot. Base the number of factors that emerge on your judgment of the results of the scree plot.
   • For the method of rotation, select Promax (see Module 18 for an explanation of why Promax is recommended).
   • Choose "sort by size" to display factor loadings.

2. Interpret the results of your factor analysis.
   a. How many interpretable factors emerged? This is the dimensionality of your scale. Label each interpretable factor by examining the items that it comprises.
   b. Which items load on each interpretable factor?
   c. Discard any items that fail to load on an interpretable factor.

EXERCISE 15.4: EXAMINING THE
RELIABILITY OF THE JOINERSHIP SUBSCALES

OBJECTIVE: To develop subscales of joinership with high internal-consistency reliability.

1. Using only those items retained following Exercises 15.2 and 15.3, conduct a reliability analysis of each dimension of the scale (as represented by the factors that emerged in Exercise 15.3) (*alternatively,* if your instructor omitted Exercise 15.3, develop scale dimensions based on your rational categorization of the items you expect to assess each of the five dimensions discussed in the prologue above). Choose the following options:
   - Compute alpha.
   - Select the options "scale if item-deleted" and "item-total correlations."

2. Examine the output for each reliability analysis. Compare the obtained alpha with the alpha estimated if each particular item was deleted. Would the alpha increase if an item were deleted from the scale? If the answer is no, retain all items. If the answer is yes, you may consider dropping the item with the lowest item-total correlation from the final version of the scale. First, however, ask yourself the following questions:
   - Would dropping the item increase the alpha substantially?
   - Is there a logical reason the item seems different from the other items loading on this factor?

If an item was dropped from a dimension, rerun the reliability analysis and repeat the process. Note that alpha is improved by dropping items with low item-total correlations.

3. Once the alphas of each dimension of the scale have been determined, compute the alpha of the overall scale.

Internet Web Site References

15.1. http://www.aom.pace.edu/rmd/1999_RMD_Forum_Method_Effects_in_Self-Reports.htm

This Web page presents a paper by Mary McLaughlin for the Academy of Management Research Methods Division titled "Controlling Method Effects in Self-Report Instruments." The article explores the influence of item context on response to an item.

15.2. http://www.amstat.org/sections/srms/brochures/survwhat.html

This Web page, presented by the American Statistical Association (ASA) Survey Research Methods section, provides an explanation of what a survey is, typical survey variations, and common uses.

Further Readings

DeVellis, R. F. (1991). *Scale development: Theory and applications.* Thousand Oaks, CA: Sage.

Fowler, F. J., Jr. (1995). *Improving survey questions: Design and evaluation.* Thousand Oaks, CA: Sage.

Gough, H. G., & Bradley, P. (1992). Comparing two strategies for developing personality scales. In M. Zeidner & R. Most (Eds.), *Psychological testing: An inside view* (pp. 215–246). Palo Alto, CA: Consulting Psychologists Press.

Jackson, D. N. (1970). A sequential system for personality scale construction. *Current Topics in Clinical and Community Psychology, 2,* 61–96.

Schuman, H., & Presser, S. (1996). *Questions and answers in attitude surveys: Experiments on question form, wording, and context.* Newbury Park, CA: Sage.

Module 16

Response Biases

Whenever we administer a psychological test, we hope to obtain reliable individual differences on the measure. Without reliable individual differences, the measure is of little use to us in predicting our outcome of interest. Sometimes, however, we find little, if any, difference between test takers' responses. Other times we may have substantially more variability in responses than we would expect based on previous administrations of the same or similar tests to comparable participants. In either possible scenario, we would want to determine *why* we obtained such different results than we had expected. There are a variety of reasons the results may be different than anticipated. In this module, we will discuss possible **response biases** that may influence the variability in test scores and, ultimately, the reliability, validity, and utility of those test scores.

Guessing on Knowledge and Aptitude Tests

One response bias that occurs with multiple-choice tests of knowledge and aptitude is guessing on items. That is, with these types of tests there is only one correct (i.e., keyed) answer and there are several distracter responses (also referred to as foils) for each item. Therefore, when a test taker answers an item correctly, it is either because he or she actually knew the answer or because he or she guessed correctly. Unfortunately, it is virtually impossible for us to know which is the case. In fact, even if you asked the respondent, he or she may not be able to tell you which was the case. Hence, one disadvantage of using multiple-choice (or constructed-response) tests is that respondents can answer an item correctly simply by guessing even though they have little or no knowledge of the subject matter being tested. Hence, in some instances, an individual's test score on a multiple-choice test may be telling you more about that person's level of test-wiseness (see Exercise 11.1) or risk-taking behavior than his or her level of knowledge in a given content area. Therefore, one needs to be careful when developing tests to make sure that clues to the correct answer are not given within the item itself (e.g., grammatical errors that give away the answer) or that the answer is not given away by another item within the same test. Following the test construction principles outlined in Module 11 will go a long way toward reducing the potential influence of test-wiseness, and thus guessing, on test scores.

Correcting for Guessing on Knowledge Tests

If we are unsure whether a given individual is answering an item correctly because he or she knows the correct answer or because he or she is guessing correctly, how can we "correct" test scores for the potential influence of guessing? There are several guessing models that can be applied to correct for the influence of guessing on test scores (see Web References 16.1–16.3). In blind guessing models, it is assumed that individuals have no idea what the correct answer is. Therefore, if there are four response options, any individual has a one in four (or 25%) chance of answering an item correctly simply by random guessing. In the past, it was thought one way to reduce this probability was to simply insert more distracters. Hence, an individual would have five, six, or possibly more options to choose from. In theory, this is a good idea. In practice, however, it became clear that it is extremely difficult and time-consuming to write distracter options that are attractive to respondents with little knowledge of the topic. As a result, it turns out that when a fifth, sixth, or additional response option is added, no one chooses it. Thus, in practice, it becomes a waste of time for test developers to rack their brains trying to come up with additional viable response options that no one is going to choose anyway.

Many test publishers have used the blind guessing model (or assumption) when correcting scores for guessing. Thus, they use a correction formula such as

$$R_c = R - \frac{W}{k - 1}$$

where R_c is the corrected-for-guessing score, R is the number of items answered correctly (right), W is the number of items answered incorrectly (wrong), and k is the number of alternatives for each question (e.g., A, B, C, D, and E would be five alternatives). Assume, for example, an individual was administered a 35-item test with each item having five response options. She attempted 32 items and answered 20 correctly. Thus,

$$R_c = R - \frac{W}{k - 1} = 20 - \frac{12}{5 - 1} = 17$$

Hence, we estimate that the individual knew 17 answers and made three lucky guesses of the 20 questions she answered correctly. Thus, you may remember being instructed when you took a standardized test (way back when) not to guess and to leave a question blank if you did not know the answer. This is because, you will notice, only items that are attempted are included in the correction formula. Thus, it will be to your disadvantage to guess on an item that you have no clue as to the correct answer (i.e., you would have to guess randomly). This advice, of course, only applies in the rare instance when a correction-for-guessing formula is used and you are truly guessing randomly.

You are probably thinking that most guessing is not really blind guessing, and you would be correct. What typically happens on any given multiple-choice question is that you are able to fairly confidently eliminate one or two options. Therefore, it is no longer a one-in-five (20%) chance of answering a question correctly for a five-option multiple-choice test question, but rather a one-in-four (25%) or one-in-three (33%) chance of getting the item correct. Another concern is that those who have the least knowledge have the most to gain from guessing. In addition, there may be certain personality characteristics associated with guessing. For example, if examinees are instructed not to guess, the more timid (or risk averse) test takers are more likely to follow the direction and not guess on items they do not know. They may do this even if they could eliminate one or two options and thus guessing would be to their advantage.

So if you are the examinee, should you guess? Yes, if you can eliminate at least one of the incorrect options. In the long run, the correction formula under-corrects in such situations. If you are the test developer or test user, should you correct for guessing? If there are no omits (i.e., everyone answers every question), then there will be a perfect correlation between the original test score and the corrected test score. Hence, it will not make much of a difference in a practical sense. However, if there are omits and your purpose for instituting a **correction for guessing** is to obtain better true scores, to discourage random guessing, or to reduce measurement error (always a good thing), then why not?

Another, less direct way to "correct" for guessing is to use **computer adaptive testing (CAT)** methods. Using CAT methods, if an individual gets an item correct (regardless of whether he knew it or whether he guessed), he then gets a harder question. However, it would be very unlikely that the individual then guesses correctly again (just by chance) on an even more difficult item. Thus, with the adaptive nature of CAT, the individual will eventually be directed back to questions of appropriate difficulty. Ultimately, then, his true underlying ability level will be accurately assessed without using a correction-for-guessing formula. This aspect of CAT is one of the reasons that the Educational Testing Service (ETS) no longer corrects for guessing on the general portion of the Graduate Record Examination (GRE). However, ETS still corrects for guessing on the subject test, which is given in paper-and-pencil format. More information on CAT is provided in Module 20.

Response Biases on Personality and Attitude Measures

A variety of different response biases can also occur on attitude measures. For example, **central tendency error** refers to the situation where the respondent tends to use only the middle of the scale and is reluctant (for whatever reason) to select extreme values. This happens when on a seven-point rating scale, for example, the respondent answers with predominantly 4s. Conversely, with **severity error** or **leniency error,** the respondent uses only the extreme ends of the continuum. Thus, again, the respondents are limiting themselves to a restricted portion of the rating scale and so engaging in response biases that will influence the reliability, validity, and utility of the resulting scores.

One of the most prominent forms of bias in attitude measurement is *acquiescence bias* (i.e., yea-saying), where respondents agree with everything that is presented in a survey. For example, you can query individuals on their attitudes regarding a variety of social issues from abortion to homosexuality to legalization of marijuana to gun ownership. Most individuals would agree with some, but probably not all, of the issues. However, the respondent who acquiesces will have a great tendency to agree with all the issues presented in your survey regardless of his or her true feelings regarding each topic. At the other end of the continuum is *nonacquiescence bias* (i.e., nay-saying), where the individual tends to disagree with everything that is presented. A common strategy to address both issues is to reverse approximately half the items on your survey so that individuals who have a tendency to acquiesce will not simply provide the highest or lowest rating for each item. That is, approximately half the items are worded positively, while the other half are worded negatively. However, you must remember to reverse score the negatively worded items so they are positive before you compute the scale scores (see Module 15).

An additional bias that can occur in personality measures in particular is *faking*. When respondents fake their answers to personality and attitude items, they are most likely trying to deliberately misrepresent themselves. For example, someone applying for a job as a salesperson may know that it is good to be extraverted to be a successful salesperson, so when the person fills out an extraversion questionnaire for employment as a car salesperson, he or she may well try to "fake good" on the extraversion dimension of a personality questionnaire to appear more extraverted than he or she really is. Alternatively, a defendant in a legal proceeding may be facing the death penalty in a capital murder trial. The only chance to avoid execution may be to "fake bad" on a personality measure (i.e., pretend he is criminally insane) in order to claim innocence by reason of insanity. In both instances, the person is not providing truthful or accurate assessments but rather trying to fake answers in order to obtain a desirable outcome.

A concept somewhat similar to faking is that of *socially desirable responding*. Paulhus (1986, 1991) discussed two forms of socially desirable responding—namely, **self-deceptive enhancement (SDE)** and **impression management (IM)**. With IM, the individual is deliberately trying to present a positive impression, similar to the faking-good situation discussed previously. The key is that the individual is consciously making a choice to respond so as to appear more socially acceptable than he or she truly is. On the other hand, an individual engaging in SDE may also be presenting himself or herself in an overly exaggerated positive light; however, the SDE individual is not conscious of doing so. For example, some three quarters of individuals typically report being above average in both intelligence and physical attractiveness. Here the individuals may not be consciously trying to deceive the questioner (although some may be trying to do so); rather, they actually believe, some obviously wrongly so, that they truly are "above average" in terms of intelligence and physical attractiveness. Social psychologists would attribute the reason individuals engage in SDE to related concepts such as self-image, self-esteem, and psychological defense mechanisms.

Another bias that occurs when individuals are rating others' behavior, or past performance (such as in performance appraisal ratings used in an organizational context), is *halo bias*. With halo bias, raters fail to discriminate among conceptually distinct aspects of the ratee's behavior. Unfortunately, it is almost impossible to determine whether the halo is true halo (i.e., the ratee really is excellent in all categories) or whether it is illusory (i.e., the ratee is very sociable, so is seen as good in all areas, even if he or she isn't). Disappointingly, there are no correction formulas for these biases as there are with knowledge tests.

We should probably make a distinction between response bias and response style. *Response biases* are measurement artifacts that emerge from the context of a particular situation. Thus, response biases can often be ameliorated with proper instructions or rater training. For example, individuals are likely to engage in IM and faking good on personality measures when a desirable outcome is attached (e.g., a job offer or academic placement). However, when the context does not involve a direct valued outcome (e.g., a career counseling session), the individual will be much less likely to engage in response biases. **Response styles,** however, are not context specific. These measurement artifacts tend to be consistent across situations and so are more difficult to reduce. For example, there are clear cultural differences in how individuals respond to attitude questions. Thus, individuals from some cultures are more likely to agree with an item (i.e., acquiesce), regardless of the content of the item. In Module 14, we discuss in more detail these and related issues with regard to cross-cultural issues in testing.

What are some of the ways we can reduce response biases? First, we must make a distinction between detecting such biases and preventing such biases. Clearly, our primary concern should be to prevent such biases in the first place. Thus, for example, it is important to have clear instructions for both test proctors and test takers. It is also important to avoid implying that one response is preferred over another. Also, whenever possible, anonymity has been shown to lead to more honest responding. In addition, research convincingly indicates that subtle wording differences (particularly in attitude and public-opinion questionnaires) can make dramatic differences in how individuals respond to a question. Test developers have also used forced-choice item formats with comparable levels of social desirability for each option. In doing so, our hope is that respondents are unable to choose the most socially desirable answer and thus will answer in a more truthful and accurate manner. However, what is considered socially desirable may change depending on the context. For example, being extraverted may be desirable for a sales position, but may be less socially desirable for an entry-level computer programmer. Respondents also tend to have a much easier time making comparative judgments rather than absolute judgments. Thus, it is better to ask, "Do you agree more with X or Y?" than to ask, "How much do agree with X? With Y?" Finally, use of unobtrusive observational measures may help to provide more accurate assessment of the constructs of interest.

No matter how much we try, however, we will not be able to totally prevent individuals from engaging in response biases. In addition, response styles are not context dependent; hence, it would be difficult to "prevent" such biases. Therefore, we must be able not only to do our best to prevent such occurrences but also to detect them once they occur. That is why popular measures such as the Minnesota Multiphasic Personality Inventory (MMPI) have several "lie" scales. In addition, there are numerous scales available to detect socially desirable responding. As Anastasi and Urbina (1997) pointed out, however, how we view such response biases has evolved over time. Initially, in the early to middle part of the 20th century, researchers assumed that any such response biases represented irrelevant error variance, and the goal was to eliminate them. By the late 20th century, however, many researchers began to see response biases such as faking, acquiescence, and socially desirable responding as their own unique traits that were worthy of measurement and study in their own right (Mersman & Shultz, 1998). Even today, however, it is still unclear how to deal with those who engage in such response biases. Should they be removed from the data set? Should their scores somehow be "corrected" for such biases? In addition, we may not even be sure what causes some of the aberrant responding we may observe. Additional factors, such as fatigue, primacy, carelessness, or item ordering effects, may be the "real" culprits. Thus, even though we have developed more and more sophisticated ways of identifying response biases, there is no consensus in the professional literature on what to do with such information once we have it.

A Step-by-Step Example of Identifying and Examining Response Biases

As a second-year graduate student, you have been asked to sit on a university-wide committee that is developing a questionnaire that will be given to faculty, staff, and students at your university to assess their attitudes regarding your university possibly converting from a quarter to a semester system. This issue has been raised numerous times in the past. In general, faculty members have been about equally split (50/50) on whether to convert to a semester system, with newer faculty members preferring to switch to semesters, while more senior faculty members generally oppose such a move. Students, though, overwhelmingly (75%+) do not want to switch from the quarter to the semester system. However, the views of the university staff have generally been much more variable, sometimes supporting and sometimes not supporting such a conversion. The administration is strongly in favor of converting to semesters; however, it refuses to do so without the support of students, faculty, and staff.

Your role on the committee is to provide input regarding how to prevent certain biases from occurring in the survey before it is administered and how to identify any biases once the data are in and ready to be analyzed. You know that there are many advantages to assessing opinions via written attitude surveys, such as their being quick, inexpensive, efficient, and flexible. You also realize, however, that poor design and careless execution of the survey can lead to biased responding. You also know that error can be both random and systematic. Random error is typically thought of in terms of sampling error. Therefore, it is important that we choose our samples appropriately. However, other committee members will be addressing the issue of appropriate sampling methods. We are charged with evaluating possible systematic errors and, in particular, issues surrounding response errors (i.e., biases).

Systematic bias can arise from administrative errors (e.g., confusing directions on how to fill out the questionnaire) or respondent error. We will focus on respondent error because that is the focus of this module. A major source of respondent error is no response at all. That is, how do we interpret unreturned surveys or returned surveys that are only half completed? Were the respondents being careless or were they trying to send a message with their lack of response? We also know that those with strong opinions are more likely to fill out and return attitude questionnaires; thus, those who are indifferent about the topic will likely be underrepresented in our final sample. Thus, it is important that we do all that we can to maximize the response rate before, during, and after the administration of the survey. Doing so will dramatically reduce nonrespondent errors.

Then there are the response biases we discussed earlier, such as acquiescence, extremity (leniency and severity), central tendency, and socially desirable responding. For example, those strongly opposed to the potential conversion may be likely to engage in severity ratings that criticize every aspect of a potential conversion, even if they do not totally agree with all such aspects, in order to ensure that their voice is heard. Others may be likely to acquiesce because they know that the administration is strongly in favor of such a conversion. In order to combat such potential response biases, we would want to guarantee anonymity, make the directions as clear and neutral as possible, and ensure that the items themselves are not worded in such a way as to elicit a response in favor of one position or another. We may even want to think about the possibility of adding some forced-choice items where each possible response is of equal social desirability; however, that may be difficult given the nature of this situation.

Assuming we have taken the safeguards mentioned previously prior to the administration of the questionnaire, we then need to identify any possible response biases or styles that may be present in the respondents' answers once we collect the data. Depending on the number of respondents, it may be unwieldy to identify individual respondents who are demonstrating specific response biases or patterns. However, we may want to break down the data by major categories such as faculty versus staff versus students. We may also want to look within subcategories, such as students within different colleges within the university or students in particular majors. However, we must be careful not to break down the data too finely, as we may be able to identify individuals (e.g., there may be only one Hispanic female who is a geology major at the university), thus violating our assurances of anonymity.

Clearly there are many details that need to be attended to when you attempt to undertake a major survey such as this one. Response biases are just a small part of the many decisions that need to be made. It is important, however, to keep potential response biases in mind as you make critical decisions along the way. For example, whether a face-to-face, mail, e-mail, telephone, or Internet survey is used can dramatically affect which response errors are likely to surface and in what fashion for each constituent group (see Web Reference 16.4). Thus, being mindful of potential response biases will help you better prevent them before the survey is administered and identify and address them once you have collected the data.

Concluding Comments

With multiple-choice constructed-response knowledge questions, there is always the possibility that individuals might guess the correct answer. Most research shows that corrections for guessing tend to underestimate the extent of guessing, in that individuals can typically eliminate one or more incorrect responses. Hence, corrections for guessing should be used sparingly. In addition, if such corrections are used, it should be made clear to the test takers what the ramifications will be if they guess randomly. Response biases and response styles on attitude questionnaires also represent possible measurement artifacts that need to be dealt with. Several suggestions are offered to prevent (or at least reduce) and identify such biases, but in the end it is difficult to assess whether such biases are true biases or illusory. Thus, how to address the issue of response biases in attitude questionnaires is still a controversial topic.

Practical Questions

1. Is correcting for guessing appropriate in college-level courses where most individuals will not be guessing randomly, but rather will almost always be able to eliminate one or more distracter options?

2. In situations where individuals are unlikely to omit any of the questions on purpose, is it appropriate to correct for guessing?

3. What other personality characteristics, besides risk taking, do you think would be associated with guessing on multiple-choice tests?

4. What other factors, besides guessing, might contribute to extremely low or high levels of variability in knowledge test scores?

5. It was noted that if a test taker can eliminate at least one of the distracters then corrections for guessing underestimate the extent of guessing. Is it possible to overestimate the extent of guessing with correction formulas? If so, how?

6. Given that you cannot guess on short-answer essay questions, would they, by default, be more reliable?

7. What is the difference between response biases and response styles?

8. What are the best ways to reduce response biases? Response styles?

Case Studies

CASE STUDY 16.1: COMPARABILITY OF DIFFERENT INTRODUCTORY PSYCHOLOGY TESTS

Ryan, a first-year PhD student, was teaching his own discussion sections of introductory psychology for the first time. At Ryan's university, the introductory psychology class consists of a 200-person lecture taught by a full-time professor in the department and ten 20-person discussion sections taught by first-year graduate students. There are five graduate students who teach two discussion sections each, every term. Every other week, the five discussion leaders for that term are to administer a 25-item quiz on the chapters covered in the lecture and discussion sections during that time frame. On the Monday before the scheduled quiz, the five discussion leaders meet with the professor and agree on the questions to be included in the quiz for that week.

Everything seemed to be going well until Ryan computed the results of the third quiz. He had noticed that students in the morning section had scored pretty much as usual, but that the grades in the afternoon section were rather odd. In particular, while he noticed that the afternoon class average was just slightly higher than the morning section's grades on the quiz for that week, what seemed really odd was that students in the afternoon section all received almost exactly the same score (i.e., all had a score of 21, 22, or 23). That is, there was basically no variability among the test scores. Figuring the students in the afternoon section probably cheated and somehow got a copy of the quiz from the morning section, Ryan started examining the quizzes more closely. However, to his surprise, he noticed that while everyone had almost the exact same score, different students answered different questions correctly. That is, not everyone answered the same two, three, or four questions wrong. Hence, it didn't appear that individuals copied off one another. This left Ryan rather perplexed. Unsure of what was going on, Ryan decided he had better check in with the other graduate student teaching assistants and see what they thought.

Questions to Ponder

1. What alternative explanation (besides cheating) do you think might explain the low variability in the afternoon section?

2. What might Ryan have done differently to reduce the possible "cheating factor"?

3. Would using a correction-for-guessing formula help Ryan in any way? If so, how?

4. Are there other statistical corrections Ryan could institute to correct for the low variability?

5. Is the low variability in test scores really a problem in a classroom situation such as this?

CASE STUDY 16.2: SUSPICIOUS SURVEY
DATA FROM A FRIEND

Dora was very excited about her committee's recent approval of her proposal for her master's thesis project. After several arduous sets of revisions, she was finally ready to collect her data. Unfortunately, the committee had added several new scales to her study and suddenly her six-page questionnaire had turned into 15 pages. As a result, the structural equation model she had proposed had also expanded. Thus, her original estimate of 150 subjects had doubled to more than 300. To add to her troubles, her target population was working parents. These were just the sort of people who didn't have time to fill out a lengthy questionnaire. Undaunted, Dora continued going to schools and day care centers to collect data, but the surveys seemed to be trickling in just a few at a time.

Just as Dora was about to throw up her hands in surrender, she had a stroke of good luck. Her friend in another city worked for a large school district as head of student counseling. Her friend said she could easily get her 100–150 parents to complete her survey. So Dora quickly mailed off 200 surveys to her friend. About six weeks later, she called her friend to check in. Her friend said she had been buried in work, but she reassured Dora that she would have the completed surveys back to her within two weeks. When Dora called her friend a month later, her friend was again rather vague on how many completed surveys she had, but the friend assured Dora once again that she would have the completed surveys mailed back to her by the end of the month. About ready to give up yet again, Dora received a box in the mail from her friend. Eagerly, she opened up the box and was shocked to see all 200 surveys inside. However, as she began entering the data that night, she noticed that all the responses were the highest value on the given scales (i.e., 5 on a five-point scale, 7 on a seven-point scale). She also noticed that while the ink color was different on some of the surveys, it seemed like the same handwriting was used on each of the 200 surveys. Did her friend simply go through and circle the highest value on all the surveys? Dora was desperate for more data, but was feeling rather uncomfortable with the current situation. Therefore, it seemed time to sit down with her thesis advisor and figure out what to do (if anything) with the "data" she recently received and where to go from here on her thesis.

Questions to Ponder

1. If you were Dora, would you use the surveys from her friend?

2. Would the data still be useful to Dora, assuming working parents, in fact, completed the data from her friend?

3. Again assuming the data are, in fact, legitimate, what response bias seems to be happening here?

4. Are there any statistical corrections that can be made to the data to make them useful?

5. If Dora were a fellow student colleague and friend, what suggestions would you provide to her with regard to collecting more data?

Exercises

EXERCISE 16.1: CORRECTION FOR GUESSING IN MULTIPLE-CHOICE KNOWLEDGE TESTS—HAND CALCULATION EXERCISE

OBJECTIVE: To practice using the correction-for-guessing formula discussed in the module overview.

Table 12.5 provides data for a 74-item multiple-choice exam from an undergraduate tests and measurements class. The first line in the table is the answer key. Determine whether each student answered each of the 74 items correctly or not, then compute a raw score (total correct) for all 35 students who provided data. (Note: Your instructor may provide this for you.) Next, using the correction formula (discussed in the overview), compute a corrected-for-guessing score for each individual. Note that all questions have four possible responses (i.e., $k = 4$).

1. What is the relationship between the uncorrected and corrected scores?

2. Does guessing seem to help some students more than others in terms of their final scores? Discuss.

3. Students in the class were not warned about the possibility of correcting for guessing. Is it fair, then, to correct for guessing in this situation? Discuss.

4. What alternatives to correcting for guessing could the instructor use to increase the quality of the test scores?

EXERCISE 16.2: CORRECTION FOR GUESSING IN MULTIPLE-CHOICE KNOWLEDGE TESTS—COMPUTER EXERCISE

OBJECTIVE: To practice using the correction-for-guessing formula discussed in the module overview with computerized data.

The data set "GMA data.sav" contains scores for 323 individuals on a 40-item general mental ability test that includes both verbal and quantitative questions. Each item has already been scored as incorrect (0) or correct (1). The data set also has a total raw score for each individual.

Demographic data are also provided. Using the correction formula (discussed in the overview), compute a corrected-for-guessing score for each individual. Note that all questions have five possible responses (i.e., $k = 5$).

1. What is the relationship between the uncorrected and corrected scores?

2. Does guessing seem to help some respondents more than others? Discuss.

3. Respondents were not warned about the possibility of correcting for guessing. Is it fair, then, to correct for guessing in this situation? Discuss.

4. What alternatives to correcting for guessing could you use to increase the quality of the test scores?

EXERCISE 16.3: IDENTIFYING RESPONSE BIASES IN ATTITUDE ITEMS

OBJECTIVE: To practice identifying response biases in attitude items.

The "Geoscience attitudes.sav" data set asks students about their attitudes toward the geosciences (archaeology, geography, and geology). The data set has 13 attitude items and 137 respondents (see Exercise 18.1 for a description of the content of each question). Examine the data set and try to identify individual cases (i.e., students) who appear to be engaging in some form of response bias. In particular, determine if any of the students are displaying signs of acquiescence, leniency, severity, central tendency, or socially desirable responding. For the latter, you will have to examine the wording of the items carefully and try to identify items that you believe to be highest in social desirability. Then determine if any student's responses appear to differ for those items identified as socially desirable as compared to the less (or non-) socially desirable items.

1. Did you identify any individuals who appear to be providing biased responses?

2. Which cases appear to be demonstrating biased responses?

3. What forms of response biases did you identify?

4. What should we do with this information once we have it?

EXERCISE 16.4: DEVELOPING TEST MATERIALS AND PROCEDURES THAT WILL (HOPEFULLY) REDUCE RESPONSE BIAS IN PARTICIPANTS

OBJECTIVE: To gain practice in developing strategies to reduce biases in responding to attitude questionnaires.

Imagine you have been asked to develop a personality test that measures antisocial behaviors. The measure will be used for three different purposes. The first purpose will be to identify high school students who are having trouble in school and thus may be referred to an alternative high school for troubled youths. The second purpose is to determine whether parolees still pose a significant risk to society if they are paroled and thus allowed to rejoin society. In the third situation, the test will be used to screen candidates applying for the job of police officer with a small municipality (15,000 residents) that uses community policing as its major crime-fighting mechanism.

1. Would you expect to find different forms of response biases in the different populations under study? If so, which biases would you see as most prominent in each of the three scenarios?

2. What strategies would you suggest to prevent response biases in each of the three scenarios?

3. What strategies would you suggest to identify response biases in each of the three scenarios once the data have been collected?

Internet Web Site References

16.1. http://www.testscoring.vt.edu/mem001.html

This Web site provides an essay on correcting for guessing on multiple-choice items by Robert B. Frary.

16.2. http://www.personal.psu.edu/users/d/m/dmr/papers/CORR4GUS.pdf

This PDF file presents a discussion of the correction-for-guessing formula by Dennis Roberts.

16.3. http://slv.math.adams.edu/ron/MathStar/StatProbs/randresp.htm

This Web page discusses useful ways of collecting nonbiased responses with regard to personal and sensitive topics by using random response methods.

16.4. http://www.psy.ohio-state.edu/social/tch62a.pdf

This PDF file presents a comparison of telephone and face-to-face interviews with a detailed discussion of various response biases.

Further Readings

Moorman, R. H. P., & Philip, M. (1992). A meta-analytic review and empirical test of the potential confounding effects of social desirability response sets in organizational behaviour research. *Journal of Occupational & Organizational Psychology, 65,* 131–149.

Paulhus, D. L. (1986). Self-deception and impression management in test responses. In A. Angleitner & J. S. Wiggins (Eds.), *Personality assessment via questionnaires: Current issues in theory and measurement* (pp. 143–165). Berlin: Springer-Verlag.

Paulhus, D. L. (1991). Measurement and control of response bias. In J. P. Robinson, P. R. Shaver, & L. S. Wrightsman (Eds.), *Measures of personality and social psychological attitudes.* San Diego, CA: Academic Press.

Schaeffer, N. C., & Presser, S. (2003). The science of asking questions. *Annual Review of Sociology, 29,* 65–88.

Advanced Topics

Module 17

Combining Predictors Using Multiple Regression

In Module 7, we said that evidence of criterion-related validity is examined by correlating test scores with corresponding criterion scores. If the test is sufficiently related to the criterion of interest, regression can later be used to predict criterion scores in a sample of people for whom we have no actual criterion values, as long as the sample is drawn from the same population used in the original validation study. Obviously, the stronger the relationship between our test and the criterion, the more accurate will be our predicted criterion score. If a test is used in this way to *predict* a criterion score, the test is often referred to as a predictor. In most cases, however, we could increase the accuracy of predicting our criterion if we expanded the number of predictors beyond one.

Multiple regression allows us to use information from numerous predictors to predict a single criterion score. For example, if we wanted to predict tomorrow's high temperature in Poughkeepsie, New York, we would want to consider a number of factors, including today's temperature in Poughkeepsie, the amount of cloud cover, last year's high temperature in Poughkeepsie on tomorrow's date, and so on. The addition of multiple predictors would likely increase the accuracy of our prediction of tomorrow's high temperature beyond the accuracy we would obtain if we relied on any single measure alone. Similarly, if we wanted to predict an applicant's potential job performance, we would desire information from multiple valid selection tests rather than just a single one. This module will discuss issues associated with combining predictors when we use multiple regression procedures.

The Multiple Regression Equation

As in the single-predictor case, in order to use multiple regression for pre-diction purposes we would first conduct a study to determine the degree to which a set of predictors is related to scores on a criterion of interest. Thus, a sample is drawn and scores on each predictor variable and criterion are collected. If the set of predictors is significantly related to the criterion, then we could use the information obtained from this original sample to produce the regression equation. As you will see below, a multiple regression equa-tion is a linear equation that includes values for each of the predictor vari-ables we choose to include. Each predictor variable receives a unique weight, or regression coefficient, based on (a) the means and standard deviations of the predictors, (b) the correlations between each of the predictors and the criterion, and (c) the correlations between the predictors themselves.

The regression equation can be presented in two forms: unstandardized or standardized. The unstandardized form of the multiple regression equa-tion uses an individual's raw scores on each test to predict a raw score on the criterion. In addition to including regression weights and predictor raw score values, the unstandardized regression equation contains a value called the *intercept,* which is the value associated with the location where the regression line crosses the Y axis. The *unstandardized* multiple regression equation is as follows:

$$\hat{Y} = b_1 x_1 + b_2 x_2 + \cdots + b_k x_k + a$$

where $\hat{Y}$ is the predicted criterion raw score, b is an unstandardized regres-sion coefficient, x is a predictor raw score, a is the intercept, and k is the number of predictors.

The standardized form of the equation requires the use of standardized predictor scores (such as z scores) to predict a standardized criterion score. The *standardized* multiple regression equation is

$$\hat{z}_y = \beta_1 z_{x1} + \beta_2 z_{x2} + \cdots + \beta_k z_{xk}$$

where $\hat{z}_y$ is the predicted standardized criterion score, β is a standardized regression coefficient, and z_x is a standardized predictor score.

It should be noted that the two versions of the regression equation are equal in terms of accuracy in prediction. However, sometimes we prefer the use of the standardized regression equation because the magnitude of the resulting standardized regression coefficients, or beta weights (β), of each predictor can be directly compared to one another because all variables are measured on a common metric.

As long as the new sample was drawn from the same population used in the development of the regression equation, the regression equation can be used to predict a criterion score for each member of a new sample of individuals. This is done by collecting predictor scores for each individual in the new sample, plugging these values into the regression equation, and computing predicted Y scores.

The Multiple Regression Equation: An Example

Let us consider a brief example of the use of the multiple regression equation, based on data in the "volunteer data.sav" data file. (*Notes:* First, you will find a more detailed description of this data set in Exercise 17.2. Second, you are encouraged to follow the computations discussed in this example using your favorite data analysis program.) From this data set, we could examine whether the variables *perceived opportunity for reward* (reward), *role clarity* (clarity), and *leader consideration* (ledcons) as a set can be used to predict an individual's level of desire to remain in the organization due to an emotional bond. This is termed *affective commitment* (affectc). An examination of the zero-order correlations reveals that *affective commitment* is highly correlated with each of the predictors: $r = .64$ with *perceived opportunity for reward,* $r = .50$ with *leader consideration,* and $r = .64$ with *role clarity.*

Because we have three predictor variables, we would also have three regression coefficients in the equation. Assuming that the terms denoted with a subscript of 1 corresponded to *perceived opportunity for reward,* those denoted with a subscript of 2 corresponded to *leader consideration,* and those denoted with a 3 corresponded to *role clarity,* the resulting unstandardized multiple regression equation for the prediction of affective commitment would be written as

$$\hat{Y} = .48x_1 + .20x_2 + .38x_3 + (-.60)$$

Let us assume that we then randomly draw a sample from the same population and wish to predict these people's scores on affective commitment. For the sake of argument, suppose that an individual from this new sample scored a value of 5.17 on *reward,* 4.20 on *leader consideration,* and 3.83 on *role clarity.* (Note that this individual just so happened to score exactly the same values as the second case of our data file.) To estimate this individual's score on *affective commitment*, we would plug these values into the regression equation:

$$\hat{Y} = .48(5.17) + .20(4.20) + .38(3.83) + (-.60)$$
$$= 2.48 + .84 + 1.46 + (-.60)$$
$$= 4.18$$

Thus, we would predict that a person with the given values on the predictor variables would have a value of 4.18 on *affective commitment*.

We would need to use the standardized version of the regression equation if we hoped to compare the magnitude of the regression coefficients across the predictor variables. In this case, the standardized regression equation is

$$\hat{z}_y = .41z_{x1} + .11z_{x2} + .40z_{x3}$$

Note that scores on *perceived opportunity for reward* and *role clarity* receive nearly equal weighting, while scores on *leader consideration* receive a lesser weight. Virtually all statistical packages will provide a test of significance of each coefficient in a regression analysis. In SPSS, for example, a table labeled "coefficients" presents not only the standardized and unstandardized regression coefficients for each predictor, but also a test of the significance of each predictor's regression weight. In this example, the regression coefficients for both *perceived opportunity for reward* and *role clarity* are statistically significant, $p < .01$. The coefficient for *leader consideration*, however, is not statistically significant, $p > .05$. This suggests that we could eliminate the *leader consideration* variable from our regression equation without a significant loss in prediction accuracy.

Let us assume in this case that we did not want to eliminate any variables from our regression equation. If we wanted to estimate the individual's score on the criterion using the standardized regression equation, we would first need to standardize each of the predictor values. If z scores were chosen, the standardized regression equation for the same individual discussed previously (i.e., a person with the same values as the individual in case 2 of the data file) would yield the following:

$$\hat{z}_y = .41z_{x1} + .11z_{x2} + .40z_{x3}$$
$$= .41(.61) + .11(.50) + .40(-.36)$$
$$= .25 + .06 + (-.14)$$
$$= .17$$

It is important to remember that in this case the predicted score on *affective commitment* for this individual is also a *z* score.

Prediction Accuracy

Because we are predicting a criterion score for an individual, you might wonder just how accurate we are in predicting this particular individual's actual level of *affective commitment*. Unfortunately, we typically will never know, unless we obtain an actual criterion score. In the creation of this example, however, we cheated a bit, and the new individual for whom we just estimated a value for *affective commitment* just so happens to have the same exact value for all variables as the second case in our data set. Because we do actually have a criterion score for this person, we could see how accurate our prediction might be in this particular case. (Note that in the real world you would want to examine this question using data from a sample that was independent of the sample the coefficients were computed on.) In the data set, the individual's actual raw score value for affective commitment is 4.29. Our prediction of 4.18 is therefore not half bad. (Incidentally, the same individual's actual *z* score for *affective commitment* is .23, compared to our predicted *z* score of .17.)

Before we become too complacent in our ability to predict scores on *affective commitment,* we might want to compute another individual's predicted criterion score as well. Let us assume that our next individual randomly drawn from the population just so happens to have the same exact predictor values as the first individual in our data set. Thus, the individual received a value of 5.00 on *perceived opportunity for reward,* a 4.70 on *leader consideration,* and a 4.33 on *role clarity.* We could again compute the individual's predicted *affective commitment* score:

$$\hat{Y} = .48(5.00) + .20(4.70) + .38(4.33) + (-.60)$$
$$= 2.40 + .94 + 1.65 + (-.60)$$
$$= 4.39$$

Well, if we had some way of knowing the *actual* criterion score for this individual, and we found that this also happened to be the same value as the individual in the first case in our data file, would we be happy with our predictive abilities? Certainly not. Taking a quick peek at the data file, we see that the actual *affective commitment* score for this individual is 2.43. That's a long way from our predicted value of 4.39, considering that the individual items comprising the criterion score were rated on a seven-point scale.

It should come as no surprise that unless our variables are perfectly reliable (which is quite unlikely) *and* as a set our predictors are perfectly related to our criterion (even less likely), we will have some error in prediction. Fortunately, in computing the regression equation, we can also derive some estimates of the overall degree of accuracy in our prediction.

In the single-predictor case, the squared correlation coefficient between the predictor and the criterion, r^2, provides an estimate of the accuracy of prediction. The larger the value of r^2, the greater the amount of reliable variance in criterion scores that can be explained by scores on the predictor. When we have multiple predictors, a similar estimate of accuracy in prediction is provided by the estimated squared **multiple correlation** coefficient, R^2. This value provides a basic estimate of how strongly the predictor set is related to the criterion. In the example prediction of *affective commitment* discussed previously, R^2 is equal to .57.

The **standard error of estimate** provides a more direct measure of the accuracy of prediction in regression. Previously, we computed a few example cases in which we compared predicted criterion scores to actual criterion scores. Because the predicted criterion scores were not identical to the actual criterion scores, we knew that we had some amount of error in prediction. Conceptually, if we subtracted the estimated criterion score from the actual criterion score (e.g., $Y - \hat{Y}$) for every individual in our sample, squared these differences, computed the average squared difference, and, finally, took the square root, we would compute the standard error of the estimate. Thus, the standard error of the estimate is the square root of the average squared deviation from the regression line. More simply, it informs us how much, on average, a predicted criterion score differs from the actual criterion score. In the example prediction of *affective commitment,* the standard error of estimate is .92.

Predictor Interrelationships

In Module 7, we said that the coefficient of determination is computed by squaring a validity coefficient and multiplying the result by 100%. If a test had a criterion-related validity of .30, we would be able to explain 9% of the reliable variance in the criterion. Unfortunately, even when using this test, we would still leave 91% of the reliable variance in the criterion unexplained—our accuracy in prediction leaves much to be desired. Ah, but I can guess what you are thinking. Why not add more and more tests (predictors) until we have explained 100% of the reliable variance in the criterion? Unfortunately, there is a little problem called *collinearity* (or multicollinearity) that interferes with this potential solution.

Let us consider a hypothetical example in which three predictors are each valid predictors of the criterion. The validity of Predictor A is $r_{xy} = .30$, of Predictor B is $r_{xy} = .40$, and of Predictor C is $r_{xy} = .20$. Figure 17.1 presents a Venn diagram representing the idealized relationships between these predictors and the criterion. If Figure 17.1 correctly reflected the relationships among the variables, we would expect the combined percentage of reliable variance accounted for in the criterion to be $R^2 = 9\% + 16\% + 4\% = 29\%$. Note that because we are using more than one predictor, we now refer to the estimated squared multiple correlation coefficient (R^2) rather than r^2.

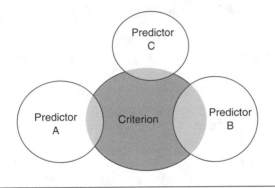

Figure 17.1   Three Orthogonal Predictors in Multiple Regression

Unfortunately, in reality, the predictors themselves are likely intercorrelated, indicating that Figure 17.1 should be revised to depict some degree of overlap between predictors. Again consider the two examples presented at the very beginning of this module. In predicting tomorrow's high temperature in Poughkeepsie, New York, it is likely there will exist relationships among the following predictors: today's high temperature, the amount of cloud cover, and last year's high temperature on tomorrow's date. Similarly, an applicant's score on several selection tests such as an interview, a measure of cognitive ability, and a measure of personality are likely to be correlated to some degree as well. *Collinearity* refers to the extent to which predictors in a regression analysis are intercorrelated. The greater the collinearity between predictors, the less each additional predictor will contribute to the explanation of unique variance in the criterion (see Web Reference 17.4 for a detailed explanation of collinearity).

Thus, a more accurate representation of the relationship among Predictors A, B, and C would produce a diagram similar to Figure 17.2.

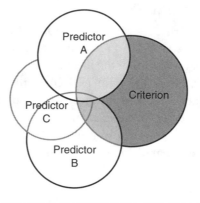

Figure 17.2   Three Oblique Predictors in Multiple Regression

In this far less attractive, but more likely scenario, each of the predictors is not only associated with the criterion but also with each other. Because we cannot "double-count" variance already explained by an earlier predictor, the unique contribution of each new predictor is lessened. Thus, the actual combined percentage of variance accounted for by the three predictors will be considerably less than 29%.

We have evidence that collinearity is a concern in our prediction of *affective commitment* as well. Recall that the zero-order correlations between *affective commitment* and each of the three predictor variables were all .50 and above. Yet when we examined the significance of the regression weights, we found that the inclusion of the variable *leader consideration* did not explain a significant portion of the variance in *affective commitment*. Inspection of the zero-order correlations both between the predictors and between the predictors and *affective commitment* helps to shed some light on this finding. While all three predictor variables were highly related to the criterion of *affective commitment*, *leader consideration* was not as highly correlated with the criterion as were the other two predictors. Further, *leader consideration* is considerably correlated with both *perceived opportunity for reward* ($r = .44$) and *role clarity* ($r = .57$). Thus, when the other two predictors are included in the regression equation, *leader consideration* fails to explain a significant portion of unique variance in *affective commitment*.

When contemplating the addition of a second, third, or fourth predictor, then, there are two factors to be considered. The first consideration is the predictor's correlation with the criterion. The second consideration is the predictor's correlation with the other predictor(s) already used. The ideal predictor will have a high correlation with the criterion and no relationship with the other predictors. In this way, the addition of this ideal predictor will explain a maximum amount of *unique variance* in the criterion—that is, variance not already explained by the predictors already in use. In multiple regression, greater beta weights are assigned to variables that explain higher amounts of unique variance in the criterion.

Stability of the Validity Coefficient

A second issue associated with the use of numerous predictors concerns the stability of the estimated squared multiple correlation coefficient, R^2. *Shrinkage* refers to the drop in validity that occurs if regression weights computed on one sample are used to predict the criterion in a second sample. Unless the sample size is very large relative to the number of predictors, some shrinkage is likely to occur. Put another way, our initial estimate of R^2 is likely to be overestimated. The **shrinkage formula** (also called *Wherry's formula*) provides an estimate of the "shrunken" squared validity coefficient for the population or what is known as the adjusted R^2:

$$\rho^2 = 1 - \left[\left(\frac{N-1}{N-k-1} \right) (1 - R^2) \right]$$

where ρ^2 is the adjusted R^2, the estimated squared population multiple correlation coefficient; N is the sample size; and k is the number of predictors.

R^2 is the estimated squared multiple correlation coefficient between the predictors and the criterion.

Using Wherry's formula, we can compute an estimate of the squared population multiple correlation coefficient for our example prediction of *affective commitment*. The sample size in this example is 120. We have three predictor variables, and, as we stated previously, R^2 is .57. Thus,

$$\rho^2 = 1 - \left[\left(\frac{120-1}{120-3-1} \right) (1 - .57) \right]$$

$$= 1 - (1.03)(.43)$$

$$= 1 - .44$$

$$= .56$$

In this example, the adjusted R^2 is nearly the same size as our original estimate of R^2, owing to our large sample size. For the sake of illustration, let us determine what the estimated squared population multiple correlation would be if our sample were composed of only 20 individuals rather than the 120:

$$\rho^2 = 1 - \left[\left(\frac{20 - 1}{20 - 3 - 1} \right)(1 - .57) \right]$$

$$= 1 - (1.19)(.43)$$

$$= 1 - .51$$

$$= .49$$

Here we see a considerable increase in the amount of shrinkage when the estimate is based on a hypothetical sample with a smaller N.

The estimated squared population multiple correlation coefficient provided by the Wherry formula can then be used to provide the *squared cross-validated correlation coefficient* (Cattin, 1980):

$$\rho_c^2 = \frac{(N - k - 3)\, \rho^4 + \rho^2}{(N - 2k - 2)\, \rho^2 + k}$$

where ρ_c^2 is the squared cross-validated correlation coefficient, N is the sample size, k is the number of predictors, and ρ is the estimated population multiple correlation (square root of the value from the Wherry formula).

The Cattin (1980) formula provides an accurate estimate of the validity of a set of predictors when used on a new sample. If the criterion-related validity coefficient is based on a sufficiently large sample, the estimated population cross-validity estimate will be very close to the originally estimated validity coefficient. However, if the validity coefficient is based on a small sample relative to the number of predictors used, the observed validity coefficient can be much larger than the more accurate cross-validity.

Our example of the prediction of *affective commitment* can be concluded as follows:

$$\rho_c^2 = \frac{(120 - 3 - 3).32 + .57}{(120 - 2(3) - 2).57 + 3}$$

$$= \frac{(114).32 + .57}{(112).57 + 3}$$

$$= \frac{37.05}{66.84}$$

$$= .55$$

Adequate Sample Size

As you can see from our example, our original estimate of the squared correlation coefficient was quite stable. This finding is due to the relatively large sample size used in the computation of the regression equation. The estimate would have been far less stable had we used a small sample size. Concern with stability of a multiple correlation coefficient is lessened when we use a large sample size (N) relative to the number of predictors (k). The problem is determining just what is meant by a "large" sample size. A common recommendation is to ensure that, at a minimum, the N to k ratio (N/k) is no smaller than 15:1. Newton and Rudestam (1999) provided additional guidelines and simple formulas for determining adequate sample size, depending on whether the primary interest is in examining the multiple correlation coefficient (R) or in examining the individual predictor variables. To scrutinize the multiple correlation coefficient, the sample size should be at least $50 + 8k$ (where k is the number of predictors). To examine the individual predictor variables, the sample size should be at least $104 + k$. For most cases, Newton and Rudestam recommended computing both formulas and then using the larger sample size as a minimum.

Concluding Comments

The issues discussed in this module only begin to touch on the complexity of multiple regression. However, the issues discussed here will hopefully sensitize you to the utility of this widely used statistical procedure to test validation and prediction. For complete coverage of multiple regression, you would do well to consult Cohen, Cohen, West, and Aiken (2002) or Pedhazur (1997).

Practical Questions

1. What factors influence the relative weighting of each predictor in an unstandardized multiple regression equation?

2. How does a standardized regression equation differ from an unstandardized regression equation?

3. If we were currently using four predictors to explain 40% of the variance in our criterion, would the addition of four more predictors with equal combined validity allow us to explain 80% of the reliable variance in our criterion? Why or why not?

4. Why do we refer to the prediction of "reliable variance" in the criterion rather than just "variance"?

5. If in question 3 you added a fifth predictor to the original regression equation, what characteristics would you want from this predictor?

6. What information is provided by the standard error of estimate?

7. If we hoped to examine the predictive ability of four independent variables, what would you recommend as the minimum sample size?

8. Why is it necessary to compute the cross-validated correlation coefficient?

Case Studies

CASE STUDY 17.1: SELECTION OF GRADUATE STUDENTS

Reflecting concerns that standardized testing was unfair, the psychology department at South East State University (SESU) decided six years ago to eliminate the requirement that prospective students submit Graduate Record Examination (GRE) scores for admission to its popular master's program. Although hired as an assistant professor only a year ago, Dr. Lisa Span already found herself questioning whether this policy was a wrong decision.

Dr. Span's main concern was the quality of the graduate students in her classes. While a number of students were highly talented academically, others appeared unable to grasp theoretical concepts, and even seemed incapable of abstract thinking. Although Dr. Span had repeatedly questioned whether these problems were a consequence of her own teaching style, her concerns with the ability of the department's graduate students were mirrored by similar concerns expressed by other faculty in the department.

In an effort to understand how students were selected for the MA program, Dr. Span investigated the criteria used by the selection committee. She found that, in the absence of GRE scores, the selection committee relied heavily on three aspects of the student's application file: grade point average (GPA) as an undergraduate, the student's one-page statement of purpose, and three letters of recommendation.

Sensing an opportunity, Dr. Span decided to determine the validity of the selection system. The department agreed to give her access to the application files of all 110 students admitted and enrolled in the MA program since the GRE was discarded from the department's grad student selection process. She was also able to obtain the GPAs these students had amassed while grad students at SESU. Although undergraduate GPA and graduate GPA were easy variables to enter into a data file, the same could not be said for the statement of purpose and the three letters of recommendation. In the end, Dr. Span decided to code the statement of purpose on a four-point scale. This scale reflected a number of characteristics, including writing ability, ability to convincingly communicate the desire to attend graduate school, undergraduate involvement in research, and relevant work experience. The three letters of recommendation were coded as a single score of 0, 1, 2, or 3, reflecting the number of letters submitted that had only positive things to say about the applicant. Thus, if an applicant received two letters that said only positive things, and one that included at least one negative comment, the applicant received a score of "2" for this predictor. While inputting the data, Dr. Span realized that the vast majority of applicants received a score of "3" on this predictor.

With much anticipation, Dr. Span ran the multiple regression analysis examining the ability of the set of predictors to explain graduate GPA. The resulting multiple correlation coefficient was $R = .31$. Stunned, Dr. Span realized that, combined, these three predictors explained very little of the performance of graduate students. She was particularly surprised that two of the three selection tests—undergraduate GPA and letters of recommendation—received very low beta weights. Indeed, the zero-order correlation between undergraduate GPA and graduate GPA was an astonishingly low $r = .13$.

By chance, Dr. Span discovered that a student's application file contained a GRE reporting form. Opening several additional application files, she found that some other students had also reported their GRE scores to SESU. Although students were not required to do so, and although they were not considered in admission, some applicants had seemingly taken the GRE for other schools and had reported their scores to SESU as well. In all, Dr. Span was able to find GRE scores for 67 students. After quickly inputting these data into her file, she was pleased to see that the correlation between GRE scores and graduate GPA was $r = .36$. Convinced that the GRE should be reinstated as a requirement for graduate application to the department, Dr. Span prepared a report to her colleagues.

Questions to Ponder

1. What percentage of variance in graduate GPA is being explained by the current entrance criteria?

2. Is there any reason to expect that letters of recommendation would have a low criterion-related validity, even before conducting the statistical analysis? Explain.

3. Which of the current entrance criteria likely has the greatest criterion-related validity? How can you tell from the given information?

4. Would it be appropriate to conclude that undergraduate GPA is unrelated to graduate GPA in the psychology master's program at SESU? Why or why not? (*Hint:* You may want to review the issues we discussed in Module 7 in answering this question.)

5. Would it be appropriate to conclude that GRE scores will act as a better predictor of graduate GPA for future graduate students at SESU than the current entrance criteria? Explain.

CASE STUDY 17.2: THE PERFECT PERSONNEL SELECTION BATTERY?

Although he'd worked in human resources (HR) for a little more than a year, Connor Maxfield had been unexpectedly promoted to oversee the selection of new employees into MiniCorp after his boss resigned last month. Although he was now responsible for filling all vacancies in the organization, relatively low-level production workers would be hired most frequently. It seemed that every month there were at least two or three of these jobs that needed to be filled. The current personnel selection system for production workers had been in place for years. Applicants were given a paper-and-pencil job knowledge test and personality inventory. Those who passed the tests were then administered a 40-minute structured interview. In searching through records in the HR department, Connor was surprised to see that, combined, these tests accounted for a mere 25% of the reliable variance in job performance. Recognizing that more than 75% of the reliable variance in job performance remained unexplained by use of the current selection system, Connor vowed to improve things.

Connor spent every night for more than a week investigating a variety of selection tests that could be used to predict the future job performance of production worker applicants. Determining that the current three tests not only made logical sense but also demonstrated good validity, Connor decided he wouldn't attempt to replace these tests. Instead, he'd add additional selection tests to the selection system until he was able to explain as close to 100% of the reliable variance in job performance as possible. He had a sneaking suspicion that measures of cognitive ability, biodata, and a work sample might go a long way to selecting the ideal candidate, but still other tests might be needed as well.

Although brief, Connor's work experience had convinced him of the importance of seeking validation evidence before implementing a new selection system. He planned to administer all of the possible new selection tests to his entire staff of production workers, which numbered 53 employees. He then expected to regress supervisor ratings onto these test scores to obtain a multiple correlation coefficient. Reflecting for a moment on his plan, Connor thought he'd better get to it—he was certainly going to be busy.

Questions to Ponder

1. What type of criterion-related validity study does Connor plan on conducting?

2. What is the criterion-related validity of the current selection system for production workers at MiniCorp?

3. Is Connor's plan to attempt to explain nearly 100% of the reliable variance in job performance feasible? Explain.

4. What practical concerns might Connor encounter even if he did find that a selection battery of six or more tests was useful in predicting job performance for production workers?

5. How should Connor go about attempting to identify additional useful predictors of job performance for production workers?

6. What minimum sample size would be recommended for conducting a criterion-related validity study with three predictors? Six predictors?

7. Given the number of production workers at MiniCorp, what method of criterion-related validity should Connor consider using?

‑◆‑═══●═══‑◆‑

Exercises

EXERCISE 17.1: DETECTING VALID
PREDICTORS (REVISITED)

OBJECTIVE: To reexamine the validity of predictors in a data set using multiple regression.

PROLOGUE: Exercise 7.2 examined a number of possible predictors of bus driver job performance. Using the entire set of predictors identified in Exercise 7.2, perform the following procedures to further examine the predictability of bus driver job performance, as indicated by the criterion of overall performance evaluation score (the variable *pescore*). As before, the relevant data set is titled "Bus driver.sav."

Perform a multiple regression analysis using *pescore* as the dependent variable and each of the six predictors identified in Exercise 7.1 as the independent variables. Choose "enter" as the method.

1. What is the sample size analyzed?

2. What is the magnitude of the estimated multiple correlation coefficient (R) obtained in this analysis?

3. What is the magnitude of the estimated squared multiple correlation coefficient (R^2) obtained in this analysis?

4. What is the magnitude of the standard error of estimate obtained in this analysis?

5. Write out the unstandardized regression equation.

6. Write out the standardized regression equation.

7. What predictors have significant regression weights?

EXERCISE 17.2: PREDICTING THE WORK
MOTIVATION OF VOLUNTEERS

OBJECTIVE: To examine the validity and cross-validity of a set of predictors.

PROLOGUE: Because volunteers are unpaid, the work motivation of these individuals can be complex. It is possible that individuals' work motivation depends on their perceptions of their own ability, along with elements of support provided by the organization. The SPSS data file "Volunteer data.sav" contains data assessed from 120 volunteers in a number of small organizations. Each volunteer completed a survey assessing the following perceptions:

Predictors

Variable Name	*Explanation of Perception*
Reward	The possible intrinsic rewards available by volunteering
Ledinit	The amount of initiating-structure provided by the volunteer's immediate supervisor
Ledcons	The amount of consideration provided by the volunteer's immediate supervisor
Clarity	The degree to which one's role and task in the volunteer organization is unambiguous
Conflict	The amount of intrarole and interrole conflict experienced as a result of volunteering
Efficacy	The degree to which the individual perceives he or she is capable of handling the assigned work in the volunteer organization
Goalid	The degree to which the individual believes the work of the volunteer organization is important
Affectc	The affective commitment of the volunteer; the degree to which the volunteer wishes to remain a part of the volunteer organization due to an emotional tie
Continc	The continuance commitment of the volunteer; the degree to which the volunteer wishes to remain a part of the volunteer organization due to perceptions of an obligation to remain in the organization

Each of the preceding scales was assessed using either a five-point or a seven-point Likert-type rating scale. An additional variable included in the data set, work motivation, will act as the criterion variable in Exercises 17.2 and 17.3.

1. Examine the correlations between each of the possible predictors of work motivation. On the whole, how highly related to one another are

these predictors? What is the range of magnitude of intercorrelation among this set of possible predictors?

2. Examine the correlations of work motivation with each of the possible predictors. Which predictors seem most highly related to work motivation?

3. Conduct a multiple regression analysis to determine the validity of the set of predictors for the criterion of work motivation. What is the magnitude of the multiple correlation coefficient (R)?

4. Which predictors have significant regression weights?

5. Compute the estimated population cross-validity of the entire set of predictors. How does this compare to the initial validity estimate?

6. Had you obtained the same regression results based on a sample of only 50 volunteers, what would be the estimated population cross-validity of this set of predictors? How does this new estimate of validity compare to the initial validity estimate, and to the cross-validated estimate based on 120 volunteers?

EXERCISE 17.3: PREDICTING SCORES USING THE REGRESSION EQUATION

OBJECTIVE: To compare the accuracy of predicted criterion scores to actual criterion scores.

PROLOGUE: Use the data set discussed in Exercise 17.2 to answer the following items.

1. Conduct a multiple regression analysis using all nine predictors. Choose method equals "enter." Write out the unstandardized regression equation that would result if all nine predictors were retained.

2. Conduct a second multiple regression analysis, this time using *only* those predictors that had significant regression weights in the previous equation. Write out the unstandardized regression equation.

3. While the standard error of estimate provides an average level of prediction accuracy, we can examine the accuracy of prediction for a single individual who is included in the data set by comparing the individual's predicted work motivation score with his or her actual reported work motivation.
   a. Use the regression equation in item 1 to compute a predicted score on work motivation for the first volunteer in the data set (i.e., for case 1).

b. Use the regression equation in item 2 to compute a predicted score on work motivation for the first volunteer in the data set (i.e., for case 1).

c. Examining the actual work motivation score for the first volunteer in the data set (i.e., the "motivate" score for case 1), which regression equation provided the most accurate prediction of work motivation for this particular volunteer?

d. Which regression equation had the smallest standard error of estimate?

4. Repeat the procedure in item 3 by randomly selecting two more volunteers in the data set and computing their predicted work motivation scores using both regression equations.

a. Do you consistently find one of these equations is more accurate?

b. If you continued this process for every individual in the data set, which equation would be more accurate? How do you know?

5. Are you surprised by either the accuracy or the inaccuracy of prediction when using the regression equations? Explain.

Internet Web Site References

17.1. http://www.statsoftinc.com/textbook/stmulreg.html

This Web page presents a brief chapter on multiple regression from Statsoft, Inc.'s electronic textbook.

17.2. http://pareonline.net/getvn.asp?v=7&n=2

This Web page presents the following reprinted article: Osborne, J. W. (2000). Prediction in multiple regression. *Practical Assessment, Research and Evaluation, 7.*

The article discusses the use of multiple regression in prediction, assumptions of multiple regression, and the issues of shrinkage and cross-validation; it also explains how to compute confidence intervals around an individual predicted criterion score.

17.3. http://davidmlane.com/hyperstat/B123219.html

This Web page, provided by Dr. David Lane, presents Rice University's HyperStat Online chapter on regression. Links are available to such topics as the standard error of estimate, shrinkage, and computing significance tests.

17.4.   http://www.tufts.edu/~gdallal/collin.htm

This Web page, provided by Dr. Gerard E. Dallal, provides a detailed discussion of collinearity.

Further Readings

Aiken, L. S., West, S. G., & Reno, R. R. (1996). *Multiple regression: Testing and interpreting interactions.* Newbury Park, CA: Sage.

Cohen, P., Cohen, J., West, S. G., & Aiken, L. S. (2002). *Applied multiple regression: Correlation analysis for the behavioral sciences* (3rd ed.). Hillsdale, NJ: Erlbaum.

Licht, M. H. (1995). Multiple regression and correlation. In L. G. Grimm & P. R. Yarnold (Eds.), *Reading and understanding multivariate statistics* (pp. 19–64). Washington, DC: American Psychological Association.

Nunnally, J. C., & Bernstein, I. H. (1994). *Psychometric theory* (3rd ed., pp. 114–208). New York: McGraw-Hill.

Pedhazur, E. J. (1997). *Multiple regression in behavioral research* (3rd ed.). Pacific Grove, CA: Wadsworth.

Module 18

Exploratory and Confirmatory Factor Analysis

F actor analysis can be used to reveal or verify the underlying dimensionality of a newly developed measure. Following administration of the measure to a large sample of respondents, we could examine the dimensionality of our scale through the use of factor analysis. If we were uncertain as to the possible dimensions underlying our scale, exploratory factor analysis (EFA) would be used. However, if we had strong theoretical expectations as to the new measure's dimensionality, then confirmatory factor analysis (CFA) could be applied. By examining how the items that comprise a scale "cluster" together, we may gain an important understanding of our operationalization of the underlying construct we are assessing.

Exploratory Factor Analysis

Do the items in our scale assess separate subdimensions, or is our scale uni-dimensional? If the scale is multidimensional, how many subdimensions are there? In the absence of strong theoretical expectations, EFA provides a way of examining these issues. Factor analysis attempts to reduce the number of factors (from the original number of items) by accounting for the intercor-relations among items. To accomplish this, EFA procedures divide item vari-ance into common, specific, and error variance. EFA attempts to extract factors based only on the common variance of the original items. The term "communality" refers to the variance that an item has in common with other items. The assumption is that there exist some underlying constructs that are responsible for the interrelationships among observed items. Consider a fictitious case in which we recently developed a brief personality inventory composed of eight items that we suspect (or perhaps, *intend to*) assess two of the Big Five personality dimensions: conscientiousness and extraversion. If there were multiple dimensions assessed by the eight items, we would expect to find that certain subsets of items would correlate highly with each other, while others would not correlate with these items but would correlate highly with each other. Thus, items assessing the personality dimension of conscientiousness would be expected to correlate highly with one another, but not correlate highly with items assessing extraversion.

EFA is used to reduce the number of interrelated items without losing too much information from the original responses. A similar but distinct procedure is called principal components analysis (PCA). In PCA, the focus is not limited to common variance but, rather, to total variance. The primary assumption of PCA is that the total variance of an item reflects both explained and error variance. Thus, the components that are formed using this procedure are linear combinations of the observed items. While mathematicians often prefer the use of PCA due to its focus on extracting total variance, most applied social science and educational researchers favor factor analysis due to its usefulness for identifying latent variables that contribute only to the common variance in a set of measured variables. Because tests are created to assess latent constructs, EFA should be preferred over PCA for test developers. (See also Web Reference 18.3 for further distinctions between EFA and PCA.)

In conducting a factor analysis, it is crucial to obtain an adequate sample size. Without adequate sample size, factor analytic results will be unlikely to generalize to other samples. How large a sample size is needed? As is the case with so many other statistical analyses, the answer is the more the better. At a bare minimum, however, we should use a sample size no smaller than 100 cases *and* a sample size relative to number of items (i.e., *N/k* ratio) of no less than 5 to 1. Velicer and Fava (1998) provide much more detailed procedures for determining appropriate sample sizes.

How Many Components or Factors Are Present in My Data?

Because EFA does not a priori specify the number of underlying dimensions in our data, we must have some way of determining the number of factors to extract. Indeed, it is possible (though perhaps unlikely) that, in the development of our measure, no particular dimensionality is hypothesized. Use of EFA is intended to determine the number of latent constructs (e.g., personality dimensions) present in our measure.

There are numerous methods of extracting factors to choose from, and each method may indicate a slightly different number of factors. Perhaps the most commonly used method of determining the number of factors extracted is also the default in most statistical analysis software packages: the Kaiser eigenvalue criterion. This method retains those factors whose eigenvalues are greater than or equal to 1.0. Although this method of determining the number of resulting factors is quite straightforward, Russell (2002) pointed out a number of problems with the use of the Kaiser criterion. One concern is that, when a large number of items are included in the factor analysis, it is likely that a relatively large number of factors with eigenvalues greater than or equal to 1.0 will be extracted, many of which will account for only a rather small percentage of the total variance.

Although not a perfect determinant of the number of factors in an EFA, the scree test (Cattell, 1966) is strongly preferred over the eigenvalue criterion. The scree test is provided as an option on most statistical software programs. Using the geological metaphor of stones that fall from a mountain (i.e., scree), the scree test provides a visual aid for determining the number of factors extracted. The magnitude of eigenvalues forms the Y axis, while the X axis presents the corresponding factor numbers. Within the plot itself, eigenvalues of each corresponding factor are plotted, and these are then connected with a line. This plot allows the user to visually determine the drop-off in the magnitude of eigenvalues from factor to factor. Typically, the user looks for an "elbow," or sudden flattening of the line. The resulting number of factors extracted is typically taken as one less than the factor associated with the elbow.

Which Items Are Loading on a Particular Factor?

Unfortunately, the factors produced by the initial extraction are difficult to interpret. The rotation of factors refers to a transformation of factor loadings into a more interpretable form. There are again multiple choices in types of rotation, but the key is to determine use of orthogonal or oblique rotations. *Orthogonal rotations* force the resulting factors to be uncorrelated. Example orthogonal rotations include Varimax and Quartimax. Quartimax is the appropriate choice when you suspect that the items on your test represent a general factor (Gorsuch, 1983), as may be the case in the development of a classroom knowledge test.

Oblique rotations allow correlations between the factors. Examples here include Direct Oblimin and Promax. Oblique rotations are appropriate when the factors are expected to be interrelated, as might be the case in the development of a measure of extraversion in which multiple facets (e.g., warmth, assertiveness, excitement seeking) of the construct are being assessed. Fabrigar,

Wegener, MacCallum, and Strahan (1999) recommended the use of oblique factor rotations. Russell (2002) pointed out that Promax allows correlations between factors only after initially performing an orthogonal Varimax rotation. Thus, uncorrelated factors would still be identified by use of a Promax rotation. Independent of which method of rotation is used, further ease of interpretation of output is aided by choosing the option to "sort by size," which arranges item loadings based on magnitude of relationship to the resulting factors rather than order of listing in the data set.

Interpreting Exploratory Factor Analysis Output

Given the number of options for conducting the factor analysis, it should not be surprising that the interpretation of the output requires some expertise as well. The following discussion describes several elements of the output using the terms employed by SPSS (SPSS, Inc., 2003). Labels may differ slightly for other statistical software packages.

The section of the output labeled "Total variance explained" provides information on the initial eigenvalues. All eigenvalues of 1.0 and above will be considered important factors when using the Kaiser criterion. The percentage of variance next to each of these values indicates the percentage of the variance in the original set of items that is captured by that particular factor. A cumulative percentage of variance accounted for by the factors is also listed. Remember that if you requested the scree plot option, the scree plot should also be consulted to determine the number of factors.

The section of the output labeled "factor matrix" provides factor-loading information computed prior to rotation of factors. "Extraction sums of square loadings" can be replicated by squaring each of the loadings on a particular factor and then summing across each of the original items. Similarly, squaring each of the loadings for an item across all of the factors and then summing will replicate extracted communalities.

The next part of the output differs depending on whether you requested an orthogonal or an oblique rotation method. With an orthogonal rotation, the output is presented in the "rotated factor matrix." With an oblique rotation, this output is presented in a "pattern matrix." Either way, this part of the output is likely to demand the greatest amount of your attention. If you chose the "sort by size" option when conducting the analysis, this matrix will display factor loadings arranged such that the item that loads highest on the first factor will be at the very top of the leftmost column, while the item with the second highest loading on the first factor will be listed next. This continues until the item with the highest loading on the second factor is presented, with subsequent item presentation following the same pattern as with the first factor. We will present a detailed example output and its interpretation later.

Typically, an item must have a loading in the range of at least .30 to be considered to load on a factor. Indeed, in conducting Monte Carlo studies, some researchers now use loadings of .4, .6, and .8 to represent low, medium, and high loadings, respectively (e.g., Enders & Bandalos, 2001). It is important to keep in mind that item loadings on a factor in one sample do not necessarily reproduce in another sample, particularly if the sample size is small relative to the number of items.

In examining the items that load on a particular factor, try to make some meaningful connection between the items. Do the items that load highly on a factor seem to have something in common? Does a single label seem appropriate for these items? If the answer to these questions is yes, then these items represent a subdimension on your scale.

Other items, however, may not load highly on a particular factor. If the test is empirically derived, it is unlikely that many of the items load onto neat, interpretable factors. That's not usually a problem for tests derived as such. On the other hand, the expectation with rationally derived tests is typically that certain general factors will emerge—namely, those consistent with the definition of the construct used to guide item generation. If this is the case, then most items should load on a limited number of interpretable factors. For rationally derived tests, items that do not load highly on any interpretable factor may be considered for elimination at this time.

On occasion, one or more items will load highly on more than a single factor. Such cross-loadings make the interpretation of factors more difficult. If only a small number of items cross-load, the items might be dropped from further consideration. Alternatively, a cross-loaded item can be inspected in terms of content and rationally categorized into the factor that is seemingly most relevant. Many significant cross-loadings, however, indicate that a smaller set of factors should likely be extracted in a subsequent factor analysis.

A Step-by-Step Example of Exploratory Factor Analysis

At the outset of this module, we discussed the possibility of factor analyzing eight items that may or may not assess the conscientiousness and extraversion dimensions of personality. To illustrate an EFA, we will select eight items chosen from Saucier's Mini-Markers scale (see Web Reference 18.1) and analyze a subset of the data using a selected sample of the Mersman-Shultz (Mersman & Shultz, 1998) data set. You are strongly encouraged to follow along with this example by accessing the data set "Personality-2.sav." This data set contains responses from 314 individuals on eight items. We will conduct a factor analysis including all eight items. To conduct this factor analysis in SPSS, choose "principal axis factoring" as the method of extraction. Choose "Promax" as the method of rotation. Select the options to display a scree plot and choose to sort factor loadings by size.

Table 18.1 presents the entire SPSS output of this EFA. Results indicate two eigenvalues above 1.0. Indeed, in this instance, both factors have eigenvalues above 2.0. The first factor accounts for 30.56% of the variance explained, while the second factor accounts for 26.72% of the variance explained. The scree plot also suggests two factors. The pattern matrix reveals that four items (disorganized, organized, sloppy, and efficient) load on factor 1, with factor loadings on this factor ranging from .79 to .43. Four items (shy, quiet, bold, and extraverted) load on factor 2, with loadings ranging from .70 to .60. None of the items cross-loads highly on both factors. Clearly, factor 1 could be labeled conscientiousness, while factor 2 could be labeled extraversion. Finally, note that the factor correlation matrix indicates that the two factors are unrelated, with $r = .059$.

Confirmatory Factor Analysis

What if you have strong expectations regarding the dimensionality of your measure? This is exactly the case for most rationally developed tests. Indeed, it is curious in the example described earlier in this module as to why (or even how) we would create personality items without knowledge of the specific personality dimensions intended. More likely, the personality items were specifically developed to assess the conscientiousness and extraversion dimensions of personality. CFA provides evidence of whether the responses of test takers are consistent with expectations regarding the scale's dimensionality.

Unlike EFA's rules for determining the number of factors that emerge, in CFA we specify a priori the number of factors that we expect to find. Further, in CFA we must specify exactly which items we expect will load on each factor. Contemporary structural equation modeling programs, such as AMOS (Arbuckle & Wothke, 1999), EQS (Bentler, 1995), and LISREL (Jöreskog & Sörbom, 1996), are typically used to conduct CFAs. Using these software packages, expected relationships between observed and latent variables are depicted through the use of a model. Figure 18.1 depicts a CFA model that we could employ to examine the eight variables previously discussed in the EFA example. The circles at the top of the model represent factors (i.e., latent constructs), while rectangles are used to represent

Table 18.1   Results of the EFA Step-by-Step Example

FACTOR
/VARIABLES bold disorgan efficien extraver organize quiet shy sloppy
/MISSING LISTWISE /ANALYSIS bold disorgan efficien extraver organize quiet
    shy sloppy
      /PRINT INITIAL EXTRACTION ROTATION
      /FORMAT SORT
      /PLOT EIGEN
      /CRITERIA MINEIGEN(1) ITERATE(25)
      /EXTRACTION PAF
      /CRITERIA ITERATE(25)
      /ROTATION PROMAX(4)
      /METHOD=CORRELATION.

Communalities

	Initial	Extraction
BOLD	.302	.372
DISORGAN	.497	.619
EFFICIEN	.244	.237
EXTRAVER	.307	.365
ORGANIZE	.465	.591
QUIET	.382	.439
SHY	.406	.500
SLOPPY	.309	.388

Extraction Method: Principal Axis Factoring

Total Variance Explained

	Initial Eigenvalues			Extraction Sums of Squared Loadings			Rotation Sums of Squared Loadings
Factor	Total	% of Variance	Cumulative %	Total	% of Variance	Cum. %	Total
1	2.445	30.560	30.560	1.894	23.679	23.679	1.803
2	2.137	26.717	57.277	1.618	20.221	43.900	1.725
3	.955	11.931	69.209				
4	.632	7.895	77.104				

(Continued)

Table 18.1 (Continued)

Factor	Total	% of Variance	Cumulative %	Total	% of Variance	Cum. %	Total
5	.580	7.250	84.354				
6	.540	6.751	91.105				
7	.403	5.034	96.139				
8	.309	3.861	100.000				

Extraction Method: Principal Axis Factoring

Scree Plot

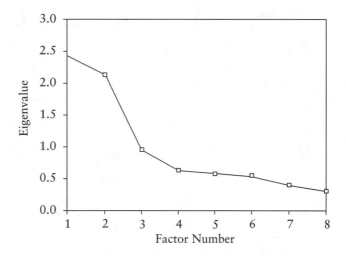

Factor Matrix

	Factor 1	Factor 2
DISORGAN	.617	−.488
ORGANIZE	.566	−.521
SLOPPY	.535	−.381
EFFICIEN	.479	−.088
QUIET	.373	.548
BOLD	.341	.505
SHY	.499	.501
EXTRAVER	.416	.438

Extraction Method: Principal Axis Factoring
2 factors extracted, 7 iterations required

Pattern Matrix

	Factor	
	1	*2*
DISORGAN	.788	−.044
ORGANIZE	.768	−.101
SLOPPY	.618	.048
EFFICIEN	.431	.204
SHY	.079	.698
QUIET	−.050	.664
BOLD	−.048	.611
EXTRAVER	.053	.598

Extraction Method: Principal Axis Factoring
Rotation Method: Promax with Kaiser Normalization
Rotation converged in 3 iterations

Structure Matrix

	Factor	
	1	*2*
DISORGAN	.786	.002
ORGANIZE	.762	−.056
SLOPPY	.621	.084
EFFICIEN	.443	.229
SHY	.120	.703
QUIET	−.011	.661
BOLD	−.012	.608
EXTRAVER	.088	.601

Extraction Method: Principal Axis Factoring
Rotation Method: Promax with Kaiser Normalization

Factor Correlation Matrix

Factor	*1*	*2*
1	1.00	.059
2	.059	1.00

Extraction Method: Principal Axis Factoring
Rotation Method: Promax with Kaiser Normalization

observed variables. Each observed variable is provided an error term (also represented in a circle). A factor loading is designated by drawing an arrow from the factor to the observed variable. The double-headed arrow between the two factors indicates that we would like to estimate the relationship between the proposed factors.

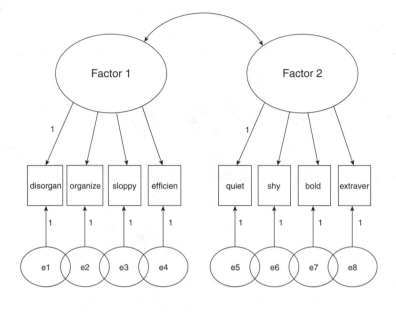

Figure 18.1   Two-Factor Structural Model for CFA Step-by-Step Example

Testing the Hypothesized Factor Model

In contrast to typical uses of EFA, CFA provides a number of indexes of how well our model actually fits the data. The problem in CFA is the decision as to which fit indexes to use to evaluate the model—there are literally dozens to choose from, though not all indexes are available from all structural equation modeling software packages. Each available index of fit addresses a slightly different issue, and no index of fit is considered to be perfect. Therefore, several fit indexes are typically reported for any given model. Perhaps the most commonly reported index of model fit is the Pearson chi-square, χ^2 (Widaman & Thompson, 2003). This index of fit indicates how likely it is that the model accurately represents the data. Good model fit is indicated by a nonsignificant chi-square. Unfortunately, the chi-square is likely to be significant if the sample size is larger than 200 regardless of model fit. Therefore, other fit indexes must also be considered. However, the chi-square statistic plays an additional important role in examining CFA model fit. In CFA, the fit of the hypothesized model is compared with the fit of at least two other models. One of these alternative models is typically a one- factor solution. Here, the CFA model is redrawn to indicate that all of the variables load on a common factor. On the opposite side of the spectrum, another alternative model is that each observed variable loads on its own, independent factor. This is termed the null, or independence, model. Most structural equation modeling programs generate fit statistics for the null model automatically when examining the hypothesized model, so it is unnecessary to draw this model (see Widaman & Thompson, 2003, for the conditions that must exist for a model to be an acceptable independence null model).

To evaluate the hypothesized model, the chi-square value obtained from the hypothesized model is subtracted from the chi-square value of one of the alternative models. Similarly, the value for the degrees of freedom of the hypothesized model is subtracted from the degrees of freedom of the alternative model. If the resulting chi-square difference value is significant, given the resulting degrees of freedom value, the hypothesized model is deemed to be a better fit than the alternative model. This process demonstrates whether the hypothesized model is a *better* fit to the data than the alternatives, but it does not provide convincing evidence that the hypothesized model is itself a *good* fit to the data. Therefore, additional fit indexes are also considered.

Another popular fit index, referred to as the goodness-of-fit index (GFI), compares the relationships between the variables obtained from the sample with those hypothesized in the model. For each relationship hypothesized in the model, any difference between the model's specification and the actual data produces a residual. If the model fits the data very well, residuals will be near zero. If the model does not fit the data, then the residuals will be larger. Good model fit is indicated by goodness-of-fit indexes greater than .90. Unfortunately, the number of parameters estimated affects this index of model fit. The GFI tends to be higher for more complex models. The adjusted goodness-of-fit (AGFI) index takes this problem into account in determining model fit, but it, too, has been deemed problematic (Kline, 1998).

Another fit index is the comparative fit index (CFI). This index indicates the proportion of improvement in fit of the hypothesized model in comparison to the null model. Obtained CFI values above .90 indicate acceptable model fit. The CFI is less influenced by sample size than are other popular incremental fit indexes such as the normed fit index (NFI). It is important to keep in mind that the fit indexes discussed here are but a sample of the evolving number of model fit indexes. Scientific consensus as to which fit indexes are most appropriate is likely to change over time.

A Step-by-Step Example
of Confirmatory Factor Analysis

The model depicted in Figure 18.1 is a graphical representation of the expected loadings of our eight-item personality scale discussed at the outset of the module. The model was built in AMOS (Arbuckle & Wothke, 1999) (see Exercise 18.3 to obtain free student versions of popular SEM software, which will allow you to follow along with the analysis described here). As with other structural equation modeling packages, AMOS includes a graphical interface that helps us to build our hypothesized model. The model in Figure 18.1 was drawn to indicate that we have two expected factors, each with four expected factor loadings. Because observed variables likely include some error in measurement, error terms are drawn to each observed variable.

In structural equation modeling, a model must be *identified* in order to be analyzed. A model is identified if, theoretically, it is possible to compute a unique estimate for each parameter in the model. If a model is not identified, then there exist an infinite number of possible solutions. This occurs when there are more parameters to be estimated than the number of variances and covariances in the model. To ensure identification, some parameters are fixed at 1.0. As can be seen in Figure 18.1, the path coefficients from each of the eight error variances and a path coefficient between each latent construct and one of the observed variables were constrained to a value of 1.0 to allow the model to be identified. Once the model is drawn and variable names are provided, it is necessary to indicate the data set we wish to analyze. The data set for this analysis is once again the "Personality-2.sav" data file. For this analysis, all defaults were used and standardized estimates were requested in the output. Finally, the estimates can be calculated.

Figure 18.2 depicts the CFA model with standardized path coefficients. As can be seen, the factors are uncorrelated. (Note this was also found in the EFA discussed previously.) In contrast, the path coefficients between the observed variables and the expected factors are sizeable. Note, however, that Kline (1998) suggested that the squared multiple correlation (R^2) for each indicator should be at least .50. Otherwise, more than half of the indicator's variance is unrelated to the factor it is expected to measure. Unfortunately, the square of several of the factor loadings depicted in Figure 18.2 is considerably less than .50. Thus, the indicators "sloppy" and "efficient" fail to meet this strict criterion for factor 1, and "bold" and "extraverted" fail to meet this criterion for factor 2. Still, we are likely more interested in examining the overall fit of the model.

Table 18.2 presents the fit indexes for the two-factor model. Given the large sample size, we may not want to rely too much on the significant

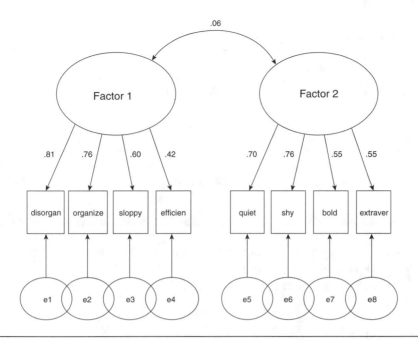

Figure 18.2   Two-Factor Structural Model for Step-by-Step Example With Path Coefficients

chi-square value, which would suggest poor model fit. While the GFI value would suggest good model fit, the AGFI and CFI suggest the model may not adequately fit the data. Finally, we would want to compare the fit of our two-factor model with the fit of a one-factor model and the null model. Table 18.2 also presents the measures of fit for each alternative model. The chi-square difference between the two-factor model and the alternative models is significant in both models. Further, as we would expect, the additional fit indexes indicate the hypothesized model provides a better fit than either of the alternative models. It is clear that the two-factor model is a much better fit than either of these two alternative models.

Concluding Comments

Volumes upon volumes have been written on factor analysis. This module is intended only to introduce readers to the issues involved in using this family of procedures. Despite the considerable literature available on factor analysis, it is often difficult to find sources that are understandable for "the rest of us." However, beginners wanting to delve deeper into factor analysis are

Table 18.2   Measures of Fit for Each Model

Model	$\chi^2(df)$	GFI	AGFI	CFI
2-Factor	100.834 (19)	.921	.850	.870
1-Factor	353.606 (20)	.751	.552	.469
Null	656.524 (28)	.628	.522	.000

Chi-square difference tests
1-factor model vs. 2-factor model: $\chi^2(1) = 252.772$, $p < .01$
Null model vs. 2-factor model: $\chi^2(9) = 555.69$, $p < .01$

strongly encouraged to read the very accessible works of Bryant and Yarnold (1995), Kline (1998), Lance and Vandenberg (2002), Tabachnick and Fidell (2001), and Russell (2002).

Practical Questions

1. Why would you want to understand the dimensionality of a scale?

2. Under what conditions might you choose to use PCA? EFA? CFA?

3. Under what conditions might you choose to use an orthogonal rotation of factors in an EFA? An oblique rotation?

4. What would you do if the expected dimensionality of your scale were very different from the results suggested by your factor analysis?

5. In conducting an EFA, describe the procedure you would follow to determine whether items found to load on a factor actually form a meaningful, interpretable subdimension.

6. In conducting an EFA, what would you do if a factor in the rotated factor (or pattern) matrix were composed of items that seem to having nothing in common from a rational or theoretical standpoint?

7. List four differences between CFA and EFA.

8. In scale construction, when would CFA be preferable to EFA? When would EFA be preferable to CFA?

9. In CFA, how would you determine if the data were consistent with your hypothesized model?

10. If the fit indexes indicated poor fit of your expected CFA model, what would you do next?

11. Upon their introduction to factor analysis, many students are likely to agree with Pedhazur and Schmelkin's (1991) assertion that factor analysis is like "a forest in which one can get lost in no time" (p. 590). Understanding, however, might be aided by identifying the elements that you find confusing. List two or three aspects of factor analysis that, if clarified, would help you to better understand this family of procedures.

Case Studies

CASE STUDY 18.1: A FIRST ATTEMPT AT EXPLORATORY FACTOR ANALYSIS

Andra was on a roll, or at least she had been until she looked at the results of her exploratory factor analysis (EFA). At the request of the chair of the psychology department, she'd been working the past few weeks on the development of a scale to assess the citizenship behaviors of graduate students. Andra based her scale on the concept of Organizational Citizenship Behavior (OCB), but she had quickly realized that the university context would require specific items that related more to grad students. She expected her Graduate Student Citizenship Behavior (GSCB) scale to have four dimensions:

- *helping behavior*—one's tendency to help other students in school-related tasks
- *conscientiousness*—following college, department, and program rules and regulations; maintaining visibility around the department; and so forth
- *professionalism*—avoiding complaining and gossiping about professors, students, and workload
- *civic virtue*—involvement in program-related activities, including serving on committees, presenting at departmental colloquia, and so on

She'd followed a rigorous process of writing items intended to assess each of these dimensions and had then asked some of the psychology department faculty to look over the items. Based on this input, she had incorporated some revisions and thrown out some items altogether. In the end, her GSCB scale was composed of 43 draft items (with at least 10 items per hypothesized dimension). After obtaining approval from the university's human subjects review board, Andra had administered the draft items to 119 undergraduate students recruited through the psychology department's subject pool. Students received extra credit in their psychology class for voluntarily participating.

Once she had completed data collection, she had excitedly entered the data into an SPSS file. After checking the accuracy of her input, Andra moved on to the exploratory factor analysis. Not exactly familiar with all the possible options, Andra clicked away at a few of the options that sounded somewhat familiar. She ended up choosing to run principal components analysis with Varimax rotation of factors. Unfortunately, the output was not very encouraging. According to the Kaiser criterion, she had seven factors. Seven. "I thought four dimensions of my scale would be complex enough, but seven," sighed Andra. She knew it was time to talk to her advisor about what to do next.

Questions to Ponder

1. The tryout sample is a crucial element in the test development process. Discuss the appropriateness of the following characteristics of Andra's sample for the development of this scale.
   a. Undergraduate students recruited through the psychology subject pool
   b. Sample size

2. Given the difficulty of obtaining a sizeable sample of graduate students, how could Andra obtain an appropriate sample?

3. Andra made a number of decisions in conducting the factor analysis. For each of the following decisions, discuss whether Andra's choice was the most appropriate option.
   a. Choosing exploratory procedures over confirmatory factor analysis
   b. Choosing principal components analysis over EFA
   c. Choosing Varimax rotation of factors
   d. Determining the number of factors based on the Kaiser criterion alone

4. If, following some modification of the analysis, Andra continued to find little support for her expected four factors, how would you suggest that she proceed?

CASE STUDY 18.2: USING CONFIRMATORY FACTOR ANALYSIS TO ANALYZE A MULTITRAIT-MULTIMETHOD MATRIX

In an article published in the *Journal of Personality*, Marsh (1990) provided evidence that confirmatory factor analysis (CFA) can be very useful in analyzing a multitrait-multimethod (MTMM) matrix—as long as care is taken to specify the correct model.

Marsh (1990) examined the construct validity of three commonly used measures of preadolescent self-concept: the 80-item Piers-Harris (PH) instrument, the 76-item Self Description Questionnaire I (SDQI), and the 28-item Perceived Competence Scale for Children (PCS). Although each of the scales examined has been found to be multidimensional, the number of previously identified dimensions differs across the scales. Marsh posited that each of the three measures assesses physical, social, and academic aspects of self-concept. Two of the three measures also include a general self-concept dimension, and two of the three measures assess other aspects of self-concept.

A sample of 290 Australian fifth graders was administered each of the scales. Marsh used the three different measures to represent different methods, while the previously identified dimensions of self-concept were taken as multiple traits. The resulting MTMM matrix was analyzed using both the Campbell-Fiske (1959) guidelines (see Module 8) and CFA.

Using the Campbell-Fiske approach, Marsh first found that similar dimensions across the measures were indeed substantially correlated with one another, providing evidence of construct validity. Second, Marsh examined whether convergent validities exceeded the correlations between different traits measured using different methods. Evidence indicated that the mean convergent validities were greater than heterotrait-heteromethod correlations for 60 out of 62 comparisons. This provided good evidence for this initial step in the examination of discriminant validity. Third, Marsh compared the convergent validities to the heterotrait-monomethod correlations. The expected pattern was found for two of the three measures of self-concept. However, mean heterotrait-monomethod correlations slightly exceeded the mean convergent validities for the PH measure. Thus, support for this criterion of discriminant validity was found for only the SDQI and PCS measures. Finally, the last Campbell-Fiske criterion was examined. This criterion argues that correlations among traits should be similar whether the methods are the same or different. Although this pattern was found for the SDQI and PCS, evidence was not supportive of the discriminant validity of the PH scales.

In reanalyzing the data using CFA, Marsh (1990) constructed four possible models to explain the data, based on Widaman's (1985) taxonomy of models that vary different characteristics of the trait and method factors. Model 1 is a trait-only model that proposes no effect of method. Model 2, the traits and uncorrelated methods factor, assumes that method effects associated with each of the measures are uncorrelated. Model 3 is a bit more complex, in that it does not assume that method effects are unidimensional across all variables assessed by a particular method. Rather, Model 3 represents method variance as correlated uniquenesses. These are correlations between pairs of variables measured by the same method once the trait effects are removed. Finally, Model 4 proposes that unidimensional method factors are correlated with each other. This model can be referred to as traits and correlated method factors.

For each of these four possible models, Marsh (1990) evaluated whether the solution was well defined for both a possible four- and a possible five-trait solution. Models 1 and 4 were found to be poorly defined for both possible solutions. Model 2 was found to be well defined for the four-trait solution, but only marginally defined for the five-factor solution. Model 3, however, was found to be very well defined for both the four- and five-factor solutions. Marsh pointed out that when method factors are considered, Model 3 typically provides solutions that are better defined than competing models. Inspection of the CFA results indicated that the correlated uniquenesses associated with the SDQI were considerably smaller than those associated with the other two measures, indicating the lesser influence of method effects for the SDQI. Although convergent validity was found for all three measures of preadolescent self-concept, evidence for discriminant validity was strongest for the SDQI.

Questions to Ponder

1. What concerns about the interpretation of an MTMM matrix are better addressed by CFA rather than the Campbell-Fiske (1959) guidelines?

2. In what ways are the four CFA models proposed by Widaman (1985) similar? In what ways do these models differ from one another?

3. What are correlated uniquenesses?

4. What might cause a CFA model to be poorly defined?

5. What methods can be used to evaluate alternative CFA models? Are some methods more appropriate than others?

6. How can researchers who use advanced statistical analyses communicate with those who are less statistically savvy?

Exercises

EXERCISE 18.1: CONDUCTING AN EXPLORATORY FACTOR ANALYSIS

OBJECTIVE: To conduct and interpret an EFA using SPSS.

PROLOGUE: The SPSS data file "Geoscience attitudes.sav" contains undergraduate responses to a survey assessing attitudes and interests related to the field of geoscience (geology, geography, and archaeology). Respondents rated their level of agreement to each of the following items using a five-point Likert-type rating scale ranging from 1 (strongly disagree) to 5 (strongly agree).

Item 1: I have a good understanding of how scientists do research.

Item 2: I consider myself well skilled in conducting scientific research.

Item 3: I've wanted to be a scientist for as long as I can remember.

Item 4: I have a good understanding of elementary geoscience.

Item 5: I'm uncertain about what course of study is required to become a geoscientist.

Item 6: I am considering majoring in geoscience.

Item 7: I'd enjoy a career in geoscience.

Item 8: I plan on taking math courses that would prepare me to major in a science.

Item 9: I would enjoy going hiking or camping.

Item 10: I would enjoy boating.

Item 11: I'd prefer to work on a science project "in the field" than in a research laboratory.

Item 12: I enjoy reading science fiction novels.

Item 13: I enjoy reading nature and travel books and magazines.

Visually inspect the preceding geoscience attitude items. Which items would you expect to load on the same factors? What labels would you provide for these supposed factors?

Using the data set "Geoscience attitudes.sav," conduct an exploratory factor analysis on the 13 items. Be sure to do the following:

- Choose principal axis factoring as your method of factor extraction.
- Choose Promax as the method of rotation.
- Ensure the extraction of factors is determined by eigenvalues greater than 1.0.
- Select the option to produce a scree plot.
- Select the option to sort factor loadings by size.
- Ensure listwise deletion of missing cases.

1. Interpret the findings of the factor analysis by completing the following:
   a. Is the sample size in the data set sufficiently large to conduct a factor analysis of the 13 items? Explain.
   b. How many factors with eigenvalues greater than 1.0 emerge from the exploratory factor analysis?
   c. What is the percentage of variance accounted for by each of these factors?
   d. What is the cumulative percentage of variance in items explained by factors with eigenvalues greater than 1.0?
   e. How many factors does the scree plot suggest? Does the scree plot provide a clear indication of the number of factors?
   f. In this particular case, do you feel the eigenvalue criterion or the scree plot is more useful for determining the number of factors present in the data?
   g. Identify which items load on each factor (use factors as determined by the eigenvalue criterion).
   h. Provide a possible label for each interpretable factor.

2. Although the exploratory factor analysis has suggested possible subscales within the geoscience attitude survey, these subscales may not have high internal consistency. Again using the data set "Geoscience attitudes.sav," compute coefficient alpha for each of the emergent factors.

a. What is the reliability of each of the factors?
b. Would deleting one or more items from a factor considerably improve internal consistency reliability? If so, delete these item(s) and recompute the reliability of the factor.
c. Which factors do you believe achieve a sufficiently high alpha to be considered viable subscales for use in research?

EXERCISE 18.2: REPRODUCING COMMUNALITIES AND EIGENVALUES

OBJECTIVE: To aid understanding of how exploratory factor analytic techniques compute extracted communalities and eigenvalues.

PROLOGUE: As discussed in the Module 18 overview, extracted communalities and eigenvalues can be computed from an unrotated factor matrix. An extracted eigenvalue is the sum of the squared loadings of the items on a factor. An extracted communality is the sum of the squared loadings for a variable across all factors. The following table is the unrotated factor matrix from the analysis requested in Exercise 18.1:

Factor Matrix

Factor

	1	2	3	4
V7	.664	−.311	−.363	7.290E–02
V3	.588	−.443	.156	−.262
V6	.557	−.531	−.247	.244
V8	.451	−.202	.101	−.263
V13	.407	.163	−.226	6.848E–02
V4	.328	2.132E–02	.264	.208
V12	.226	7.399E–03	−3.869E–02	−.212
V9	.571	.605	−9.928E–02	−.154
V10	.423	.578	−8.521E–02	−.164
V11	.278	.435	−.246	.312
V2	.461	2.486E–03	.612	.176
V1	.315	.215	.424	9.492E–02
V5	−3.964E–03	−5.199E–03	−9.033E–02	−6.165E–02

Extraction Method: Principal Axis Factoring 4 factors extracted, 20 iterations required

Using information presented in this table, compute the following. Be sure to write out the relevant equation for each.

1. The extracted eigenvalue for factor 1.

2. The extracted eigenvalue for factor 2.

3. The extracted communality for item 1.

4. The extracted communality for item 2.

Note that you can verify your computations by comparing your computed values with those presented in the output of the exploratory factor analysis produced in Exercise 18.1.

EXERCISE 18.3: TUTORIAL IN STRUCTURAL EQUATIONS MODELING

OBJECTIVE: To provide a brief introduction to common structural equation modeling programs.

LISREL and EQS are two popular structural equations modeling programs for conducting confirmatory factor analysis (CFA). The links below provide access to free demonstration versions of these software programs and introductory user guides. Choose one of these structural equation modeling programs and perform the following activities.

For LISREL, download the free student version and the "Getting started with the Student Edition of LISREL" Word file at http://www .ssicentral.com/other/download.htm.

Once the LISREL files have downloaded, open the "Getting started" file and refer to Section 3: Fitting a Measurement model to SPSS data. This provides a step-by-step example of how to conduct a CFA in LISREL. Note that the depress.sav and depress0.spl files needed to conduct the step-by-step CFA example using LISREL should be in the directory, "c:/lisrel854_student/turorial" on your computer's hard drive once the demonstration files are downloaded.

For EQS, download the free demonstration version of the software and the "User's Guide Summary for EQS 5.7 for Windows demo version" PDF file at http://www.mvsoft.com/demos.htm.

Once the EQS files have been downloaded, open the "User's Guide Summary." A description of how to conduct a CFA begins on page 19.

Internet Web Site References

18.1. http://www.uoregon.edu/~gsaucier/gsau.htm

This Web page presents a link to Dr. Gerard Saucier's 40-item Mini-Markers measure of the Big Five personality dimensions.

18.2. http://www.unc.edu/~rcm/book/factornew.htm

This Web page provides access to a 500-page manuscript on exploratory factor analysis by Drs. Ledyard Tucker and Robert MacCallum.

18.3. http://www.statsoftinc.com/textbook/stfacan.html

This Web page presents the chapter on principal components and factor analysis from Statsoft, Inc.'s electronic textbook.

18.4. http://www.siu.edu/~epse1/pohlmann/factglos/

This Web page presents a glossary of factor analysis terms by Dr. John T. Pohlmann.

Further Readings

Bryant, F. B., & Yarnold, P. R. (1995). Principal components analysis and exploratory and confirmatory factor analysis. In L. G. Grimm & P. R. Yarnold (Eds.), *Reading and understanding multivariate statistics* (pp. 99–136). Washington, DC: American Psychological Association.

Fabrigar, L. R., Wegener, D. T., MacCallum, R. C., & Strahan, E. J. (1999). Evaluating the use of exploratory factor analysis in psychological research. *Psychological Methods, 3,* 272–299.

Klem, L. (2000). Structural equations modeling. In L. G. Grimm & P. R. Yarnold (Eds.), *Reading and understanding more multivariate statistics* (pp. 227–260). Washington, DC: American Psychological Association.

Kline, R. B. (1998). *Principles and practice of structural equation modeling.* New York: Guilford Press.

Lance, C. E., & Vandenberg, R. J. (2002). Confirmatory factor analysis. In F. Drasgow & N. Schmitt (Eds.), *Measuring and analyzing behavior in organizations: Advances in measurement and data analysis* (pp. 221–254). San Francisco: Jossey-Bass.

Pedhazur, E. J., & Schmelkin, L. P. (1991). *Measurement, design, and analysis: An integrated approach* (pp. 590–694). Hillsdale, NJ: Erlbaum.

Russell, D. W. (2002). In search of underlying dimensions: The use (and abuse) of factor analysis in *Personality and Social Psychology Bulletin*. *Personality and Social Psychology Bulletin, 28,* 1629–1646.

Tabachnick, B. G., & Fidell, L. S. (2001). *Using multivariate statistics* (4th ed.). Boston: Allyn & Bacon.

Thompson, B. (2000). Ten commandments of structural equation modeling. In L. G. Grimm & P. R. Yarnold (Eds.), *Reading and understanding more multivariate statistics* (pp. 227–260). Washington, DC: American Psychological Association.

Widaman, K. F., & Thompson, J. S. (2003). On specifying the null model for incremental fit indices in structural equation modeling. *Psychological Methods, 8,* 16–37.

Module 19

Item Response Theory

In Module 12, we discussed classical test theory item analysis (CTT-IA) where the focus was on how difficult and discriminating each item on a given test was within a particular sample. Under the CTT-IA framework, items on a given test are retained or discarded based on how difficult they are, as estimated by the percentage of respondents answering the item correctly—the p value—and how well they discriminate among our examinees, as estimated by an item-total correlation—the point-biserial correlation coefficient. In addition, our estimate of a person's underlying true score (or ability level) is simply the sum of the number of items correct, regardless of which items the individual answered correctly. CTT-IA has been a workhorse over the years for test developers and users who want to improve the quality of their tests. Given no other information, CTT-IA can be useful for local, small-scale test development and revision. However, there are newer, more psychometrically sophisticated models of item responding that provide much more useful and generalizable information to test developers and users who want to improve the quality of their tests, namely, item response theory.

Item Response Theory Versus Classical Test Theory

Item response theory (IRT) (sometimes referred to as modern test theory to contrast it with CTT) models provide more item, person, and test information than the CTT-IA procedures outlined in Module 12. In fact, Embretson and Reise (2000) viewed CTT-IA principles as being special cases of the more general IRT model. As such, many of the CTT-IA principles that we all know and love (e.g., the principle that the longer a test is the more reliable it will be as demonstrated by the Spearman-Brown prophecy formula) are simply not true under IRT. Thus, IRT is not simply a refinement of CTT-IA principles; rather, it is a new and different way of looking at the entire psychometric process, albeit one that is much more mathematically and conceptually complex, and, as a result, requires a new and deeper level of thinking to appreciate.

Ellis and Mead (2002) noted that, to control error in test development, "CTT's approach resembles that of standardization (or matching) and randomization used in experimental design. IRT, on the other hand, relies on mathematical models to make statistical adjustments to test scores for 'nuisance' properties (e.g., difficulty, discrimination, and guessing) of items" (p. 333). Other distinctions between CTT and IRT noted by Ellis and Mead include IRT's focus on items rather than the overall test score, using nonlinear rather than linear models, as well as differences in how item parameters such as difficulty, discrimination, and guessing are estimated. Overall, Ellis and Mead provided a balanced comparison of the CTT-IA and IRT approaches to item analysis. In the end, Ellis and Mead "advocate that the CTT and IRT approaches be combined in conducting an item analysis" (p. 324), and they demonstrated how to do so in their chapter by applying both techniques to the analysis of a Spanish translation of a reasoning scale.

Given its complexity, we will not delve into the major underpinnings and nuts and bolts of IRT models here. Excellent overview chapters and articles (e.g., Ellis & Mead, 2002; Zickar, 1998) and comprehensive discussions (e.g., Hambleton, Swaminathan, & Rogers, 1991; Hulin, Drasgow, & Parsons, 1983; Lord, 1980) can be found in the extant literature. One of our favorites is Embretson and Reise (2000), who provided a very readable, nontechnical book-length introduction to IRT. They covered all the major current topics in IRT and concluded with a useful chapter that gives an overview of the major IRT software programs, including the XCALIBRE program used in this module. Thus, we provide only a broad overview of the topic, and, as a consequence, we refer the reader to the preceding references (as well as others cited later and in Module 20) for more detailed discussions of the major current issues surrounding IRT, as well as detailed explications of its major underpinnings.

General Overview of Item Response Theory

IRT uses information from both the individuals (test takers) and the item to determine the likelihood of a person with a given level of ability (referred to as theta, θ, in IRT parlance) responding correctly to a given item. That is, IRT represents a set of probabilistic models that allow us to describe the relationship between a test taker's θ level and the probability of a correct response to any individual item. Early IRT models (in the 1940s–1970s or so) were developed to examine dichotomous data (scored 0 = incorrect and 1 = correct) that focused primarily on mental abilities. However, researchers eventually realized that such models could easily be applied to other dichotomous data such as those used in many personality and attitude scales (e.g., agree/disagree or yes/no). By the 1980s, IRT models were being developed to examine polytomous data (more than two response options), such as Likert-type response scales of 1–5 (1 = strongly agree to 5 = strongly disagree). In this module, however, we will only discuss IRT models that use dichotomous responses (Zickar, 2002, provided a chapter-length overview on estimating polytomous item formats). In addition, we will assume unidimensionality of θ, as is traditional; however, newer multidimensional IRT models are becoming increasingly available.

A major advantage of IRT over CTT-IA is that IRT models provide test and item information that are parameter invariant. That is, the information provided by IRT models regarding item parameters (e.g., item difficulty and discrimination), unlike that provided by CTT-IA, is invariant to the sample used to generate the item and test information. This is because the mathematical model used to derive item parameters in IRT (i.e., the logistic or normal ogive model) is derived based on the estimated latent trait (θ) and not the test taker's total score. Thus, information obtained from one sample using IRT models, assuming it is sufficiently large but not necessarily representative of the target population, will be equivalent to that obtained from another sample, regardless of the average ability level of the examinees who took the two tests. The same cannot be said for CTT-IA.

For example, under the CTT-IA framework, an item measuring developmental psychology theories taken from an examination in an upper-division developmental psychology class may be viewed as very difficult for introductory psychology students, of moderate difficulty for students in the upper-division developmental psychology class, and as extremely easy for students in a graduate-level developmental psychology class. However, IRT would provide a single (invariant) estimate of difficulty and discriminability, regardless of which individuals were used to calibrate the item. In addition, under CTT-IA such items on the test would differentiate students in the upper-division developmental psychology class fairly well; however, they would not differentiate students in the introductory psychology or graduate-level class very well.

In addition, responses in IRT are assumed to be locally independent. What does that mean, you ask? Basically, it means that a test taker's response, for any given level of θ, is a function of only his or her level of θ. This is what is known as a strong assumption in IRT. CTT-IA does not make any such assumption. Thus, under the CTT-IA framework, responses may be due to factors other than ability level, such as exposure to a previous item on the test. These strong assumptions in IRT of parameter invariance and **local independence** allow researchers to compare the measurement equivalence of tests that are made up of different items. This opens the door for the development of computer adaptive tests (CATs), which we discuss in Module 20. In addition, it allows for the analysis of item bias (also to be discussed in Module 20) as well as the determination of the conditional (based on θ level) standard error of measurement.

Running IRT analyses, as with the confirmatory factor analysis (CFA) procedures discussed in Module 18, requires special software that is typically not part of most major statistical packages such as SPSS, SAS, and STATA. Embretson and Reise (2000) concluded their book with a chapter that compares and contrasts the major IRT programs available. Until very recently, most were DOS-based programs that were not very user-friendly. However, most major IRT programs now have Microsoft Windows versions that are easier to learn and use. As a result, IRT analyses should be easier to produce—if not to understand.

Item Response Functions

Information in IRT models is often depicted in graphical form as item response functions (IRFs) or **item characteristic curves** (ICCs). Three such IRFs are plotted in Figure 19.1 based on data from Wiesen (1999), which will be discussed later in the step-by-step example. Note, however, that the item numbers presented here do not match the items on the Wiesen Test of Mechanical Aptitude (WTMA). These item response functions are nonlinear regressions (sometimes called S curves because of their shape) of the likelihood of responding affirmatively to an item given the individual's θ level (Zickar, 1998). Most items follow a cumulative normal distribution ogive. While IRFs can take several forms, the three-parameter logistic (3-PL) model is the most general. Under this model, the three parameters of discrimination (a_i—the slope of the IRF, typically .5 to 1.5), difficulty (b_i—the point of inflection on the IRF, where the curve switches from accelerating to decelerating, typically -2.0 to $+2.0$), and pseudo-guessing (c_i—where the lower asymptote crosses the ordinate or y axis, typically 0 to .20) are estimated. These parameters can be estimated in various ways. The most common practice is to use marginal maximum likelihood (MML) procedures to estimate the item parameters. In a two-parameter logistic (2-PL) model, the c_i parameter is assumed to be zero, while a_i and b_i are estimated. In the one-parameter logistic (1-PL) model, also called the Rasch model, c_i is set to zero, while the a_i parameter is assumed to be constant ($a_i = 1.0$) across items; thus, only the b_i (difficulty) parameter is estimated.

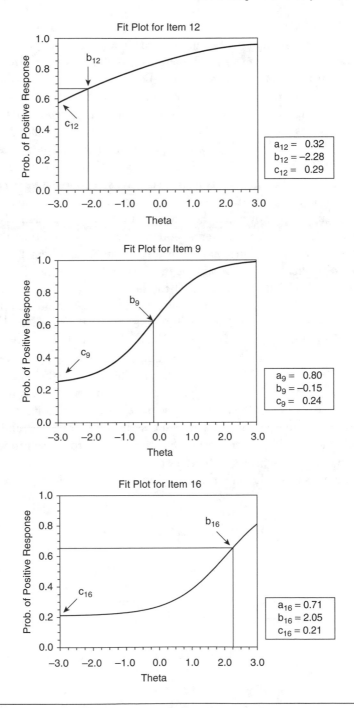

Figure 19.1   Item Response Functions for Three Items From a Mechanical Comprehension Test

Examining Figure 19.1, you can see that the first item (Item 12) is a relatively easy item. How can you tell? The b_i (difficulty) parameter is very low at -2.28. This means that a test taker only needs a very low (roughly 2.28 standard deviations below the mean) ability level (θ value) to have about an equal chance of answering this item correctly or incorrectly. In addition, the small a_i (discrimination) value (.32) indicates that it tends not to differentiate the test takers very well. This is seen by the very flat nature of the curve. Finally, the c_i (pseudo-guessing) parameter is somewhat deceptive in this graph. Typically, the line crosses the y axis at about the value of the c_i parameter. However, given this item is so easy, someone with even a θ value less than -3.00 has a better than 50/50 chance of getting this item correct.

Figure 19.1 shows that the second item (Item 9) is a relatively harder item. The b_i (difficulty) parameter is moderate at $-.15$. In addition, the a_i (discrimination) value indicates that this is a better item than Item 12 at discriminating test takers, particularly in the middle of the score range (between say -1.0 and $+1.0$). That is, the slope of the line at the point of inflection is much steeper than it was for Item 12. Finally, the c_i (pseudo-guessing) parameter is more intuitive for this item, as the curve crosses the y axis at about the value of the c_i parameter (.24). Overall, then, this would be a very good item for distinguishing individuals in the middle range of θ (i.e., it's a keeper).

The third item (Item 16) is the most difficult of the three items. Its b_i (difficulty) parameter is rather high at 2.05. As with Item 9, the a_i (discrimination) value for Item 16 indicates that it is better at discriminating test takers, however, this time at higher score ranges (between, say, 1.0 and 3.0). The c_i (pseudo-guessing) parameter in this case appears to be right on target, as the curve crosses the y axis at the value of the c_i parameter (.21). Overall, then, this would be a useful item for distinguishing individuals in the upper range of θ.

Item Information Functions

In CTT-IA, the concept of reliability applies to the entire test, whereas, with IRT, each item is assessed for the information it provides. As discussed in Module 5, the reliability estimate is used in CTT-IA to compute the standard error of measurement (SEM), which, in turn, is used to build confidence intervals around individual scores. In CTT-IA, however, the SEM is assumed to be the same at all ability levels. This is highly unlikely, in that extremely high or low scores will likely have more measurement error than moderate scores. In IRT, the SEM can be estimated for different ability levels, thus giving us much more accurate estimates of an individual's underlying ability, particularly at the extremes of the score distributions.

Figure 19.2 provides examples of item information functions (IIFs) for the previous three items. An IIF represents the amount of information that a given item contributes to a test's measurement precision. In general, the higher the value of a_i, the more information the item provides in estimating θ near the value of the difficulty parameter (b_i). Not surprisingly, then, the first item (Item 12) provides the most information for individuals at lower score ranges (θ between less than -3.0 and about 0.0), as it is a very easy item. The second item (Item 9) provides the most information for individuals in the middle range of θ (between -1.0 and $+1.0$). Finally, the third item (Item 16) provides the most information for individuals at the upper ranges of θ (from 1.0 to $+3.0$). When we are building a test, we want items with a variety of difficulty levels. We also want items with high discrimination values. Thus, we would most likely keep Items 9 and 16; however, we would only keep item 12 if we could not find other easy items with better discrimination values. Because most traits we study tend to follow roughly a normal distribution, we would want to have more items of moderate difficulty (such as Item 9) than items of high or low difficulty, although, again, we need a wide range of difficulty levels. In addition, if we were working with special populations, such as gifted or mentally disabled students, we would clearly need more items at the appropriate ends of the distributions.

A Step-by-Step Example of Conducting an Item Response Theory Analysis

Wiesen (1999) discussed the administration, scoring, development, and validation (among other things) of the Wiesen Test of Mechanical Aptitude (WTMA)—PAR Edition. This test is similar to tests such as the Bennett Mechanical Comprehension Test (BMCT), the Differential Aptitude Test—Mechanical Reasoning (DAT-MR), Science Research Associates Mechanical Concepts Test, the Career Ability Placement Survey—Mechanical Reasoning (CAPS-1MR), and Applied Technology Series—Mechanical Comprehension (ATS-MTS3) (see Wiesen, 1999, Appendix F, p. 45). These tests measure (to varying degrees) an individual's ability to learn mechanical and physical principles. Given many of these tests are well established with known reliability, validity, and utility, why is there a need for yet another mechanical aptitude/comprehension test? Wiesen (1999) noted that the WTMA "was developed to achieve four goals: (a) to measure mechanical aptitude using questions based on common everyday objects and events rather than those encountered primarily in academic physics or chemistry courses, (b) to present modern test content, (c) to minimize gender and racial/ethnic bias in

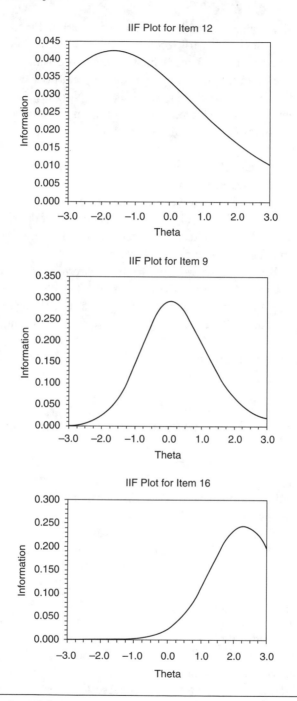

Figure 19.2   Item Information Functions for Three Items From a Mechanical Comprehension Test

test content, and (d) to provide a tool for further academic research on mechanical aptitude" (p. 1).

The WTMA consists of 60 questions that measure three broad classes of object types (kitchen, nonkitchen household, and other everyday objects) of 20 questions each. Each question has three options (A, B, and C). The sample question on the WTMA is typical of most items on the test. It shows two pitchers of water (one labeled A, the other B) with different amounts of ice in them. The question asks, "Which pitcher of water will stay cold longer? (A) A, (B) B, or (C) There is no difference." In addition to the three broad classes of object types, there are eight mechanical/physical principles of seven to eight items each (basic machines, movement of objects, gravity, basic electricity/electronics, transfer of heat, basic physical properties, miscellaneous, and academic). The programs RASCAL (1-PL) and XCALIBRE (2-PL and 3-PL) were used to analyze the items from the 20-item everyday-objects scale. Exercise 19.2 gives the URL for the software publisher, which includes a review of the XCALIBRE program that was published in the journal *Applied Psychological Measurement*. In addition, Embretson and Reise (2000) provided an overview of the XCALIBRE program, and other similar programs, in Chapter 13 of their book.

Table 19.1 displays the output of a Rasch analysis using the RASCAL for Windows 95, Version 3.5, IRT program (Assessment Systems Corporation, 1996). Page 1 of the abridged printout displays basic information such as the number of items (20), examinees lost to editing (i.e., individuals with extreme scores, of 0 or 20 in this case; 15 examinees), how the scale was centered (on difficulty in this case), scale adjustment information, and the change in average difficulty parameter after each loop (iteration). The RASCAL program stops looping when the change is less than .05. Page 2 displays the difficulty parameter estimates (the only parameter estimated in the Rasch model) for all 20 items on the scale. Also reported on this page are the standard errors for each item difficulty, chi-square values, and scaled difficulty levels (which rescale the θ values to a scale with a mean of 100 and a standard deviation of 10). Examining the difficulty column, we can see that Item 15 is the easiest item in that a person with a θ value of -1.851 (or a scaled score of only 83) has about a 50/50 chance of answering this item correctly. In CTT-IA terms, Item 15 has a p value of .93 (i.e., 93% of respondents answered the item correctly). On the other hand, Item 45 is the most difficult item. For this item, a θ value of 2.086 (or a scaled score of 119) would be needed to have a 50/50 chance of correctly answering this question. Item 45 has a p value of only .30. Although IRT b_i (difficulty) parameters and CTT-IA p values do not always coincide; in general, the higher the p value the lower the b_i value.

Table 19.1   RASCAL IRT Computer Output for a Difficulty Scale

---

```
            RASCAL for Windows95 (tm) Version 3.50          Page   1
Copyright (c) 1982 - 1996 by Assessment Systems Corporation
              Rasch Model Item Calibration Program
```

The number of items was 20

Items lost to editing: 0

Total remaining items: 20

Examinees lost to editing: 15

Total remaining examinees: 1544

Scale Centered on: Difficulty

Model: Logistic [D = 1.0]

Correction for Bias in Final Estimates: YES

Scale Adjustment   Multiplicative Constant =   9.1000
Information: Additive Constant   = 100.0000

On loop 1 the average difficulty parameter change was   0.2075

On loop 2 the average difficulty parameter change was   0.0454

On loop 3 the average difficulty parameter change was   0.0042

On loop 4 the average difficulty parameter change was   0.0004

RASCAL converged after 4 Loops

(Continued)

RASCAL for Windows95 (tm) Version 3.50   Page 2
Copyright (c) 1982 - 1996 by Assessment Systems Corporation

Rasch Model Item Calibration Program

Item	Difficulty	Std. Error	Chi Sq.	df	Scaled Diff
4	-0.997	0.079	40.800	10	91
5	-1.677	0.100	21.864	10	85
6	0.941	0.056	26.360	10	109
10	0.778	0.056	34.184	10	107
11	0.360	0.058	14.328	10	103
13	-0.059	0.062	16.687	10	99
14	-0.991	0.079	32.349	10	91
15	-1.851	0.107	9.489	10	83
17	0.474	0.058	47.541	10	104
24	-0.495	0.069	13.345	10	95
29	1.901	0.058	135.453	10	117
30	-0.632	0.071	57.034	10	94
31	-0.197	0.064	20.531	10	98
37	0.808	0.056	67.305	10	107
38	-1.438	0.091	23.863	10	87
45	2.086	0.059	16.686	10	119
48	0.291	0.059	22.330	10	103
54	1.404	0.056	30.707	10	113
58	-1.647	0.099	24.425	10	85
60	0.941	0.056	32.458	10	109

(Continued)

RASCAL for Windows95 (tm) Version 3.50   Page   3
Copyright (c) 1982 - 1996 by Assessment Systems Corporation

Rasch Model Item Calibration Program

Raw Score Conversion Table

Number Correct	(Theta) Ability	Std. Error	Freq-uency	Cum Freq	Percentile	Scaled Score
0	*****	*****	1	1	1	***
1	-3.55	1.076	0	1	1	68
2	-2.74	0.796	0	1	1	75
3	-2.21	0.680	1	2	1	80
4	-1.80	0.616	1	3	1	84
5	-1.44	0.576	6	9	1	87
6	-1.12	0.550	11	20	1	90
7	-0.82	0.532	19	39	3	93
8	-0.54	0.521	31	70	5	95
9	-0.27	0.514	51	121	8	98
10	0.00	0.512	78	199	13	100
11	0.27	0.513	104	303	20	102
12	0.54	0.519	139	442	29	105
13	0.82	0.531	193	635	41	107
14	1.12	0.548	230	865	56	110
15	1.43	0.575	205	1070	69	113
16	1.79	0.616	181	1251	81	116
17	2.21	0.682	157	1408	91	120
18	2.74	0.799	95	1503	97	125
19	3.55	1.080	42	1545	99	132
20	*****	*****	14	1559	99	***

(Continued)

```
                RASCAL for Windows95 (tm) Version 3.50          Page  4
        Copyright (c) 1982 - 1996 by Assessment Systems Corporation

      ITEM BY PERSON DISTRIBUTION MAP
                                                        Numbers of
                                                      Items / People
          ITEMS                        PERSONS

                        +   -4.0  +                      0  /    0
                        |   -3.8  |                      0  /    0
                        |   -3.6  |                      0  /    0
                        |   -3.4  |                      0  /    0
                        |   -3.2  |                      0  /    0
                        +   -3.0  +                      0  /    0
                        |   -2.8  |                      0  /    0
                        |   -2.6  |                      0  /    0
                        |   -2.4  |                      0  /    0
                        |   -2.2  |                      0  /    1
                        +   -2.0  +                      0  /    0
                  #####|   -1.8  |                      1  /    1
             #########|   -1.6  |                      2  /    0
                  #####|   -1.4  |                      1  /    6
                        |   -1.2  |#                     0  /   11
             #########|   -1.0  |                      2  /    0
                        |   -0.8  |#                     0  /   19
                  #####|   -0.6  |##                    1  /   31
                  #####|   -0.4  |                      1  /    0
                  #####|   -0.2  |###                   1  /   51
                 #####+<  0.0  +#####                  1  /   78
                  #####|    0.2  |#######               1  /  104
             #########|    0.4  |                      2  /    0
                        |    0.6  |#########             0  /  139
             #########|    0.8  |###########           2  /  193
             #########+   1.0  +                      2  /    0
                        |    1.2  >|###############      0  /  230
                  #####|    1.4  |############          1  /  205
                        |    1.6  |                      0  /    0
                        |    1.8  |############          0  /  181
             ##########|   2.0  +                      2  /    0
                        |    2.2  |##########            0  /  157
                        |    2.4  |                      0  /    0
                        |    2.6  |                      0  /    0
                        |    2.8  |######                0  /   95
                        +   3.0  +                      0  /    0
                        |    3.2  |                      0  /    0
                        |    3.4  |                      0  /    0
                        |    3.6  |###                   0  /   42
                        |    3.8  |                      0  /    0
                        +   4.0  +                      0  /    0
        +----+----+----+----+--------+----+----+----+----+
        20  15   10    5          5   10   15   20
             Percent of                Percent of
               Items                   Examinees
```

Summary Information:	Average Difficulty	S.D. Difficulty	Average ability	S.D. ability
(Theta Metric)	-0.00	1.19	1.18	0.95
(Scaled Score Metric)	100.0	10.9	110.7	8.6

(Continued)

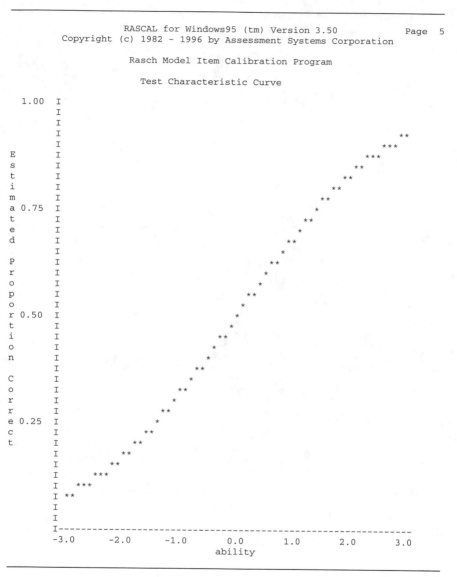

(Continued)

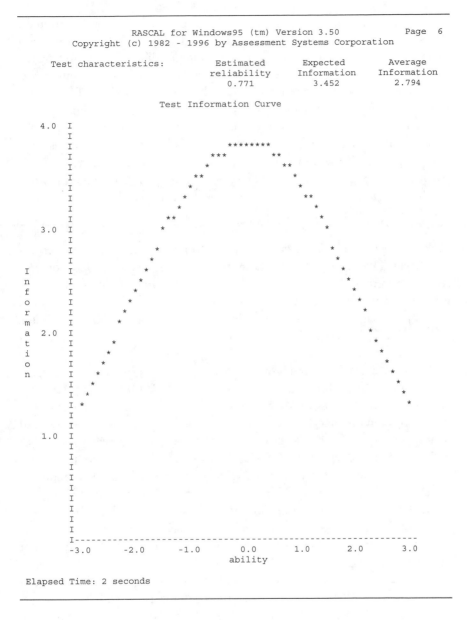

```
                    RASCAL for Windows95 (tm) Version 3.50              Page  6
          Copyright (c) 1982 - 1996 by Assessment Systems Corporation

      Test characteristics:          Estimated        Expected        Average
                                    reliability     Information     Information
                                       0.771           3.452           2.794
```

Test Information Curve

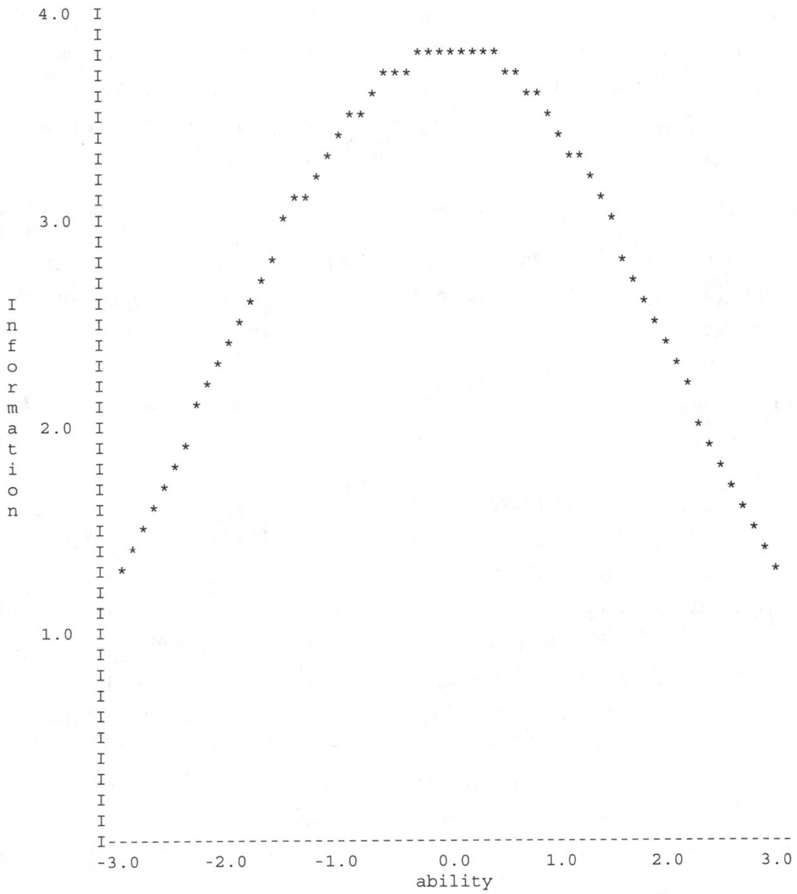


```
Elapsed Time: 2 seconds
```

Page 2 of the RASCAL printout displayed in Table 19.1 also provides chi-square values for each item as an indicator of how well each item fits the Rasch model. For 10 degrees of freedom, a value greater than 18.3 may indicate a lack of fit to the model (alpha = .05). In this output, 15 of the 20 items exceed the critical value of chi-square. However, the chi-square value is highly dependent on sample size, which, in this case, is rather large ($N = 1544$).

Hence, chi-square may not be an appropriate indicator of fit in this instance. We will test items against the 2-PL and 3-PL IRT models later on to see if items display a better fit. Page 3 provides an item **calibration** by showing the frequency of the θ values and scaled scores associated with the number correct. This appears to have resulted in a slightly negatively skewed (i.e., easy) test. Page 4 of the printout shows how well items and persons line up with one another by displaying back-to-back histograms of items and persons both mapped on θ. The fact that items generally have lower values than persons provides further evidence that this was a relatively easy test for this particular sample. At the bottom of page 4, summary information is provided for the average difficulty, standard deviation of difficulty, average ability, and standard deviation of ability.

Pages 5 and 6 display the test characteristic curve (test response function, TRF) and test information curve (**test information function, TIF**), respectively. The TRF is a graphic representation of the estimated proportion correct for different levels of θ. The TIF displays the amount of psychometric information provided by (i.e., effectiveness of) the test at different levels of θ. The top of page 6 also displays estimates of the test reliability, expected information (for a normal distribution), and average information (for a rectangular distribution).

Table 19.2 displays the abridged output for a two-parameter marginal maximum likelihood IRT analysis using the XCALIBRE for Windows 95/NT, Version 1.10, IRT program (Assessment Systems Corporation, 1995). As can be seen on page 1 of the output in Table 19.2, the model converged in four loops (iterations). The mean number of items correct was 13.914 with a standard deviation of 2.917. The estimate KR-21 reliability is .600 (lower than that for the Rasch analysis). However, all 1,559 respondents were included in this analysis. The top part of page 2 of the printout displays the a_i, b_i, and c_i parameter estimates as well as residual values and CTT-IT values of percentage correct (PC) and point-biserial item-total correlations (PB). The PBt column displays the item-theta correlation, the IRT equivalent of the item-total correlation. The third column (Flg) "flags" items that have $a_i < .30$, $b_i > 2.95$ or < -2.95, and $c_i > .40$ with a P. A flag of R indicates a standardized residual statistic greater than 2.0 (thus possibly indicating a poor fit of the item to the 2-PL IRT model). Notice that only one item (Item 38) has an R flag; however, six items had a P flag: Items 15, 30, and 38 for having extreme b_i (difficulty) values and Items 29, 37, and 60 for having extreme (low) a_i (discrimination) values. The former items might be replaced with more moderate difficulty items, while the latter items might be replaced with better discriminating items. In general, however, most items appear to fit well with the 2-PL model.

Finally, pages 3 and 4 display the test information curve (test information function, TIF) and the test characteristic curve (test response function, TRF), respectively. The TIF displays the amount of psychometric information provided by (i.e., effectiveness of) the test at different levels of θ. The top of page 3 also displays estimates of the test reliability, expected information (normal distribution), and average information (rectangular distribution). The TRF is a graphic representation of the estimated proportion correct for different levels of θ.

Table 19.2   XCALIBRE 2-PL IRT Computer Program Output

```
           XCALIBRE (tm) for Windows95/NT -- Version 1.10        Page  1
    Copyright (c) 1995 by Assessment Systems Corporation, All Rights Reserved
        Marginal Maximum-Likelihood IRT Parameter Estimation Program

            *****  CONFIGURATION INFORMATION  *****

          Item Parameter Priors: COMMON

          Allow Priors to Float: YES

                IRT Model Used: 2-parameter

      Maximum Number of Loops: 12

      Starting Prior Distribution Moments:

              Mean       SD
         a   0.0000   0.0000
         b   0.0000   1.0000
         c   0.0000   0.0000

      NOTE:  *** will be printed when the c standard error value > 0.10

The number of items was:    60

The maximum parameter change on loop 1 was      0.987
The maximum parameter change on loop 2 was      0.137
The maximum parameter change on loop 3 was      0.056
The maximum parameter change on loop 4 was      0.041

Mean Number-Correct Score =    13.914
Number-Correct Standard Deviation =     2.917
K-R 21 Reliability = 0.600

The number of examinees was 1559


 Final Parameter Summary Information:
          Mean       SD

Theta    0.00     1.00
   a     0.50     0.16
   b    -1.28     1.37
   c     0.00     0.00
```

(Continued)

XCALIBRE (tm) for Windows95/NT -- Version 1.10   Page 2
Copyright (c) 1995 by Assessment Systems Corporation, All Rights Reserved
Marginal Maximum-Likelihood IRT Parameter Estimation Program

FINAL ITEM PARAMETER ESTIMATES

Item	Lnk	Flg	a	b	c	Resid	PC	PBs	PBt	N	Item name
4			0.78	-2.06	0.00	0.42	0.87	0.45	0.47	1559	
5			0.66	-2.91	0.00	0.74	0.93	0.34	0.34	1559	
6			0.52	-0.25	0.00	0.57	0.54	0.45	0.47	1559	
10			0.56	-0.43	0.00	0.89	0.58	0.46	0.50	1559	
11			0.53	-0.98	0.00	0.65	0.67	0.44	0.46	1559	
13			0.57	-1.42	0.00	0.54	0.74	0.44	0.46	1559	
14			0.69	-2.20	0.00	0.48	0.87	0.41	0.43	1559	
15		P	0.57	-3.00	0.00	1.26	0.94	0.25	0.25	1559	
17			0.70	-0.70	0.00	0.46	0.64	0.52	0.57	1559	
24			0.53	-2.03	0.00	0.59	0.81	0.39	0.39	1559	
29		P	0.27	1.55	0.00	1.62	0.34	0.22	0.18	1559	
30		P	0.31	-3.00	0.00	1.53	0.83	0.19	0.15	1559	
31			0.57	-1.59	0.00	0.61	0.77	0.43	0.44	1559	
37		P	0.25	-0.74	0.00	1.40	0.57	0.25	0.17	1559	
38		RP	0.44	-3.00	0.00	2.02	0.91	0.17	0.15	1559	
45			0.39	1.44	0.00	0.78	0.30	0.34	0.35	1559	
48			0.33	-1.49	0.00	0.94	0.68	0.30	0.27	1559	
54			0.33	0.47	0.00	1.11	0.44	0.32	0.29	1559	
58			0.69	-2.78	0.00	0.20	0.93	0.36	0.35	1559	
60		P	0.29	-0.39	0.00	1.17	0.54	0.30	0.23	1559	

ITEM PARAMETER ESTIMATES W/STANDARD ERRORS

Item	Lnk	Flg	a	a error	b	b error	c	c error	Resid	Item name
4			0.78	0.045	-2.06	0.068	0.00	N/A	0.42	
5			0.66	0.044	-2.91	0.100	0.00	N/A	0.74	
6			0.52	0.069	-0.25	0.062	0.00	N/A	0.57	
10			0.56	0.064	-0.43	0.059	0.00	N/A	0.89	
11			0.53	0.056	-0.98	0.065	0.00	N/A	0.65	
13			0.57	0.049	-1.42	0.066	0.00	N/A	0.54	
14			0.69	0.044	-2.20	0.075	0.00	N/A	0.48	
15		P	0.57	0.042	-3.00	0.104	0.00	N/A	1.26	
17			0.70	0.055	-0.70	0.051	0.00	N/A	0.46	
24			0.53	0.044	-2.03	0.080	0.00	N/A	0.59	
29		P	0.27	0.070	1.55	0.119	0.00	N/A	1.62	
30		P	0.31	0.044	-3.00	0.127	0.00	N/A	1.53	
31			0.57	0.047	-1.59	0.069	0.00	N/A	0.61	
37		P	0.25	0.104	-0.74	0.124	0.00	N/A	1.40	
38		RP	0.44	0.041	-3.00	0.110	0.00	N/A	2.02	
45			0.39	0.058	1.44	0.087	0.00	N/A	0.78	
48			0.33	0.061	-1.49	0.100	0.00	N/A	0.94	
54			0.33	0.093	0.47	0.094	0.00	N/A	1.11	
58			0.69	0.045	-2.78	0.094	0.00	N/A	0.20	
60		P	0.29	0.104	-0.39	0.107	0.00	N/A	1.17	

(Continued)

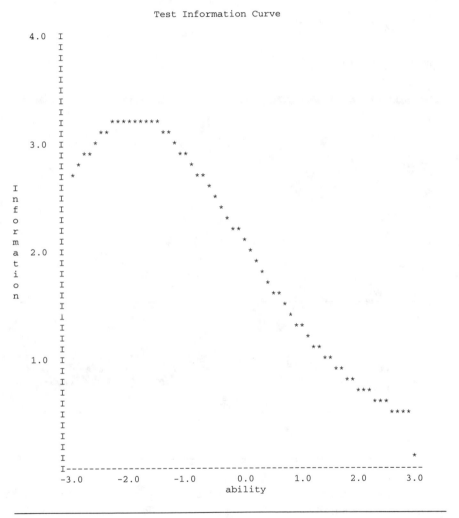

(Continued)

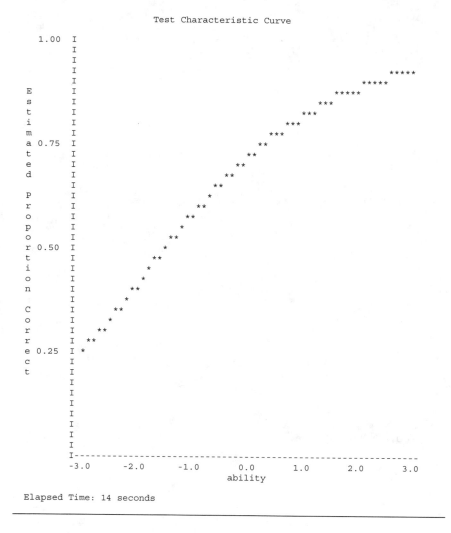

```
         XCALIBRE (tm) for Windows95/NT -- Version 1.10         Page 4
    Copyright (c) 1995 by Assessment Systems Corporation, All Rights Reserved
            Marginal Maximum-Likelihood IRT Parameter Estimation Program


                         Test Characteristic Curve

         1.00  I
               I
               I
               I
               I                                                *****
               I                                              *****
      E        I                                            *****
      s        I                                          ***
      t        I                                        ***
      i        I                                      ***
      m        I                                    ***
      a  0.75  I                                  **
      t        I                                **
      e        I                              **
      d        I                            **
               I                          **
      P        I                         *
      r        I                       **
      o        I                     **
      p        I                    *
      o        I                  **
      r  0.50  I                 *
      t        I               **
      i        I              *
      o        I             *
      n        I           **
               I          *
      C        I        **
      o        I       *
      r        I     **
      r        I   **
      e  0.25  I *
      c        I
      t        I
               I
               I
               I
               I
               I
               I
               I
               I---------------------------------------------------------
               -3.0      -2.0      -1.0      0.0       1.0      2.0      3.0
                                         ability

      Elapsed Time: 14 seconds
```

Table 19.3 displays the abridged output for a three-parameter marginal maximum likelihood IRT analysis using the XCALIBRE for Windows 95/NT, Version 1.10, IRT program (Assessment Systems Corporation, 1995). As can be seen on page 1 of the output, the model took 12 loops (iterations) to converge. In general, 3-PL models do take longer to converge, as more parameters need to be estimated for each item. The upper portion of page 2 indicates that the items fit the model rather well. No items have an R flag, and only two items have P flags (both Items 15 and 38 have b_i difficulty values of −3.00—slightly less than the −2.95 cutoff). By the way, note that this is the table that provided the IRT parameter information for Items 9 (Item 17 here), 12 (Item 30 here), and 16 (Item 45 here) depicted in Figures 19.1 and 19.2. Can you see how the values in Figures 19.1 and 19.2 match the values in page 2 of Table 19.3 if you match up the numbers above?

Table 19.3   XCALIBRE 3-PL IRT Computer Program Output

```
              XCALIBRE (tm) for Windows95/NT -- Version 1.10        Page  1
       Copyright (c) 1995 by Assessment Systems Corporation, All Rights Reserved
             Marginal Maximum-Likelihood IRT Parameter Estimation Program

                      *****  CONFIGURATION INFORMATION  *****

              Item Parameter Priors: COMMON

              Allow Priors to Float: YES

                    IRT Model Used: 3-parameter

          Maximum Number of Loops: 12

          Starting Prior Distribution Moments:

                    Mean        SD
              a     0.0000    0.0000
              b     0.0000    1.0000
              c     0.0000    0.0000


          NOTE:  ***  will be printed when the c standard error value > 0.10

      The number of items was:    60

      The maximum parameter change on loop 1 was      1.886
      The maximum parameter change on loop 2 was      0.428
      The maximum parameter change on loop 3 was      0.118
      The maximum parameter change on loop 4 was      0.115
      The maximum parameter change on loop 5 was      0.107
      The maximum parameter change on loop 6 was      0.095
      The maximum parameter change on loop 7 was      0.084
      The maximum parameter change on loop 8 was      0.075
      The maximum parameter change on loop 9 was      0.067
      The maximum parameter change on loop 10 was     0.060
      The maximum parameter change on loop 11 was     0.054
      The maximum parameter change on loop 12 was     0.049

      Mean Number-Correct Score =    13.914
      Number-Correct Standard Deviation =     2.917
      K-R 21 Reliability = 0.600

      The number of examinees was 1559

       Final Parameter Summary Information:
             Mean       SD

      Theta   0.00     1.00
        a     0.58     0.15
        b    -0.56     1.66
        c     0.27     0.02
```

(Continued)

```
           XCALIBRE (tm) for Windows95/NT -- Version 1.10          Page  2
       Copyright (c) 1995 by Assessment Systems Corporation, All Rights Reserved
           Marginal Maximum-Likelihood IRT Parameter Estimation Program
```

FINAL ITEM PARAMETER ESTIMATES

Item	Lnk	Flg	a	b	c	Resid	PC	PBs	PBt	N	Item name
4			0.79	-1.67	0.27	0.29	0.87	0.45	0.49	1559	
5			0.65	-2.58	0.27	0.74	0.93	0.34	0.36	1559	
6			0.64	0.52	0.25	0.22	0.54	0.45	0.45	1559	
10			0.77	0.31	0.26	0.46	0.58	0.46	0.49	1559	
11			0.59	-0.23	0.27	0.10	0.67	0.44	0.45	1559	
13			0.62	-0.79	0.26	0.17	0.74	0.44	0.47	1559	
14			0.73	-1.72	0.27	0.33	0.87	0.41	0.46	1559	
15		P	0.54	-3.00	0.28	0.52	0.94	0.25	0.26	1559	
17			0.80	-0.15	0.24	0.38	0.64	0.52	0.56	1559	
24			0.55	-1.39	0.28	0.14	0.81	0.39	0.40	1559	
29			0.70	2.46	0.27	0.71	0.34	0.22	0.15	1559	
30			0.32	-2.28	0.29	1.13	0.83	0.19	0.16	1559	
31			0.60	-0.96	0.27	0.17	0.77	0.43	0.45	1559	
37			0.33	1.07	0.32	1.09	0.57	0.25	0.16	1559	
38		P	0.38	-3.00	0.29	1.25	0.91	0.17	0.15	1559	
45			0.71	2.05	0.21	0.50	0.30	0.34	0.31	1559	
48			0.39	-0.26	0.30	0.55	0.68	0.30	0.27	1559	
54			0.49	1.68	0.27	0.63	0.44	0.32	0.27	1559	
58			0.69	-2.45	0.28	0.25	0.93	0.36	0.38	1559	
60			0.39	1.17	0.31	0.68	0.54	0.30	0.21	1559	

ITEM PARAMETER ESTIMATES W/STANDARD ERRORS

Item	Lnk	Flg	a	a error	b	b error	c	c error	Resid	Item name
4			0.79	0.054	-1.67	0.072	0.27	***	0.29	
5			0.65	0.051	-2.58	0.105	0.27	***	0.74	
6			0.64	0.095	0.52	0.073	0.25	0.077	0.22	
10			0.77	0.087	0.31	0.062	0.26	0.079	0.46	
11			0.59	0.085	-0.23	0.073	0.27	0.099	0.10	
13			0.62	0.068	-0.79	0.071	0.26	***	0.17	
14			0.73	0.054	-1.72	0.077	0.27	***	0.33	
15		P	0.54	0.050	-3.00	0.126	0.28	***	0.52	
17			0.80	0.075	-0.15	0.057	0.24	0.092	0.38	
24			0.55	0.060	-1.39	0.085	0.28	***	0.14	
29			0.70	0.109	2.46	0.157	0.27	0.052	0.71	
30			0.32	0.062	-2.28	0.142	0.29	***	1.13	
31			0.60	0.066	-0.96	0.075	0.27	***	0.17	
37			0.33	0.125	1.07	0.145	0.32	0.079	1.09	
38		P	0.38	0.050	-3.00	0.140	0.29	***	1.25	
45			0.71	0.090	2.05	0.110	0.21	0.051	0.50	
48			0.39	0.113	-0.26	0.108	0.30	***	0.55	
54			0.49	0.092	1.68	0.120	0.27	0.064	0.63	
58			0.69	0.052	-2.45	0.099	0.28	***	0.25	
60			0.39	0.112	1.17	0.129	0.31	0.075	0.68	

(Continued)

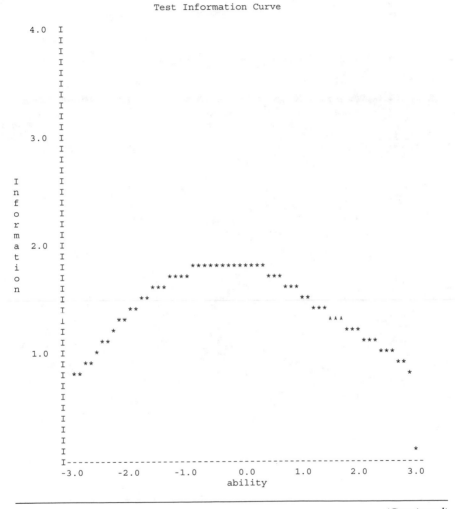

(Continued)

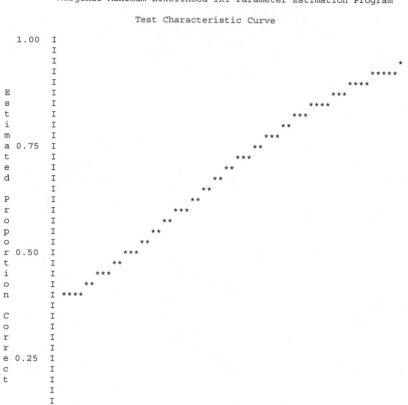

```
         XCALIBRE (tm) for Windows95/NT -- Version 1.10          Page 4
Copyright (c) 1995 by Assessment Systems Corporation, All Rights Reserved
         Marginal Maximum-Likelihood IRT Parameter Estimation Program

                        Test Characteristic Curve

        1.00  I
              I
              I
              I                                                              *
              I                                                       *****
              I                                                    ****
    E         I                                                 ***
    s         I                                              ****
    t         I                                           ***
    i         I                                         **
    m         I                                      ***
    a  0.75   I                                    **
    t         I                                 ***
    e         I                               **
    d         I                             **
              I                           **
    P         I                         **
    r         I                      ***
    o         I                    **
    p         I                  **
    o         I                **
    r  0.50   I             ***
    t         I           **
    i         I         ***
    o         I       **
    n         I ****
              I
    C         I
    o         I
    r         I
    r         I
    e  0.25   I
    c         I
    t         I
              I
              I
              I
              I
              I
              I
              I--------------------------------------------------------------
              -3.0      -2.0      -1.0      0.0       1.0      2.0      3.0
                                       ability

Elapsed Time: 28 seconds
```

Finally, pages 3 and 4 display the test information curve (test information function, TIF) and the test characteristic curve (test response function,
TRF), respectively. The TRF is a graphic representation of the estimated
proportion correct for different levels of θ. The TIF displays the amount of
psychometric information provided by (i.e., effectiveness of) the test at different levels of θ. The top of page 3 also displays estimates of the test reliability, expected information (normal distribution), and average information

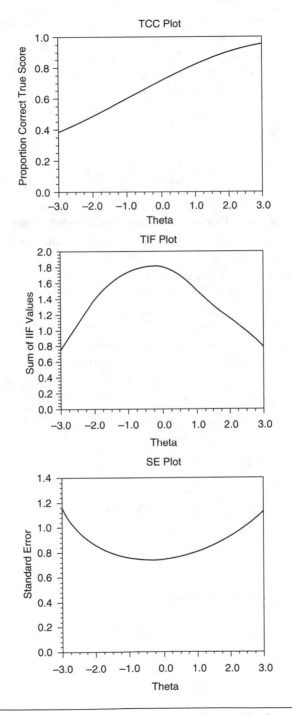

Figure 19.3   Test Information, Characteristic, and Error Plot for a Mechanical
Comprehension Test

(rectangular distribution). Figure 19.3 also displays a better looking version of the same test characteristic curve (TCC) on page 4 and the test information function (TIF) on page 3. More important, however, it also displays a standard error plot showing how the standard error of θ increases rather dramatically as ability (θ) increases in either direction.

Concluding Comments

Classical test theory item analysis (CTT-IA) can be useful, especially in small-sample, local (e.g., classroom) situations. Such procedures can greatly facilitate the construction of new tests and the evaluation and revision of existing tests in these limited situations. However, a major problem with CTT-IA is that the parameter estimates of difficulty and discriminability are sample dependent. In local situations, this may not be as big an issue because the test takers may not differ much in ability level from one administration to another. However, for tests and instruments that are developed with the intention of being used across a wide span of ability levels, use of CTT-IA may at best be incomplete and at worse misleading. Thus, item response theory (IRT) models, whose parameter estimates are sample invariant, are more appropriate and informative when constructing, evaluating, administering, and scoring tests. In addition, IRT models allow for use of computer adaptive testing (CAT) techniques of test administration, thus allowing each "test" to be tailored to the individual's ability level, as well as estimation of item bias. Both of these issues will be discussed in the next module.

Practical Questions

1. What are the major advantages of IRT over CTT-IA?

2. How do you determine the difficulty, discrimination, and pseudo-guessing parameters in IRT? How are they different from CTT-IA?

3. When might it be preferable to use CTT-IA instead of IRT?

4. What are the advantages and disadvantages of the 1-PL, 2-PL, and 3-PL IRT models?

5. What advantages do IRFs (i.e., graphs) have over simply examining the item parameters in table form?

6. What does it mean to say that item and person parameters are invariant (i.e., locally independent) in IRT models, but not in CTT-IA?

7. What unique information do IRFs and IIFs provide for test development and revision?

Case Studies

CASE STUDY 19.1: ANALYSIS OF A HIGH SCHOOL ENGLISH PROFICIENCY EXAM USING ITEM RESPONSE THEORY

Elena, a first-year educational measurement graduate student, vaguely remembered a discussion of item response theory (IRT) in her undergraduate tests and measurements class, but never thought that she might actually conduct such a study one day. The whole concept of IRT seemed so complex and appeared to require a level of mathematical sophistication that was well beyond her. In addition, the item response function (IRF) graphs she remembered seemed like the apparent random lines she recalled seeing on her father's oscilloscope when she was a child. How could she possibly understand all of it, let alone help a professor conduct such a study using IRT?

However, she had recently agreed to serve as a paid graduate research assistant for Professor Koshino in the college of education. Professor Koshino was contracted to help a large local school district evaluate the English competency exit exam it had recently developed and administered to seniors in the district's four high schools. The district graduated more than 2,500 students each year from its four high schools combined. Not surprisingly, students varied widely in their English ability, both within and across schools. Given the large sample sizes and wide ability ranges, Professor Koshino decided that IRT would be a good way to examine items on the test to determine which items should be kept and which should be revised or discarded. However, Professor Koshino was no expert in IRT. He was hoping he could just turn over the analysis part of the project to Elena and some other graduate students in the educational measurement PhD program. However, Elena and the other graduate students were feeling rather uncomfortable trying to apply what little they had learned about IRT so far to this very real life situation. It seemed time to sit down and have a frank discussion with Professor Koshino.

Questions to Ponder

1. What would be the advantages and disadvantages of using CTT-IA in this situation instead of IRT?

2. What would be the advantages and disadvantages of using the 1-PL IRT model? The 2-PL IRT model? The 3-PL IRT model?

3. Where should Elena start to "get up to speed" with the IRT procedures?

4. Should the four high schools be analyzed separately or together?

5. What should Elena and Professor Koshino be focusing on in their IRT computer printouts?

6. What advantages are there to examining the item response functions (IRFs) in this situation?

CASE STUDY 19.2: CREATION OF A
CERTIFICATION EXAM FOR CORRECTIONS AGENTS

Dr. Agars was recently hired by the state of California as a senior research analyst in the Department of Corrections (DoC). His degree was in industrial and organizational (I/O) psychology, with a minor in forensic psychology, while his undergraduate degree was in criminal justice. Thus, his boss knew that Dr. Agars had some expertise in psychological testing as well as the job duties of a parole agent. The DoC was recently mandated by the state legislature to develop a certification exam for parole agents. Corrections in the state of California are a $5.2 billion industry, by far the largest in the United States. A large part of the reason for the exorbitant cost is that 66% of the 125,000 annual parolees from the state's 33 prisons are reincarcerated before their three-year parole is up. That's more than twice the national average. It's not all that surprising, however, because 75% of parolees have drug or alcohol problems, 50% are illiterate, and 80% have no job when they get out. Thus, the goal of the state legislature in passing the certification requirement was to hire additional parole agents (who typically have a load of between 80 and 100 ex-convicts at any one time) to work more closely with current felons to prepare them for their eventual release from prison. This, the legislature hopes, will dramatically reduce the number of reincarcerated felons, thus more than making up for the cost of new parole agents. However, there is no way of knowing if the current parole agents are qualified to perform these additional functions, hence, the new certification requirement.

The Department of Corrections has close to 1,000 applicants for the parole agent job each year. Thus, the DoC typically offered the civil service exam for parole agents four times a year. However, with the certification prerequisite, there will be an additional requirement that individuals not only pass the civil service exam to be a parole agent, they must also pass a new certification exam. In addition, current parole agents will need to take and pass the as yet to be implemented certification exam.

The State Personnel Board has hundreds of multiple-choice test items that it has given to tens of thousands of job applicants over the last 20 years (when it started its electronic scoring procedures) for the job of parole agent. The DoC would like to create a computerized version of the certification test that could be offered on an as-needed basis. Professor Agars knows a little about computer-based testing, but is by no means an expert. However, given the DoC was interested in continuous testing and there were lots of questions and data to get things started, it seemed to Dr. Agars that using item response theory (IRT) to create a computer adaptive test (CAT) would be a logical choice. Use of IRT would allow the test to be tailored (or adapted) to each test taker. In addition, because each individual would, in a sense, have his or her own exam with a different mixture of questions, unlike the state civil service exam, problems with cheating and remembering items would be minimized. Thus, applicants who had already passed the state civil service exam for parole agent could come into a testing center at a designated time and take the certification exam. Finally, using IRT to create a CAT version of the certification exam would also allow individuals currently in the position to take the certification exam multiple times over a short time period until they passed. Thus, it seemed using IRT to create a CAT version of the certification exam was a logical choice. When Dr. Agars presented the idea to his boss, not only was his boss excited about the idea, he wanted to know if he could also do the same thing (i.e., use IRT to create a CAT) for the civil service exam for parole agents. Suddenly, Dr. Agars was beginning to wonder what he had gotten himself into.

Questions to Ponder

1. Does it appear that IRT is a viable option for creating a written exam (CAT or paper-and-pencil) in this situation?

2. Given the changing nature of the job of parole agent, should Dr. Agars be using questions from prior civil service exams for the selection of new parole agents?

3. Are there any unique issues concerning the use of IRT for certification and/or licensing exams? If so, what are they?

4. Would the development and use of a test using IRT procedures be any different for the civil service exam (which typically rank orders job applicants) and the certification exam (which typically sets a pass point and those above are "certified" while those falling below the pass point are not "certified")?

5. Based on the information presented in the case study, does it appear that a new certification exam is the answer to the state's reincarceration problem? What unique information do you think it will provide?

6. What would be the advantage of using IRT methods over CTT-IA procedures to develop the certification test in this instance?

7. Should the applicants and current incumbents be treated any differently in this situation?

Exercises

EXERCISE 19.1: AN ITEM
RESPONSE THEORY ONLINE TUTORIAL

OBJECTIVE: To become familiar with IRT through an interactive, self-paced, online tutorial.

BACKGROUND: In the module overview, we discussed the key elements of IRT and how it differs from (and expands upon) classical test theory item analysis (CTT-IA). Using the following Web addresses, explore an interactive IRT Web site where you can adjust each of the three major item parameters and see how altering each of these parameters affects the resulting item characteristic curves.

An online, interactive, computer adaptive testing tutorial can be found at the following address:

http://edres.org/scripts/cat/catdemo.htm

There are several activities to explore at this Web site that will help you better understand the concepts and logic underlying IRT and CAT. For example,

1. You can take an actual CAT, altering your true score (θ), which items you answer correctly or incorrectly, and so on, and seeing how each affects your θ estimate.

CAT Demo: http://edres.org/scripts/cat/startcat.htm

2. You can alter a_i, b_i, and/or c_i and see what happens to the ICCs (item characteristic curves, or IRFs) for a given item across the different levels of θ.

Interactive IRT mini-tutorial: http://edres.org/scripts/cat/genicc.asp

a. What happens to the item response function when you adjust the level of a_i (*item discrimination*)?

b. What happens to the item response function when you adjust the level of b_i (*item difficulty*)?

c. What happens to the item response function when you adjust the level of c_i (*pseudo-guessing*)?

EXERCISE 19.2: 1-PL (RASCH), 2-PL, AND 3-PL COMPUTER RUNS

OBJECTIVE: To provide a brief introduction to common IRT programs by downloading a demo version and running 1-PL (Rasch), 2-PL, and 3-PL models for example data.

1. The Web site http://www.assess.com provides information on several IRT programs, including BILOG-MG, MULTILOG, TESTFACT, PARSCALE, RASCAL, and XCALIBRE. The Web site has demonstration versions of RASCAL and XCALIBRE available for download. To download the demonstration versions of these two programs, click on "software" and scroll down to Rasch Analysis (choose RASCAL) and IRT (choose XCALIBRE), respectively.

2. Once the respective programs are downloaded and installed on your computer, start the RASCAL program. You should get a screen that looks like Figure 19.4a. From the menu at the top, select "Configure" then "Go." This will open the "Analysis Options Configuration Window" (see Figure 19.4b). When you click on the icon of a file folder next to "Input data file name," you should get a dialog box that lists a file named "sample1.dat." Click on this file and click on "OK." Then click on the icon of the file folder next to the "Analysis output file name." There should be a file named "sample1.out." Click on this file. The program will ask if you want to overwrite the existing file, click "no." It will then allow you to rename the file. Rename the file to "Sample2.out" and make sure that it is in the same directory as the input data file. The default options are to use "difficulty" and "logistic" so keep those settings. Next, click on "OK" (with a green check mark) in the upper right hand corner of the "Analysis Options Configuration Window" (see Figure 19.4b). This will take you back to the main screen (Figure 19.4a). Next, click on the icon of the computer in the upper left of Figure 19.4a. This will run the analysis. The program should run in one to two seconds and converge in four loops (iterations). The screen that appears next will tell you how to print out and/or view your analyses on screen. Print out your results of "Sample2.out" so that you can answer the questions at the end.

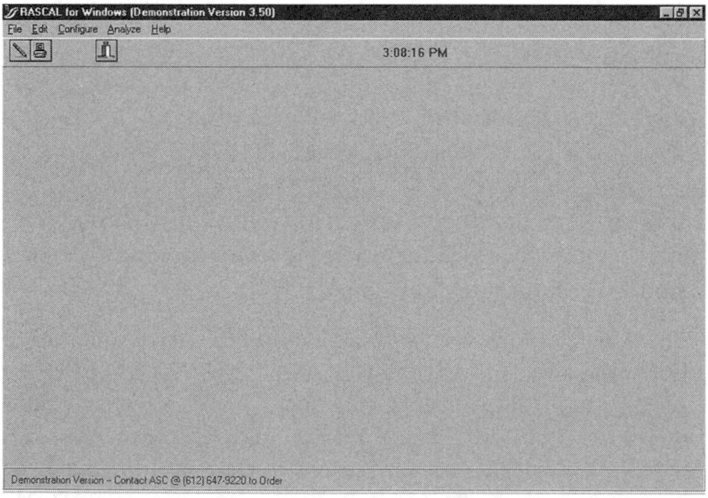

Figure 19.4a   Initial RASCAL IRT Computer Program Window

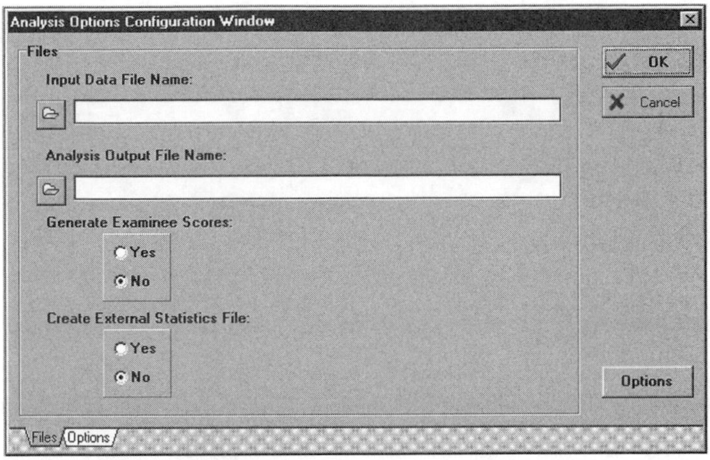

Figure 19.4b   Analysis Configuration Window in RASCAL IRT Computer Program

3. Next, start the XCALIBRE program. You should get a screen that looks very much like Figure 19.4a for the RASCAL program; however, it will say "XCALIBRE for Windows (Demonstration Version 1.0)" at the top. From the menu at the top, select "Configure" then "Go" (just as you did in step 2). This will again open the "Analysis Options Configuration Window" as before. When you click on the icon of a file folder next to "Input data file name," you should once again get a dialog box that lists a file named "sample1.dat." Click on this file. Then click on the icon of the file folder next to the "Analysis output file name." There should be a file named "sample1.out." Click on this file. The program will ask if you want to overwrite the existing file, click "no." Rename this file "Sample3.out." Next, click on the "options" button and change only the "IRT Model" value to two-parameter (see Figure 19.5). Keep all other default options the same. Next, click on "OK" (with a green check mark) in the upper right hand corner of the "Analysis Options Configuration Window" (see Figure 19.4b). This will take you back to the main screen. Next, click on the icon of the computer in the upper left of the main screen. This will run the analysis. The program should run in less than 15 seconds (depending on the speed of your computer) and converge after three loops (iterations). The screen that appears next will tell you how to print out and/or view your analyses on screen. Print out your results of "Sample3.out" so that you can answer the questions below.

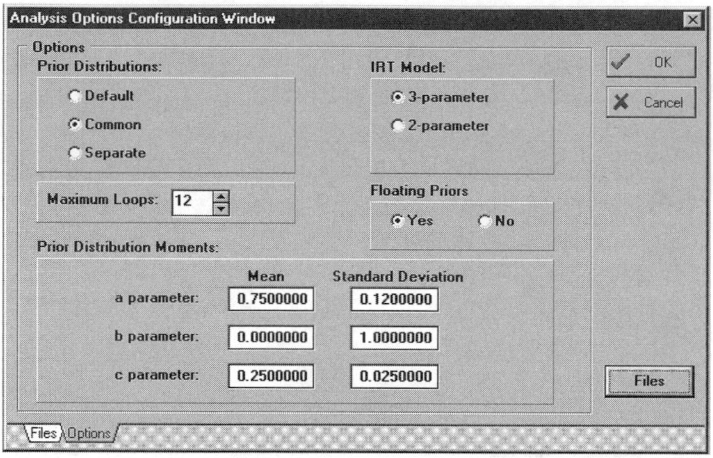

Figure 19.5   Analysis Options Configurations Window for XCALIBRE
IRT Computer Program

4. Repeat step 3, but now choose the three-parameter option. Again, keep all other defaults options the same. Rename the output file "Sample4.out." Next, click on "OK" (with a green check mark) in the upper right hand corner of the "Analysis Options Configuration Window" (see Figure 19.4b). This will take you back to the main screen. Next, click on the icon of the computer in the upper left of the main screen. This will run the analysis. The program should run in less than 15 seconds (depending on the speed of your computer) and converge after three loops (iterations). The screen that appears next will tell you how to print out and/or view your analyses on screen. Print out your results.

Questions

a. What are the basic descriptive statistics for the data? (N, average number correct, number of items, etc.)

b. How many items were flagged in the 2-PL model with an R? With a P? Why were they flagged?

c. How many items were flagged in the 3-PL model with an R? With a P? Why were they flagged?

d. Which of the three models seems to best fit the data? What did you base your answer on?

EXERCISE 19.3: ITEM RESPONSE
THEORY LITERATURE SEARCH

OBJECTIVE: To become familiar with applications of IRT in the literature.

Either individually or in small groups, perform a literature search to find a recent empirical article that provides an example of the application of IRT to an applied testing situation. Then write a brief summary and/or make a short presentation to the class summarizing the application of IRT with a focus on critiquing the use of IRT for that particular application.

Internet Web Site References

19.1. http://edres.org/irt/baker/

This Web page presents links to an electronic text by Frank Baker titled "The Basics of Item Response Theory."

19.2. http://work.psych.uiuc.edu/irt/tutorial.asp

This Web page, from the IRT Modeling Lab at the University of Illinois at Urbana-Champaign, provides a tutorial on IRT.

19.3. http://www.psych.umn.edu/psylabs/CATCentral/

This Web page, developed by David Weiss and his colleagues at the University of Minnesota, provides an excellent introduction to IRT from the basics to advanced methods.

Further Readings

Ellis, B. B., & Mead, A. D. (2002). Item analysis: Theory and practice using classical and modern test theory. In S. G. Rogelberg (Ed.), *Handbook of research methods in industrial and organizational psychology* (pp. 324–343). Malden, MA: Blackwell.

Embretson, S. E., & Reise, S. P. (2000). *Item response theory for psychologists.* Hillsdale, NJ: Erlbaum.

Hambleton, R. K., Swaminathan, H., & Rogers, H. J. (1991). *Fundamentals of item response theory.* Newbury Park, CA: Sage.

Hulin, C. L., Drasgow, F., & Parsons, C. K. (1983). *Item response theory: Applications to psychological measurement.* Homewood, IL: Dow Jones Irwin.

Lord, F. M. (1980). *Applications of item response theory to practical testing problems*. Hillsdale, NJ: Erlbaum.

Wiesen, J. P. (1999). *WTMA™ Wiesen Test of Mechanical Aptitude™ (PAR edition) professional manual*. Odessa, FL: Psychological Assessment Resources.

Zickar, M. J. (1998). Modeling item-level data with item response theory. *Current Directions in Psychological Science, 7,* 104–109.

Zickar, M. J. (2002). Modeling data with polytomous item response theory. In F. Drasgow & N. Schmitt (Eds.), *Measuring and analyzing behavior in organizations: Advances in measurement and data analysis* (pp. 123–156). San Francisco: Jossey-Bass.

Module 20

Applications of Item Response Theory

Computer Adaptive Testing and Differential Item Functioning

wo major applications of item response theory (IRT) noted in Module 19 were the development of computer adaptive tests (CATs) and the examination of differential item functioning (DIF). There are numerous other less-well-known applications of IRT beyond these, such as measuring change over time, that unfortunately we do not have the space, or expertise, to expand on here. However, given the technical—and, to many, mysterious—nature of IRT, we believe it is important to discuss at least a few of the more prominent applications of this procedure. In doing so, we hope to demonstrate IRT's practical relevance and entice you to learn more about IRT and its application to a variety of measurement issues. As with IRT itself, however, both of these topics are rather involved. Therefore, we provide only a brief overview of these topics and refer you to Camilli and Shepard (1994), Embretson and Reise (2000), and Raju and Ellis (2002) for more detailed discussions on the nuts and bolts of implementing such procedures in practice.

Computer Adaptive Testing

The vast majority of tests that we both take and administer, whether measuring cognitive ability or achievement or aptitude or attitude, are administered in the traditional paper-and-pencil format. Increasingly, however, we are seeing tests being administered via computer. When a paper-and-pencil test is simply transferred from paper to a computer, it is commonly referred to as **computer-based testing (CBT)**. Such tests may provide many practical advantages, including immediate scoring with no need for a separate answer sheet, use of multimedia questions, and easier creation of test score databases. However, there is no real psychometric advantage to simply transferring a paper-and-pencil test to a CBT. Conversely, when item response theory (IRT), as discussed in Module 19, is used to develop, administer, and score computerized tests, then there are distinct psychometric, as well as practical, advantages.

In particular, computer adaptive tests (CATs), as compared to traditional paper-and-pencil tests, are both more effective and more efficient. By effective, we mean that CATs are generally more accurate in estimating individuals' ability levels. Another way of thinking of it is that CATs tend to have less measurement error than traditional paper-and-pencil tests because the tests are specifically tailored to an individual's estimated ability level. In addition, traditional tests based on classical test theory (CTT) assume that measurement error is uniform across the ability score distribution. As discussed in Module 19, IRT makes no such assumption. Instead, measurement error is estimated for all levels of ability. As a result, individuals with moderate trait levels tend to have less measurement error than individuals with extreme trait levels, thus providing more psychometrically accurate estimates of ability in the moderate ability range for most tests.

CATs are also more efficient because they are tailored to the individual's ability level; thus test takers do not have to answer as many questions as in a traditional paper-and-pencil test to obtain comparable, or better, estimates of ability. That is, the questions become easier or harder as test takers correctly, or incorrectly, answer each question. As a result, most CATs tend to be about half as long (i.e., 50% shorter) than their paper-and-pencil counterparts and yet have equal or better measurement properties. In addition, because individuals with low ability are not wasting their time answering extremely difficult questions and, conversely, individuals with high ability levels are not wasting their time answering questions that are extremely easy for them, CATs are more efficient. This efficiency is gained by the fact that each item in a CAT provides more useful information than a typical paper-and-pencil test, thus allowing the test user to more efficiently distinguish test takers at various levels of ability (Embretson & Reise, 2000).

In addition to the practical advantages noted previously for CBTs (e.g., use of multimedia, no need for separate answer sheets, easier creation and maintenance of test score databases), CATs also have the practical advantage of year-round testing. For example, back in the authors' day, the Graduate Record Examination (GRE) was administered only a few times a year in paper-and-pencil format. As a result, in order for the first author to meet certain graduate admissions application deadlines, he ended up having to go to Canada to take his GREs. Now that the GRE is administered continuously via CAT, it is simply a matter of making an appointment and paying your fee, of course. In addition, because a CAT is tailored to each test taker, each individual takes a unique test. Thus, the ability to cheat on the test or to remember one's answers from a previous administration is extremely low. Another advantage is that test takers typically receive their scores in minutes. Again, in the authors' day, it was an anxious few months before GRE results were received. Assuming the test taker is comfortable using a computer, the CAT is likely to be a less stressful testing environment than the traditional experience of mass testing in a crowded school gymnasium. Thus, overall, there are many practical and psychometric advantages to CATs over traditional paper-and-pencil tests.

As you might guess, however, CATs pose some potential challenges, as well. For example, in most cases, a CAT requires many questions to be available at all ability ranges. As noted in Module 11, it can be very difficult and time consuming to create a single good item, let alone a cadre of good items for each level of ability. In addition, CAT is based on IRT, which is a model-based theory. If your data do not meet the assumptions of the model or simply do not fit your proposed model very well, then the results obtained from the CAT will likely not possess all of the advantages noted previously. As a result of these practical and technical constraints, CATs have until recently been limited to large-scale testing operations, such as the Educational Testing Service (ETS) and the U.S. military.

So how does a CAT actually work? (Web Reference 20.1 provides an excellent interactive discussion of CATs.) With CATs, the test is adapted to an individual's level of ability as she progresses through the test. For example, a test taker is typically first given an item of moderate difficulty (i.e., $\theta = 0.0$ or between, say, $-.50$ and $+.50$). If the person is known to be substantially above or below average on the trait being measured, however, an appropriately harder or easier item can be used to begin the testing session. Assuming, though, that we start with a moderately difficult item and the individual answers the first item correctly, her θ level is assessed (presumably as being above the mean) and she is given a more difficult item (i.e., $\theta > 0.0$), whereas if she answers the first item wrong, she is given an easier item (i.e., $\theta < 0.0$). This adaptive form of question administration is continued until a certain predetermined level of confidence (i.e., standard error of measurement) in the estimate of the individual's level of ability (θ) is obtained.

As you might surmise, early estimates of θ based on a small number of responses will have much higher measurement error. In addition, individuals who respond in an unsystematic fashion will also have a lot of measurement error associated with their θ value. As a result, some individuals may need only a few items to accurately estimate their ability level, while others, who may be responding less systematically, may require many more items. In some instances, the computer is preprogrammed to administer a minimum and/or maximum number of items. As a result, there may be some instances where an individual's ability level (θ) is unable to be estimated with enough precision within the maximal number of allowable questions or time limit. Thus, that individual would most likely have to retake the examination in order to obtain a valid score on the trait being assessed.

Several prominent examples of the use of CAT include the Graduate Record Examination (GRE) general exam, which you may well have taken yourself in CAT form; the Armed Services Vocational Aptitude Battery (ASVAB), used to select and place armed services recruits; and the National Council Licensure Examination for Registered Nurses (NCLEX-RN) (see Web Reference 20.2 for more examples of CATs). In all three examples, IRT is used to develop and administer CAT versions of the respective tests. That is, the test developers have written and calibrated a wide range of items with varying levels of difficulty (b_i). In addition, item discrimination (a_i) for most items will be high at designated levels of ability. There is an important difference in these three tests, however. For the former two, the goal is to estimate as precisely as possible a test taker's level of ability (θ). For the NCLEX-RN (or any licensing exam, for that matter), the goal is not a precise estimate of θ, but rather to estimate if θ is above or below a given critical passing score. Thus, licensing exams administered via CAT may require fewer items because of the goals of the measurement process (i.e., pass/fail); however, when the test taker's θ level is very close to the cutoff point, a CAT may actually require more questions to confidently establish a pass/fail grade than would be required if we were simply estimating θ. Thus, with traditional tests we typically desire a wide range of items with varying difficulty levels, whereas with licensing examinations we need many more items that are near the cutoff score.

Differential Item Functioning

As noted throughout this book, starting in Module 1, psychological and educational testing is as much a political process as it is a psychometric process. As a result, individuals who do not receive valued outcomes as a result of testing may well claim that it was due to the test itself being biased. In Module 10, we discussed the issue of test bias and how best to estimate it. What happens, however, once a test is found to display evidence of test bias? Do we discard the entire test? Hopefully not. As you have seen throughout this book, the test development and validation process is a long and arduous one. Therefore, we do not want to simply discard an entire test that may have been years in the making, especially one with well-established and promising psychometric properties. Conversely, we do not want to be administering tests that display clear evidence of test bias. So what is the alternative?

It may well be that only a few items on the test are the major contributors to the observed test bias. Therefore, we would want to establish whether individual items are biased and modify or discard those particular items and replace them with items that display less (hopefully no) bias. So how does one go about identifying biased items? Detection of item bias is a holistic process that involves both qualitative and quantitative evidence. In this module, we are going to focus on a particular form of quantitative or empirical evidence for item bias known as **differential item functioning (DIF)**. (In Exercise 20.3, you will perform a qualitative item bias review.) An item displays DIF when individuals from different groups with the same ability level (θ) have different probabilities of correctly answering an item. While we can look at more than two groups, we will focus here on comparing only two groups at one time, typically referred to as the focal and referent groups. For example, if you wanted to see if certain cognitive ability items were biased against women, women would be identified as the focal group and men would be identified as the referent group. Thus, groups can be based on most characteristics; however, demographic groups based on gender, race, ethnicity, religion, and disability are typically used as individuals in these groups are protected under major civil rights laws.

Before we discuss the IRT approach to item bias, it should be noted that other non-IRT methods are common and have a long history (see Web Reference 20.3). For example, the Mantel-Haenszel (M-H, chi-square) technique has been used extensively to assess item bias. Here, a 2 (focal versus referent group) by 2 (pass/fail) table is set up for each item. The resulting table is tested for statistical significance using the M-H statistic. A significant

M-H statistic would be an indication of item bias. However, remember the definition of *item bias* is that those test takers with equal ability have a different chance of answering a given item correctly based on group membership. Therefore, the M-H tables must be set up separately for different total test scores. In most practical situations, however, we will have too few (and sometimes no one) from a particular group at a given score level. Therefore, in practice, score groups (e.g., deciles or quartiles) may be established instead of individual raw scores in order to obtain adequate sample sizes.

Another prominent non-IRT technique for estimating item bias is the use of logistic regression (LR). With LR, one predicts the item outcome (i.e., pass/fail) using three predictors: (1) the total test score, (2) the variable that designates group membership, and (3) the interaction term between total test score and group membership. If the regression weight for group membership is significant, but the interaction is not, this is referred to as uniform DIF (Raju & Ellis, 2002). Uniform DIF occurs when the item differs in difficulty level across the focal and referent groups but is not different in terms of discrimination. Alternatively, if the regression weight for the interaction between group membership and total test score is significant (regardless of whether the group membership weight is significant by itself), then this is an indication of nonuniform DIF. As you might guess, nonuniform DIF means that the item displays both differences in difficulty and discrimination for individuals in different groups with the same ability levels. This procedure is analogous, though not the same, to the use of moderated multiple regression (MMR) to establish test bias in the form of slope and intercept bias (i.e., uniform DIF being similar to intercept bias and nonuniform DIF being similar to slope bias). With item-level data, however, we are evaluating **measurement bias** (i.e., if the item represents the underlying construct equally well for different groups). Conversely, with test bias, we are establishing **predictive bias** (i.e., if the test differentially predicts some criterion of interest). Thus, while item and test bias are similar, they represent the evaluation of fundamentally different forms of bias.

Several IRT-based methods for detecting DIF are discussed by Raju and Ellis (2002). These include a visual inspection of differences in item response functions (such as those displayed in Figure 19.1) for the focal and referent groups on a given item. Similar to the LR procedure discussed previously, both uniform and nonuniform DIF can be found. Uniform DIF would be present when the b_i (difficulty) parameters differ for the two groups, whereas differences in the a_i (discrimination) parameters would indicate nonuniform DIF. This can be seen when the two IRF curves cross one another. An actual test of the significance of the difference in these parameters is available using

Lord's chi-square statistic. Thus, inspection of the IRFs provides visual evidence of the DIF, and Lord's chi-square provides statistical evidence; however, neither procedure provides an actual index of the amount of DIF present. Raju and Ellis (2002) discussed several statistics that actually map the differences in area between the two IRFs and thus serve as an index of the level of DIFs.

Before item parameters from different groups can be compared, however, the two groups must first be linked. That is, the scores from different groups must be equated so that the item parameters represent meaningful differences and not just artifacts associated with the two distributions. An in-depth discussion of linking item parameters is beyond the scope of this overview. Briefly, however, a subset of items from your scale is used as the linking items to equate the tests. The problem with this is deciding which items to use. Ideally, you will want to use items that do not display DIF. To determine DIF, however, you must first do the linking procedure. As a result, most IRT users run an iterative process where DIF items are identified, then removed, and the linking study is run again until no DIF items are identified. The remaining items are then used for linking purposes. Alternatively, newer IRT programs (e.g., BILOG-MG) use a likelihood ratio procedure that allows for multigroup IRT modeling, thus ameliorating the need for the linking step (Embretson & Reise, 2000). These procedures are relatively new, however, and their accuracy compared to the more traditional linking procedures is still unknown. In summary, regardless of which DIF procedure is used, our key goal is to identify, and remove if necessary, items that have different levels of difficulty and/or discrimination across groups that have the same ability level.

Concluding Comments

Item response theory (IRT) procedures still remain a mystery to many classically trained psychologists. However, use of IRT is becoming more prominent as specialty software becomes more user-friendly and less technical references are available to explain its basic principles. In addition, as new graduates who have wider exposure to IRT enter the field, its use should continue to increase. As a result, application of IRT models is clearly becoming more widespread, yet by no means mainstream. Therefore, our goal in writing this module was not so much to provide technical details on the applications of IRT, but rather to pique your interest in the possible applications of IRT and to provide a few examples of how IRT can be applied.

Practical Questions

1. What are the major advantages of CAT administration over traditional paper-and-pencil test administration?

2. Could CAT be used in small-scale applications? If so, explain how.

3. What is the difference between a test that is simply administered on a computer (sometimes called computer-based testing, CBT) and a computer adaptive test (CAT)?

4. How do DIF procedures extend CTT-IA analyses?

5. What are the advantages and disadvantages of using non-IRT DIF versus IRT-based DIF?

6. Why do we need to equate item parameters before running a DIF analysis?

7. How do item bias and test bias procedures differ? How are they similar?

Case Studies

CASE STUDY 20.1: EXPLAINING COMPUTER ADAPTIVE TESTING TO A LAY AUDIENCE

Scott, a second-year graduate student in educational measurement, had just gotten off the phone with his sister Gail, who had recently finished her nursing degree. Gail and her friend, Tammy, had taken the CAT version of the National Council Licensure Examination for Registered Nurses (NCLEX-RN) a few weeks earlier. Gail and Tammy had just received their results. Gail had passed and Tammy had failed. Passing this licensing exam is required of all nursing students who hope to practice as registered nurses in a given state within the United States. While Gail was glad that she had passed, she was disappointed for her friend Tammy. Gail didn't really understand how the CAT worked, and, reflecting back on their conversation, Scott felt he had had a difficult time trying to explain it to her.

"It doesn't seem fair that Tammy and I actually took different tests. Don't the tests have to contain the same items to be able to compare them?" asked Gail.

"Well, it doesn't have to," Scott began as he tried to explain. "The test is called 'adaptive' because it adapts to your ability level."

"How does a computer know what my ability level is if I haven't taken the test yet?" asked Gail, somewhat perplexed.

"Well, the computer starts with a moderately difficult item and then, depending on whether you answer that one correctly or not, it gives you an easier item if you get it wrong, or a harder item if you get it correct," Scott explained. "Then the computer uses that information to compute an estimate of your ability in nursing," Scott added.

"But how could it do that with just a few questions?" Gail wondered out loud.

"Well, the estimate of your ability isn't very good at first. That's why the computer has to give you more than just a couple of questions," Scott tried to explain. "In fact, I just looked up information on the NCLEX-RN on the Internet and it says that they have to administer a minimum of 75 questions."

"I kind of understand, but I still don't know why Tammy had to answer so many more questions than I did and she still failed. In fact, she was there for five hours and it only took me about half that time to complete the test," said Gail, somewhat frustrated.

"Well, you must have been more consistent in your responding than Tammy. In addition, for a licensing exam, the key is to score above the cutoff score, so as soon as the computer is relatively confident that you are above the cutoff score it will stop administering questions. So, my guess is that the computer was able to say with confidence that you were above the cutoff, but it took much longer for Tammy. In fact, the information I found on the NCLEX-RN says the maximum time limit is five hours, so Tammy simply ran out of time and never reached the maximum number of 265 questions," Scott explained.

"Ah, I think I'm starting to understand," said Gail with a wry smile on her face. "But, I still don't understand why Tammy and I couldn't just answer the same questions."

Somewhat discouraged, Scott said, "Okay, let me try to explain it to you another way. . . . "

Questions to Ponder

1. If you were Scott, how would you go about explaining what a CAT was to Gail?

2. What are some of the major differences between a CAT and a paper-and-pencil test that might highlight the advantages of CAT over paper-and-pencil testing for Gail?

3. Are there other reasons that Tammy might have had to answer more questions than Gail? Is there a better way to explain this than what Scott said?

4. What other stopping procedures might a CAT use to decide when to end the testing session besides a maximum number of items or a time limit? Will it be different for licensing exams versus other more traditional testing situations?

5. Are there other examples of the use of CAT that you can think of that might help Gail better understand what a CAT is?

CASE STUDY 20.2: DIFFERENTIAL ITEM FUNCTIONING

Web Reference 20.3 explains how the Educational Testing Service identified differential item functioning (DIF) on an analogy question from the SAT exam. The question was an analogy that asked: "Strawberry: Red as (a) peach:ripe, (b) leather:brown, (c) grass:green, (d) orange:round, or (e) lemon:yellow." The test question demonstrated DIF against Hispanic test takers in that they were more familiar with lemons that are green, not yellow. As a result, they were more likely to select option (c) instead of the correct answer, option (e). The procedure ETS used to determine DIF was a statistic developed by psychometricians at ETS called the Delta statistic, which compares how difficult different groups found the item. In addition to the DIF analysis, ETS also gathered a panel of experts who were the ones who identified that Hispanic examinees would be more likely to associate lemons with being green and not yellow. Thus, this item was ultimately discarded as the question was intended to assess one's knowledge of analogies, but for at least one group, Hispanics, it was more an assessment of one's knowledge of different fruit colors.

Questions to Ponder

1. What additional information might use of IRT procedures for DIF analysis provide that are not available with use of the Delta statistic?

2. Psychometricians at ETS no doubt know a lot about IRT procedures. In fact, ETS psychometricians were among the earlier pioneers in IRT research and development. Why, then, do you think they opted not to use IRT procedures to assess DIF in this instance?

3. As noted in the module overview, in order to perform IRT DIF procedures item parameters need to be linked or equated across groups. Do you think such equating would also be required if other statistics, such as ETS's Delta procedure, are used to establish DIF?

4. If you plotted the item response functions (i.e., ICCs) for the different ethnic groups noted in this example, what do you think you are likely to see?

5. Could this item be revised instead of simply being discarded? If so, how?

Exercises

EXERCISE 20.1: ITEM RESPONSE THEORY AND COMPUTER ADAPTIVE TESTING ONLINE TUTORIAL

OBJECTIVE: To become familiar with IRT and CAT through an interactive, self-paced, online tutorial.

BACKGROUND: In the module overview, we discussed the key elements of IRT and how it can be applied to computer adaptive testing and differential item functioning. Using the following Web addresses, explore an interactive IRT Web site where you can adjust each of the three major item parameters and see how altering each of these parameters affects the resulting item characteristic curves.

An online, interactive, computer adaptive testing tutorial can be found at the following Internet Web address:

http://edres.org/scripts/cat/catdemo.htm

There are several activities to explore at this Web site that will help you better understand the concepts and logic underlying IRT and CAT. For example,

1. You can take an actual CAT, altering your true score (θ), which items you answer correctly or incorrectly, and so on, and seeing how each affects your θ estimate.

CAT Demo: http://edres.org/scripts/cat/startcat.htm

EXERCISE 20.2: ITEM
BIAS/FAIRNESS REVIEW

OBJECTIVE: To provide an opportunity to use item bias/fairness review to critically evaluate test items for possible bias.

The Web page http://pareonline.net/getvn.asp?v=4&n=6 by Ronald Hambleton and H. Jane Rogers is titled "Item Bias Review." The page provides a number of questions test creators can ask themselves in order to reduce bias in test items. After reviewing the brief write-up at the Web site, use the "Sample questions addressing fairness" and the "Sample bias questions" to review the 13 organizational behavior items found in Table 12.4 for possible item bias with regard to both gender (men versus women) and race/ethnic group (Caucasian versus African American and Caucasian versus Hispanic).

1. Did you find any questions that appear to demonstrate bias based on sex? If so, which items and on what basis do they appear to show bias?

2. Did you find any questions that appear to demonstrate bias based on race (Caucasian versus African American)? If so, which items and on what basis do they appear to show bias?

3. Did you find any questions that appear to demonstrate bias based on ethnic group status (Caucasian versus Hispanic)? If so, which items and on what basis do they appear to show bias?

EXERCISE 20.3: A CAT/DIF
LITERATURE SEARCH

OBJECTIVE: To become familiar with the CAT and DIF literature.

Either individually or in small groups, perform a literature search to find a recent empirical article that provides an example of the application of IRT to an applied testing situation that specifically addresses computer adaptive testing (CAT) or differential item functioning (DIF). Then write a brief summary and/or make a short presentation to the class summarizing the application of IRT with a focus on critiquing the use of IRT for that particular application of CAT or DIF.

Internet Web Site References

20.1. http://edres.org/scripts/cat/catdemo.htm

This Web page provides a detailed explanation of CAT, along with an interactive IRT tutorial.

20.2. http://www.psych.umn.edu/psylabs/CATCentral/

This Web page, developed by David Weiss and his colleagues at the University of Minnesota, provides an excellent introduction to IRT from the basics to advanced methods. Once at the Web site, click on "Current CAT research programs" on the left to see current applications of CAT.

20.3. http://www.ets.org/research/dif.html

This Educational Testing Service (ETS) Web page provides a simple explanation of differential item functioning (DIF).

20.4. http://pareonline.net/getvn.asp?v=4&n=6

This Web page provides a brief overview of item bias.

Further Readings

Camilli, G., & Shepard, L. A. (1994). *Methods for identifying biased test items.* Thousand Oaks, CA: Sage.

Embretson, S. E., & Reise, S. P. (2000). *Item response theory for psychologists.* Hillsdale, NJ: Erlbaum.

Murphy, K. R., & Davidshofer, C. O. (2001). *Psychological testing: Principles and applications* (5th ed., pp. 236–251). Upper Saddle River, NJ: Prentice Hall.

Raju, N. S., & Ellis, B. B. (2002). Differential item and test functioning. In F. Drasgow & N. Schmitt (Eds.), *Measuring and analyzing behavior in organizations: Advances in measurement and data analysis* (pp. 156–188). San Francisco: Jossey-Bass.

Appendix A
Course-Long Exercise
on Psychological
Scale Development

This continuing exercise will require you and your classmates to apply information from many of the modules that comprise this book. The intent of this continuing exercise will be to develop a rationally derived measure of typical performance of your choosing. Development will progress through test specifications, item writing, administration of the scale, consideration of issues related to reliability and validity, item refinement through use of exploratory factor analysis, and specification of test scoring. In the end, you will be encouraged to create a test manual that outlines the development of your measure.

This continuing exercise has elements of both group and individual work. In a group with other classmates, you will choose a psychological construct to measure, decide on test specifications, develop items, obtain both subject matter expert (SME) ratings and responses to items, and construct data files. Individually, you will then be responsible for making decisions based on the SME ratings, examining the reliability and dimensionality of the scale, discarding items, proposing methods for examining the scale's validity, and creating the test manual.

Important note: In creating this book, the authors have followed what we consider to be a logical organization of the material needed to understand the process of test construction. The order in which the modules are presented, however, is not likely to be the order in which a test developer creates a test. For the purpose of this continuing exercise, we suggest conducting the continuing exercise in the following order:

Group Work	Relevant Module
Part 1: Introduction	Module 1
Part 2: Test preparation and specification	Module 4
Part 3: Item writing and administration	Module 15
Individual Work	Relevant Module
Part 4: Examining subject matter expert ratings	Module 6
Part 5: Exploratory factor analysis	Module 18
Part 6: Reliability analysis	Module 5
Part 7: Criterion-related validity	Module 7
Part 8: Construct validity	Module 8
Part 9: Development of a test manual	Uses information from all modules

PART 1: INTRODUCTION (MODULE 1)

Objective: To gain experience in all steps of development of a rationally derived psychological measure of typical performance.

In part 1 of this continuing exercise, we ask you to begin looking forward to and mentally preparing for some of the activities that will go into the development of a measure of typical performance. It's likely going to be more work than you think. Now is a good time to begin to identify a psychological construct that you might like to operationalize.

PART 2: TEST PREPARATION AND SPECIFICATION (MODULE 4)

Objective: To begin development of a psychological measure by developing test specifications.

By this time, your instructor has specified how many people will comprise a group for the initial parts of this continuing exercise, and you have hopefully determined who your group members will be. We're about to get started on this project in earnest.

1. Together with your group members, identify a psychological construct that could benefit from additional measurement. Perhaps consider a construct that:
   - is currently not well measured,
   - is currently available only from a test publisher,

- could be useful for an upcoming research project or thesis,
- captures your interest.

2. Clearly define the domain to which this test will apply. Carefully consider each of the subquestions (2a–2d) presented in the overview of Module 4. (*Note: This is the most important step of this continuing exercise.*)

3. Choose the item format that will be used. This is an important element of test specifications. For this continuing exercise, choose a Likert-type rating scale for your items. Determine the scale anchors that will be used.

PART 3: ITEM WRITING AND
ADMINISTRATION (MODULE 15)

Objective: To develop quality items to assess a psychological construct.

1. Determine how many items will be written.

Great! You finally get to write some items. Before you do, we must consider an important dilemma concerning how many items should be written. On the one hand, the more items your group develops, the better. That way, after conducting some analyses, you will be able to discard poor items without worrying too much about ending up with too few items in the final scale. On the other hand, with a class exercise such as this, we often have a limited sample to which we can administer our scale. Because some important statistical procedures such as exploratory factor analysis require a large sample size relative to the number of items, we'd like to ensure that we don't have too many items.

So what's the plan? We recommend the following. Determine the largest possible tryout sample size your group will commit to obtaining (your instructor will likely give you a minimum sample size). Then divide that number by 5. The resulting number is the number of items your group will want to create for initial administration. Let's say, for example, the sample size of your tryout sample will be 180. Because at a minimum we'll want to ensure five respondents per item (see Module 18), then we divide 180 by 5 and determine that we need to include no more than 36 items in the initial draft.

If your group has six members, then each person is responsible for drafting six items (36 total items divided by 6 members = 6 items each). In planning how many items to create, your group may want to specify that each member should initially draft more than the minimum number of items so that, as a group, you can select the best items to be initially administered to the tryout sample. Continuing with the example, each of the six group members might want to draft nine items initially, for a group total of 54 items. Together, the group can then decide which 36 of the 54 possible items should be administered to the tryout sample.

2. Write items to assess the construct specified in part 2.

To ensure quality items, remember to do the following:

- Review your definition of the construct.
- Write items to assess each of the dimensions of your construct (if multidimensional).
- Ensure that some items are worded such that disagreement with the item indicates endorsement of the construct (i.e., include items that will be reverse scored).
- Review the item-writing tips presented in Module 15.

3. As a group, determine the set of items that will be administered to the tryout sample.

4. Obtain subject matter expert (SME) ratings of the items.

SMEs should be asked to rate each of your draft items. Several scales could be used, including the rating scale used to assess the CVR as discussed in the overview of Module 6. Here, each SME rates whether the item is "essential," "useful," or "not necessary" to the operationalization of the theoretical construct. Alternatively, you could use a scale of relevance to the intended construct that includes anchors such as "not at all relevant," "somewhat relevant," "relevant," and "highly relevant." Your instructor may have additional suggestions and will specify the minimum number of SME ratings your group should obtain.

When obtaining SME ratings, ensure the following:

- SMEs are presented a clear definition of your construct.
- SMEs are informed that items that assess the opposite pole of your construct (i.e., reverse-scored items) are just as relevant to your construct as other items.
- SMEs understand they are making judgments about the items themselves. They are not being administered the items.

5. Administer the items to your tryout sample.

6. Construct two data sets. One should contain all of the SME responses obtained by group members; the other should contain all of the responses of the tryout sample obtained by group members.

This is the last step of the group work phase of the project. From here on, you will be making all important decisions on your own (or perhaps with some advice from your instructor).

PART 4: EXAMINING SUBJECT
MATTER EXPERT RATINGS (MODULE 6)

Objective: To refine the draft scale by using information provided by SME ratings.

1. Using the SME ratings data file created by your group, compute the mean and standard deviation of all items.

2. Determine a cut score that you believe reflects SME judgments that the item is too low in relevance to be included for further consideration. There are no rules of thumb here—you'll have to rely on your own judgment. Keep the following in mind when determining what cut score to use:
   - Be sure you are able to justify your choice of a cut score. Why do you think all items at or above this mean should be included for further analysis, while all other items should be discarded?
   - Use the same cut score for all items on the scale. Even if you expect your scale to be multidimensional, use a single cut score across all items.
   - Do not set your cut score so high that you eliminate too many items. Remember, additional items may be dropped following reliability and/or factor analysis.

3. Eliminate from further consideration those items that do not meet your cut score. Use only those items that are at or above your cut score for all remaining parts of this continuing exercise.

PART 5: EXPLORATORY
FACTOR ANALYSIS (MODULE 18)

Objective: To examine the dimensionality of the remaining scale items.

1. Using the tryout sample data file, conduct an exploratory factor analysis of those items that were retained following examination of the SME ratings. Use the following options found within your data analysis software:
   - Choose the principal axis factoring method.
   - Choose Promax as the method of rotation.
   - Request a scree plot. Determine the number of factors by examining your scree plot.
   - Choose "sort by size" to display the factor loadings.

2. Examine the output from your factor analysis. Does the output support the expected dimensionality of your scale? Which items are loading on the major factors? Can you provide a logical label for the group of items loading on a particular factor?

It is often the case that exploratory factor analysis does not support the expected dimensionality of a newly created scale. Perhaps you expected a multidimensional scale and found that almost all of the items load on a single factor. Perhaps you expected a single dimension, and the items form distinct, interpretable factors. If the initial exploratory factor analysis suggests a very different factor structure from what you expected, you may want to conduct an additional factor analysis requesting a specified number of factors to be extracted. Does the new factor analysis provide a more logical grouping of items? Select the output from the factor analysis that seems to make the most logical sense for the remaining steps of this part of the continuing exercise.

3. Interpret the results of your factor analysis.
    a. How many interpretable dimensions emerged? This is the dimensionality of your scale. Label each interpretable factor by examining the items that comprise it.
    b. Which items load on each interpretable factor?
    c. Delete items that fail to load on any interpretable factor. Only those items that are retained should be used in the remaining parts of the continuing exercise.

PART 6: RELIABILITY ANALYSIS (MODULE 5)

Objective: To develop scales with high internal consistency reliability.

Using only those items still retained in the tryout sample, conduct a reliability analysis of each dimension of the scale. Choose the following options:

* Compute alpha.
* Select the options "scale if item-deleted" and "item-total correlations."

1. Examine the output for each reliability analysis. Compare the obtained alpha with the alpha estimated if each particular item were deleted. Would the alpha increase if the item were deleted from the scale? If the answer is no, you will obviously retain the item. If the answer is yes, you may consider dropping the item from the final version of the scale. First, however, ask yourself the following:
    * Would dropping the item increase alpha substantially?
    * Is there a logical reason the item seems different from the other items loading on this factor?

If an item was dropped from a dimension, rerun the reliability analysis and repeat the process. Note that alpha is improved by dropping items with low item-total correlations.

2. Once the alphas of each dimension of the scale have been determined, compute the alpha of the overall scale.

PART 7: CRITERION-RELATED VALIDATION (MODULE 7)

Objective: To propose appropriate criteria to assess the criterion-related validity of the scale.

Identify criteria that *could* be used to assess the criterion-related validity of your newly developed scale. Consider the following:

- Ensure that the criteria you propose are practical, relevant, and reliable.
- Justify why your recommended criteria would be useful for validating your scale.
- Determine whether the proposed criterion-related validation design will be concurrent, predictive, or postdictive.

PART 8: CONSTRUCT VALIDATION (MODULE 8)

Objective: To propose appropriate measures to provide evidence of the construct validity of the scale.

Identify psychological measures that *could* be used to provide evidence of the construct validity of your newly developed scale. Consider the following:

- In part 2, you specified constructs that were related to your measure. Accepted measures of these constructs could be used to provide evidence of the convergent validity of your scale.
- Psychological measures that you expect to be unrelated to your scale, but that are measured on a similar Likert-type scale, would be useful in examining the discriminant validity of your newly developed scale.
- It is important to explain why the measures you are recommending could be useful for providing evidence of the convergent and discriminant validity of your scale.

PART 9: DEVELOPMENT OF A TEST MANUAL

Objective: To conclude the experience of the development of a psychological measure by production of a written report.

This final part of this continuing exercise asks you to document the entire process you conducted in developing your psychological measure. Be sure to include the following:

- Clearly define the psychological construct.
- Identify the number of SMEs used and the size and characteristics of the tryout sample.

- Document and discuss the procedures you followed in each step of the scale's development, including revisions.
- Discuss the decision points you encountered in the development of the scale and justify the decisions you made.
- Discuss the proposed validation of your scale.
- Use appendixes to present the items in the initial scale, as well as the final version of the scale.
- Include any additional elements suggested by your instructor in your test manual and/or appendixes.

Appendix B
Data Set Descriptions

This appendix contains a description of all the computerized data files needed for the exercises used in this book. All data files can be found in electronic (SPSS) format at www.sagepub.com/shultzdatasets and the Instructor's Resources CD-ROM available from Sage Publications. The exercises that use each data set are listed in parentheses after the data set name. Data sets are listed in alphabetical order.

BUS DRIVER.SAV (EXERCISES 3.3, 7.2, AND 17.1)

This data set consists of 1,441 incumbent bus drivers who completed a job analysis questionnaire, as well as personality and ability tests, as part of a large-scale employment test validation project. Job performance criteria were also collected and are included in this version of the data set. This version of the data set represents only a fraction of the 1,375 variables that made up the entire data set for the large-scale study.

Variable	Description
rand id#	Random ID number
r_hpi	Hogan Personality Inventory reliability (e.g., integrity) subscale
st_hpi	Hogan Personality Inventory stress tolerance subscale
so_hpi	Hogan Personality Inventory service orientation subscale
jobtitle	Current job title
	1 = Light bus driver
	2 = Heavy bus driver
	3 = Replacement bus driver
	4 = Driver trainee
	5 = Training supervisor

tenure   Years on current job
             1 = Less than 1 year
             2 = 1–5 years
             3 = 6–10 years
             4 = 11–15 years
             5 = More than 15 years

degree   Level of education
             1 = Less than high school
             2 = High school degree
             3 = Some college
             4 = College degree
             5 = Graduate-level work

race   Racial category
             1 = Asian
             2 = Black
             3 = Filipino
             4 = Hispanic
             5 = Native American
             6 = Pacific Islander
             7 = White
             8 = Other

sex   Sex of bus driver
             0 = Male
             1 = Female

time   Full- or part-time driver
             1 = Full time
             2 = Part time

sickdays   Number of sick and personal days in last year
srti   Number of self-reported traffic incidents in last year
drivetst   Score on driving performance test
pescore   Overall performance evaluation score
age   Age in years
TF001   Task 1—Frequency (following response scale used for all
             TF items)
             1 = Almost never
             2 = Hardly ever
             3 = Regularly
             4 = Often
             5 = Very often

TT001   Task 1—Relative time spent (following response scale used for
             all TT items)
             1 = Almost none
             2 = Little
             3 = Moderate

	4 = Much
	5 = Almost always
TI001	Task 1—Importance (following response scale used for all
	TI items)
	1 = Unimportant
	2 = Borderline
	3 = Important
	4 = Very important
	5 = Critical
TF002	Task 2—Frequency
TT002	Task 2—Relative time spent
TI002	Task 2—Importance
TF003	Task 3—Frequency
TT003	Task 3—Relative time spent
TI003	Task 3—Importance
TF004	Task 4—Frequency
TT004	Task 4—Relative time spent
TI004	Task 4—Importance
TF005	Task 5—Frequency
TT005	Task 5—Relative time spent
TI005	Task 5—Importance
TF006	Task 6—Frequency
TT006	Task 6—Relative time spent
TI006	Task 6—Importance
TF007	Task 7—Frequency
TT007	Task 7—Relative time spent
TI007	Task 7—Importance
TF008	Task 8—Frequency
TT008	Task 8—Relative time spent
TI008	Task 8—Importance
TF009	Task 9—Frequency
TT009	Task 9—Relative time spent
TI009	Task 9—Importance
TF010	Task 10—Frequency
TT010	Task 10—Relative time spent
TI010	Task 10—Importance

GEOSCIENCE ATTITUDES.SAV (EXERCISES 16.3 AND 18.1)

This data set has 15 variables (items) measured on 137 cases. Respondents rated their level of agreement to each of the following items using a five-point Likert-type rating scale ranging from 1 = strongly disagree to 5 = strongly agree.

Variable	Description
item 1	I have a good understanding of how scientists do research.
item 2	I consider myself well skilled in conducting scientific research.
item 3	I've wanted to be a scientist for as long as I can remember.
item 4	I have a good understanding of elementary geoscience.
item 5	I'm uncertain about what course of study is required to become a geoscientist.
item 6	I am considering majoring in geoscience.
item 7	I'd enjoy a career in geoscience.
item 8	I plan on taking math courses that would prepare me to major in a science.
item 9	I would enjoy going hiking or camping.
item 10	I would enjoy boating.
item 11	I'd prefer to work on a science project "in the field" than in a research laboratory.
item 12	I enjoy reading science fiction novels.
item 13	I enjoy reading nature and travel books and magazines.
sex	Participant sex
	1 = Female
	2 = Male
classyr	Class year
	1 = HS frosh or sophomore
	2 = HS junior or senior
	3 = College frosh or sophomore
	4 = College junior or senior

GMA DATA.SAV (EXERCISE 16.2)

These data come from a study by Mersman and Shultz (1998) on the fakeability of personality measures, which consisted of 323 students who worked at least part time.

Variable	Description
g1–g40	The 40 general mental ability (GMA) items
	0 = Incorrect
	1 = Correct
gsum	Total score on the GMA scale
gender	Sex of respondent
	1 = Female
	2 = Male
age	Age of respondent in years
ethnicity	Respondent's race/ethnicity
	1 = Caucasian
	2 = Hispanic

3 = African American
4 = Asian
5 = Native American
6 = Other
7 = Filipino
8 = Asian Pacific Islander

class   Academic rank of respondent
1 = Freshman
2 = Sophomore
3 = Junior
4 = Senior
5 = Graduate student

JOINERSHIP DATA RECODED.SAV (EXERCISES 15.3 AND 15.4)

Each of the items below shares the following five-point Likert-type response scale: 1 (strongly disagree), 2 (disagree), 3 (neither agree nor disagree), 4 (agree), and 5 (strongly agree). An "R" indicates that the item has already been recoded. There are 230 subjects in the data set. (See the description of Exercises 15.2–15.4 in Module 15 for the actual items and a more detailed description of the data set.)

Variable	Description
item1–item42R	Scores for each of the 42 items
age	Age in years
gender	Gender
	1 = Male
	2 = Female

JOINERSHIP RATIONAL RATING.SAV (EXERCISE 15.2)

Subject matter expert (SME) rational ratings ($N = 35$) for the 42 items in the Joinership study described in Module 15, Exercises 15.2–15.4.

Variable	Description
r1–r42	Rational rating for the 42 items
age	Age in years
gender	Gender
	1 = Male
	2 = Female

MECHANICAL COMPREHENSION.SAV
(EXERCISES 2.1 AND 10.2)

This data set was from an applied research project where 474 current employees of a large automobile manufacturer completed two tests of mechanical aptitude. Job performance data (supervisory ratings) were also collected on all 474 employees. A variety of demographic information was also collected.

Variable	Description
id	Employee code
sex	Sex of employee
	0 = Male
	1 = Female
	9 = Missing value
age	Age of employee
edlevel	Education
	0 = Missing value
	1 = Less than HS
	2 = HS diploma or GED
	3 = Some college
	4 = Associates degree
	5 = Bachelors degree
	6 = Graduate or professional degree
work	Work experience in years
jobcat	Job category
	0 = Missing value
	1 = Clerical
	2 = Office trainee
	3 = Security officer
	4 = College trainee
	5 = Exempt trainee
	6 = MBA trainee
	7 = Technical
minority	Minority classification
	0 = White
	1 = Nonwhite
	9 = Missing value
sexrace	Sex and race classification
	1 = White males
	2 = Minority males
	3 = White females
	4 = Minority females

mech1	Current mechanical aptitude test score
mech2	Proposed mechanical aptitude test score
perf	Job performance rating

         1 = Unacceptable
         2 = Well below standard
         3 = Below standard
         4 = Meets standard
         5 = Above standard
         6 = Well above standard
         7 = Outstanding

NOMONET.SAV (EXERCISE 8.4)

These data are from an applied project where 255 individuals completed several psychological tests.

Variable	Description
overt	Overt integrity measure
cogab	Cognitive ability measure
masked	Personality-based integrity measure

PASSING SCORE.SAV (EXERCISE 13.3)

This data set contains data on 200 student scores for a graduate statistics exam.

Variable	Description
final	Final exam grade in graduate statistics—ideal
final2	Final exam grade in graduate statistics—realistic
desig	Designation as successful or unsuccessful

         1 = Successful
         2 = Unsuccessful

PERSONALITY.SAV (EXERCISE 10.1)

These data come from a study by Mersman and Shultz (1998) on the fakeability of personality measures, which consisted of 323 students who worked at least part time.

Variable	Description
im	Impression management scale score
sd	Social desirability scale score

conmean1   Mean on con scale for honest
conmean2   Mean on con scale for fake
intmean1   Mean on intellect scale for honest condition
gender   Sex of respondent
       1 = Female
       2 = Male
age   Age of respondent in years
ethnicity   Respondent's race/ethnicity
       1 = Caucasian
       2 = Hispanic
       3 = African American
       4 = Asian
       5 = Native American
       6 = Other
       7 = Filipino
       8 = Asian Pacific Islander
class   Academic rank of respondent
       1 = Freshman
       2 = Sophomore
       3 = Junior
       4 = Senior
       5 = Graduate student

PERSONALITY-2.SAV (MODULE 18 OVERVIEW)

This data set is a subset of the study by Mersman and Shultz (1998) that examined the fakeability of personality measures. This subset of the larger data set consists of responses from 314 students who worked at least part time. Eight personality variables from Saucier's (1994) Mini-Markers scale (see Web Reference 18.1) in this subset of the data use the following nine-point rating scale: 1 = extremely inaccurate, 2 = very inaccurate, 3 = moderately inaccurate, 4 = slightly inaccurate, 5 = ?, 6 = slightly accurate, 7 = moderately accurate, 8 = very accurate, and 9 = extremely accurate.

Variable	*Description*
bold	Bold
disorgan	Disorganized
efficien	Efficient
extraver	Extraverted
organize	Organized
quiet	Quiet
shy	Shy
sloppy	Sloppy

RELIABILITY.SAV (EXERCISE 5.1)

This data set consists of a small subset of data from Wave 1 (1992) of the Health and Retirement Study (http://hrsonline.isr.umich.edu). This subset includes 1,560 persons who had retired "early" as of 1992.

Variable	Description
V1	DS (depression scale)—Depression
	1 = All the time
	2 = Most
	3 = Some
	4 = None
V2	DS—Tiring
V3	DS—Restlessness
V4	DS—Happiness (R)
V5	DS—Loneliness
V6	DS—People unfriendly
V7	DS—Enjoyed life (R)
V8	DS—Sadness
V9	DS—People dislike me
V10	DS—Can't get going
V11	DS—Poor appetite
V12	DS—Lots of energy (R)
V13	DS—Tired
V14	DS—Rested when woke up (R)
V15	LS (life satisfaction)—House
	1 = Very satisfied
	2 = Somewhat satisfied
	3 = Even
	4 = Somewhat dissatisfied
	5 = Very dissatisfied
V16	LS—Neighborhood
V17	LS—Health
V18	LS—Financial
V19	LS—Friendships
V20	LS—Marriage
V21	LS—Job
V22	LS—Family life
V23	LS—Way handle problems
V24	LS—Life as a whole
V25	Reason retired (RR)?—Bad health
	1 = Very important
	2 = Moderately important
	3 = Somewhat important
	4 = Not important at all

V26	RR—Health of family member
V27	RR—Wanted to do other things
V28	RR—Didn't like to work
V29	RR—Didn't get along with the boss
V30	RR—Didn't need to work/had sufficient income
V31	RR—Couldn't find any work
V32	RR—My work not appreciated
V33	RR—My spouse was about to retire
V34	RR—Employer policy toward older workers
V35	Good about retirement (GAR)—Lack of pressure

        1 = Very important
        2 = Moderately important
        3 = Somewhat important
        4 = Not important at all

V36	GAR—Being own boss
V37	GAR—Taking it easy
V38	GAR—Having time with spouse
V39	GAR—Spending more time with kids
V40	GAR—Spending more time on hobbies
V41	GAR—Time for volunteer work
V42	GAR—Having chance to travel
V43	Bad about retirement (BAR)—Boring/too much time

        1 = Bothered a lot
        2 = Bothered somewhat
        3 = Bothered a little
        4 = Bothered not at all

V44	BAR—Not productive/useful
V45	BAR—Missing co-workers (0 = didn't work)
V46	BAR—Illness/disability
V47	BAR—Not enough income
V48	BAR—Inflation
sex	Sex of respondent

        1 = Male
        2 = Female

age	Age of respondent

SALES.SAV (EXERCISE 7.3)

A sales manager hoping to improve the personnel selection process for the position of product salesperson compiled the data file with variables listed below consisting of scores on three tests as well as a job performance score and demographic data for 229 sales employees.

Variable	Description
sex	Sex of employee
	0 = Female
	1 = Male
ethnic	Ethnicity of employee
	0 = Caucasian
	1 = African American
w1–w50	Each indicates the employee's score on a separate item on the test of cognitive ability
	0 = Incorrect
	1 = Correct
cogab	Employee's total cognitive ability score
sde	Employee's score on a test assessing one's level of self-deception
impress	Employee's score on a test of impression management
selling	Number of products employee sold in the past month

VOLUNTEER DATA.SAV (EXERCISE 17.2)

This data set contains data assessed from 120 volunteers in a number of small organizations. Each of the volunteers completed a survey assessing the following perceptions.

Variable	Description
reward	Perceived reward
ledinit	Leader-initiating structure
ledcons	Leader consideration
clarity	Role clarity
conflict	Role conflict
efficacy	Job-related self-efficacy
goalid	Goal identification
affectc	Affective commitment
continc	Continuance commitment
motivate	Work motivation

References

AERA/APA/NCME. (1999). *Standards for educational and psychological testing.* Washington, DC: American Educational Research Association.

Aiken, L. S., West, S. G., & Reno, R. R. (1996). *Multiple regression: Testing and interpreting interactions.* Newbury Park, CA: Sage.

Albermarle Paper Company v. Moody. (1975). 422 U.S. 405.

Allen, M. J., & Yen, W. M. (1979). *Introduction to measurement theory.* Monterey, CA: Brooks/Cole.

Anastasi, A., & Urbina, S. (1997). *Psychological testing.* Upper Saddle River, NJ: Prentice Hall.

Arbuckle, J. L., & Wothke, W. (1999). *AMOS 4.0 user's guide.* Chicago: SPSS.

Arnold, B. R., & Matus, Y. E. (2000). Test translation and cultural equivalence methodologies for use with diverse populations. In I. Cuellar & F. A. Paniagua (Eds.), *Handbook of multicultural mental health: Assessment and treatment of diverse populations* (pp. 121–136). San Diego, CA: Academic Press.

Arvey, R. D., & Faley, R. H. (1988). *Fairness in selecting employees* (2nd ed.). New York: Addison-Wesley.

Assessment Systems Corporation. (1995). *XCALIBRE user's manual, version 1.1 for Windows 95.* St. Paul, MN: Author.

Barrett, G. V., Phillips, J. S., & Alexander, R. A. (1981). Concurrent and predictive validity designs: A critical reanalysis. *Journal of Applied Psychology, 66,* 1–6.

Barrett, R. S. (1992). Content validation form. *Public Personnel Management, 21,* 41–52.

Barrett, R. S. (1996). Content validation form. In R. S. Barrett (Ed.), *Fair employment strategies in human resource management* (pp. 47–56). Westport, CT: Quorum Books/Greenwood.

Beehr, T. A. (1986). The process of retirement: A review and recommendations for future investigation. *Personnel Psychology, 39,* 31–55.

Bentler, P. M. (1995). *EQS structural equations program manual.* Encino, CA: Multivariate Software.

Berk, R. A. (Ed.). (1982). *Handbook of methods for detecting test bias.* Baltimore: Johns Hopkins University Press.

Berk, R. A. (1986). A consumer's guide to setting performance standards on criterion-referenced tests. *Review of Educational Research, 56,* 137–172.

Biddle, R. E. (1993). How to set cutoff scores for knowledge tests used in promotion, training, certification, and licensing. *Public Personnel Management, 22,* 63–79.

Bishop, G. F., Oldendick, R. W., Tuchfarber, A. J., & Bennett, S. E. (1980). Pseudo-opinions on public affairs. *Public Opinion Quarterly, 44,* 198–209.

Bloom, B. S. (Ed.). (1956). *Taxonomy of educational objectives: The classification of educational goals: Handbook I, cognitive domain.* New York: Longmans, Green.

Bornstein, R. F. (1996). Face validity in psychological assessment: Implications for a unified model of validity. *American Psychologist, 51,* 983–984.

Brown, D. C. (1994). Subgroup norming: Legitimate testing practice or reverse discrimination. *American Psychologist, 49,* 927–928.

Bryant, F. B. (2000). Assessing the validity of measurement. In L. G. Grimm & P. R. Yarnold (Eds.), *Reading and understanding more multivariate statistics* (pp. 99–146). Washington, DC: American Psychological Association.

Bryant, F. B., & Yarnold, P. R. (1995). Principal components analysis and exploratory and confirmatory factor analysis. In L. G. Grimm & P. R. Yarnold (Eds.), *Reading and understanding multivariate statistics* (pp. 99–136). Washington, DC: American Psychological Association.

Burns, R. S. (1996). Content validity, face validity, and quantitative face validity. In R. S. Barrett (Ed.), *Fair employment strategies in human resource management* (pp. 38–46). Westport, CT: Quorum Books/Greenwood.

Camilli, G., & Shepard, L. A. (1994). *Methods for identifying biased test items.* Thousand Oaks, CA: Sage.

Campbell, D. T., & Fiske, D. W. (1959). Convergent and discriminant validation by the multitrait-multimethod matrix. *Psychological Bulletin, 56,* 81–105.

Campion, M. A., Outtz, J. L., Zedeck, S., Schmidt, F. L., Kehoe, J. F., Murphy, K. R., & Guion, R. M. (2001). The controversy over score banding in personnel selection: Answers to 10 key questions. *Personnel Psychology, 54,* 149–185.

Cascio, W. F., Alexander, R. A., & Barrett, G. V. (1988). Setting cutoff scores: Legal, psychometric, and professional issues and guidelines. *Personnel Psychology, 41,* 1–24.

Cattell, R. (1966). The meaning and strategic use of factor analysis. In R. B. Cattell (Ed.), *Handbook of multivariate experimental psychology* (pp. 174–243). Chicago: Rand McNally.

Cattin, P. (1980). Estimation of the predictive power of a regression model. *Journal of Applied Psychology, 65,* 407–414.

Chan, D., Schmitt, N., DeShon, R. P., & Clause, C. S. (1997). Reactions to cognitive ability tests: The relationships between race, test performance, face validity perceptions, and test-taking motivation. *Journal of Applied Psychology, 82,* 300–310.

Code of Fair Testing Practices in Education. (1988). Washington, DC: Joint Committee on Testing Practices.

Cohen, J. (1988). *Statistical power analysis for the behavioral sciences* (2nd ed.). Hillsdale, NJ: Erlbaum.

Cohen, P., Cohen, J., West, S. G., & Aiken, L. S. (2002). *Applied multiple regression: Correlation analysis for the behavioral sciences* (3rd ed.). Hillsdale, NJ: Erlbaum.

Cohen, R. J., & Swerdlik, M. E. (2002). *Psychological testing and assessment: An introduction to test and measurement* (5th ed.). Boston: McGraw-Hill.

Cole, D. A. (1987). Utility of confirmatory factor analysis in test validation research. *Journal of Consulting and Clinical Psychology, 55,* 584–594.

Cole, M., Gay, J., Glick, J., & Sharp, D. W. (1971). *The cultural context of learning and thinking.* New York: Basic Books.

Cortina, J. M. (1993). What is coefficient alpha? An examination of theory and applications. *Journal of Applied Psychology, 78,* 98–104.

Crocker, L. M., & Algina, J. (1986). *Introduction to classical and modern test theory.* Belmont, CA: Wadsworth.

Cronbach, L. J. (1970). *Essentials of psychological testing* (3rd ed.). New York: Harper & Row.

Cronbach, L. J., & Meehl, P. E. (1955). Construct validity in psychological tests. *Psychological Bulletin, 52,* 281–302.

DeVellis, R. F. (1991). *Scale development: Theory and applications.* Thousand Oaks, CA: Sage.

Doering, M., Rhodes, S. R., & Schuster, M. (1983). *The aging worker: Research and recommendations.* Thousand Oaks, CA: Sage.

Dove, A. (1971). The "Chitling" Test. From L. R. Aiken, Jr. (Ed.), *Psychological and educational testings.* Boston: Allyn & Bacon.

DuBois, D. A., & DuBois, C. L. Z. (2000). An alternate method for content-oriented test construction: An empirical evaluation. *Journal of Business and Psychology, 15,* 197–213.

Ebel, R. L. (1982). Proposed solutions to two problems of test construction. *Journal of Educational Measurement, 19,* 267–278.

Ebel, R. L., & Frisbie, D. A. (1986). *Essentials of educational measurement.* Englewood Cliffs, NJ: Prentice Hall.

Eid, M. (2000). A multitrait-multimethod model with minimal assumptions. *Psychometrika, 65,* 241–261.

Ekstrom, R. B., & Smith, D. K. (Eds.). (2002). *Assessing individuals with disabilities in educational, employment, and counseling settings.* Washington, DC: American Psychological Association.

Ellis, B. B., & Mead, A. D. (2002). Item analysis: Theory and practice using classical and modern test theory. In S. G. Rogelberg (Ed.), *Handbook of research methods in industrial and organizational psychology* (pp. 324–343). Malden, MA: Blackwell.

Embretson, S. E., & Reise, S. P. (2000). *Item response theory for psychologists.* Hillsdale, NJ: Erlbaum.

Enders, C. K., & Bandalos, D. L. (2001). The relative performance of full information maximum likelihood estimation for missing data in structural equation models. *Structural Equation Modeling, 8,* 430–457.

Fabrigar, L. R., Wegener, D. T., MacCallum, R. C., & Strahan, E. J. (1999). Evaluating the use of exploratory factor analysis in psychological research. *Psychological Methods, 3,* 272–299.

Feldman, J. M., & Lynch, J. G. (1988). Self-generated validity and other effects of measurement on belief, attitude, intentions, and behavior. *Journal of Applied Psychology, 73,* 421–435.

Forsyth, D. R. (1998). *Group dynamics* (3rd ed.). Belmont, CA: Wadsworth.

Fouad, N. A., & Chan, P. M. (1999). Gender and ethnicity: Influence on test interpretation and reception. In J. W. Lichtenberg & R. K. Goodyear (Eds.), *Scientist-practitioner perspectives on test interpretation.* Needham Heights, MA: Allyn & Bacon.

Fowler, F. J., Jr. (1995). *Improving survey questions: Design and evaluation.* Thousand Oaks, CA: Sage.

Frisby, C. L. (1998). Culture and cultural differences. In J. Sandoval, C. L. Frisby, K. F. Geisinger, J. D. Scheuneman, & J. R. Grenier (Eds.), *Test interpretation and diversity: Achieving equity in assessment.* Washington, DC: American Psychological Association.

Ghiselli, E. E., Campbell, J. P., & Zedeck, S. (1981). *Measurement theory for the behavioral sciences.* New York: W. H. Freeman.

Glass, G. V. (1976). Primary, secondary and meta-analysis of research. *Educational Researcher, 5,* 388.

Glass, G. V., McGaw, B., & Smith, M. L. (1981). *Meta-analysis in social research.* Beverly Hills, CA: Sage.

Gorsuch, R. L. (1983). *Factor analysis* (2nd ed.). Hillsdale, NJ: Erlbaum.

Gottfredson, L. S. (1994). The science and politics of race-norming. *American Psychologist, 49,* 955–963.

Gough, H. G., & Bradley, P. (1992). Comparing two strategies for developing personality scales. In M. Zeidner & R. Most (Eds.), *Psychological testing: An inside view* (pp. 215–246). Palo Alto, CA: Consulting Psychologists Press.

Graham, J. R. (1977). *The MMPI: A practical guide.* New York: Oxford University Press.

Graham, J. R. (1999). *MMPI-2: Assessing personality and psychopathology* (3rd ed.). New York: Oxford University Press.

Guildford, J. P. (1954). *Psychometric methods.* New York: McGraw-Hill.

Guion, R. M. (1965). Synthetic validity in a small company: A demonstration. *Personnel Psychology, 18,* 49–63.

Guion, R. M. (1978). "Content validity" in moderation. *Personnel Psychology, 31,* 205–213.

Haladyna, T. M. (1999). *Developing and validating multiple-choice test items* (2nd ed.). Mahwah, NJ: Erlbaum.

Hambleton, R. K., Swaminathan, H., & Rogers, H. J. (1991). *Fundamentals of item response theory.* Newbury Park, CA: Sage.

Haney, W. M., Madaus, G. F., & Lyons, R. (1993). *The fractured marketplace for standardized testing.* Boston: Kluwer.

Hothersall, D. (1990). *History of psychology* (2nd ed.). New York: McGraw-Hill.

Hulin, C. L., Drasgow, F., & Parsons, C. K. (1983). *Item response theory: Applications to psychological measurement.* Homewood, IL: Dow Jones-Irwin.

Hunter, J. E., & Schmidt, F. L. (1990). *Methods of meta-analysis: Correcting error and bias in research findings.* Newbury Park, CA: Sage.

Hunter, J. E., Schmidt, F. L., & Jackson, G. B. (1982). *Meta-analysis: Cumulating research findings across studies.* Beverly Hills, CA: Sage.

Impara, J. C., & Plake, B. S. (1997). Standard setting: An alternative approach. *Journal of Educational Measurement, 34,* 353–366.

Jackson, D. N. (1970). A sequential system for personality scale construction. *Current Topics in Clinical and Community Psychology, 2,* 61–96.

Jöreskog, K. G., & Sörbom, D. (1996). *LISREL 8: User's reference guide.* Chicago: Scientific Software International.

Kenny, D. A., & Kashy, D. A. (1992). Analysis of the multitrait-multimethod matrix by confirmatory factor analysis. *Psychological Bulletin, 112,* 165–172.

Kim, J. E., & Moen, P. (2001). Moving into retirement: Preparation and transitions in late midlife. In M. E. Lachman (Ed.), *Handbook of midlife development* (pp. 487–527). New York: Wiley.

Klem, L. (2000). Structural equations modeling. In L. G. Grimm & P. R. Yarnold (Eds.), *Reading and understanding more multivariate statistics* (pp. 227–260). Washington, DC: American Psychological Association.

Kline, R. B. (1998). *Principles and practice of structural equation modeling.* New York: Guilford.

Lammlein, S. E. (1987). *Proposal and evaluation of a model of job knowledge testing.* Unpublished doctoral dissertation, University of Minnesota, Minneapolis.

Lance, C. E., & Vandenberg, R. J. (2002). Confirmatory factor analysis. In F. Drasgow & N. Schmitt (Eds.), *Measuring and analyzing behavior in organizations: Advances in measurement and data analysis* (pp. 221–254). San Francisco: Jossey-Bass.

Landy, F. J. (1986). Stamp collecting versus science: Validation as hypothesis testing. *American Psychologist, 41,* 1183–1192.

Lawshe, C. H. (1952). What can industrial psychology do for small business? *Personnel Psychology, 5,* 31–34.

Lawshe, C. H. (1975). A quantitative approach to content validity. *Personnel Psychology, 28,* 563–575.

Licht, M. H. (1995). Multiple regression and correlation. In L. G. Grimm & P. R. Yarnold (Eds.), *Reading and understanding multivariate statistics* (pp. 19–64). Washington, DC: American Psychological Association.

Linn, R. L. (Ed.). (1989). *Educational measurement* (3rd ed.). New York: American Council on Education/Macmillan.

Lipsey, M. W., & Wilson, D. B. (2001). *Practical meta-analysis.* Thousand Oaks, CA: Sage.

Lonner, W. J. (1990). An overview of cross-cultural testing and assessment. In R. W. Brislin (Ed.), *Applied cross-cultural psychology* (pp. 56–76). Newbury Park, CA: Sage.

Lord, F. (1980). *Applications of item response theory to practical testing problems.* Hillsdale, NJ: Erlbaum.

Maclure, M., & Willett, W. C. (1987). Misinterpretation and misuse of the kappa statistic. *American Journal of Epidemiology, 126,* 161–169.

Marsella, A. J., & Kameoka, V. A. (1989). Ethnocultural issues in the assessment of psychopathology. In S. Wetzler (Ed.), *Measuring mental illness in psychometric assessment for clinicians* (pp. 231–256). Washington, DC: American Psychiatric Press.

Marsh, H. W. (1990). Confirmatory factor analysis of multitrait-multimethod data: The construct validation of multidimensional self-concept responses. *Journal of Personality, 58,* 661–692.

Marsh, H. W. (1991). Confirmatory factor analysis of multitrait-multimethod data: A comparison of alternative models. *Applied Psychological Measurement, 15,* 47–70.

Maurer, T. J., & Alexander, R. A. (1992). Methods of improving employment test critical scores derived by judging test content: A review and critique. *Personnel Psychology, 45,* 727–762.

McKeachie, W. J. (1994). *Teaching tips* (9th ed.). Lexington, MA: D. C. Heath.

Mersman, J. L., & Shultz, K. S. (1998). Individual differences in the ability to fake on personality measures. *Personality and Individual Differences, 24,* 217–227.

Messick, S. (1989). Validity. In R. Linn (Ed.), *Educational measurement* (3rd ed., pp. 13–103). New York: Macmillan.

Messick, S. (1995a). Validity of psychological assessment: Validation of inferences from persons' responses and performances as scientific inquiry into score meaning. *American Psychologist, 50,* 741–749.

Messick, S. (1995b). Standards of validity and the validity of standards in performance assessment. *Educational Measurement: Issues and Practice, 14,* 5–8.

Millman, J., & Greene, J. (1989). The specification and development of tests of achievement and ability. In R. L. Linn (Ed.), *Educational measurement* (3rd ed., pp. 335–366). New York: American Council on Education/Macmillan.

Moorman, R. H. P., & Philip, M. (1992). A meta-analytic review and empirical test of the potential confounding effects of social desirability response sets in organizational behaviour research. *Journal of Occupational & Organizational Psychology, 65,* 131–149.

Murphy, K. R., & Davidshofer, C. O. (2001). *Psychological testing: Principles and applications.* Upper Saddle River, NJ: Prentice Hall.

Newton, R. R., & Rudestam, K. E. (1999). *Your statistical consultant: Answers to your data analysis questions.* Thousand Oaks, CA: Sage.

Nunnally, J. C., & Bernstein, I. H. (1994). *Psychometric theory* (3rd ed.). New York: McGraw-Hill.

Ory, J. C., & Ryan, K. E. (1993). *Tips for improving testing and grading.* Newbury Park, CA: Sage.

Osterlind, S. J. (1998). *Constructing test items: Multiple-choice, constructed-response, performance, and other formats.* Boston: Kluwer.

Padilla, A. M. (2001). Issues in culturally appropriate assessment. In L. A. Suzuki, J. G. Ponterotto, & P. J. Meller (Eds.), *Handbook of multicultural assessment: Clinical, psychological, and educational applications* (2nd ed.). San Francisco: Jossey-Bass.

Paulhus, D. L. (1986). Self-deception and impression management in test responses. In A. Angleitner & J. S. Wiggins (Eds.), *Personality assessment via questionnaires: Current issues in theory and measurement*. Berlin: Springer-Verlag.

Paulhus, D. L. (1991). Measurement and control of response bias. In J. P. Robinson, P. R. Shaver, & L. S. Wrightsman (Eds.), *Measures of personality and social psychological attitudes*. San Diego, CA: Academic Press.

Pearson, K. (1903). Mathematical contributions to the theory of evolution XI: On the influence of natural selection on the variability and correlation of organs. *Philosophical Transactions of the Royal Society, Series A, 200*, 1–66.

Pedhazur, E. J. (1997). *Multiple regression in behavioral research* (3rd ed.). Pacific Grove, CA: Wadsworth.

Pedhazur, E. J., & Schmelkin, L. P. (1991). *Measurement, design, and analysis: An integrated approach*. Hillsdale, NJ: Erlbaum.

Raju, N. S., & Ellis, B. B. (2002). Differential item and test functioning. In F. Drasgow & N. Schmitt (Eds.), *Measuring and analyzing behavior in organizations: Advances in measurement and data analysis* (pp. 156–188). San Francisco: Jossey-Bass.

Reid, R. (1995). Assessment of ADHD with culturally different groups: The use of behavioral rating scales. *School Psychology Review, 24*, 537–560.

Resnick, L. B., & Resnick, D. (1992). Assessing the thinking curriculum: New tools for educational reform. In B. R. Gifford & M. C. O'Connor (Eds.), *Changing assessments: Alternative views of aptitude, achievement and instruction* (pp. 37–75). Boston: Kluwer.

Rodriguez, M. C. (2002). Choosing an item format. In G. Tindal & T. M. Haladyna (Eds.), *Large-scale assessment programs for all students: Validity, technical adequacy, and implementation* (pp. 213–231). Mahwah, NJ: Erlbaum.

Rothstein, H. R., McDaniel, M. A., & Borenstein, M. (2002). Meta-analysis: A review of quantitative cumulation methods. In F. Drasgow & N. Schmitt (Eds.), *Measuring and analyzing behavior in organizations: Advances in measurement and data analysis*. San Francisco: Jossey-Bass.

Russell, D. W. (2002). In search of underlying dimensions: The use (and abuse) of factor analysis. *Personality and Social Psychology Bulletin, 28*, 1629–1646.

Saad, S., & Sackett, P. R. (2002). Investigating differential prediction by gender in employment-oriented personality measures. *Journal of Applied Psychology, 87*, 667–674.

Sackett, P. R., Laczo, R. M., & Lippe, Z. P. (2003). Differential prediction and the use of multiple predictors: The omitted variables problem. *Journal of Applied Psychology, 86*, 1046–1056.

Sackett, P. R., & Wilk, S. L. (1994). Within-group norming and other forms of score adjustment in preemployment testing. *American Psychologist, 49*, 929–954.

Samuda, R. J. (1998). Cross-cultural assessment: Issues and alternatives. In R. J. Samuda, R. Feuerstein, A. S. Kaufman, J. E. Lewis, R. J. Sternberg, & Associates, *Advances in Cross-Cultural Assessment*. Thousand Oaks, CA: Sage.

Sandoval, J., Scheuneman, J. D., Ramos-Grenier, J., Geisinger, K. F., & Frisby, C. (Eds.). (1998). *Test interpretation and diversity: Achieving equity in assessment.* Washington, DC: American Psychological Association.

Saucier, G. (1994). Mini-marker: A brief version of Goldberg's unipolar big-five markers. *Journal of Personality Assessment, 63,* 506–516.

Schaeffer, N. C., & Presser, S. (2003). The science of asking questions. *Annual Review of Sociology, 29,* 65–88.

Schmidt, F. L., & Hunter, J. E. (1977). Development of a general solution to the problem of validity generalization. *Journal of Applied Psychology, 62,* 529–540.

Schmidt, F. L., & Hunter, J. E. (1980). The future of criterion-related validity. *Personnel Psychology, 33,* 41–60.

Schmidt, F. L., & Hunter, J. E. (1996). Measurement error in psychological research: Lessons from 26 research scenarios. *Psychological Methods, 1,* 199–223.

Schmidt, F. L., & Hunter, J. E. (2001). Meta-analysis. In N. Anderson, D. S. Ones, H. K. Sinangil, & C. Viswesvaran (Eds.), *Handbook of industrial, work and organizational psychology* (Vol. 1, pp. 51–70). Thousand Oaks, CA: Sage.

Schmidt, F. L., Hunter, J. E., & Urry, V. W. (1976). Statistical power in criterion-related validity studies. *Journal of Applied Psychology, 61,* 473–485.

Schmitt, N. (1996). Uses and abuses of coefficient alpha. *Psychological Assessment, 8,* 350–353.

Schmitt, N., Gooding, R., Noe, R. A., & Kirsch, M. (1984). Meta-analyses of validity studies published between 1964 and 1982, and the investigation of study characteristics. *Personnel Psychology, 37,* 407–422.

Schmitt, N., & Klimoski, R. (1991). *Research methods in human resource management.* Cincinnati, OH: Southwest.

Schmitt, N., & Ostroff, C. (1986). Operationalizing the "behavioral consistency" approach: Selection test development based on a content-oriented strategy. *Personnel Psychology, 39,* 91–108.

Schmitt, N., & Stults, D. M. (1986). Methodology review: Analysis of multitrait-multimethod matrices. *Applied Psychological Measurement, 10,* 1–22.

Schuman, H., & Presser, S. (1996). *Questions and answers in attitude surveys: Experiments on question form, wording and context.* Newbury Park, CA: Sage.

Schwarz, N. (1999). Self-reports: How the questions shape the answers. *American Psychologist, 54,* 93–105.

Shultz, K. S. (1995). Increasing alpha reliabilities of multiple-choice tests with linear polychotomous scoring. *Psychological Reports, 77,* 760–762.

Shultz, K. S., Morton, K. R., & Weckerle, J. R. (1998). The influence of push and pull factors in distinguishing voluntary and involuntary early retirees' retirement decision and adjustment. *Journal of Vocational Behavior, 53,* 45–57.

Shultz, K. S., & Taylor, M. A. (2001, August). The predictors of retirement: A meta-analysis. In K. S. Shultz & M. A. Taylor (Co-Chairs), *Evolving concepts of retirement for the 21st century.* Symposium conducted at the 109th Annual Conference of the American Psychological Association, San Francisco.

Society for Industrial and Organizational Psychology, Inc. (2003). *Principles for the validation and use of personnel selection procedures* (4th ed.). Bowling Green, OH: Author.

Spearman, C. (1904). General intelligence: Objectively determined and measured. *American Journal of Psychology, 15,* 201–293.

Sperber, A. D., Devellis, R. F., & Boehlecke, B. (1994). Cross-cultural translation: Methodology and validation. *Journal of Cross Cultural Psychology, 25,* 505–524.

SPSS, Inc. (2003). *SPSS 11.5 base user's guide.* Chicago: Author.

Steenkamp, J.-B. E. M., & Baumgartner, H. (1998). Assessing measurement invariance in cross-national consumer research. *Journal of Consumer Research, 25,* 78–90.

Sternberg, R. J., & Grigorenko, E. L. (2001). Ability testing across cultures. In L. A. Suzuki, J. G. Ponterotto, & P. J. Meller (Eds.), *Handbook of multicultural assessment: Clinical, psychological, and educational applications* (2nd ed., pp. 335–358). San Francisco: Jossey-Bass.

Styers, B., & Shultz, K. S. (2002, April). Perceived reasonableness of employment testing accommodations for persons with disabilities. Paper presented at the annual conference of the Society for Industrial and Organizational Psychology, Toronto.

Sussmann, M. (1986). The validity of validity: An analysis of validation study designs. *Journal of Applied Psychology, 71,* 461–468.

Tabachnick, B. G., & Fidell, L. S. (2001). *Using multivariate statistics* (4th ed.). Boston: Allyn & Bacon.

Tenopyr, M. L. (1977). Content-construct confusion. *Personnel Psychology, 30,* 47–54.

Thompson, B. (2000). Ten commandments of structural equation modeling. In L. G. Grimm & P. R. Yarnold (Eds.), *Reading and understanding more multivariate statistics* (pp. 227–260). Washington, DC: American Psychological Association.

Torgerson, W. S. (1958). *Theory and methods of scaling.* New York: Wiley.

Traub, R. E. (1994). *Reliability for the social sciences: Theory and application.* Thousand Oaks, CA: Sage.

Trochim, W. (2000). *The research methods knowledge base* (2nd ed.). Cincinnati, OH: Atomic Dog.

Trochim, W. M. (2003). *The research methods knowledge base* (2nd ed.) [On-line]. Retrieved from http://trochim.human.cornell.edu/kb/index.htm

Tuckman, B. W. (1988). *Testing for teachers* (2nd ed.). New York: Harcourt, Brace, Jovanovich.

van der Ven, A. H. G. S. (1980). *Introduction to scaling.* New York: Wiley.

Vaughn, K. W. (1951). Planning the objective test. In E. F. Lindquist (Ed.), *Educational measurement* (pp. 159–184). Washington, DC: American Council on Education.

Velicer, W. F., & Fava, J. L. (1998). Effects of variable and subject sampling on factor pattern recovery. *Psychological Methods, 2,* 231–251.

Wanous, J. P., Sullivan, S. E., & Malinak, J. (1989). The role of judgment calls in meta-analysis. *Journal of Applied Psychology, 74,* 259–264.

Widaman, K. F. (1985). Hierarchically nested covariance structure models for multitrait-multimethod data. *Applied Psychological Measurement, 9,* 1–26.

Widaman, K. F., & Thompson, J. S. (2003). On specifying the null model for incremental fit indices in structural equation modeling. *Psychological Methods, 8,* 16–37.

Wiersma, W., & Jurs, S. G. (1990). *Educational measurement and testing* (2nd ed.). Boston: Allyn & Bacon.

Wiesen, J. P. (1999). *WTMA™ Wiesen Test of Mechanical Aptitude™ (PAR edition) professional manual.* Odessa, FL: Psychological Assessment Resources.

Wiggens, G. (1989, May). A true test: Towards a more authentic and equitable assessment. *Phi Delta Kappan,* 803–813.

Williams, R. L. (1972). *The black intelligence test of cultural homogeneity.* St. Louis, MO: Black Studies Program, Washington University.

Wonderlic, Inc. (2002). *Wonderlic Personnel Test and Scholastic Level Exam user's manual.* Libertyville, IL: Wonderlic.

Zickar, M. J. (1998). Modeling item-level data with item response theory. *Current Directions in Psychological Science, 7,* 104–109.

Zickar, M. J. (2002). Modeling data with polytomous item response theory. In F. Drasgow & N. Schmitt (Eds.), *Measuring and analyzing behavior in organizations: Advances in measurement and data analysis* (pp. 123–155). San Francisco: Jossey-Bass.

Glossary of Key Terms

B elow we provide definitions for key terms used within this text, as well as other key terms used more broadly in the field of psychological measurement and psychometrics. Please be aware that multiple definitions of these key terms can be found in the extant literature on psychological testing. Therefore, we have tried to strike a balance between technical and common usage, but given the nature of the book, we have emphasized the former. Note that italicized words within the definitions of key terms below are also defined elsewhere in this glossary.

Ability The capacity for performing different tasks, acquiring knowledge, or developing skills within cognitive, psychomotor, or physical domains. In *classical test theory,* ability is represented by the true score. In modern test theory (*IRT*), ability is represented by a theoretical value (theta, θ).

Ability Testing The use of *tests* to determine an individual's current level of ability in cognitive, psychomotor, or physical domains.

Accommodation In testing and assessment, the adaptation of an assessment device, testing procedure, or the substitution of one device for another, to make the test more appropriate for individuals with special needs (e.g., a physical disability such as blindness).

Achievement Test A test that emphasizes what an individual currently knows or can do with regard to a particular subject matter.

Acquiescence A *response style* characterized by agreement with whatever is presented in a given assessment device.

Adaptive Testing A form of testing that individually tailors the presentation of test items to the *test taker*. See also *Computer Adaptive Testing* (*CAT*).

Adverse Impact A situation where individuals in one group (typically a "protected group" under federal statute) pass a test at a substantially different rate than other comparable groups. The "80% rule" is typically applied to establish adverse impact.

Alternate Forms Reliability An estimate of the degree to which the items used on two versions of the same assessment device are associated with one another. Also called *Parallel Forms Reliability.*

Anchor Test or Items A common set of items from two forms of a test that allows a test user to equate the two forms of the test. Creating an anchor test is necessary when *item response theory* procedures are used to investigate the possibility of *item bias*.

Aptitude Test A test that emphasizes innate potential and informal learning, and is used to predict future performance and/or behavior.

Armed Services Vocational Aptitude Battery (ASVAB) A series of tests used for military selection and placement. The ASVAB consists of 10 subtests that assess individuals' strengths and weaknesses in aptitudes including general science, arithmetic reasoning, word knowledge, paragraph comprehension, numerical operations, coding speed, auto and shop information, mathematics knowledge, mechanical comprehension, and electronics information.

Assessment A broad method of obtaining information that may include the use of test scores, as well as other information that describes individuals, objects, or some other target of the assessment.

Attitude One's disposition, thoughts, and/or feelings regarding a particular stimulus that is relatively stable in nature.

Back Translation The translation of a test, which has already been translated from its original language, back into its original language. The original test and the back-translated version are then compared to determine the quality of the translation.

Banding A procedure for setting a *cutoff score* where scores within a particular range are treated as equivalent. The range of scores is typically determined based on statistics such as the *standard error of measurement*.

Battery A combination of several tests given in sequence in order to obtain a combined assessment score. See also *Armed Services Vocational Aptitude Battery (ASVAB)*.

Bias Variance in test scores due to deficiencies or *contamination* that differentially affects scores within different groups of individuals, such as men versus women or minority versus majority *test takers*.

Bivariate Distribution A joint distribution for two variables. This can include two tests or a test and a criterion variable. Bivariate distributions are typically visualized using a *scatterplot* graph.

Calibration In *item response theory,* the process of estimating the parameters (i.e., difficulty, discrimination, and guessing) for an item. In equating test scores, the process of setting test statistics (i.e., *central tendency, variability,* and shape) in order to equate scores across distributions.

Central Tendency A statistical estimate of the "average" or "typical" score in a given distribution. Examples include the arithmetical *mean, median,* and *mode.*

Central Tendency Error When an evaluator rates *test takers* using only the central portion of a rating scale regardless of the test takers' actual level of performance.

Classical Test Theory (CTT) A theory of testing that says that any observed score is a function of an individual's true score plus error. The basis for common estimates of *reliability, validity,* and estimations of error, such as the *standard error of measurement.*

Coefficient Alpha An estimate of test *reliability* based on the intercorrelations among items.

Coefficient of Determination The squared value of a bivariate correlation coefficient. It represents the percentage of variance in one variable that is attributable to variance in the other variable.

Compensatory Scoring The combining of several test scores where high scores on one test can offset low scores on another.

Composite Score The combining of individual test scores into a single score based on some specified formula, such as unit weighting or empirically derived regression weights.

Computer Adaptive Testing (CAT) A form of assessment where the test is administered via computer and the items administered are tailored to each individual based on his or her responses to previous items. See also *Item Response Theory (IRT).*

Computer-Based Testing (CBT) A method of test administration where a test is administered (and possibly scored) on a computer, thus allowing for branching of items and use of multimedia materials.

Concurrent Validity Providing evidence for the *validity* of a measure by determining the degree of association between it and a *criterion* that is presently available.

Confidence Interval The estimation of a population parameter (e.g., a population mean) by creating an interval that is determined based on a designated probability value (e.g., critical Z value) and a standard error statistic (e.g., standard error of the mean).

Constant Ratio Model A model of test *fairness* where the proportion of individuals successful on the *criterion* must be equal to the number who pass the test *cutoff score* across designated subgroups in order for the test to be considered fair.

Constituents, Testing Individuals or stakeholders who have a vested interest in the testing process. These include the *test taker, test developer, test user,* and society as a whole.

Construct A characteristic or *trait* that individuals possess to differing degrees that a test is designed to measure.

Construct Equivalence The degree to which a given *construct* measured by a given test is comparable across different cultural or linguistic groups or the degree to which a given *construct* is the same across different tests.

Construct Validity The evidence gathered to support the inferences made regarding the scores obtained on an assessment instrument and the degree to which they represent some intangible characteristic of the *test taker.* The extent to which a measurement instrument assesses the hypothesized *construct* of interest.

Contamination The extent to which irrelevant sources of systematic variance account for a portion of the total variance in test scores.

Content Domain The set of knowledge, skills, abilities, related characteristics, and behaviors that are proposed to be measured by a given assessment device.

Content Validity The degree to which the content of a given measure is representative of the hypothesized *content domain,* as judged by *subject matter experts (SMEs).*

Content Validity Index (CVI) A quantitative index of the average CVR value across items for a given test. See Module 6 for the formula for, and the interpretation of, the CVI.

Content Validity Ratio (CVR) A quantitative index of the degree to which *subject matter experts (SMEs)* agree in their ratings of item content. See Module 6 for the formula for, and the interpretation of, the CVR.

Convergent Validity A way of supporting the *construct validity* of a measure by demonstrating the association between theoretically similar measures of the same *construct* or *trait.* See also *Multitrait-Multimethod Matrix (MTMM)* and *Divergent Validity.*

Correction for Attenuation A formula that yields an estimate of relationship between two variables if they are both measured without error (i.e., the population relationship).

Correction for Guessing A procedure/formula used with multiple-choice items to better estimate a person's true score by removing from their observed score that portion that is a function of guessing (see Module 16 for the correction-for-guessing formula).

Correlation Coefficient A statistical index of the degree of association between two variables.

Criterion The yardstick by which a test or test scores are assessed. Alternatively, an outcome of interest (e.g., job performance) that the test is predicted to be associated with.

Criterion Contamination The extent to which irrelevant variance contributes to the measure of a *criterion* of interest.

Criterion Deficiency The extent to which important and relevant variance is missing from a *criterion* of interest.

Criterion-Referenced Testing Deriving meaning of a test score by comparing it to a given standard. Contrast with *Norm-Referenced Testing.*

Criterion-Related Validity The degree of association between a *test* and *criterion* variable.

Critical Score The specific point on a distribution of scores that distinguishes successful from unsuccessful *test takers.* Unlike the *cutoff score,* which may have many factors influencing it (e.g., size of the test applicant pool, number of openings), the critical score is *criterion referenced* and thus should be the same regardless of other contextual factors.

Cross-Validation The application of a set of scoring weights derived from one sample of *test takers* to another sample of test takers in order to assess the stability of the weights across samples.

Cutoff Score The designated point in a distribution of scores where individuals at or above the point are considered successful on the test, while those below are considered unsuccessful. It is distinguished from the *critical score* in that it may be based on a variety of contextual factors in addition to *criterion-referenced* test performance.

Descriptive Statistics A collection of statistical procedures used to summarize a sample of data. Includes measures of *central tendency*, dispersion or *variability*, and shape.

Differential Item Functioning (DIF) When individuals in different groups, who possess the same level of estimated ability or total test score, respond differently to a given test item.

Discriminant Validity See *Divergent Validity*.

Divergent Validity A way of supporting the *construct validity* of a measure by demonstrating the association between theoretically dissimilar measures of the same *construct* or *trait*. Also referred to as discriminant validity. See also *Multitrait-Multimethod Matrix (MTMM)* and *Convergent Validity*.

Domain Sampling When items are selected for a *test* so that they represent a specified universe or area of interest.

Equivalent Forms Reliability See *Alternate Forms Reliability*.

Expectancy Charts A graphical technique that expresses the *validity coefficient* as the ability of a *test* to make correction predictions.

Face Validity The extent to which a *test* or *assessment* device appears to be valid.

Factor Analysis A set of statistical procedures by which a set of items is reduced to a fewer number of factors, based on the interrelationship among the items. If item-factor relationships are specified a priori, it is known as confirmatory factor analysis; if not, it is designated as exploratory factor analysis.

Fairness A sociopolitical concept where the outcome of the testing process is examined separately for various subgroups of *test takers*. Several definitions of fairness have been proposed over the years (e.g., constant ratio, equal probability, conditional probability, constant ratio), but no consensus definition currently exists.

False Negative A term used to define those individuals who are not selected or do not pass a test, but would have been successful had they been selected or passed.

False Positive A term used to define those individuals who were selected or passed a test, but ended up not being successful once selected.

Frequency Distribution A tabular representation of individual test scores in terms of how frequently a given score occurs in a given distribution of scores.

General Mental Ability (GMA) One's capacity to learn and reason across a wide variety of situations and content domains.

Generalizability Theory Estimates of *reliability* that extend classical forms of reliability by using analysis of variance (ANOVA)–like procedures to assess the generalizability of test scores beyond a given sample of persons, items, or other related study dimensions.

Grouped Frequency Distribution A tabular representation of groups of test scores in terms of how frequently each group of scores occurs in a given distribution of scores.

Heteroscedasticity Unequal variability along the entire range of the regression line.

Hit Rate The proportion of *test takers* who are accurately identified as possessing a given *trait* or characteristic purported to be measured by a test. Contrast with *False Negatives* and *False Positives*.

Homoscedasticity Equal variability along the entire range of the regression line.

Impression Management (IM) The degree to which a *test taker* responds in a socially desirable fashion in order to purposefully inflate his or her test score.

Incremental Validity The extent to which additional *predictors* added to a *multiple regression* prediction equation improve the overall *predictive validity* of the multiple predictors.

Individual Differences The dissimilarity observed on a single *construct* or *trait* of interest across individuals (*inter-individual differences*) or within the same individual over time or across constructs (*intra-individual differences*).

Intercept Bias A form of *predictive bias* where the prediction lines for each group are parallel, but cross the *y* axis (the intercept) at different points. Contrast with *Slope Bias*.

Internal Consistency A reliability estimate based on the intercorrelation (i.e., homogeneity) among items on a *test,* with *alpha* being a prime example.

Inter-Rater Reliability The extent to which two or more raters agree in their assessment of target objects, such as individuals.

Inter-Individual Differences An analysis of a single construct across *test takers* common with *norm-referenced testing.*

Interquartile Range A statistical measure of variability or dispersion equal to the difference between the 75th percentile and the 25th percentile of a distribution of scores. This measure of variability is typically computed for ordinal-level data or highly skewed interval-level data.

Interval Scale The level of measurement where the distance between score points is uniform, but the zero point on the scale is arbitrary.

Intra-Individual Differences An analysis of a single construct within a given *test taker* over time or an analysis of multiple constructs within the same individual.

Item Analysis Statistical procedures used to assess the properties of *tests* and specific test items. Statistics calculated typically include *item difficulty, item discrimination,* item-total correlations, and related indexes.

Item Characteristic Curve (ICC) A mathematically derived function used in *item response theory* models to depict the probability of correctly answering a given item for various levels of ability (designated as theta). Also called item response curves (IRCs) or item response functions (IRFs).

Item Difficulty An item analysis statistic that quantifies how easy or difficult an item is by computing the percentage of respondents who answered the item correctly or the difference in percentages between high and low scoring groups. The former is typically referred to as the *p* value, while the latter is called the *d* statistic for contrasting groups.

Item Discrimination An item analysis statistic that quantifies the degree to which *test takers* answer an item correctly is associated with their total test score. Typically computed using biserial, point-biserial, tetrachoric, or phi coefficients, depending on the nature of the data.

Item Response Theory (IRT) A mathematical model of the relationship between performance on a test item and the test taker's level of the construct being assessed, typically designated as θ. The probability of a given response for a given level of θ is typically determined using a logistic function that resembles a cumulative normal distribution (i.e., ogive).

Kappa Statistic An index of the degree of inter-rater agreement for nominal scales.

Kurtosis A statistical index of the degree to which scores in a distribution are clumped together. A distribution of test scores that has a positive kurtosis (i.e., the distribution of scores piling up in the center) is said to be leptokurtic. A distribution of test scores that has a kurtosis of zero (i.e., the distribution of scores closely follows a normal distribution) is said to be mesokurtic. A distribution of test scores that has a negative kurtosis (i.e., the distribution of scores is very flat, as in a uniform distribution) is said to be platykurtic.

Leniency Error A form of systematic rater error in which the rater is being insufficiently critical of the individual being assessed. Contrast with *Severity Error.*

Likert Scale A procedure for scaling individuals where items typically have five response options (e.g., 1 = Strongly Disagree to 5 = Strongly Agree). Individual item responses are then summed to get a total score.

Local Independence A term used in *item response theory* to indicate that item characteristics or parameters are independent of the sample used to derive those characteristics.

Mean The arithmetic average of a distribution of scores.

Measurement The systematic quantification of a characteristic of *test takers* according to clearly explicated rules.

Measurement Bias When test items do not represent the underlying *construct* they are intended to measure equally well for different subgroups of *test takers.*

Measurement Theory See *Psychometrics*.

Median The middle score (50th percentile) of a distribution of scores.

Mental Measurements Yearbook (MMY) A reference volume that publishes reviews and critiques of a wide variety of tests and assessment instruments.

Meta-Analysis A statistical method for quantitatively reviewing and summarizing findings from empirical studies within a given area.

Mode The most frequently occurring score of a distribution of scores.

Moderator Variable A variable that explains additional variance in a *criterion* of interest beyond that of the selected *predictor* variable due to its nonlinear (i.e., interactive) association with the predictor variable.

Modern Test Theory A theory used to explain the relationship between individuals' responses to test items and their underlying *traits* or *abilities*.

Multidimensional Scaling A statistical procedure where the number of dimensions underlying a *construct* are identified and then quantified (i.e., scaled).

Multiple Correlation The degree of association among three or more variables.

Multiple Regression The use of two or more *predictor* variables in predicting a *criterion* variable.

Multitrait-Multimethod (MTMM) Matrix A matrix used to depict the relationship among variables representing two or more *traits*, as well as two or more methods. The MTMM is used to provide evidence of the *construct validity* of a test.

Nominal Scale A scale of measurement where values represent qualitative (rather than quantitative) differences.

Norm-Referenced Testing Deriving the meaning of a test score by comparing it with the test scores of other *test takers*. Contrast with *Criterion-Referenced Testing*.

Normal Distribution A theoretical, symmetrical distribution of scores.

Ordinal Scale The scale of measurement where data are ordered or ranked.

Parallel Forms Reliability See *Alternate Forms Reliability*.

Percentile Rank The percentage of *test takers* who score lower than a given score within a given sample of scores.

Phi Coefficient An index of association between two dichotomously scored variables.

Pilot Testing Administration of a test or test items to a sample of *test takers* in order to evaluate the test or items in terms of the clarity or appropriateness of instructions, items, options, or other test characteristics, thus allowing for necessary changes to be made before full-fledged testing occurs.

Point-Biserial Correlation Coefficient A Pearson product moment correlation coefficient of the degree of association between a dichotomous variable (e.g., pass/fail) and a continuous variable (e.g., job performance measured in dollar sales).

Postdictive Validity The degree of association between test scores measured in the present and criterion scores that were already measured (e.g., current test scores and prior absenteeism rates).

Power Test A test that has a very comfortable time limit, thus allowing the typical individual to complete the test within the allotted time. Contrast with *Speed Test*.

Predictive Bias When a test score systematically under- or overpredicts a criterion of interest for designated groups.

Predictive Validity The degree of association between test scores measured in the present and criterion scores measured in the future (e.g., current test scores and future promotions).

Predictor A measure, often a test, used to predict a criterion of interest, such as job or school performance.

Psychometrician The name given to an individual who has extensive advanced formal training in the area of psychological measurement and assessment.

Psychometrics The science of the assessment of individual differences. Usually refers to the quantitative aspects of psychological measurement. Also called *Measurement Theory*.

Qualitative The degree to which variables differ in terms of type.

Quantitative The degree to which variables differ in terms of amount.

Range A *descriptive statistic* that estimates the variability or dispersion of a set of scores. Defined as the difference between the highest and lowest score in a distribution.

Ratio Scale The scale of measurement where the intervals are equal and the zero point represents the complete absence of the construct of interest.

Regression Coefficient In linear regression analysis, an index of the linear relationship between a *predictor* and *criterion* variable. In unstandardized form, its size is influenced by the variance of the two variables.

Reliability The degree to which test scores are free of measurement error for a given group of *test takers*. Also the extent to which test scores are consistent over time or across forms of the test.

Reliability Coefficient The quantification of the degree of association between two parallel tests.

Response Biases The extent to which *test takers* respond to test items in such a way as to create construct-irrelevant error in the test scores. These *biases* are typically associated with the context of the testing situation. Examples include test takers engaging in guessing on multiple-choice knowledge tests, faking on personality measures, or impression management tactics in interviews.

Response Styles The extent to which *test takers* respond to test items in such a way as to create construct-irrelevant error in the test scores. These biases are typically associated with personality or cultural characteristics of the test taker. Examples include *acquiescence, leniency,* and *severity* response errors in attitude measures.

Restriction of Range A situation where test scores do not represent the entire possible range for a given variable, thus resulting in a deflated *correlation coefficient.*

Scaling Quantification of *constructs* according to a designated set of rules.

Scatterplot A graphical depiction of the relationship between two variables in which individuals' scores are shown simultaneously on the same graph.

Selection Ratio An index reflecting the proportion of individuals who are selected, compared to all those assessed, as a result of the use of some assessment device.

Self-Deceptive Enhancement (SDE) The degree to which a *test taker* responds in a socially desirable fashion, which is not purposeful but inflates his or her test score regardless.

Severity Error A form of systematic rater error in which the rater is being overly critical of the individual being assessed. Contrast with *Leniency Error.*

Shrinkage Formula A correction statistic used in *multiple regression* that adjusts the index of fit (e.g., R^2) due to the fact that the regression weights for a given sample are maximized for that sample and as a result are likely to be lower than in any other sample. The correction becomes more pronounced as the number of *predictor* variables in the multiple regression equation increases.

Skewness An index of the degree to which a distribution of scores is symmetrical about a central value. A distribution of scores with a skew of zero generally follows a normal distribution A negatively skewed distribution has scores piled in the upper end of the distribution, while a positively skewed distribution has scores piled in the lower end of the distribution.

Slope Bias A form of *predictive bias* where the prediction lines for at least two groups are not parallel and as a result have different predictive power for the two groups. Contrast with *Intercept Bias.*

Spearman-Brown Prophecy Formula An equation that estimates the *reliability* of a set of items if the number of the items is increased or decreased by a given factor.

Speed Test A test that has a short time limit where most candidates will not be able to complete the instrument. Contrast with *Power Test.*

Split-Half Reliability Coefficient An estimate of reliability created by correlating two halves of a given test. This figure is then corrected by using the *Spearman-Brown prophecy formula.*

Standard Deviation An index of the degree of dispersion of a set of scores about their *mean.*

Standard Error of Estimate An index of the degree of error associated with using one variable to predict another variable. Sometimes referred to as the standard error of prediction.

Standard Error of Measurement An index of the degree to which scores will vary over repeated assessments across parallel tests.

Stanine A standard score distribution with nine values, which has a *mean* of 5 and a *standard deviation* of approximately 2.

Statistical Artifacts Negative characteristics of an empirical study (e.g., small sample size, use of unreliable measures, restriction of range) that distort the results of the study. In *meta-analysis,* researchers often correct for such artifacts within each study.

Subgroup Analysis An analysis of the relationship between a *predictor* variable and a *criterion* variable separately for different subgroups (e.g., men versus women) in order to determine if *moderator variables* differentially influence the predictor-criterion relationship across subgroups.

Subgroup Norming The separate ranking of individuals within subgroups based on their test scores as compared to only members within their group.

Subject Matter Expert (SME) An individual with expertise in a given area who provides expert ratings or assessments as part of a measurement process.

Technical Manual A document produced by *test developers* (e.g., test publishers) that explains the development of the test, its administration, and the *psychometric* evidence available to support inferences made from use of the test.

Test An assessment device based on a sample of *test-taker* behavior.

Test Battery A collection of *tests* and/or *assessment* devices that is used to assess a wide range of psychological constructs. For an example, see *Armed Services Vocational Aptitude Battery (ASVAB).*

Test Developer The individual or group of individuals (i.e., *constituents*) responsible for the creation of the test and for documentation that supports the inferences to be drawn from use of the test (e.g., *technical manual*).

Test Information Function (TIF) A mathematical function in *item response theory* of the relationship between *ability level* and the reciprocal of the conditional measurement error variance. The TIF is equivalent to reliability scores in classical true score theory.

Test-Retest Reliability The assessment of *reliability* by correlating the scores of two administrations of the same test on the same groups of individuals after a given period of time between test administrations.

Test Taker The individual (i.e., *constituent*) who is assessed by the measurement device.

Test User The individual or agency (i.e., *constituent*) responsible for administration and, possibly, scoring, interpretation, and implementation decisions based on the test.

Trait A persistent or enduring characteristic of an individual that is often represented by his or her score on a test purported to measure that trait.

True Score Theory The *classical test theory* that an individual's true score (T, i.e., underlying attribute) is a function of his or her observed score (X) and measurement error (E), depicted as $T = X + E$.

T **score** A standardized score that has a *mean* of 50 and a *standard deviation* of 10.

Utility In *measurement theory,* the degree to which a test proves useful in terms of its *psychometric* properties (e.g., *validity*) and cost-effectiveness (e.g., cost, ease of use).

Validation The process of gathering, analyzing, and reporting theoretical and empirical evidence that supports the intended uses of a *test* or *assessment* device.

Validity The body of theoretical and empirical evidence gathered to support the intended uses of a *test* or *assessment* device.

Validity Coefficient An index of the degree to which inferences drawn from the use of a *test* are appropriate. Typically depicted as a *correlation coefficient* between test scores and a criterion variable.

Validity Generalization The degree to which the *validity coefficients* established in one setting for a given population generalize to other settings and populations.

Variability The extent to which test scores are distributed. Typically depicted as the extent to which test scores differ from some central value, such as the *mean* or *median*.

Variance A statistical measure of variability or dispersion equal to the arithmetic average of the squared difference between each score in the distribution and the mean of the distribution. This measure of variability requires interval-level data.

Z score A standardized score with a *mean* of zero and a *standard deviation* of one.

Author Index

429

Subject Index